Other Books by James Gabler

An Evening with Benjamin Franklin and Thomas Jefferson: Dinner, Wine, and Conversation. Travel back in time to 18th century Paris and dine with two wine and food enthusiasts who changed the world for the better, and over wine listen to them tell in their own words the most interesting stories of their lives, stories to fascinate anyone interested in history, travel, wine or politics.

Wine into Words: A History and Bibliography of Wine Books in the English Language, 2nd edition. "The ultimate wine library." Hugh Johnson. "Magisterial bibliography." Robin Garr. "A must for every wine lover." Robert Mondavi. "A prodigious and essential achievement." Robert M. Parker, Jr.

The Secret Formula, a novel. The prize is the Coca-Cola secret formula and money beyond the wildest dreams. Can a young woman and a limousine driver pull off the greatest heist of all time and walk away multimillionaires?

God's Devil, a novel. An American priest's obsessive quest to become Pope and change the Catholic Church. He lets nothing stand in his way.

Be Your Own Wine Expert. A beginner's guide that makes learning about wine fun.

Dine with Thomas Jefferson and Fascinating Guests, a fact-based account of 25 dinners at Monticello, the White House, Paris, London, Philadelphia, and the French wine country.

Passions

The Wines and Travels of
THOMAS JEFFERSON

James M. Gabler

Bacchus Press
Palm Beach, FL

Copyright © 2016 by James M. Gabler

All rights reserved including the right of reproduction in whole or in part in any form by any means, electronic, multimedia, or mechanical, including photocopying, recording or by any information storage and/or retrieval system, without the prior written permission of the publisher, Bacchus Press Ltd. and the author.

First Edition: 1995
Library of Congress Catalog Card Number 95-94318
International Standard Book Number

Cover design and maps by Wilma M. Rosenberger
Typesetting by Maureen Cutajar (gopublished.com)

For information on ordering copies of this book or other Bacchus Press publications call: 410-960-1002

Published and Distributed by:
Bacchus Press Ltd
146 Sunset Avenue, #3
Palm Beach, FL 33480
410-960-1002
bacchuspr@aol.com

To Anita, Morgan, Tricia

Contents

List of Illustrations and Maps..ix
Preface...xiii
Chapter One   Emerging Passions 1
Chapter Two   Jefferson in Paris 15
Chapter Three   London and the English Countryside 35
Chapter Four   A Romantic Interlude....................................49
Chapter Five   Burgundy and the Wine Country 59
Chapter Six   The Rhone Valley and its Wines.....................71
Chapter Seven   A Peep Into Elysium: Roman Grandeur...........81
Chapter Eight   Italy and the Riviera 95
Chapter Nine   Provence and Languedoc 103
Chapter Ten   Bordeaux: its Wines and Vineyards 115
Chapter Eleven   The Wine Connoisseur 129
Chapter Twelve   Holland, The Rhine Valley and Champagne ..139
Chapter Thirteen   The French Revolution Begins 157
Chapter Fourteen   Wine Consultant and Secretary of State........167
Chapter Fifteen   Wines in the White House 195
Chapter Sixteen   The Vintage Years 209
Chapter Notes..229
Appendices
    Appendix A   Jefferson's Favorite Wines—Available Today..................287
    Appendix B   The White House Wine Cellar with Annotations...........293
    Appendix C   Currency Values—Equivalents 299
    Appendix D   Wine Measures...301
    Appendix E   Jefferson's Travel Box with Comments..........................303
Glossary 307
Index...315

List of Illustrations and Maps

Bust of Thomas Jefferson by Jean-Antoine Houdon
—Museum of Fine Arts Boston..Cover
Monticello—Thomas Jefferson Memorial Foundation, Inc. 2
Map of Philadelphia in 1777-Photograph courtesy of
The Old Print Gallery, Washington, D.C. 7
Jefferson and Franklin, from Trumbull's Declaration of Independence
—Library of Congress Collection 8
Encampment of General Riedesel's Prussian Troops near Charlottesville,
VA—Photograph courtesy of The Old Print Gallery, Washington, D.C. ...9
Chevalier de Chastellux—Library of Congress Collection 10
Martha Jefferson—Library of Congress Collection..................................11
Grillé de Chaillot—Bibliothéque Nationale 16
Place Louis XV—Bibliothéque Nationale 17
Map of Paris and Environs—A. Vuillemin Geographe 18
John Paul Jones—Library of Congress Collection 20
Lafayette—A. Vuillemin Geographe 22
Hotel de Salms—Boston Athenaeum 23
Interior of the Underground Circus at the Palais Royal
—Boston Athenaeum 24
Jefferson's Diplomatic Calling Card
—Thomas Jefferson Memorial Foundation, Inc. 26
Versailles—A. Vuillemin Geographe 27
Hotel de Langeac, south side along the Champs-Elysées
—Bibliothéque Nationale..31
Count Buffon—A. Vuillemin Geographe...33
The King's Garden—Boston Athenaeum 34
White Lion Inn—Shakespeare Birthplace Trust 41
Shakespeare's Birthplace—Shakespeare Birthplace Trust..........................41
St. Paul's Cathedral—Appleton, European Guide Book 1872..................45

Portrait of Thomas Jefferson by Mather Brown
—Library of Congress Collection 46
John Trumbull—Library of Congress Collection 49
Vue du Théatre Francais—Boston Athenaeum 50
Jefferson, Miniature by John Trumbull
—The Metropolitan Museum of Art.. 50
Versailles and its Gardens—Boston Athenaeum 51
Church of St. Genevieve
—Thomas Jefferson Memorial Foundation, Inc. 52
Maria Cosway—Bibliothéque Nationale... 53
Halle Aux Bleds—Bibliothéque Nationale... 53
Château de ST. Germain-en-Laye—Boston Athenaeum 55
Pavillon de Bagatelle—Boston Athenaeum 55
Auxerre—A. Vuillemin Geographe 61
Dijon—A. Vuillemin Geographe 61
Jefferson's Diagram of the Towns and Vineyards of Burgundy
—Library of Congress Collection 62
Clos de Vougeot—Confrerie des Chevaliers du Tastevin 63
Burgundy Wine Bottles—A. Vuillemin Geographe 65
Château de Laye—Christian de Fleurieu, owner 69
Lyon—A. Vuillemin Geographe 71
Map Northern Rhone—Wilma M. Rosenberger 72
Triumphal Arch in Orange—18th Century Print 78
Map Southren Rhone—Wilma M. Rosenberger 78
Pont du Gard—A. Vuillemin Geographe 81
Hôtel du Louvre—Author 82
Graeco-Roman Theatre—Author 84
Marseilles—A. Vuillemin Geographe 88
Ollioules Pass—Author 90
Turin—Appleton, European Guide Book 1872 97
Map of Italy—Wilma M. Rosenberger 99
Avignon—Guillaume Atger for Editing 103
Fountain of Vaucluse—Musée Pétrarque 105
Cette—A. Vuillemin Geographe... 110
Pierre Paul Riquet—A. Vuillemin Geographe 111
Vintage in the South of France—The Vernon Gallery 112
Toulouse—A. Vuillemin Geographe... 113
Bourdeaux—A. Vuillemin Geographe 116
Château Haut-Brion—Property of Château Haut-Brion 116
Theatre at Bordeaux—Appleton, European Guide Book 1872.................................... 118
Château Latour—From T.G. Shaw's, *Wine, The Vine and The Cellar* 119
Château Yquem—From T.G. Shaw's, *Wine, The Vine and The Cellar* 120

Preface

Map Bordeaux Wine Regions—Wilma M. Rosenberger	122
La Rochelle—A. Vuillemin Geographe	124
Nantes—A. Vuillemin Geographe	125
Map Loire Valley—Wilma M. Rosenberger	125
Tours—A. Vuillemin Geographe	126
Orleans—A. Vuillemin Geographe	127
Château Marguax—From T.G. Shaw's, *Wine, The Vine and The Cellar*	130
Mont Valerien and The Hermitage—Bibliothéque Nationale	134
View of the Paris Countryside—Boston Athenaeum	134
Château Lafite—From T.G. Shaw's, *Wine, The Vine and The Cellar*	136
Cologne Cathedral—Appleton, European Guide Book 1872	143
Map of the Mosel—Wilma M. Rosenberger	144
Map of the Rheningau and Rheinhessen—Wilma M. Rosenberger	145
Heidelberg Castle—Appleton, European Guide Book 1872	150
Jefferson's Topographical Sketch of the Champagne Wine Villages—Massachusetts Historical Society	153
Gouverneur Morris—Library of Congress Collection	161
Bastille—A. Vuillemin Geographe	164
President's Washington's Carriage—Photograph courtesy of The Old Print Gallery, Washington, D.C.	169
Houdon's Statue of George Washington, Capitol, Richmond, VA—Virginia State Library	170
Maryland State House at Annapolis—Maryland State Archives	174
A Modern view of Annapolis from State House Dome—Author	174
Ruins of Fort Ticonderoga—W.H. Bartlett	180
Bennington, 1793—Bennington Museum	182
Map of Portugal Wine Areas	187
The President's House—Maryland State Society	197
Jefferson's Dinner Invitation—Thomas Jefferson Memorial Foundation, Inc.	198
English, Burgundy, and Bordeaux Wine Bottles—Colonial Williamsburg Foundation	201
William Short—Library of Congress Collection	204
Portrait of Jefferson at 62 by Rembrandt Peale—Library of Congress Collection	205
Château de la Rochefoucauld—A. Vuillemin Geographe	206
Monticello—Don Swann	209
Parlor at Monticello—Thomas Jefferson Memorial Foundation, Inc.	210
Dining Room, Monticello—Thomas Jefferson Memorial Foundation, Inc.	211
Artimino—Author	216
The Port of Leghorn—The Vernon Gallery	216
Bedroom and Study, Monticello	

—Thomas Jefferson Memorial Foundation, Inc. 218
Jefferson Wine Glasses—Thomas Jefferson Memorial Foundation, Inc. 223
Houdon's But of Lafayette—Virginia State Library 227

Preface

This is a biography of Thomas Jefferson at leisure, enjoying two of his passions—wine and travel. I have tried to capture Jefferson in the act of living and to let him and his contemporaries speak for themselves. The journeys you are about to take with Jefferson are, for the most part, based on original sources: his letters, memorandum books, receipts, and the correspondence and diaries of his contemporaries. To provide a perspective of what Jefferson saw, I have also referenced, when necessary, the travel accounts of his contemporaries and near contemporaries. In addition I have personally followed his footsteps throughout Europe and the United States. These experiences have allowed me to contemporize what he saw and drank.

Thomas Jefferson had such a galaxy of interests and accomplishments that he is sometimes referred to as the Leonardo da Vinci of America. Many of his interests were so intensely pursued that they can be classified as passions. Clearly, wine was a life-long passion; he called it a "necessary of life." However his wine interests went far beyond drinking wine. He was interested in its viticulture—making notes on German and Italian grape growing and examining "the details relative to the most celebrated wines of France." He planted vineyards at Monticello and experimented with grape growing in his Paris garden on the Champs-Elysées with vine cuttings from such famous vineyards as Montrachet, Chambertin, Clos de Vougeot, Hochheim and Rudesheim. He encouraged Philip Mazzei, John Adlum and others in their vineyard efforts and accurately predicted that America would, some day, make wines as good as those of France. He was a wine adviser to Presidents Washington, Adams, Madison and Monroe.

Throughout his life he was an advocate of the virtues of wine, arguing that "No nation is drunken where wine is cheap; and none sober, where the dearness of wine substitutes ardent spirits as the common beverage." His wine advice to merchants and friends opened channels for the importation of wine into the United States from France, Italy, Portugal and Spain. To encourage the importation of wines he effectively lobbied for a reduction in U.S. taxes while serving as Secretary of State, as President and later in retirement.

Jefferson was the most knowledgeable wine connoisseur of his age and his tastes in wine covered the world: France, Germany, Italy, Cyprus, Hungary, Madeira, Portugal, Spain and, of course, America. He seldom drank a wine he didn't like but he had clear favorites including: Haut-Brion, Lafite, Latour, Margaux, Yquem, Chambertin and Schloss Johannisberg. These wines remain favorites with wine lovers today.

At a White House dinner in 1962 President Kennedy told a group of Nobel prize winners that "this is the most extraordinary collection of talent, of human knowledge, that has ever gathered together in the White House—with the possible exception of when Thomas Jefferson dined alone." But, as you will learn, Jefferson, when President, rarely dined alone. Dinner conversations, whether at the White House, Monticello or at his Paris villa on the Champs-Elysées, spanned the range of human knowledge with an emphasis on his passions—architecture, gardening, music, wine and his years in France.

His love for travel speaks for itself with trips to London and the English countryside, Paris, Amsterdam, Frankfurt, Heidelberg, Strasbourg, New York, Philadelphia and Washington. His three and a half month trip through southern France took him through beautiful Provence, over the Alps into Italy, along the French and Italian Rivieras, with visits to the great Roman antiquities of Gaul, the vineyards of Burgundy, Bordeaux, Cote Rotie, Hermitage and the Loire Valley. One year later he traveled to Holland and down the Rhine with tastings at famous German vineyards.

In his lifetime Jefferson was accused of being aloof and my initial studies left me with that impression. But somewhere in my research and travels, probably as I followed him through the wine country, a fellowship developed between us and I came to know a much more accessible Jefferson. I hope that *this* Jefferson comes through because it is a warmer side of this amazing man that is seldom encountered—in *vino veritas.*

As the more than 900 source notes attest, a significant amount of research went into the writing of this book. I invite your attention to the Chapter Notes that appear at the end of the text because they provide citations for the factual sources drawn upon; they contemporize the wines he drank and the places he visited; they give biographical sketches of important authors; and they add significant follow-through information.

A word about the book's organization. Since this is an account of Jefferson's wine and travel interests, it is presented chronologically. The political background of his life has been filled in only to the extent that it seemed necessary to the themes of wine and travel. As careful and meticulous as Jefferson was about almost everything, he was not a careful speller and often relied on phonetic spellings. Therefore I have followed the practice of using the modern spelling of places and wines followed in brackets by Jefferson's spelling. Subsequently, when the same word again appears, I have usually used the modern spelling without further identification.

John Donne said that no man is an island unto himself and, in writing a book such as this, I can attest to the accuracy of that aphorism. I have relied on the assistance of many individuals and institutions who, if not mentioned here, are identified in the Chapter Notes.

I especially want to acknowledge and thank Lucia Stanton, Director of Research at Monticello, for her advice and making available Jefferson's unpublished annotated memorandum books and other information; Zanne Macdonald at Monticello for re-

Preface

search assistance; Dr. William Franklin for translating most of the French documents and letters and his help with the phonetic pronunciations in the Glossary; Alfonso Baldi for his comments on the uses Jefferson might have made of the chemicals he carried in his travel box; Wilma M. Rosenberger for the cover design and maps; Steven Meyer for typesetting; my late wife, JoAnn, for her significant writing contributions; my daughter, Morgan, for spending a large part of her 1992 summer college vacation helping with research at the Library of Congress; my brother Robert Gabler and Gwinn Owens for editing the manuscript; JoAnn Stolley and Charles Wunder; John Catanzariti, Robert M. Parker, Jr., and Warren Winiarski for agreeing to read the manuscript and comment for attribution but especially for their enthusiastic support and constructive criticism; Irene Graziano, for the hundreds of lonely hours spent typing and retyping the manuscript; and my wife, Anita, for her research assistance and the understanding and encouragement that kept me going.

I am particularly grateful to The Thomas Jefferson Memorial Foundation at Monticello; the Library of Congress; Maryland Archives; Alderman Library, University of Virginia; American Philosophical Society, Philadelphia; Massachusetts Historical Society; and Loyola College in Baltimore for providing research facilities and assistance.

Jim Gabler

CHAPTER ONE

Emerging Passions

Thomas Jefferson was fascinated by the whole range of human experience. No topic seemed to bore him. His interest in wine and travel was indicative of his wide-ranging curiosity. "Among Jefferson's contemporaries in America," writes Julian Boyd, "if not among all who preceded and followed him, only Franklin could be said to approach him in the extent and variety of his inquiry. To catalogue the areas of his explorations is to list most of the principal categories of knowledge—law, government, history, mathematics, architecture, medicine, agriculture, languages and literature, education, music, philosophy, religion and almost every branch of the natural sciences from astronomy through meteorology to zoology."[1]

He evolved slowly into the Renaissance man. As a student at William and Mary College he studied fifteen hours daily, including vacations.[2] He found intellectual companionship with Dr. William Small, his professor of natural and moral philosophy, who introduced him to many of the concepts that would lead to his belief in the rights of man. Small brought him into a select circle of that day's intellectuals, including 35-year-old George Wythe, a scholarly lawyer, who had educated himself in Latin, Greek, mathematics and philosophy.[3]

Jefferson's friendship with Small, whom he had grown to respect as the teacher-student relationship developed, was ended by his professor's return to England in 1764. Wythe took the six-foot-two, 19-year-old Jefferson into his Williamsburg law office after he had finished the two-year course of study at William and Mary in 1762. Jefferson and Wythe would travel the entire revolutionary trail together, both signing the Declaration of Independence. Their relationship ended only with Wythe's death in 1806, poisoned by a grandnephew.

His legal training under Wythe did not encompass the traditional apprentice relationship, for there are no receipts recorded for money exchanged and there were no articles of apprenticeship. But there was the special training that experience provides, such as listening to "the sublime eloquence" of Patrick Henry when he spoke in the Virginia House of Burgesses.[4]

Passions

On the social side Jefferson traveled in Virginia Royal Governor Francis Fauquier's circle of educated older men, including Small and Wythe, who enjoyed music, literature, and knowledge. The surroundings at the Royal Palace in Williamsburg were suitable for the regal cachet they embodied; muskets lined the paneled hallways as a symbol of kingly authority; a formal ballroom glittered with chandeliers and a polished pianoforte. In the dining-room, hand-painted wallpaper with butterflies and birds flying two by two and an owl sitting alone illustrated the oriental aphorism, "Love and beauty fly side by side; wisdom flies alone."

The young, red-haired Jefferson also found more proletarian entertainment, spending freely at coffeehouses and drinking punch in Raleigh's, Campbell's, Charlton's, Vaughan's and other taverns. He was seeing plays, winning and losing at backgammon, buying a horse that pleased his demanding eye, seeing a tiger in a traveling curiosity show and dreaming of spending two or three years traveling through Europe.[5]

His law practice grew. He recorded in his account books, employment in over 300 cases between 1767–1770, although client payments were another matter. Jefferson's account books idealistically list as "total profits," the figure he billed. What he collected was far different as net receipts show. For the years 1767 through 1772, he billed 2,119 pounds, collected 797 and had outstanding 1,322.[6]

Exactly when he decided to design and build his own house is not recorded but the first mention of Monticello (little mountain) is noted in his *Garden Book* on August 3, 1767. Why a bachelor lawyer who practiced law in Williamsburg, and had a family estate at Shadwell (near Charlottesville), wanted to build a 35-room house astride a mountaintop, a long and arduous horse ride away from the valley, is unknown, but at the age of twenty-four this became his ambition, soon to be translated into a life-long passion.

The price? Jefferson never considered it. His home, which survives intact today, has a cannon-ball clock at the front entrance, with the days of the week painted on the wall. And when the space was not large enough for Saturday, he cut a hole through the floor and put Saturday in the basement. He felt it should have a special silver coffee urn, so he designed and had one made. He made detailed sketches of nearly every item, including how to hang the draperies—famous now as the Jeffersonian drape, a simple length of fabric falling gracefully at the glass windows and doors. An automatic door

Monticello

2

operated by a gear beneath the floor opens into the drawing room. An ice-house was stocked so that ice lasted all summer. If fresh fish were needed for dinner they were retrieved from a pond and prepared in the kitchen beneath the mainhouse. As his house progressed, his plans for a library seemed hopeless when his books and personal papers were ruined in a fire that destroyed his home at Shadwell where he lived with his mother and sisters. He began rapidly replacing the books, leading to a 20,000 volume library that later became the nucleus for the Library of Congress.

A wine cellar, 17½ feet long, 15 feet wide and 10 feet high, was laid out near a cider room. The dimensions indicated far more ambitious plans than his wine inventory of 1769: 83 bottles of rum, 15 bottles of Madeira, 4 bottles of "Lisbon wine for common use" and 54 bottles of cider.[7]

A home, a profession: the only missing element was a wife. She was soon to join him at Monticello. His account book shows tips for the servants at the home of John Wayles, a prominent and wealthy attorney, whose daughter Martha had returned home in 1768 with an infant son following the death of her husband, Bathurst Skelton, two years after their marriage.[8]

The 28-year-old Jefferson and 23-year-old widow were married on New Year's Day, 1772, at John Wayles' home, *The Forest*, and two weeks later arrived early in the morning hours at Monticello on horseback in a snowstorm. It is perhaps apocryphal but Jefferson's great-granddaughter, Sarah N. Randolph, reports that they found a bottle of wine "on a shelf behind some books" which they drank before retiring on their Monticello honeymoon night.[9]

It was to be the first of many bottles that he would enjoy at home with family and friends. In his account book of September 15, 1772, he records liquors and bottles on hand, including "about three gallons rum and a half hogshead [27½ gallons] Madeira, 72 bottles of Madeira, 37 bottles of Lisbon wine, 29 bottles small beer, 10 bottles of port and 31 bottles of miscellaneous in the closet." The year earlier he recorded 10 dozen bottles of port so, in the intervening year, 110 bottles of port had been consumed.[10]

In November, 1773 Philip Mazzei, one of the most interesting men to enter Jefferson's life, landed in Virginia with his wife-to-be, Mrs. Joseph Martin, her twelve-year old daughter and ten Italian vignerons. Mazzei arrived with a plan to cultivate in the colonies popular European products such as vines, olive trees, and the eggs of silk worms to make silk. To help Mazzei in his viticultural project, a Virginia merchant, Thomas Adams, who had become friendly with Mazzei in London, acquired from the Virginia Assembly 1,000 acres for him. Mazzei found the land offer unacceptable because it was divided into many parcels and separated by great distances.[11] Adams, who was building a home in Augusta County, about 160 miles northwest of Williamsburg, offered to sell Mazzei land adjoining his estate and Mazzei set out with Adams to examine the property. Monticello being on their way, they stopped to visit Jefferson, arriving late at night. Early the next morning Jefferson and Mazzei went for a walk and Mazzei found the vineyard land he had been looking for—a 400-acre tract adjoining Monticello to the east. He named it "Colle." Jefferson described the land that Mazzei selected as "having a southeast aspect and an abundance of lean and meagre spots of stony and red soil, without sand, resembling extremely the Cote of Burgundy from Chambertin to Montrachet where the famous wines of Burgundy are made."[12] Jefferson later said that Mazzei was right "in preferring the southeastern face of this ridge of mountains. It is the first ridge, from the sea, begins on the north side of the James River and extends northeasterly, thro' the state under the different names, in different parts of it, of the Green Mountain, Southwest Mountains and Bull Run Mountains."[13]

What they talked about on this morning stroll along Monticello's hillsides was not recorded, but it sparked a lifetime friendship and caused Jefferson to become a partner in Mazzei's vineyard project. As Mazzei remembered in his autobiography, "By the time we returned home, everyone was up. Looking at Mr. Jefferson, Mr. Adams said: 'I see by your expression that you've taken him away from me. I knew you would do that.' Jefferson smiled, without looking at him, but, staring at the table, said: 'Let's have breakfast first and then we'll see what we can do.'"[14]

Whether on that morning walk or later, Jefferson would learn that Mazzei had grown up in a mountain village in Tuscany. As a young man he studied medicine at the Santa Maria Nuova Hospital in Florence, but was dismissed for drinking wine before taking communion on Holy Thursday. Undeterred, he went to Leghorn (now Livorno) and established a successful medical practice. But ever restless, Mazzei left Italy for Smyrna, Turkey, where he continued the practice of medicine for two and a half years. Bored with life in Smyrna, and armed with a supply of Turkish opium and a few other local products, Mazzei sailed for England in December, 1755. In London he sold his Turkish goods for a sizable profit, rejected offers to resume his medical practice, and made a living giving Italian language lessons to the British gentry. The profits from the sale of the Turkish goods gave him the idea of opening a shop specializing in wines, silks, olive oil, anchovies, parmesan cheese and other Italian products that were almost impossible to buy in London.[15]

His introduction to Americans living in London came about by accident. The Grand Duke of Tuscany sent an order for two Franklin stoves. Knowing Benjamin Franklin was then living in London, the enterprising Mazzei knocked on Franklin's door and persuaded Franklin to help him find the stoves. Through Franklin, Mazzei met Thomas Adams, in London, and Adams introduced Mazzei to his circle of Virginians. Mazzei, whose political persuasions were in tune with the growing American rebellious spirit, succumbed to the urgings of Franklin and Adams to go to America to live.[16]

Jefferson, who envisioned the production of quality wine in America and especially in Virginia, encouraged Mazzei's experiment. But Mazzei needed more than land; he needed money. From his fertile mind evolved a partnership "for the purpose of raising and making wine, oil, agruminous plants and silk."[17] A share in the new venture was set at fifty pounds sterling. The experiment in viticulture so captured the imagination of Virginia's landed gentry that original subscribers included such prominent men as George Washington, George Mason, Governor Earl Dunmore, Thomas Randolph, Thomas Adams, John Park Custis (Washington's stepson) and Jefferson. Jefferson later acquired a second share by buying out the interest of Thomas Randolph. Mazzei was given four shares and the right "to use for his table or household, such necessaries, as may be raised on the lands of the company."

The ebullient Mazzei, a natural raconteur, was a frequent dinner guest at Monticello. He loved to tell how he had single-handedly improved the quality of Italian wines drunk in England. He recalled that when he first opened his shop in London the English told him that Tuscan wine was a pleasant summer drink but it did not keep. Mazzei remembered as a child that his grandfather would never drink a wine less than a year old. Believing that Tuscan wines spoiled because they were mishandled by English merchants Mazzei ordered wine from his Italian cousins, but over the summer his wine also spoiled. Later on a trip through Burgundy he observed the vinification and noted that the Burgundians did not adulterate their wines. When he explained this difference to an Italian wine dealer, "he admitted that our forefathers never adulterated wines. He pointed out, too, that the inhabitants of Chianti treated wine much less than others did and that some did not treat it at all."[18] Mazzei purchased a large quantity of unadulterated wines from this wine dealer and less than a third spoiled.

On another trip to Florence, Mazzei discovered an excellent red wine from Carmignano[19] produced on a small vineyard owned by a tailor by the name of Cartei. Mazzei offered to buy his entire vintage and to pay him eleven percent more than his asking price on condition that Cartei not strengthen his wine with alcohol. But the tailor-vintner would not agree, explaining that if he did not strengthen his wine it would not be good and he would lose prestige.

Mazzei finally succeeded in buying Cartei's vintage and, after bottling it in London, it improved with age. He enjoyed telling the story of a friend who at dinner had his servant "bring in a bottle of Burgundy, one of Bordeaux, and one of Cartei's wine, which had been bottled for six or seven years. The guests expressed a preference for Cartei's wine and they were amazed to learn that it was nothing more than the famous wine of Carmignano."[20]

Mazzei began his Virginia wine-making adventure with his enthusiasm heightened by what he saw on his arrival. Shortly after settling in at Colle, Mazzei "learned from his men, who had explored the woods, that they had observed two hundred varieties of wild grapes. I myself had observed thirty six on my own property—good, fair, and bad. I chose six of the best to make two barrels of wine, one of which I saved for myself and the other I gave to my men. They did not drink the wine but sold it for a shilling a bottle." Mazzei's enthusiasm was not diminished by a murderous late frost that struck the Charlottesville area in May, 1774, killing the vines. Two months later he was writing, "In my opinion, when the country is populated in proportion to its size, the best wine in the world will be made here. It must be remembered that the grapes from which I made the two barrels of wine were picked from the top of a tree in a very dense woods, and the vine had a tremendous number of branches. When I pulled the cork three months later, it was like the sparkling wine of Champagne. I do not believe that nature is so favorable to growing vines in any country as this. I measured two of which were more than a foot and a half in circumference. The shoots of the lugliola grape produced branches of such length that my good Vicenzo Rossi told me, 'Master, don't write of this to our village, because they won't believe it, and you'll pass for a liar....'"[21]

War intervened and Mazzei's vineyard was disbanded when he went to Europe as a financial agent for the State of Virginia. Before leaving Mazzei rented his estate, Colle, to the interned German General Riedesel, "whose horses in one week destroyed the whole labour of three or four years," according to Jefferson.[22]

An Englishman, Isaac Weld, visited Mazzei's estate after it was disbanded and concluded that the experiment failed because "the vines which the Italians found growing here were different, as well as the soil, from what they had been in the habit of cultivating, and they were not much more successful in the business than the people of the country."[23] Weld went on to presage that "We must not, however, from hence conclude that good wine can never be manufactured upon these mountains. It is well known that the vines, and the mode of cultivating them, vary as much in different parts of Europe as the soil in one country differs from that in another. It will require some time, therefore and different experiments, to ascertain the particular kind of vine, and the mode of cultivating it, best adapted to the soil of these mountains."[24]

With the demands of Monticello Jefferson's law practice seemed a drain on his energies rather than a successful enterprise, so in August, 1774, he turned his practice over to Edmund Randolph. He was enjoying the pleasures of home, stocking alcohol for some guests, but for himself and friends with similar tastes he preferred light wines, Madeira, beer, port and cider. In February he was recording in his account book the number of bottles a new pipe of Madeira yields, the amount of ullage that occurs after seven years of aging Madeira, and the fact that a "bottle holds 15 common wine glasses."[25]

When Jefferson and an elite circle of other colonial leaders met in congressional session in Philadelphia during the summer of 1775, it was not with reconciliation with England in mind. Their Rubicon had been crossed and there was no turning back. The search was on for a commander-in-chief. Washington, who arrived dressed in his military uniform, was the unanimous choice. The day after the news of Bunker Hill came Washington set out for Boston as the Commander of the American Army.[26]

During his forty-three days in Philadelphia Jefferson lodged with a cabinetmaker, Benjamin Randolph. A typical day of congressional sessions, at what became known as Independence Hall, began at nine and usually did not end until four or five. Occasionally they worked into the night. Jefferson's long days of drafting documents, of listening to arguments of each state's delegates, were broken by meals at "Smith's," better known as the City Tavern, on Second Street near Walnut. Hypercritical John

Adams called it "the most genteel one in America." The tavern was operated by Daniel Smith whose Tory-Loyalist colors came to light when the British occupied Philadelphia from September, 1778 to June, 1779. When the British evacuated Philadelphia, Smith was forced to flee with them, leaving 1800 pounds sterling in property and taking in possessions only what he could carry.

The City Tavern was built by subscription by a group of prominent Philadelphians, who felt the thriving city of 40,000 needed an elegant place for public entertainment. It became a dining and meeting place for Congress. The tavern cook prepared meals in a kitchen described as serving French and English cuisine. The menu included fowl, rib roast, plum pudding, bread, ale, beer, wine or brandy, fruit, with little cakes or candies as dessert. The meats were roasted over spits that were turned by the movement of dogs confined in the basement in circular cages.

On May 7, 1776, Jefferson left Monticello for Philadelphia for his third congressional session. He traveled what was known as the upland route, through Frederick and Taneytown, Maryland, York and Lancaster, Pennsylvania, and arrived May 14. He took his old lodgings on Walnut Street but eight days later rented an apartment on the second floor of a new three-story brick house on the south west corner of Market and Seventh Streets. His apartment consisted of a bedroom and a parlor, divided by a stairway.[27]

Within less than a month of his arrival he was cast into a major role—an appointment by Congress with Benjamin Franklin, John Adams, Roger Sherman, and Robert Livingston to draft a Declaration of Independence.[28] Jefferson was asked to write the document. With "neither book nor pamphlet while writing it" he finished the task in less than seventeen days. With just a few changes by Franklin and Adams, it was

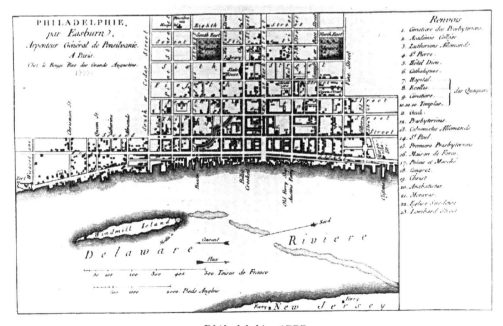

Philadelphia, 1777

submitted to Congress on June 28th. After a string of debates and changes by Congress (Jefferson thought Congress weakened the Declaration) toward the evening of July 4th a vote was taken and the Declaration was adopted.[29] Earlier that day Jefferson found time to steal away from the debates and buy a thermometer and seven pairs of women's gloves.[30] He stayed on for two more months but left Congress in September because of concerns for his wife's health.

In the fall of 1778 Jefferson proposed sending Mazzei to Europe as a special agent of Virginia. The Virginia legislature approved the idea and a few months later, after Mazzei had signed an oath of allegiance to Virginia, he was on his way to France. Mazzei had convinced Jefferson that the Duke of Tuscany had "ten million crowns lying dead in his treasury," a part of which Mazzei thought he could borrow for the United States.[31]

In January 1779, over 4,000 British and German captured soldiers were marched from Boston into the Charlottesville area as interned prisoners following the surrender of General John Burgoyne at Saratoga.[32] Jefferson and his wife, Martha, became friends with several of the Prussians, especially Major General Baron Frederick Adolphus Riedesel (1738-1800) who in February moved into Mazzei's house at Colle with his wife, the Baroness Friderikc von Riedesel, and their three small daughters. War and politics were put aside as music furthered their friendship. Jefferson played the violincello, with a young German, Captain Baron de Geismar, on the violin and the Baroness singing Italian arias. Jefferson was befriended by Geismar ten years later when he traveled down the Rhine visiting the German vineyards.

From June 1, 1779, to May 31, 1781, Jefferson served as Governor of Virginia but when his second term expired he refused reappointment and retired to Monticello. Four days later, at sunrise on June 4, Virginia's "Paul Revere," in the guise of a neighbor named Jouett, rode up the mountain to warn Jefferson and his guests that a British cavalry of 250 men under the command of Colonel Tarlton was in Louisa, only thirty miles away. Jouett then rode on to Charlottesville to warn the legislature. Tarlton sent a detachment under the command of Major McCleod on to Monticello to capture Jefferson. When they arrived the house was vacant, and they found but one slave, Martin, standing on a plank on the portico under which he had just finished stashing the family

Jefferson and Franklin, from Trumbull's Declaration of Independence.

ENCAMPMENT of the CONVENTION ARMY

silver with the help of another slave, Ceasar. McCleod and his troops followed Tarlton's orders not to damage Monticello, but they are said to have helped themselves to some of Jefferson's wines.

Jefferson's estate at Elk Ridge, that Cornwallis occupied for ten days, did not receive the same gentle treatment. Jefferson later reported that Cornwallis' troops destroyed all the growing crops of corn and tobacco, burned the barns and fences, took all the livestock, and carried off twenty-seven slaves. Regarding his slaves Jefferson said: "Had this been to give them freedom, he would have done right; but it was to consign them to inevitable death from the small-pox and putrid fever, then raging in his camp." Feeling that Cornwallis' actions expressed a particular hatred for him, Jefferson went on to add, "[he] treated the rest of the neighborhood in much the same style, but not with that spirit of total extermination with which he seemed to rage over my possessions."[33]

In the spring of 1782, on Jefferson's thirty-ninth birthday, the Marquis de Chastellux, a major general in the French Expeditionary Forces,[34] paid a visit to Monticello, and as he rode up the mountain he had no difficulty recognizing Jefferson's house on one of the summits. "[T]his house, of which Mr. Jefferson was the architect, and often the builder, is constructed in an Italian style, and is quite tasteful, although not however without some faults; it consists of a large square pavilion, into which one enters through two porticoes ornamented with columns. The ground floor consists chiefly of a large and lofty salon, or drawing room, which is to be decorated entirely in the antique style; above the salon is a library of the same form; two small wings, with only a ground floor and attic, are joined to this pavilion, and are intended to communicate with the kitchen, offices, etc. which will form on either side a kind of basement topped by a terrace ... Mr. Jefferson is the first American who has consulted the Fine Arts to know how he should shelter himself from the weather."[35]

Chastellux, at forty-eight, had already gained a reputation throughout France as the author of the two-volume work *Public Happiness*, as a philosopher, scientist, and soldier. Chastellux's intellectual interests were so similar to Jefferson's that their feelings and opinions were, as Chastellux said, "in agreement and who understand each other at the first hint—all these made my four days spent at Monticello seem like four minutes."

Chastellux described Jefferson as "a man, not yet forty, tall, and with a mild and pleasing countenance, but his mind and attainments could serve in lieu of all outward graces; an American, who without ever having quitted his own country, is Musician, Draftsman, Surveyor, Astronomer, Natural Philosopher, Jurist, and Statesman; a Senator of America, who sat for two years in that famous Congress which brought about the Revolution and which is never spoken of here without respect . . . a Governor of Virginia, who filled his difficult station during the invasions of Arnold, Phillips, and Cornwallis; and finally a Philosopher, retired from the world and public business . . . a gentle and amiable wife, charming children whose education is his special care, a house to embellish, extensive estates to improve, the arts and sciences to cultivate— these are what remain to Mr. Jefferson, after having played a distinguished role on the stage of the new world, and what he has preferred to the honorable commission of Minister Plenipotentiary in Europe."[36]

Chastellux walked with Jefferson through a park that adjoined Monticello and watched while Jefferson fed deer Indian corn that they ate out of his hand. On another evening Chastellux and Jefferson "were conversing . . . over a bowl of punch after Mrs. Jefferson had retired. Our conversation turned on to the poems of Ossian . . . the book was sent for and placed near the bowl, where by their mutual aid the night far advanced imperceptibly upon us."[37]

Jefferson's account book entry on September 6, 1782 is one of the few in which he uses a term of endearment, for as a public man he was enormously private about his emotions. On his wife Martha's death, he wrote simply, "My dear wife died this day at 11:45 a.m." His reaction to his wife's death was one of profound sorrow. He is reported to have had fainting spells and to have stayed alone for three weeks, finally emerging from a "stupor of mind" that had rendered him "as dead to the world as she was whose loss occasioned it."[38] He never remarried.

Chevalier de Chastellux

Emerging Passions

Two months after his wife's death he accepted an appointment to serve with Benjamin Franklin and John Adams in Paris as a peace commissioner. He reached Philadelphia two days after Christmas, expecting to sail on a French vessel with Chastellux and General Rochambeau, but his departure was delayed for months because the British fleet had the port blockaded.[39] Thinking passage from Baltimore might be easier, he traveled there but a combination of winter storms and an effective blockade of that port kept him from sailing. As he waited for clearance, news reached America that a provisional peace treaty had been negotiated leading to the suspension of his appointment.

Shortly after returning to Monticello he was notified that the Virginia Assembly had elected him a delegate to Congress, to begin service in the fall. Arriving in Trenton on November 3, he learned the next day that Congress was adjourning to reconvene m Annapolis, Maryland, on November 26.

In Annapolis he lodged with a "Mrs. Gheeseland", but on February 25, 1783, he moved with James Monroe "to Mr. Dulany's house" which they rented together until Jefferson's departure from Congress eleven weeks later. They were there to work and to ratify the Treaty of Peace proposed by Benjamin Franklin, John Adams and John Jay. Partout, a French chef, prepared their meals including beef, turkey, duck, veal and oysters with cider and wine purchased at Mann's tavern.[40]

Mann's tavern was located just down the hill from the Maryland State House and fronted on what is now Main Street. Only two months before Jefferson's arrival in Annapolis, George Mann had purchased the former residence of Lloyd Dulany out of a sale of confiscated loyalist property. Mann, an experienced innkeeper, had enhanced his reputation in April, 1783, when he provided enormous quantities of food and drink for the city's premature celebration of the Treaty of Peace between America and England.[41] The formal signing of the treaty by Congress did not take place until January 14th of the following year.

Martha Jefferson.

The original tavern was expanded in 1787, and when Jefferson and Madison stayed at Mann's seven years later it contained three large dining rooms, barroom, dressing room on the first floor, sitting room, eight lodging rooms on the second floor, a kitchen, wash house, billiard room, a garden with an icehouse, a stable for fifty horses and a garret room for servants.[42]

Jefferson was a member of the committee appointed by Congress to make arrangements for

General George Washington's stay in Annapolis when he arrived late in December, 1783, to resign his commission as Commander-in-Chief of the Continental Armies. By all accounts the committee performed its task remarkably well. The *Maryland Gazette* reported the festivities beginning with a cannon salute on Washington's arrival. "On Friday evening last, his Excellency General Washington with his suite, arrived here on his way to Mount Vernon. His Excellency was met a few miles from this city by the Honorable Generals Gates and Smallwood, and several of the principal inhabitants, who attended him to Mr. Mann's, where apartments had been prepared for his reception."[43] A member of Washington's entourage was his aide-de-camp, thirty-one-year-old David Humphreys. This was Jefferson's first meeting with Humphreys, but in less than eight months Humphreys would be a permanent member of Jefferson's household in Paris—Jefferson as a commissioner along with Benjamin Franklin and John Adams, and Humphreys as the secretary of the American legation.

The day before the resignation ceremony Congress hosted a dinner in Washington's honor at Mann's tavern for over 200 "distinguished guests." After dinner, glasses were raised in thirteen toasts beginning with "to the United States," and ending with "to the long health and happiness of our illustrious general." The Congressional Committee did not quibble over Mann's bill of $644, calling "the entertainment . . . exceeding plentiful, the provisions and liquors good in their kind."

The next morning the small gallery of the State House was jammed with people anxious to witness this historic event. As the clock struck twelve, and Thomas Mifflin, President of the Continental Congress, called upon Washington to speak. "The spectators all wept," wrote James McHenry to his fiancée, "and there were hardly a member of Congress who did not drop tears . . . The General's hand . . . shook as he read."[44] George Washington reached into his pocket for the commission and handed it to President Miffiin.

With the ratification of the Articles of Peace on January 14, 1784, an era had ended and the colonial revolutionists became presidents, diplomats, judges and just plain private citizens. For Jefferson, it would be a new country. His appointment on May 7 by Congress as a Commissioner to France to join Benjamin Franklin and John Adams disrupted his household in Annapolis. "Sold Co. Monroe my books and household things at Annapolis," he writes in his account book. Collecting his salary due as a congressional delegate, Jefferson left Annapolis on May 11.

Three days later he was in Philadelphia to pick up his oldest daughter Martha (Patsy) who would accompany him to France. His two younger children, Maria (Polly) and Lucy Elizabeth, were left in Virginia in the care of Jefferson's sister-in-law and her husband, Elizabeth and Francis Eppes.

Leaving Philadelphia on May 28, Jefferson and his daughter spent twenty-two days in leisurely traveling through New Jersey, New York (six days in New York City), Connecticut, Rhode Island and Massachusetts before arriving in Boston on June 18. With Martha in the care of the family of John Lowell, Jefferson took off alone for a six-day journey along the seacoasts of Massachusetts and New Hampshire. His avowed purpose in all this travel was a sort of learning process about the commercial possibilities of these regions and how this information might help him in the negotiation of foreign trade treaties.

On his return to Boston he visited Samuel Adams and his wife. Jefferson knew that the initial sparks of revolution had been ignited by Sam Adams in the coffee houses of Boston ten years earlier. What these two patriots talked about was not recorded, but they obviously enjoyed themselves because seventeen years later when Samuel Adams wrote to congratulate Jefferson on his election as President, he added: "My dear Mrs. Adams will not suffer me to close this letter till I let you know that she recollects the pleasure and entertainment you afforded us when you were about to embark for France."[45]

CHAPTER TWO

Jefferson in Paris

On July 5, 1784, the 41-year-old Jefferson, his 11-year-old daughter Martha (Patsy), and an 18-year-old slave-servant, James Hemings, sailed from Boston for France on the *Ceres*. This was the beginning of a five-year adventure that Jefferson would always cherish. During his stay in Europe he would acquire a depth of knowledge and an appreciation of wines that no American of his time would rival.

There were only six other passengers and one of those was the owner of the ship, Nathaniel Tracy. Martha was to recall later that the food aboard was excellent. Four days before sailing her father had the foresight to buy forty-eight bottles of Hock (a white German wine) for the voyage, which he no doubt shared with his fellow passengers. They had perfect weather and their twenty-day passage was unusually fast. Jefferson amused himself on a daily basis by recording in his account book various weather data, whale and shark sightings, and a study of *Don Quixote* in Spanish.

When the *Ceres* arrived at West Cowes on the Isle of Wight, Martha was sick. The following day they landed at Portsmouth, England, and, after taking lodgings at Bradley's Crown Inn, Jefferson engaged a Dr. Meek to treat his daughter. With Martha feeling better, Jefferson spent July 29 visiting three neighboring towns. When Martha was fit to travel they sailed for France. After a stormy passage across the Channel, they landed at Le Havre on July 31 and lodged at Mahan's l'Aigle d'Or. The new commissioner soon found that French hospitality had its price. "It cost papa as much to have his baggage brought from the shore to the house, which was about a half square apart, as the bringing it from Philadelphia to Boston."[1]

After three days in Le Havre they traveled the post roads to Rouen and lodged in the old section of town at the Hotel Pomme de Pin. Apparently their food and accommodations were better than that experienced by an English traveler of the same period, Arthur Young,[2] who described it as "that dirty, impertinent, cheating hole." Young remembered a dinner at the Pomme de Pin so sparse that by the time the food reached him there was almost nothing left. Young left the table hungry and longing for an English meal where he could get a "piece of meat which would, literally speaking, outweigh this whole dinner."[3]

Rouen with its narrow, crooked streets, its 15th-and-16th century stone and timber-gabled houses, Gothic Cathedral, Palais de Justice, Hotel de Ville and busy quays obviously captured Jefferson's interest because he remained there two days.[4]

On August 5 the Jeffersons left for Paris and spent the next two days traveling through the picturesque Seine Valley and the medieval towns of Point Saint-Ouen, Vaudreuil, Gaillon, Vernon, Vonnieres, Mantes, Meulan, and Triel. This part of the trip was later described by young Martha as "the most beautiful country I ever saw in my life, it is a perfect garden ... and when ever we stopped we were surrounded by the beggers."[5] Stopping in Mantes to visit the Gothic Church of Notre Dame, "which had as many steps to go to the top as there are days in the year," and said to have been erected as a result of a bequest from William the Conqueror, they lodged for the night in the village of Triel.[6]

The next day they approached Paris by way of Saint-Germain-en-Laye, Marly and Nanterre, seeing along the way a spectrum of palaces, bridges, towns, woods and hillsides in vines and wheat. They crossed the Seine at the Pont de Neuilly and rode down the Champs-Elysées stopping at the Grillé de Chaillot, one of twenty-four barriers or tollhouse gates that ringed Paris for the purpose of levying taxes on all goods coming into the city. Within a year Jefferson would live in the mansion directly across from the Grillé de Chaillot.[7]

GRILLE DE CHAILLOT.

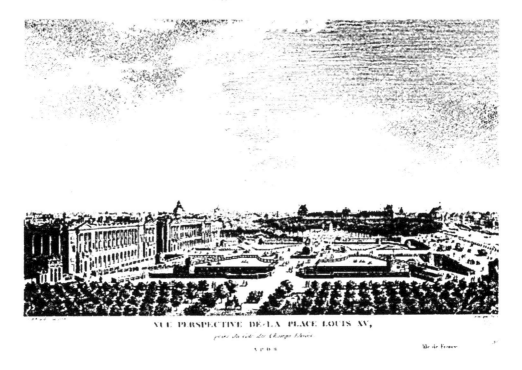
VUE PERSPECTIVE DE LA PLACE LOUIS XV,

Entering Paris their carriage continued down the Champs-Elysées to Place Louis XV (now Place de la Concorde), past the gardens of the Tuileries, and along Rue Saint Honore to Rue de Richelieu where they took rooms at the Hotel d'Orleans, located on the same street as the Bibliotheque du Roi (now the Bibliotheque Nationale) and opposite the Palais Royal.

Six days later the newly appointed commissioner took another temporary home at a fashionable hotel with the same name on the Left Bank, acquired a new wardrobe, arranged for his daughter Martha's admission to a fashionable school, the Convent of Panthemont. Having attended to these practical matters, he went on a wine-buying spree.[8] Before his second week ended he had purchased 276 bottles of wine.[9]

Four days after his arrival Jefferson visited Benjamin Franklin, who lived in the suburb of Passy, "a neat village" about two miles from Paris. Franklin had come to France in late 1776 to obtain money and arms for the American Revolution and to forge, if possible, an alliance with France. He was successful in achieving all of these goals and in so doing had become the most popular and respected foreigner in Europe. Even John Adams, who was jealous of Franklin, admitted that his "reputation was more universal than that of Leibnitz or Newton or Frederick or Voltaire; and his character more beloved and esteemed than any or all of them."

Franklin occupied a portion of a spacious estate known as the Hotel de Valentinois, owned by a wealthy merchant, Le Ray de Chaumont. The mansion stood on the top of a hill with terraced gardens leading down to the Seine and a view looking back to Paris.

This was the first of many visits for Jefferson who frequently dined with Franklin. Franklin's waistline became as ample as his bounty as a host: he had contracted with his *maitre d'hotel* to furnish for each of his dinners a joint of beef, veal or mutton, fowl or game; two vegetables with hors d'oeuvres of butter, pickles and relishes; and for desserts—fruits, fruit preserves, cheeses, biscuits, bonbons and ice cream. As they drank wines selected from Franklin's cellar of over 1,100 bottles, including red Bordeaux, Burgundies, sparkling Champagnes and sherries, the two diplomats relaxed in elegant but simple surroundings.[10]

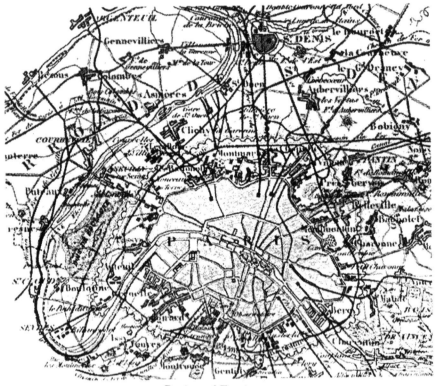

Paris and Environs

Jefferson's visit with Benjamin Franklin on August 10 coincided with John Adams' arrival in France from London with his wife Abigail, his nineteen-year-old daughter Abigail, and his seventeen-year-old son, John Quincy. After a temporary residence of four days in Paris at the Hotel d'York, Adams moved his family into a mansion in the village of Auteuil (about a mile from Franklin's residence in Passy) which bordered the Bois de Boulogne far "distant from the putrid streets of Paris." Adams found the pure air of the country and the silence of Auteuil far more enjoyable than the constant roar of carriages "like incessant rolls of thunder" that resounded through his Paris hotel windows. His frequent walks and rides through the Bois de Boulogne soon made him "master of this curious forest."[11]

A few days later Jefferson and his daughter and the Adams family were guests of Thomas Barclay,[12] and dinner was served in the "French style." Dinner in the French style was, in the words of Abigail Adams, a "very curious" custom. "When company are invited to dine, gentlemen meet, they seldom or never sit down, but are standing or walking from one part of the room to the other, with their swords on, and their *chapeau de Bras,* which is a very small silk hat, always worn under the arm. These they lay aside while they dine, but resume them immediately after . . . . At dinner the ladies and gentlemen are mixed, and you converse with him who sits next you, rarely speaking to persons across the table, unless to ask if they will be served with anything from your side. Conversation is never general as with us or when company quit the table, they fall into téte-a-téte of two, when the conversation is in a low voice, and a stranger, unacquainted with the customs of the country, would think that everybody had private business to transact. And on with the conversation very pleasantly, with scarcely a word from any other person, til we had finished our ice cream. When the wine began to pass round the table a little more freely, all their tongues began to be in motion."[13]

After two months in temporary quarters Jefferson moved to a handsome house in the Cul-de-Sac Taitbout, in what is presently the vicinity of the Opera.[14] The house came unfurnished and Jefferson purchased furniture, dishes, carpets, etc. His friend Thomas Barclay helped stock his wine cellar with "2 casks of very good Brandy two years old, each cask containing 42 gallons."[15] He assembled a household staff consisting of Marc, the *maitre d' hotel,* Le-grand, *valet de chambre,* and Saget, the *frotteur,* whose sole job was to keep the red tile or parquet floors clean by whirling around the rooms with brushes strapped to his feet "dancing here and there like a Merry Andrew."[16] During the year that he resided at the Cul-de-Sac Taitbout all of his meals were catered, and his slave-servant James Hemings was apprenticed to several caterers to learn the skills of French cooking.[17] James later became a cook at Jefferson's mansion on the Champs-Elysées.

With a house of his own, Jefferson offered free room and board to thirty-one-year-old David Humphreys who had been appointed by Congress to the post of Secretary to the American Legation.[18] Upon hearing of Humphrey's appointment as Secretary, George Washington wrote Jefferson, "In him you will find a good scholar, natural and acquired abilities, great integrity, and more than a share of prudence." [19] Another young protege was John Quincy Adams. Their relationship was so close that John Adams later wrote Jefferson, "I call him our John because, when you were at the Cul-De-Sac at Paris, he appeared to me to be almost as much your boy as mine."[20] During the nine months that John Quincy was in Paris he spent as much time with Jefferson as Jefferson could spare, and confided, "I spent the evening with Mr. Jefferson whom I love to be with, because he is a man of very extensive learning, and pleasing manners."[21]

The one who was most like a son to Jefferson was twenty-five-year-old William Short, also a native Virginian and a graduate of William and Mary College. Jefferson had been one of Short's examiners when he was admitted to the Virginia Bar, and when Short learned that Jefferson had been appointed a commissioner to Paris he offered to come abroad and serve as Jefferson's private secretary.[22] Although no such position existed at the time of his arrival in November, Short became a resident of Jefferson's household. Short soon discovered that neither Franklin, Adams, Jefferson, nor anyone else in the American circle spoke fluent French, so in order to become fluent in French he went off to live for four months with a French family in St. Germain-en-Laye.[23]

Another who became an intimate of Jefferson's household was the mysterious Charles Williamos. During Jefferson's first year in Paris a close friendship developed between the diplomat and this expatriate Englishman. Just days before leaving Paris in May 1785, Abigail Adams wrote: "I have returned from Mr. Jefferson's. When I got there, I found a pretty large company.... Mr. Williamos, of course, as he always dines with Mr. Jefferson."[24]

Benjamin Franklin and John and Abigail Adams gave frequent dinner parties that were attended by Jefferson and other members of the American contingent and their French friends, such as the Lafayettes and the Abbes Arnoux, Chalut and Mably. It was through the Adamses that Jefferson became friendly with the Abbes whose aristocratic connections proved helpful to Jefferson. Abbe Arnoux provided him with letters of introduction when he took his three-and-a-half month trip through southern France two-and-a-half years later.

Another member of the American circle who dined at the Adamses' was John Paul Jones who was in Paris in connection with collecting prize money that was due him and his crew. He was, in the eyes of Abigail Adams, somewhat of a disappointment. "From the intrepid character he justly supported in the American Navy, I expected to have seen a rough, stout, warlike Roman—instead of that I should sooner think of wrapping him up in cotton wool, and putting him into my pocket, than sending him to contend with cannon-balls. He is small in stature, well proportioned, soft in his speech, easy in his address, polite in his manners, vastly civil, understands all the etiquette of a lady's toilet as perfectly as he does the masts, sails and rigging of his ship. Under all this appearance of softness he is bold, enterprising, ambitious and active ... he is said to be a man of gallantry and a favorite amongst the French ladies ... he knows

John Paul Jones

how often the ladies use the baths, what color best suits a lady's complexion, what cosmetics are most favorable to the skin."[25]

Dinner at the Adamses' was always accompanied or followed by wine. John Adams had acquired an early taste of French hospitality and French wines when he landed at Bordeaux six years earlier and was invited aboard a French vessel to have dinner with the captain. "The first dish was a fine French soup, which I confess I like very much. Then a dish of boiled meat. Then the lights of a calf, dressed one way and the liver another. Then roasted mutton. Then fricased mutton. A fine salad and something very like asparagus, but not it. The bread was very fine, and it was baked on board. We had then prunes, almonds, and the most delicate raisins I ever saw. Dutch cheese—then a dish of coffee—then a French cordial—and wine and water, excellent Claret with our dinner. None of us understood French—none of them English . . ."[26]

The following day he received his first lesson on the Bordeaux wine hierarchy from J. C. Champagne, a negociant from Blaye, who rated Châteaux Margaux, Haut-Brion, Lafite and Latour the best wines of Bordeaux and referred to them as "First Growths." That afternoon, Adams dined "in the fashion of the country. We had fish and beans and salad, and Claret and Champagne and Mountain Wine."[27] The "mountain wine" referred to by Adams is known today as Malaga. It was called mountain wine in the 18th century because the grapes were grown in the mountainous regions surrounding the town of Malaga. It is a sweet wine made principally from the Pedro Ximenes grape.[28]

Young Abigail Adams (known as Nabby), nineteen and single, sized up all of the young men and recorded her impressions in her diary. She thought that as a group the Americans were too stiff and reserved and that they would be better off adopting some of the French ease of manner. She found David Humphreys too "soldier like." On her second meeting with Humphreys she noted him to be "a sensible man, I believe, but his address is not agreeable." Later when Humphreys presented her with a copy of his poem, "Armies of the America," Nabby was surprised to learn that he was a poet and noted in her diary, "Col. Humprheys has taken the most effectual means of gaining my good opinion; no more reflections upon the stiffness of his manner must proceed from me."[29]

William Short, on the other hand, had some of that ease of French manner that Nabby admired, and she found him sociable and pleasant "without the least formality or affectation of any kind. He converses with ease and says many good things." Nabby's diary entries clearly show, however, that she had no romantic interests in either Humphreys or Short.

Jefferson was probably present at Franklin's villa when Franklin's lady friend, the famous Madame Helvetius, whom Franklin called, "our lady of Auteuil," shocked Abigail Adams by her appearance and behavior. Abigail recalls Madame Helvetius entering the room "with a careless, jaunty air. Upon seeing ladies who were strange to her she bawled out, 'ah, Mon Dieux! Where is Franklin? Why did you not tell me there were ladies here? How I look!' Her hair was frizzled, over it she had a small straw hat with a dirty gauze half-handkerchief tied over it... She carried on the chief of conversation at dinner, frequently locking her hand into the Doctor's [Franklin's] and sometimes spreading her arms upon the backs of both gentlemen." She was seated between John Adams and Franklin. "Then throwing her arm carelessly about the Doctor's neck... I should have been greatly astonished if the Doctor had not told me that in this lady I would see a genuine French woman and one of the best women in the world. For this I must take the Doctor's word, but I should have set her down as a very bad one, although 60 years of age and a widow. After dinner she threw herself on a settee where she showed more than her feet," to which daughter Nabby added, "odius indeed do our sex appear when divested of those ornaments, with which modesty and delicacy adorn them."[30]

Jefferson's introduction into the highest circles of French society by Chastellux, the Marquis de Lafayette, Abbes Arnoux and Chalut, and to a lesser extent by Franklin and Adams, was a new and exciting experience for the "savage of the mountains of America," as he described himself.[31] French society, having become accustomed to the friendly pioneer image of Benjamin Franklin, who bit the tops off his asparagus, made a mush of his eggs and wore a beaver cap—some said even to bed—found Jefferson aloof and austere on first meeting but "warming to intelligent conversation."[32]

Jefferson made exhaustive efforts to blend into the French social scene, eventually acquiring a mansion on Champs Elysées, six servants, a chariot, horses, clothing suitable for the style-conscious French, dishes, glasses, furnishings, books and, of course, wines. The French intelligentsia responded to Jefferson by welcoming him into the upper reaches of their society. They were pleased to meet the author of *The Declaration of Independence* and *Notes on the State of Virginia*, and were intrigued by details of how the colonists lived, entertained, farmed, and structured their politics.

His coterie of friends consisted mainly of aristocratic French liberals: Chastellux, Lafayette and his wife, Louis-Alexandre, the Duke of Rochefoucauld, his young wife Rosalie and wealthy mother, the Duchess d'Anville, the mathematician and permanent secretary of the French Academy, Marquis de Condorcet, the scientist Lavoisier, Countess d'Houdetot, Countess de Tesse, Madame Helvetius, Madame de Corny, and the Abbes Mably, Chalut, and Arnoux. Other distinguished friends were Baron Grimm, Beaumarchais, Marmontel, Count Buffon, Houdon, Necker, Mirabeau, Malesherbes, Jacques-Louis David, and the King's foreign ministers, Counts Vergennes and Montmorin. Many of these friends formed the nucleus of a powerful group of elite French aristocrats who helped to initiate events that unleashed the French Revolution, which eventually resulted in their own destruction.

Jefferson's social acceptance was far more easily achieved than his diplomatic mission—negotiations for treaties of commerce with almost every European country. Some countries hesitated over formal recognition of the United States that had declared itself an equal. Would they alienate powerful Britain? Would they give their own people encouragement for rebellion? While the three American diplomats worked with those who did recognize them, Jefferson explored his new environment. He combed bookstalls along the Left Bank for bargains that would become part of his wide-ranging collection, eventually the nucleus of the Library of Congress; he wandered the streets of Paris absorbing its architecture; he took daily walks through the Bois de Boulogne; he sampled the pleasures of the Palais Royal; he attended dinner parties at the homes of his fellow ministers and new French friends, attended concerts, plays, operas; he shopped the elegant stores that lined Rue Saint-Honore; and he made almost daily visits to the Tuileries Gardens that stretched toward Place Louis XV and faced the Seine. Here, surrounded by the beauty of its gravel walks, beds of flowers, raised terraces, marble statues, rows of trees and water basin, he viewed the construction of a mansion whose architectural beauty had "violently smitten" him. Known as the Hotel de Salm [now the Palais de la Legion d'Honneur], it was going up directly across the Seine from the Tuileries Gardens.[33] The Château des Tuileries (torn down in 1841) and its gardens were the settings for Sunday and holiday evening *Concerts Spirituels* performed by many of the best musicians of the day. Six livres got Jefferson the best seat in the house where an orchestra of fifty-eight performed Hayden symphonies and shorter selections.

The Palais Royal was the center of the city's social life and the most interesting place for entertainment and shopping in all Europe. Four years before Jefferson's arrival the palace had passed into the hands of the Duke of Chartes who engaged the famous French architect, Victor Louis, to transform it into a pleasure center unlike anything else in the world.[34] When Jefferson first visited the Palais Royal it had only recently opened to the public. In a letter to a friend he described it as "a particular building lately erected here, which

VUE DE L'HÔTEL DE SALM.

has greatly enriched the owner of the ground, has added one of the principle ornaments to the city and increased the convenience of his inhabitants."[35]

The Palais Royal was enclosed on three sides by elegant apartment houses and along the lower levels were arcaded galleries extending from below to above ground level which housed cafes, restaurants, coffee houses, all kinds of shops, art galleries, theatres, gambling-houses and other facilities for "every vice." The most popular theatre was the *Varietes Amusantes*, and as its name indicates, it featured a variety of plays and other performances. The Duke of Chartes' private art gallery was open to the public and it contained many masterpieces by Raphael, Rubens, Rembrandt and other famous artists.[36] One of Paris' historians, Sebastien Mercier, said of the Palais Royal "there is no spot in the world comparable to it. Visit London, Amsterdam, Madrid, Vienna, you will see nothing like it: a prisoner could live here free from care for years with no thought of escape."[37]

A colonnade ran around the whole square in the middle of which was a huge garden. In the middle of this garden, as Jefferson noted, "the Palais Royal is gutted, a considerable part in the center of the garden being dug out, and a subterranean circus begun wherein will be equestrian exhibitions, etc."[38] Shade was created by triple rows of small trees. Walking in the garden during daylight hours was a fashionable Parisian pastime. It was the place to hear the latest gossip, observe women's fashions, and to see and be seen. It was a favorite haunt of Americans in Paris and, in particular, of young John Quincy Adams who loved to walk in the gardens because "This place furnishes a vast fund of entertainment to an observer. It is the most frequented walk in Paris. At every hour of the day, and of the night too, you will never fail of finding company there, and it is very curious to see the different dresses and appearances of the people you find there."[39] In the evening it was a different scene: "a mother dare not cross the noisy gallery with her two daughters; the virtuous wife, the honest citizeness, dare not be seen beside the bold courtesans, whose finery, manners, bearing, and often even their words, force one to flee, bemoaning the general corruption of both sexes."[40]

Jefferson was so impressed with the Palais Royal that he discussed the possibility of becoming involved with a similar project in Shockoe Hill in Richmond.[41] He often came to the Palais Royal for sightseeing, visiting art galleries, attending the theatre, buying books and dining at its many restaurants and cafes. Five years later these cafes became the focal point for revolutionary rhetoric.

Just before Christmas, 1784, Jefferson made his first wine contact with John Bondfield, the American Counsel in Bordeaux, who had been recommended to him by Franklin.[42] He ordered 144 bottles of "such wine" as he had drunk at Benjamin Franklin's home and another gross to be sent to his brother-in-law, Francis Eppes, in Virginia.[43] In April Bondfield acknowledged the order stating that he had forwarded "four cases containing 36 bottles each of our First Growth per the messagerie," and that a similar shipment had been sent to Eppes in Virginia.[44] Jefferson wasted little time in drinking some of the wine. His summary journal of letters under date of May 20, 1785, acknowledges receipt of the wine and adds, "wine good."

On New Year's Eve Jefferson attended a dinner party given by John and Abigail Adams. After dinner the Adams family drove into Paris and welcomed the New Year at Jefferson's place. The next day the future presidents traveled to Versailles to attend the Grand Couvert, a tradition held by the King and Queen on New Year's Day to receive foreign ambassadors. Later that month Jefferson canceled a dinner invitation with the Adamses after learning from Lafayette, who had just returned from America, the sad news of the death of his youngest daughter, Lucy Randolph. That same evening young Nabby entered in her diary, "Mr. Jefferson is a man of great sensibility and paternal affection. His wife died when this child was born, and he was almost in a confirmed state of melancholy; confined himself from the world, and even from his friends for a long time; this news has greatly affected him and his daughter."[45]

Although Jefferson had not been feeling well for several months, on February 7 he invited the Adams family to his place in the Cul-de-Sac to "see all Paris, which was to be seen on the streets today, it being the last day the one of the Carnival," a pre-lenten fete that culminated in a masked ball. The carnival consisted of hundreds of people wearing masks roaming around in the streets while thousands looked on. John Quincy did not find it entertaining, noting in his diary: "With reason our Parisians are called by all the rest of the nation eadauds [frivolous persons] de Paris, for nothing can be conceived more stupid but than this carnival amusement."[46] After dinner, Jefferson invited the Adamses to go to the masked ball which began at 1 a.m. and continued to 6 a.m., but his invitation was not accepted because young Nabby "had but little curiosity to go, the description of those who have seen it has not given me spirit enough to spend all the night to be perhaps not gratified."[47]

On Sunday, March 27, Paris reverberated from the sound of fireworks in celebration of the birth of the Duke of Normandy. Two days later, when Jefferson and Adams attended Ambassadors Day at Versailles, the Duke received "all of the ambassadors and ministers, though only two days old; he was lying on a bed, attended by two or three ladies."[48]

The next day while walking in the Palais Royal gardens, John Quincy, the American artist Benjamin West and two other American friends, found their conversation turning from the Prince's title as Duke of Normandy to his parentage. They speculated on the rumor, common at the time, that the Duke might be a bastard like a predecessor Duke of Normandy, William the Conqueror.[49]

Three days later the King came to Paris and at the Cathedral of Notre Dame assisted in the *Te Deum,* which was sung in thanks for the Duke's birth. Madam Lafayette had invited Jefferson and the Adams family to share her seats at the ceremony and, as they drove through the streets packed with people in every window and doorway, Jefferson mentioned to young Nabby that he supposed there were as many people in the streets as there were in the State of Massachusetts.

The ceremony apparently amused Jefferson because the next day he wrote Short in St. Germain-en-Laye, "you lost much by not attending the *Te-deum* at Notre Dame yesterday. It bids defiance and description. I will only observe to you in general that there were more judges, ecclesiastics and Grands seigneurs present, than Genl. Washington had of simple soldiers in his army, when he took the Hessians at Trenton, beat the British at Princeton, and hemmed up the British army at Brunswick a whole winter."[50]

On May 2 Franklin sent a letter to Adams advising that Paul Randolph Randall, a New York lawyer, had arrived in Paris with the commission papers from Congress appointing Adams minister to the Court of St. James's. Immediately after dinner Adams with his son went to the Hotel d'Orlean where Randall was staying and picked up his commission. They then went to Jefferson's and found that he had received his commission as sole minister to France along with confirmation that Benjamin Franklin's resignation had been accepted by Congress.[51] Adams was elated by his appointment as the first American minister to the Court of St. James's but had one regret. He knew immediately that he would miss the beauty of his home in Auteuil and lamented, "What shall I do in London for *my* garden, *my* park, *my* river, and *my* plain? You see I call all the environs of Auteuil mine, and with good reason, for I will lay a wager they have given me more pleasure in the last nine months than they ever afforded their legal and royal proprietors for a century."[52]

On Sunday, May 8, John and Abigail Adams gave a farewell dinner for their American colleagues, and this was followed the next day with dinner at the Lafayettes. On the way home Jefferson, John and Abigail Adams and others in the party went shopping. Nabby and Paul Randolph Randall remained in one of the carriages. When a young girl wearing a gauze veil passed their carriage, Randall commented that the blush of innocence

Jefferson's Diplomatic Calling Card

would make for a better veil, which brought from Nabby the retort that "there were few of those known in Paris."[53]

Tuesday was Ambassadors Day at the Court of Versailles, but John Adams' attendance on this Tuesday was unlike any other that he had made because he came to take his leave of Court. Jefferson, who was to make this weekly journey over the next fifty-two months, often combined it with a side visit to Chaville, the country estate of his friend Madame de Tesse, who shared his passion for architecture, gardening, and Roman antiquities.[54]

John Adams, an enthusiastic wine drinker, had accumulated during his stays at The Hague and Paris a large supply of wines. In fact, just before receiving word that he had been appointed America's first minister to England, he had ordered 500 bottles of French wine. Upon his arrival in London on May 26, he was told, to his chagrin, that diplomatic immunity could not save him from paying the English duty of six to eight shillings (about $1.75) on every bottle of wine brought into the country. In a state of shock he frantically wrote Jefferson beseeching him to stop the shipment of all his wines except one case of Madeira and Frontignan adding: "I am sorry to give you this trouble but I beg you to take the wine, at any price you please. Let your Maitre d'Hotel judge, or accept it as a present or sell it at Vendue i.e. let Petit dispose of it as he will...."[55] In a follow-up letter Adams pleaded: "For mercy sake stop all of my wine but the Bordeaux and Madeira and Frontenac. And stop my order to Rouen for 500 additional bottles. I shall be ruined, for each minister is not permitted to import more than 5 or 600 bottles which will not more than cover what I have at The Hague which is very rich wine and my Madeira, Frontenac and Bordeaux at Auteuil."[56] The day before receiving Adams' first urgent message, Jefferson had arranged for the shipment of his wines. On getting Adams' plea, he immediately dispatched his *maitre d'hotel*, Petit, to stop the boat leaving Paris for Rauen but Petit was not in time. The boat was just departing.[57]

The letters which flew back and forth between Jefferson and Adams about arrangements for Adams' wine preceded in presence, if not importance, other diplomatic correspondence. Jefferson also reported the arrival for Adams of a 60-gallon cask of wine that held 215 bottles of red wine from Gaillac, probably Cahusac, which he could not taste and determine its quality because "it is in a cask within a cask," a security measure. Adams advised that this cask of wine was not paid for but he had sampled it and it was a good wine "and very, extremely cheap." He asked Jefferson to take it for himself which Jefferson did—"cheerfully."[58] Finally, on July 16, Adams notified Jefferson that he had written to the U.S. Consul in Rouen, Anthony Garvey, to forward all of his wine "as I believe I shall easily obtain an order to receive it without paying duties."[59] The Adams wine crisis was over.

After a year in Paris, Jefferson wrote his friend Charles Bellini, a professor of modern languages at William and Mary College, some of his impressions "on the vaunted scene of Europe!" He observed that the great mass of people suffered under physical and moral oppression and that, among his aristocratic friends, conjugal love had no existence and domestic happiness was utterly unknown. Still, "were I to proceed to tell you how much I enjoyed their architecture, sculpture, painting, music, I should want words. It is in these arts they shine."[60]

Jefferson, who was a frequent dinner guest at the homes of these rich and privileged people, said that "in the pleasures of the table, they are far before us, because with good taste they unite temperance."[61] Arthur Young went a step further and said of French food, "There is but one opinion ... for every man in Europe, that can afford a great table, either keeps a French cook, or one influenced in the same manner ... [T]here is not better beef in the world than at Paris. Large handsome pieces were almost constantly on the considerable tables I have dined at. The variety given by their cooks, to the same thing, is astonishing; they dress an hundred dishes in an hundred different ways, most of them excellent; and all sorts of vegetables have a flavourness and flavours." These lavish meals were often served with knives, forks and spoons of gold.[62]

Paris, for all its beauty, had its ugliness. Two percent of the population, the clergy and nobility, owned or controlled ninety-eight percent of the nation's wealth. Much of the rest of the nation lived in poverty. Beggars and prostitutes crowded Parisian streets causing the new minister to observe, "It is difficult for a young man to refuse it where beauty is begging in every street."[63] Although mansions lined the streets in fashionable areas, and the nobility and clergy rode through those streets in gilded carriages, there were "no sidewalks. The carts, cabrioles, and carriages. run up to the very houses. You must save yourself by bracing flat against the wall.... Most of the streets are paved as Albany and New York were before the Revolution with an open gutter in the middle. Some arched in the middle, and a little gutter to each side.... It is fine sport for the cabriolet and hack drivers to run a wheel in one of these gutters, always full of filth, and bespatter fifty pedestrians who are braced against the wall."[64]

In the summer of 1785, Jefferson's friend and old Virginia neighbor, Philip Mazzei, arrived in Paris and "went at once to see Jefferson.... I took an enjoyable and interesting walk, arriving about an hour before dinner. I had informed him of my arrival at Lorient, as soon as I landed; and I wrote to him from Nantes also. So he expected me daily. Nevertheless, our meeting was moving to both. We had many things to say, and we had a great deal of time at our disposal, for on that day no one came to dine with him, and his secretary, Mr. Short, was at dinner with the Countess de Tesse, cousin of the Marquis de la Fayette. After discoursing on public matters, we spoke about our own affairs." The next day they called on Marmontel and then paid their respects to

Lavoisier, Condorcet, and the Duke of Rochefoucault before returning home to dine with Short.[65]

It was about this time that Jefferson acquired a pedometer and made calculations of the length of his stride in both winter and summer that revealed he walked at a fast pace, in excess of four miles an hour.[66] Jefferson's thoughts on exercise are well expressed in a letter to his future son-in-law. "If the body be feeble, the mind will not be strong. The sovereign invigorator of the body is exercise, and of all the exercises walking is best. A horse gives but a kind of half exercise, and a carriage is no better than a cradle. No one knows, till he tries, how easily a habit of walking is acquired. A person who never walked three miles will in the course of a month become able to walk 15 or 20 without fatigue. I have known great walkers and had particular accounts of many more; and I never knew or heard of one who was not healthy and long lived . . . not less than two hours a day should be devoted to exercise, and the weather should be little regarded. A person not sick will not be injured by getting wet."[67]

The physically fit Jefferson made walking his principal form of exercise and established the routine of leaving work at noon for a two hour walk through the Bois de Boulogne.[68] Jefferson did not leave a description of what he saw on these daily walks but John Adams, who considered the Bois de Boulogne his private sanctuary, penned a vivid account. "The Gate, by which you enter the Bois de Boulogne, from the Village of Auteuil . . . I turn to the left and follow the Path, which runs in sight of the Stone Wall of 12 feet high which bounds the Forest, until I come to a Gate which they call Porte Royal, out of which you go to Versailles. From this Gate I follow the Path which runs near the Boundary Stone Wall, until I come to the Gate which opens into the Village of Boulogne. I pursue to this Path by the Wall until I come to the Pavilion of Bagatelle, belonging to the Comte D'Artois. The Estate of the Comte is separated from the Forest only by a Treillage or a kind of Picketted Wooden Fence. Having passed the Bagatelle you come to the Royal Castle of Madrid, passing this you go out of the Wood into the Grand Chemin, by the Gate called Porte Neuilly, near the new Bridge of that name.

But by the Forest from the Grand Chemin, you come to the Gate, which is called Porte Maillot, at the Plain de Sablons. By following the Grand Road from this Gate, you come to the Royal Castle of Muet, at Passy, near which is the Gate by which you enter the Forest from Passy. By following the Path near the Stone Wall, which bounds the Wood, You come to the Gate, at Auteuil, by which We first entered the Forest.

"Near the Center of the Forest, is a Circle, of clear Ground, on which are no Trees or Shrubs. From the Center of this Circle, proceed Avenues in all Directions. One goes to the Porte Royale, another to the Village of Boulogne, another to the Castle of Madrid, another to the Castle of Muet at Passy, and another to the Gate of Auteuil.

"In riding over this Forrest, you see some neat Cattle, some Horses, a few Sheep, and a few Deers, Bucks, Does and Fawns, now and then a Hare and sometimes a few Partridges."[69]

This was the summer that Jefferson started what would become an annual Fourth of July party, and all Americans in Paris and many of his French friends were invited. The next day he wrote a scathing letter to Charles Williamos, ending their friendship. Although Jefferson never explained why, it is believed that France's foreign minister, Vergennes, convinced him that Williamos was a British spy. Williamos' rambling reply adds nothing to explain the sudden and unexpected dissolution of their friendship, although he does allude to a small pension he was receiving from the British crown.[70]

Facing a longer stay in Paris than originally expected, Jefferson had appointed Short his private secretary and began looking for a residence more suitable to his position as Minister Plenipotentiary. In October, 1785, he moved into his new home, the Hotel de Langeac, located on the Champs-Elysées and Rue de Berri, and across the street from the Grillé de Chaillot.[71] This was a new but fashionable area and Jefferson was pleased with his new home, writing John Adams: "I have at length procured a house in a situation much more pleasant to me than my present . . . it suits me in every circumstance but the price . . . it has a clever garden to it."[72] It was a much larger house than the one he had occupied in the Cul-de-Sac with a garden, stables, horses, carriages, a cook, and even a regular coachman. It served not only as his home but also as the American Legation where he transacted official business.

Over the next four years the Hotel de Langeac became the scene of many dinners where France's best wines were served to an appreciative coterie of friends, both American and French.

The entrance to the house was through a courtyard that faced the Rue de Berri, with servants' quarters and stables on the other side of the courtyard. Jefferson's dining room interconnected a circular room with a skylight, a petit salon, and a larger salon that looked out onto a garden where he grew "Indian corn for the use of my own table, to eat green in our manner."[73]

Jefferson's dinner guests could view the Champs-Elysées through three windows draped with blue silk damask. A fifteen-foot dining room table could seat twenty and was ornamented with silverware, biscuit figurines, and a crenelated porcelain bucket *(seau crenele)* used for cooling wine glasses. Wines from Jefferson's cellar made their rounds in beautiful crystal decanters. Jefferson's interest in serving wine in decanters had early origins as is evidenced from the engraved dartouche and grapevine motifs that festooned an English decanter recovered from the drywell at Monticello and dating from the 1760s.[74]

Eleven days after moving into his new mansion he made his first visit to Fontainebleau, a royal palace located about forty miles south of Paris. Fontainebleu was used almost exclusively by the King for hunting boar in the surrounding forests. Writing by his hotel fireside after dinner, Jefferson entered into "conversation" with James Madison. "I set out yesterday morning to take a view of the place. As soon as I had got clear of the town I fell in with a poor woman walking at the same rate with

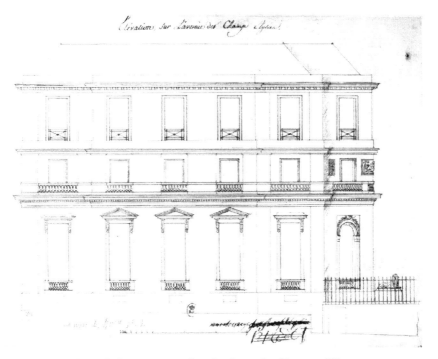

Hotel de Langeac, south side along the Champs-Elysées

myself and going the same course. Wishing to know the condition of the laboring poor I entered into conversation with her, which I began by inquiries for the path which would lead me into the mountains: and thence proceeded to enquires into her vocation, condition and circumstance. She told me she was a day laborer, at 8 sous or 4d sterling the day; that she had two children to maintain, and to pay rent of 30 livres for the house ... that often she could get no employment, and of course was without bread. As we walked together near a mile and she had so far served me as a guide, I gave her, on parting 24 sous. She burst into tears of gratitude which I could perceive was unfeigned, because she was unable to utter a word. She probably never before received so great an aid. This little *attendnssement*, with the solitude of my walk led me into a train of reflections on that unequal division of property which occasions the numberless instances of wretchedness which I had observed in this country and is to be observed all over Europe. The property of this country is absolutely concentered in a very few hands ... I am tomorrow to go to Mr. Malesherbes (an uncle of the Chevalr. Luzerne's) about 7 leagues from hence, who is the most curious man in France as to his trees. He is making for me a collection of the vines from which the Burgundy, Champagne, Bordeaux, Frontignac, and other the most valuable wines of this country are made."[75]

Lafayette, who at nineteen had defied his King to impetuously serve in America, continued in France his zealous efforts in behalf of all things American. In Jefferson Lafayette found an echoing voice, sharing memories of the Revolution, an interest in

France's political and social structure and Gallic cuisine and wines. They frequently met at one another's homes for dinner, and on at least one occasion their conversation turned to ordering wine, for in January, 1786, the two agreed to share the expense of a pipe of Madeira.

Lafayette had acquired a taste for Madeira in America and, by all accounts, the Madeira drunk by our founding fathers was far better than the present-day product. It was discovered that Madeira was improved by long sea voyages when casks were stowed as ballast in ships that sailed world-wide. With the demand for Madeira increasing, the aging process was simulated by storing it in heated rooms of up to 120 degrees Fahrenheit. Perhaps it is apocryphal, but Cyrus Redding reports that the maturity of such a voyage was also achieved by plunging well-corked bottles of Madeira "into a trench filled with fermenting horse-dung."[76]

Following up on their decision to purchase a pipe of Madeira, Jefferson wrote Francis Lewis, a New York wine merchant: "Finding it impossible to get good and genuine Madeira wine here I have concluded it most convenient to import it from America, and particularly from New York where it is generally to be had good, and may be sent readily by the packet. The acquaintance I have had the honor of having formerly with you encourages me to trouble you with this commission . . . as nobody knows better how to chuse what is good. I would prefer that which is of the nut quality, and of the very best. If you will be so good as to send me a pipe [110 gallons] of such . . . You are the best judge whether it would come better in bottles, or in a cask; and if in a cask, whether the precaution of one cask within another be necessary."[77]

Three months later Lewis received Jefferson's order and "upon inquiry found that the best Madeira Wine in this City for sale is eight years old, of which I shall pick the best out of forty Pipes." Lewis apparently took the precaution of shipping the wine "one cask within another" because he mentions that he was shipping it "cased."[78] It was obviously "the very best" because at a cost of 1075 livres, or about two and a half livres per bottle, it was expensive.[79]

In France, Jefferson could choose from that country's famous wines rather than being limited as in America to Madeira, Port, Lisbon, cider, beer or home-brewed products. The cuisine was a different matter; although he enthusiastically endorsed French cooking, he did not completely "abjure his native vittles" as Patrick Henry later accused him of doing. He was not even above getting them illegally, writing to Alexander Donald in Richmond for "a dozen or two of hams" to be sent by a captain, who "must pretend the hams to be a part of his private stores, or they will be seized . . . I have it in contemplation to write to Mr. Eppes for some of a particular kind of cider which he makes, and in like manner to trouble you with it." Jefferson never got the hams because Donald could not find a captain willing to risk losing his ship to satisfy Jefferson's longing for home-smoked hams.[80]

On New Year's Eve he received a letter from the world famous naturalist Count Buffon, who had served since 1739 as the Intendant of the King's Garden and Cabinet, inviting Jefferson and Chastellux to dinner on a day of their convenience.[81]

This was the first of several invitations to dine with Count Buffon, whose practice it was "to remain in his study til dinner time, and receive no visitors under any pretense; but his house was open and his grounds, and a servant showed them very civilly and invited all strangers and friends to remain to dine. We saw Buffon in the garden, but carefully avoided him, but we dined with him, and he proved himself then, as he always did, a man of extraordinary powers in conversation. He did not declaim; he was singularly agreeable."[82]

Jefferson's valet, Marc, ended his lack-luster wine stewardship, selecting for Jefferson more than 700 bottles of no particular distinction in 1784-85. He was dismissed in July, 1786, for stealing. This began Bondfield's guidance and acquisitions for one of the outstanding cellars of that period. In a letter to Bondfield in January, 1786, Jefferson ordered 12 dozen bottles of red Bordeaux and 12 dozen bottles of *"vin de Grave* of fine quality" leaving to Bondfield's judgment whether it should come in bottles or in casks.[83] He also had Bondfield send Francis Eppes 36 pint bottles of Frontignac. Jefferson's friend Thomas Barclay reported that Bondfield filled this order by purchasing two hogsheads of Haut-Brion "wine for you, and fined it before I reached Bordeaux, so he has robbed me of any share in the merit of that purchase."[84] Learning that Jefferson was in England and not knowing when he would return, Bondfield deliberately delayed shipping the wine until June. When Jefferson received the wine in August he reported to Bondfield, "We find the red wine excellent. The Graves is a little hard."[85] Actually, the red wine that Bondfield sent Jefferson was not Haut Brion but 144 bottles of 1783 Leoville (now three vineyards: Leoville-LasCases, Leoville-Poyferre and Leoville-Barton) at a cost of two livres per bottle. The twelve dozen bottles of Graves also arrived packed thirty-six bottles to a case from the vineyards of President du Roy.[86] Du Roy owned at the time the vineyard now known as Château de Suduiraut, a sweet Sauternes, but he owned other vineyard properties and, because Jefferson said it was a Graves and "a little hard," it probably came from one of du Roy's other vineyards.

In spite of his preference for French wines, he was still curious about the vines he had left growing at Monticello. "How does my vineyard come on? Have there been grapes enough to make a trial of wine?," he wrote Antonio Giannini, who had emigrated with Philip Mazzei. "If there should be, I should be glad to receive here a few bottles of the wine."[87] The vines were "improving marvelously," Giannini replied, but no wine had been made "because each year the grapes are picked before they are ripe, which is very harmful to the vines." He promised to make wine and send some to Jefferson in Paris in the autumn.[88] Giannini did not stay long enough to keep his promise because on June 21, 1786, he sent a letter to Jefferson about the possibility of selling Italian cloth in Virginia. Although Jefferson's Garden Book

VUE DU JARDIN DU ROI
du côté de la Rivière, en face de l'Arsenal

shows that he planted vines at Monticello as early as March 28, 1771, and continued to grow grapes in two small vineyards located just below the main house, there is no evidence that he ever produced a bottle of wine from his viticultural efforts.[89]

CHAPTER THREE

London and the English Countryside

On February 27, 1786, William Stephen Smith arrived in Paris from London with a message from his soon to be father-in-law, John Adams, urging Jefferson to come to London to assist in negotiating a commerce treaty with Portugal and to meet the minister from Tripoli, in hopes of reaching an accord protecting against the seizure of American ships by the Barbary pirates. In earlier letters to the Adamses, Jefferson had expressed a desire to visit England, and Adams' request afforded the perfect opportunity.[1]

Smith, as described by his future mother-in-law, Abigail Adams, was: "tall, slender, and a good figure, a complexion naturally dark, but made still more so by seven years service in the field, where he reaped laurels more durable than the tincture of a skin. He appears a gentleman in every thought, word, and action; domestic in his attachments, fond in his affections, quick as lightning in his feelings, but softened in an instant; . . . he loves his country, and is willing to devote his talents to the service of it."[2]

That evening Smith accompanied Jefferson to the Opera Masquerade Ball. The Masquerade Ball was held on Sunday nights throughout the winter following a concert, and there was dancing from 1 a.m. to 6 a.m. Although it was known as a "masquerade," the participants wore masks and dominoes (a hood with a mask) rather than fancy dress.[3] Jefferson had attended this ball on other occasions but, on this night, according to Smith, a predatory Dutch Baroness had set her evening's hopes on snaring Jefferson. When Jefferson "had made his escape she fastened her talons on me."[4]

A week later Jefferson and Smith left Paris by way of Chantilly, Breteuil, Abbeville and Montreuil and arrived in Calais on March 8. They took rooms and had dinner at Pierre Dessin's popular inn, Hotel d'Angleterre. Dessin, who had become famous through Lawrence Sterne's portrait of him in *A Sentimental Journey*,[5] provided the traveler with more than good food and comfortable lodging; he changed money and rented all types of carriages, English as well as French.[6]

The next morning they crossed the channel to Dover. Their developing friendship, combined with the beauty of their trip through the Kentish countryside, made the two-day journey from Dover to London a pleasant one. Crossing London Bridge on March 11, Jefferson arrived in London for what would be his first and only visit. He immediately visited the Adamses but did not stay with them at their handsome house on Grosvenor Square. He lodged nearby at No. 14 Golden Square, a fashionable area.[7]

Jefferson's next forty-eight days were spent in diplomatic negotiations, shopping London's establishments, visiting its historic sites, meeting new friends such as John and Lucy Paradise and American artists John Trumbull and Mather Brown, visiting publishers and bookshops, buying books, sitting for his portrait,[8] being presented to the King and Queen, and traveling through the English countryside. His evenings included the theatre, the opera and concerts, a ball at the French Embassy, dinners at the homes of the Adamses and their friends, a visit to one of London's pleasure-haunts, the Ranelagh, and a late evening at Dolly's Chop House.

The Adams-Jefferson diplomatic efforts were unsuccessful. Although they negotiated and signed a treaty with Portugal, the Portuguese minister, Chevalier de Pinto, had not received authority to sign, and when he submitted the treaty for approval, it was rejected.[9] The price demanded for peace by the Tripolian minister was far too high and these negotiations were abandoned. Jefferson came away convinced that the best solution to the Barbary pirates' menace was war, and in a letter to Adams a few months later he opined: "However if it is decided that we shall buy a peace, I know no reason for delaying the operation, but should rather think it ought to be hastened. But I should prefer the obtaining it by war."[10]

On the morning of March 17, Adams took Jefferson to the Court of St. James's Palace and presented him to King George III and Queen Charlotte. Ten years earlier the King had read Jefferson's scorching denunciation of him in the Declaration of Independence, and he had neither forgotten nor forgiven. Jefferson poignantly describes their reception: "On my presentation... to the King and Queen at their Levees, it was impossible for anything to be more ungracious than their notice of Mr. Adams and myself. I saw at once that the ulcerations in the narrow mind of that mulish being left nothing to be expected on the subject of my attendance."[11]

Adams remembered the King turning his back on them. "A hint which, of course, was not lost upon the circle of his subjects in attendance."[12] And, indeed, it was not, for though Jefferson was entertained at dinners by a few Englishmen who were American sympathizers, he was ignored during the remainder of his stay by members of the British ministry.[13]

It is not surprising that working under such conditions, their attempts to negotiate acceptable trade arrangements with England were futile. Jefferson expressed his frustrations in a letter to Madison on the eve of his departure for Paris: "With this nation nothing is done; and it is now decided that they intend to do nothing with us. The king is against a change of measures; his ministers are against it, some from principle, others from attachment to their places, and the merchants and people are against it. They sufficiently value our commerce; but they are quite persuaded they shall enjoy it on their own terms."[14]

With time available he shopped for a variety of items including a walking stick, cotton stockings, knives, a thermometer, protractor, globe, telescope, solar microscope, boots, tools, saddlery, pocket pistols, hydrometer, chess set, fish knife, books, and he also sat for his portrait by Mather Brown.[15]

On March 18 he attended the opera at the King's Theatre in Hay Market and saw Antonio Salieri's comic opera *La Scuola de Gelosi*. Three days later Jefferson, William Smith and Richard Peters, a friend from the United States who was visiting London, spent the evening at the famous London chop house, Dolly's, in Paternoster Row.[16]

Early the next morning Jefferson left for Windsor Castle where he spent the day sightseeing the castle and its gardens and having dinner.

It was about this time that Jefferson first met the American painter John Trumbull.[17] Trumbull, twenty-nine years old, was an aspiring American artist who was studying in London under Benjamin West. He had distinguished himself during the Revolutionary War as an officer and had served for a short period as General Washington's aide-de-camp. Jefferson immediately became interested in Trumbull when he learned of his plan to devote himself to painting the great events of the American Revolution. In his autobiography Trumbull recalled his meeting with Jefferson in London: "He encouraged me to persevere in this pursuit, and kindly invited me to come to Paris, to see and study the fine arts there, and to make his house my home during my stay. I now availed myself of this invitation and went to his house, at the Grillé de Chaillot, where I was most kindly received by him . . . . I employed myself, with untiring industry, in examining and studying whatever had relation to the arts . . . Mr. Jefferson joined our party almost daily; and here commenced his acquaintance with Mrs. Cosway."[18]

In company with the Adams family, Jefferson dined with John and Lucy Paradise at their home in Charles Street on Cavendish Square. This was probably the first time that Jefferson had met the Paradises to whom he was to become a friend, advisor and protector as a result of their personal and financial difficulties.[19] At nine o'clock that evening the whole party went to the French Ambassador's Ball "where were two or three hundred people, chiefly ladies."[20]

The next day saw Jefferson getting his first sight of the English landscape gardens, journeying to Enfield Chase, laid out by William Pitt, Earl of Chatham. These buildings and gardens no longer survive. He then visited Moor Park, near Rickmansworth.[21] As he approached the house at Moor Park, he saw behind it a flat lawn of about 30 acres with three distinct and different hills as a backdrop. He thought the house superb with the front a Corinthian portico of four columns and a terrace with four Corinthian pilasters but felt that the walk that surrounded the lawn destroyed its unity.[22]

On April 2 Jefferson and William Stephen Smith began a two day landscape garden tour of Surrey and Middlesex. Their first stop was at Chiswick where they saw the house and gardens of the Earl of Burlington.[23] The house was an imitation of the Villa Capra at Vicenca, by Palladia, Jefferson's chief architectural mentor.[24] Still, Jefferson thought the octagonal dome of the house gave an "ill effect," and the six acre garden contained too much ornamental art, especially in its use of obelisks.[25]

A garden that Jefferson was eager to see was Alexander Pope's in Twickenham, designed by William Kent and by Pope.[26] Pope, known today for his poetry, was almost as famous during his lifetime for his contributions to landscape gardening. The garden surrounding his villa was known throughout England.[27] Jefferson noted that the house was about thirty yards from the Thames, with a grotto under the street that extended level to the river. In the center of the garden was a mound with a spiral walk-around, and an obelisk that Pope had dedicated to his mother.[28]

Their next stop was Hampton Court, the largest royal palace in Great Britain and the former residence of Henry VIII and his six wives. Its famous gardens, laid out by Lancelot "Capability" Brown"[29] were dismissed by Jefferson with the comment, "Old fashioned. Clipt yews grown wild."[30] The palace and its now well-clipped yew hedge gardens are still open to the public.

From Hampton Court they traveled south to Esher Place and Claremont. The gardens at both places were the works of William Kent, although the Claremont grounds had been improved by "Capability" Brown. The Esher gardens consisted of about 45 acres of "a most lovely mixture of concave and convex" (meaning hills and dales) with its main attraction being "clumps of trees." At Claremont, which was contiguous to Esher Place, Jefferson found "nothing remarkable."[31]

Their last stop was at Painshill Park near Cobham, one of the most famous landscaped gardens of the 18th century. Jefferson described Painshill as 323 acres of "garden and park." Painshill was laid out in the form of a semi-circle between a river, which defined its outward boundary, and the park. The gardens bordered the river and the estate-house stood on a hill above the park. On a second hill there was a large vineyard. On the side of another hill was a hermitage and tower that looked down on an artificial lake. Just above the lake was a Gothic building with a winding path to the lake and a walkway embellished with bridges, a ruined arch and a grotto. Jefferson's notes make reference to a beautiful Doric temple near the tower called the Temple of Bacchus "with a fine portico in the front, a rich *alto relievio* in the pediment, and on each side a range of pilasters." Jefferson thought the dwelling house ill-situated and its architecture "incorrect."[32] They spent the night at the Postman's Arms in Weybridge and dined on veal cutlets, mutton chops, beer and wine.[33]

Jefferson had one day of rest before leaving on April 4 with John Adams on a six-day tour through the English countryside. During this trip they visited magnificent landscaped gardens and battle sites, sharing thoughts and meals and wines. Although they would both live another 40 years, never again would they experience such intimacy and friendship. Ten years later they would be locked in political enmity which

Adams would win to become the second President of the United States, only to lose that office to Jefferson four years later.

In the late 18th century roads in England between cities and towns were essentially well-graded, and the stagecoach was a highly developed form of travel, with a 200-year tradition. In addition to the regular stagecoach, many of the inns served as posting-houses where the traveler could rent a chaise (a closed body four-wheeled carriage) and horses for a few pence per mile. The horses were used for distances of about six to ten miles and were left at another posting-inn where new horses were hired. Each inn branded its horses so they could be identified and returned.[34] Since this was an expensive way to travel it was usually used by upper-class gentlemen, and was the method employed by Adams and Jefferson.

Innkeeping in England was more than a mere occupation or trade; as practiced by many innkeepers it was an honorable calling. Eighteenth century inns often did not have common dining rooms. Affluent travelers, such as Adams and Jefferson, usually dined in private rooms with the common traveler taking his meals in the kitchen.[35]

The English landscape gardens that Jefferson and Adams visited were the antithesis of earlier formal English gardens they were familiar with in colonial America as well as the strictly defined gardens surrounding French palaces and châteaux. Pleasure gardening, as Jefferson called it, had emerged as the rave in 18th century England and was best associated with the gardens designed by William Kent and Lancelot "Capability" Brown.[36]

Their first day took the two Americans through Twickenham and then to Woburn where they visited Woburn Farm (a revisit for Jefferson), a pleasure garden of about 35 acres that was "merely a highly ornamented walk through and round the divisions of the farm and kitchen garden."[37] Not a trace remains today.

From Woburn they traveled to Caversham where they inspected Major Marsac's garden and park of 431 acres, the work of "Capability" Brown. The English countryside from Caversham to Reading was a prelude to the scenic beauty that would surround them for the next six days. In Reading they lodged at the Bear Inn on Bridge Street,[38] an important hostelry at that time. They had for dinner chicken, potatoes, tarts and custards, accompanied by punch, porter and sherry wine.[39]

In the morning they rented horses and traveled the turnpike road to Wallingford, Thame, and Wooton. In the late 17th century tolls were established for bridges, causeways, and along the heaviest traveled roads. At first these toll roads were not barred or obstructed, but because some travelers would dash past the toll collector without paying, laws were enacted giving local authorities the power to block the roadway with a turnpike. The turnpike consisted of metal pikes fastened to a metal frame which formed a barrier when placed across the road. After the traveler paid the toll, the frame was turned on a pivot, clearing the way. Later in the 18th century the pikes were replaced with ordinary tollgates that we are still faced with in one form or the other. Since turnpikes were used on the most heavily traveled roads, the term became synonymous with the main road and survives today.[40]

The owner of the Wooton gardens employed only two workers to keep the more than 300 acres in order, and they found the gardens "much neglected." They lodged in Buckingham and paid almost twice as much for their beer and wine as they did for their dinners of veal chops and mutton steaks.[41]

Although Jefferson's travel receipts do not identify the specific wines they drank with their dinners, they were expensive, usually costing twice as much as their meals. There are two explanations: the quantity and quality of the wines. The English imposed exorbitant duties on French wines during the entire 18th century and these taxes caused French wines to cost more than wines from Germany, Portugal and Spain. Jefferson and Adams, both lovers of French wines, when given the choice would have invariably selected claret or Burgundy or Champagne.[42]

Early in the morning they traveled to the pleasure-gardens at Stowe. They approached the Stowe gardens along a magnificent avenue of elms with the mansion and a Corinthian arch in the distance. Because the arch was not a part of the house and had no independent "destination," Jefferson thought it broke up a pleasing prospect and created an ill-effect. The Stowe gardens, with the imprint of both Kent and Brown on them, were probably the best known gardens in England at the time. Jefferson and Adams climbed to the top of the 115 foot Lord Cobham's Pillar for the view.[43]

On the way to Banbury they stopped at Edgehill where the first great battle of the Civil War (1642-1651) was fought between the forces of the King and Parliament. The battlefield is now covered with trees. In Banbury they stayed at the William Pratt Inn and had beer and wine with their dinner. Following dinner they changed their chaise and horses and traveled to Shakespeare's birthplace, StratfordUpon-Avon.[44]

Jefferson's inn receipt does not reveal the name of the inn where they stayed for the evening, but Adams identified it as being "three doors" from Shakespeare's birthplace, and it is almost certain that it was The White Lion Inn, operated by John Payton on Henley Street. This was the town's leading inn and was located "three doors" from Shakespeare's birthplace. Although the White Lion Inn was known for its excellent dinner fare, Jefferson and Adams had dined earlier and ordered only lemonade and tea before retiring.[45]

Jefferson's only mention of their stay in Stratford-Upon-Avon was to record in his account book paying one shilling each to see Shakespeare's birthplace and gravesite. It is curious that he did not comment on his Shakespearean experience because, in addition to owning all of Shakespeare's works, he considered Shakespeare and Alexander Pope two of the greatest English poets.[46] Adams, however, thought Stratford-Upon-Avon "interesting, as it is the scene of the birth, death, and sepulcher of Shakespeare. Three doors from the inn is the house where he was born, as small and mean as you can conceive. They showed us an old wooden chair in the chimney corner where he sat. We cut off a chip according to custom. A mulberry tree that he planted has been cut down and is carefully preserved for sale. The house where he died has been taken

White Lion Inn

Shakespeare's Birthplace

down, and the spot is now only yard or garden. The curse upon him who should remove his bones, which is written on his gravestone, alludes to a pile of some thousands of human bones which lie exposed in that church.[47] There is nothing preserved of this great genius which is worth knowing; nothing which might inform us what education, what company, what accident, turned his mind to letters and the drama. His name is not even on his gravestone. An ill-sculptured head is set up by his wife, by the side of his grave in the church. But paintings and sculpture would be thrown away on his fame. His wit, fancy, his tastes and judgment, his knowledge of nature, of life and character, are immortal."[48]

In the morning they rented a chaise and horses and visited Birmingham and "viewed a manufactury of paintings on wallpaper," probably a business for the production of decorated *papier mâché* ceiling panels, tea trays and tables. After dinner at the Swan Tavern, they set out for the gardens at Leasowes situated between Birmingham and Stourbridge.[49]

Leasowes consisted of a 150-acre grazing farm encircled by a walk that looked like a common field path. After the opulence of Stowe, Jefferson was disappointed in the plainness of the gardens. Eleven years earlier Leasowes had been described as abounding in attractive winding walks, "serpentnizing" paths and a variety of romantic scenes,[50] but at the time of Jefferson's visit its grandeur was a thing of the past.[51]

Their next stop was Stourbridge where they stayed at John Wiley's Talbot Inn on High Street. The inn's origins date back to the 16th century and it was Stourbridge's most famous coaching inn during the 18th century. It was owned by John Wiley until 1793. It still operates as a hotel (now the Talbot Hotel) and though such modern amenities as televisions, telephones, radios and hair dryers are standard in the all the rooms, much of its 17th and 18th century character remains.[52]

On the morning of April 8 they rented a chaise and horses to Bromsgrove and visited the 1,000 acre garden and park at Hagley, located between the Clent and Witchbury hills. The estate house was in a hollow between the hills. The Witchbury hills rose in three swells, the summits of which provided striking views of the countryside, the Hagley estate-house, the town of Stourbridge and the ruins of the Dudley Castle. The view from the Clent hills took in the Black Mountains of Wales and the towns of Worcester, Birmingham, and Stourbridge.[53]

In Worcester, they visited battle sites which Adams recorded as "curious and interesting to us, as scenes where free men had fought for their rights." Adams became annoyed, even indignant, because the people in the neighborhood appeared to be ignorant of the fact that Worcester was the scene of Oliver Cromwell's final victory in 1651 over Charles II during England's bloody Civil War. Provoked, he asked: 'And do Englishmen so soon forget the ground where liberty was fought for? Tell your neighbors and your children that this is holy ground; much holier than that on which your churches stand. All England should come and pilgrimage to this hill once a year."[54]

Worcester's well-paved streets, public walks and cathedral showed its affluence from flourishing trades in gloves, carpets and china. They dined at Worcester's most expensive and popular inn, the Hop-Pole. It was located on Foregate Street on the road from Holyhead to Bath and Bristol.[55]

Leaving Worcester they rode through the hamlets of Moreton, Lynston and lodged at Woodstock, a "neat" little town that served as a convenient stop for a visit to the gardens at Blenheim Palace. Jefferson's tavern receipt does not tell us at which inn they stayed but the Bear Inn and Marlborough Arms were both excellent.[56] The next morning they visited the gardens at Blenheim. Blenheim Palace had been built by the British nation for the Duke of Marlboro in commemoration of his defeating the French at Blenheim in 1704. The colossal house measures almost three football fields in length. The gardens were revised in the 1760's by "Capability" Brown. Jefferson noted that the grounds consisted of 225 acres with gardens, lakes, and a park stocked with deer and sheep. He found the lakes "very beautiful and very grand," but overall he was disappointed, complaining of too many temples and fountains and too few seats, and trees scattered thinly over the grounds.[57]

In Oxford they visited several of the colleges, and then went on to High Wycombe where they dined at the Antelope Inn on mutton chops accompanied by beer and wine. Following dinner they traveled as far as Uxbridge, lodging at the White Hart Inn before returning to London the next day.[58]

During his tour of the English landscaped gardens, Jefferson carried a copy of Thomas Whateley's, *Observations on Modern Gardening*, whose descriptions of the gardens Jefferson called "models of perfect elegance and classical correctness and remarkable for their exactness." Jefferson's main inquiries were directed "chiefly to such practical things as might enable me to estimate the expense of making and maintaining a garden [at Monticello] in that style."[59] A few days following his return to Paris he wrote his friend John Page, "the gardening in that country is the article in which it surpasses all the earth. I mean their pleasure gardening. This indeed went far beyond my ideas."[60]

Gardening was another of Jefferson's lifelong passions. On his return to America he prepared elaborate plans for landscaping the lawns and the gardens at Monticello. Although many of his ideas for landscaping were never realized, they were always in his mind. Two years after retiring as President he wrote Charles Wilson Peale: "No occupation is so delightful to me as the culture of the earth and no culture comparable to that of the garden. Such a variety of subjects, some one always coming to perfection, the failure of one thing repaired by the success of another."[61]

Shortly after returning to London, Adams and Jefferson crossed the Blackfriars Bridge to see John Viny's "manufacture of Patent Wheels made of bent Timber." Viny made cartwheels by bending saplings. Adams found Viny's inventions for boiling and bending timber "very ingenious." Viny had gotten to know Benjamin Franklin during Franklin's stay in London fifteen years earlier and Viny's loud praise of Franklin annoyed Adams who found Viny "very vain."[62] Jefferson was unimpressed with Viny's bent-timber wheels, noting that farmers in New Jersey had long practiced the art of making cartwheels by bending saplings into circles, probably from reading Book IV of the *Iliad,* "because ours are the only farmers who can read Homer."[63]

The next day Abigail and John Adams and Jefferson visited the Tower of London. Jefferson left no clue as to any emotions he felt as he inspected this fortress of royal murder and intrigue. On April 14, and again in the company of the Adams family, he left for Kew, a pleasant village in Surrey ten miles from London and known then and now for its botanical gardens. Near the garden and facing the Thames was Kew Palace, a favorite residence of the royal family. His notes of this visit are technical and illustrated by a sketch of an Archimedes screw for raising water. He knew, however, what to expect since he owned a copy of Sir William Chambers book, *Chambers's View of Kew Gardens.*[64]

Three days later he went to the Ranelagh in Chelsea, one of London's main pleasure haunts. Here kings, ambassadors, statesmen, literati, nobility, ladies of fashion and prostitutes mingled at masquerades, banquets, dances, parties, and other fetes. This was a sharp departure in style from his usual evenings at the theatre, opera, concerts and dining with the Adams family and their friends.

The main building, the Rotunda, 185 feet in diameter and nearly 200 feet high, was described by Horace Walpole as "a vast amphitheatre, finely gilt, painted and illuminated, into which everybody who loves eating, drinking, staring or crowding is admitted for 12 *pence.*" It was divided into three stories with private boxes for those who wanted privacy. As one visitor remarked, "We never tire of Ranelagh, for every night we may see the men and women whose letters and diaries we have read, whose portraits by Hudson, Richardson, and, above all, by Hogarth, have already been painted and who are going to *be* painted by Ramsay, Reynolds, and Gainsborough. Ranelagh is enormously popular, and although it is no farther than Chelsea, our coach may be over an hour in getting there, particularly in May, for May is the height of the season at the Gardens." An evening at the Ranelagh is no longer possible. It was closed in 1805 and the site purchased by The Royal Hospital.[65]

The next day he went on a tour of Buckingham House, built by John Sheffield, Duke of Buckingham, in 1703, and the site of the present palace. When Jefferson visited, Buckingham House was owned by the royal family and was used as an occasional residence. Jefferson saw in the salon room seven of Raphael's preparatory designs for the tapestries in the Sistine Chapel. They can now be seen in the Victoria and Albert Museum. Later that day he saw Sir Ashton Lever's (1729-1788) extraordinary natural history collection at Leicester House on Leicester Square, and then went to witness trick horseback riding at the Amphitheatre Riding House located on Westminster Bridge Road. That evening he dined at the Adamses with fellow Americans and friendly Englishmen.[66]

Jefferson probably accompanied John Adams the next day on a visit to several of London's booksellers and publishers whose offices were located in an area around Paternoster Row. Paternoster Row parallels Christopher Wren's great masterpiece,

St. Paul's Cathedral, on the north. A favorite gathering spot for publishers and booksellers was the Chapter coffee-house just off Paternoster Row. This may have been the scene of their conversations with publishers Stockdale, Cadel and Dilly that caused Adams to write in his diary, "Seeds were sown, this day, which will grow." That evening Jefferson went to Covent Garden, on the site of what is now the Royal Opera House, and saw William Congreve's tragedy, *The Mourning Bride* and the *Two Misers*, a musical farce by Kane O'Hara.[67]

Early on April 20, the Adams family and Jefferson drove to Brentford in Middlesex by way of Hyde Park and Kensington Gardens along avenues bordered by elms. Brentford was directly across the Thames from the Kew Gardens, and a ferry operated between the two villages. Here they visited Osterly and Syon [Sion] House, two mansions remodeled by Robert Adam. The mansion house and grounds at Osterly had been the seat of the Child banking dynasty, but because Mrs. Child had gone to the races, they could not get tickets to see the interior of the mansion. The owner's absence caused Adams to comment: "The beauty, convenience, and utility of these country seats, are not enjoyed by the owners. They are mere ostentations of vanity. Races, cocking, gambling draw away their attention." At Syon House, which had been a nunnery in the 15th century, the pleasure gardens repeated the winding walks, greenhouses, hot houses, and clumps of trees that they viewed at Osterly.[68] That evening he went to the Royal Theatre at Drury Lane to see Sarah Siddons (1755-1831) play Portia in *The Merchant of Venice*. He had first seen her perform in John Delap's *The Captive* two days after his arrival in London.[69] Two nights later he saw her again in her most popular role of *Lady Macbeth*. In between these Shakespearean plays he spent an evening at a music hall known as Sadler's Wells where he watched the feats of tumblers, strongmen, and rope dancers; all relieved by ballets and pantomime.[70]

Two days prior to leaving London, never to return, he visited the British Museum with John and Abigail Adams and William Smith. They were given a personal tour by Edward Whitker Grey, the botanist and keeper of the collections of natural history and antiquities. Later he visited the James Lee nursery and bought his French horticultural friend, Malesherbs,[71] seventeen kinds of shrubs and trees. In the morning he visited his favorite London bookseller, John Stockdale, in Piccadilly, and spent for books four times as much as he paid Mather Brown to paint his portrait.[72]

Before leaving for Paris on April 26, he stopped by Robert Cannon's tailor shop and paid him for, "A pr. Sattin florentine breeches," "a waistcoat Silk Strip'd," "A pr. Nankeen riding breeches," "A waistcoat and breeches buff Kersymere Gilt butts.," and "2 pr. buff ribdelure breeches Gilt Buttons."[73] On his return trip to Paris he was accompanied as far as Greenwich by his new friend, John Paradise. He stopped here to see the Royal Observatory and Wren's hospital which was being rebuilt. He arrived at

Jefferson at 45 by Mather Brown

Dover a little before midnight, and then was detained for a day and a half by bad weather and contrary winds.[74] He spent part of this layover seeing Dover Castle. Had the weather been better, he would have had a splendid view from Dover Castle of the harbor and the coast of France.

Thinking of his friend on the road alone, William Smith sent Jefferson a note. "A quarter before 4 and we are seated as usual round the fire expecting the summons to dinner. The pleasure at it will be lessened by an apprehension that yours today will be rather solitary."[75] Actually, the winds had become favorable and Jefferson crossed the channel to Calais in three hours, had dinner at Pierre Dressin's Hotel d'Angleterre and was on the road between Calais and St. Omer at the moment Smith penned his note.[76] Within two days he was at his home on the Champs Elysées.

CHAPTER FOUR

A Romantic Interlude

On returning to France Jefferson remembered that he had not received some Portuguese wines ordered from Jean Baptiste Pecquet in Lisbon. In a note reminding Pecquet of his order he expressed the hope of getting "them more genuine and of better quality from you." When the wines arrived, Jefferson was disappointed in how little Malmsey had been included, "only 30 bottles of Malvoisie de Madeira in the parcel . . . I will beg the favor of you to send me six dozen bottles more of that kind of wine of what is old and good."[1] The merchant house in Lisbon quickly responded that Pecquet was "awaiting your new order so that he will know the amount of each quality of wine you want. In order not to slow down the transaction any more, we will send you a sample of each kind of wine . . . by way of a French vessel which goes to Rouen all the time, with orders to make sure it reaches you." Jefferson's memorandum book shows that he received 72 bottles of Malmsey, but at a cost of almost 6 livres a bottle it was very expensive. This may account for why he never re-ordered, while in France, wines directly from Portugal.[2]

On August 2 the American painter, John Trumbull, arrived in Paris and stayed with Jefferson. The next five weeks were a whirlwind of sights and activities for the young artist and his indefatigable host. With Jefferson as his guide, Trumbull moved in the highest intellectual and social circles and saw Paris from a perspective that he would not have otherwise obtained. He met Count de Moustier, later to become the French Ambassador to the United

Vue du Théatre Francais

States, Count de Vergennes, the King's foreign minister "and other great men of the day."³ He visited the homes of several noblemen who had assembled art collections but saw none more extraordinary than the Duke of Chartes' collection at the Palais Royal, which he thought "magnificent, and in good taste."⁴ On Saturday evening they saw Paris' newest and most successful comedy, *Le Mariage de Figaro,* by Beaumarchais⁵ at the Comedie Francaise, Paris' largest theatre, with over 1,900 seats, located on the Left Bank near the Luxembourg Palace and Gardens. The next day, Jefferson, Trumbull, and probably William Short, walked from Jefferson's Champs-Elysées mansion to the village of Suresnes and witnessed a ceremony known as the Crowning of the Rosiere Suresnes-the crowning with roses of "the most amiable, industrious, and virtuous maiden of the parish."⁶

Trumbull toured the collection of the great French sculptor, and Jefferson's friend, Jean Antoine Houdon.⁷ He visited Jacques-Louis David at his apartments in the Louvre, the Bibliotheque du Roi (now the Bibliotheque Nationale), and the Hotel des Invalides and found its dome "one of the most beautiful pieces of architecture" in existence. He toured the Luxembourg Palace and its gardens, the King's Gardens, the Sorbonne, and the churches of Notre Dame, St. Sulpice, and St. Genevieve.

On August 12 in the company of Richard and Maria Cosway, Charles Bulfinch⁸ and others, Trumbull traveled to Versailles and was overwhelmed by the royal

Jefferson, by John Trumbull

A Romantic Interlude

art collection. "I had no imagination of ever seeing such works in existence."[9] On another artistic level he was astounded by the grandeur of the gardens of Versailles saying they "must be seen; they cannot be described."[10] The next day he revisited the Louvre and saw a part of the royal collection housed there, which he called, "numberless inestimable things."[11] That evening Trumbull and Jefferson dined with Abbes Chalut and Arnoux at their home in Passy.

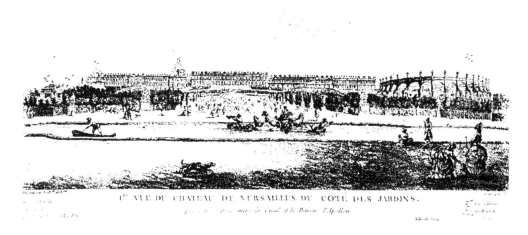

Trumbull had brought with him the first two paintings of his Revolutionary War series, *The Death of General Warren at the Battle of Bunker's Hill* and *The Death of General Montgomery in the Attack on Quebec.* Jefferson said these two paintings were "the admiration of the connoisseurs" and called Trumbull's talents "almost unparalleled."[12] Whether Jefferson conveyed these thoughts to Jacques-Louis David is unknown, but David was sufficiently curious about the young American's artistic talents to return Trumbull's visit by going to see Trumbull's *Bunker's Hill* and *Quebec* at Jefferson's mansion on the Champs-Elysées.

Jefferson would not have considered Trumbull's visit to Paris complete without showing him the architectural beauty of the Hotel de Salm. Part of another day was spent in Passy visiting the Hotel de Valentinois, Benjamin Franklin's residence for seven years. From the garden there was a view of Paris which Trumbull found "very beautiful."[13]

A different perspective of Paris was achieved by climbing to the top of the scaffolding of the new but unfinished church of St. Genevieve. Trumbull found "the view of Paris ... magnificent and vast; it was a very fine day, so that the eye, without interruption, wandered over the immense extent of the buildings, which lay beneath it. The Tuileries, the Louvre, with the Church of Notre Dame, St. Sulpice, the dome of the Invalides, the Bastille ... towering above the dwelling houses. The extent of the city; the vast and opulent country, terminating partly in rough and broken hills, partly in fine champaign, ornamented with the palaces of Meudon and St. Cloud; the aqueduct of Marly, the Convent of Mount Calvaire, and a number of other splendid buildings, formed together a *coup d'oeil* [view] entirely superior to anything I have heretofore seen."[14]

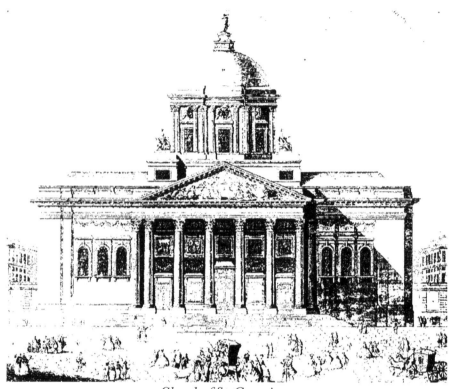
Church of St. Genevieve

Jefferson had all the qualities that attract women: wealth, good looks, intelligence, position, power, fame, an incredible range of interests and yet, since his wife's death four years earlier, his life had lacked any romantic involvement. A romantic interlude was around the corner in the person of the beautiful, blond, musically and artistically talented twenty-seven-year-old Maria Cosway. She appeared one day in August through the invitation of John Trumbull. She was married to Richard Cosway, at that time the most famous painter of miniatures.

Jefferson's attention was riveted on Maria from the time they met beneath the dome of the Halle aux Bleds, the newly completed Parisian grain market. He changed his plans, including dinner with the Duchesse de la Rochefoucauld, by "lying messengers," and whisked away the Cosways and Trumbull for dinner at the Palais Royal and a ride to the royal park at Saint Cloud. On their return to Paris they visited Ruggieris, which featured elaborate displays of fireworks combined with pantomimes. "The Forges of Vulcan beneath Mount Etna" and "The Combat of Mars" were on the program on this summer night, and afterwards they attended a performance by the famous harpist Krumpholtz at the Tuileries Gardens.[15] This first day together was a prelude to many spent over the next three weeks on trips together, soon without Richard Cosway, and then without Trumbull, who had left for a German vacation. The lonely ambassador and the lively Maria were together almost daily with romantic outings along the Seine and the environs of Paris.

A Romantic Interlude

Maria Cosway

Halle aux Bleds

Jefferson recalled those days when he asked Maria to "paint me the day we went to St. Germains." "How beautiful was every object! The Pont de Neuilly, the hills of the Seine, the rainbows of the machine of Marly, the terraces of St. Germain, the châteaux, the gardens, the statues of Marly, the pavilion of Lucienne. Recollect to Madrid, Bagatelle, the King's garden, the Dessert, How grand the idea excited by the remains of such a column! The spiral staircase too was beautiful. The wheels of time moved on with a rapidity of which those of our carriage gave but a faint idea, and yet in the evening, when one took a retrospect of the day, what a mass of happiness we travelled over!"[16]

Their journey of twelve miles to St. Germain-en-Laye took them up the Champs-Elysées, past the Bois de Boulogne and across the Seine at the Pont de Neuilly. The Pont de Neuilly is a beautiful stone bridge that spans the Seine at the Bois de Boulogne. Jefferson thought it the handsomest bridge in the world.[17] The road then turned west and followed the Seine on their left and hills and valleys on their right, cultivated principally in vines and wheat.

The Château de Madrid bordered the Bois de Boulogne as did the Bagatelle, a Neo-classic pavilion built in 1777. It is now the property of the City of Paris and open to visitors.[18] The rainbows of Marly were created by the famous hydraulic machine constructed a hundred years earlier by Louis XIV to carry water from the Seine to the gardens of Versailles and Marly. From the terrace of the royal château at St. Germain they could see Mont Calvaire and Paris.[19]

The "Dessert" that Jefferson and Maria visited on September 16,[20] was *Le Desert de Retz*, the country estate of a Farmer-General, M. de Manville, located four miles from St. Germain on the edge of the forest of Marly. The grounds included a garden, an obelisk, a pyramid and a huge "column house." Nothing survives of the "Dessert" except the ruined column house which has been classified an historic monument.[21]

Their romantic outings ended when Jefferson attempted to jump over a fence along the Seine and laid himself up for weeks with a dislocated wrist.[22] Even though he knew Maria and her husband were leaving Paris for Antwerp on October 5, he sent a note to her that morning: "I have passed the night; in so much pain that I have not closed my eyes. It is with infinite regret therefore that I must relinquish your charming company for that of the Surgeon whom I have sent for to examine into the cause of this change. I am in hopes it is only the having rattled a little too freely over the pavement yesterday [with Maria]. If you do not go today I shall still have the pleasure of seeing you again." Maria's reply, by return messenger, was that she would be leaving that morning. "I am very, very sorry . . . for having been the cause of your pains in the [night]; And why was I not more friendly to you and less to Myself by preventing your giving me the pleasure of your Company? You repeatedly said it wou'd do you no harm, I felt interested and did not insist. We shall go I believe this Morning, Nothing seems ready, but Mr. Cosway seems More dispos'd then I have seen him all this time."[23]

A Romantic Interlude

IIe VUE DU CHATEAU DE St GERMAIN EN LAYE,
prise du Parterre du côté du Nord.

VUE DU PAVILLON DE BAGATELLE

The emotionally controlled Jefferson, uncharacteristically left his sick bed and accompanied the Cosways as far as St. Denis and "having performed the last sad office of handing you into your carriage at the Pavilion de St. Denis, and seeing the wheels get actually into motion, I turned on my heel and walked, more dead than alive, to the opposite door, where my own was awaiting me."[24]

Returning home, the anguished diplomat sat by his fireside and wrote to Maria, with his left hand, his famous love letter, "My Head and My Heart." The ensuing months saw letters back and forth between Maria and Jefferson, in English, in Italian; passionate, scolding, and ultimately cooling. The affair, never intimate, was more of Jefferson's head than his heart. They would meet again.

This same summer Jefferson met a fellow American whose past achievements and ambitions fascinated him-John Ledyard, navigator, explorer and soldier of fortune. Broke and living outside of Paris in St. Germain-en-Laye, Ledyard was a frequent dinner guest at Jefferson's table. In a letter to a relative he tells of taking "a walk to Paris this morning, and saw the Marquis de la Fayette . . . . I make these trips to Paris often; sometimes to dine with this amiable Frenchman, and sometimes with our minister, who is a brother to me . . . I find at our minister's table between fifteen and twenty Americans, inclusive of two or three ladies. It is very remarkable, that we are neither despised nor envied for our love of liberty, but very often carressed."[25]

It may have been over wine that Jefferson suggested to Ledyard the "enterprise of exploring the 'Western part of our continent, by passing thro St. Petersburg to Kamschatka, and procuring a passage thence' in some of the Russian vessels to Nootka Sound, whence he might make his way across the continent to America; and I undertook to have the permission of the Empress of Russian solicited . . . . The Empress refused permission at once, considering the enterprise as entirely chimerical. But Ledyard would not relinquish it."[26] After being expelled from Russia, Jefferson last heard from Ledyard in 1789 as "he was just then plunging into the unknown regions of Africa, probably never to emerge again."[27]

In early October Trumbull wrote Jefferson from Antwerp, and after noting that the Cosways had arrived there early in the morning, he described with the eye of an artist his experience in "the wine country of Champagne, very beautiful, rough and finely cultivated. At Épernay I saw one of the great wine cellars and tasted the finest wine I ever saw."[28]

The injury to his wrist had caused Jefferson to postpone a trip he had planned through southern France. But, as time passed, the cause of his delay became the trip's *raison d'etre* as he wrote friend after friend telling that he would be traveling to southern France to bathe his injured wrist in the curative mineral waters at Aix-en-Provence.[29]

Two weeks before leaving Paris he received notice that a barrel of Cahuzac wine holding the equivalent of 250 bottles was on its way from Bordeaux. Assured that the wine was of excellent quality, he arranged for its passage[30] into Paris along with some other wines by requesting a passport for "three barriques of common wine and one of wine de liqueur, one of which is arrived at Paris, and the other three are soon expected there. They are for my own use."[31]

CHAPTER FIVE

Burgundy and the Wine Country

After two and a half years in France, Jefferson's enchantment with his work had dulled to lambent acceptance. His duties were perfunctory: confined to "the receipt of whale-oils, salted fish and salted meats on favorite terms; the admission of our rice on equal terms with that of Piedmont, Egypt and the Levant; a mitigation of the monopolies of our tobacco . . . ." With his wrist failing to heal and his romance with Maria Cosway cooling to friendship, never were there more compelling reasons for a vacation.

Traveling alone in his own carriage drawn by three horses, his venture into the south of France began on February 28, 1787, with rain, hail and snow as traveling companions. The Parisian custom of nightly gatherings for dinner and conversation were behind him as he avoided "good dinners and good company. Had they been my objects, I should not had quitted Paris."[1]

There were three methods of traveling by road in France, all of which utilized posthouses. These were franchises of the king and were way-stations along the roads. They provided horses, drivers, postillions, guides and, usually, overnight lodging. The distance between posthouses was approximately ten miles and the average speed about seven and a half miles an hour. The safety of these public roads was overseen by the *marechaussee*, mounted troops engaged by the King for this purpose.[2]

The usual method of travel was by *diligence* or stagecoach. For a fixed price the passenger was provided a seat in the coach and meals on the road until the final destination. The obvious drawbacks were crowded conditions (usually eight persons to a carriage), the inability to select traveling companions, and being the captive of the *diligence* schedule which often meant being hurried out of bed at three in the morning.

Another way was to hire a *voiture* or carriage. This allowed the traveler to control his time schedule and traveling companions, but it was more expensive.

The third method, and the one employed by Jefferson and the nobility, was to provide one's own carriage but to rely on the posthouses for horses, guides and, when in remote areas, room and board.

As Jefferson traveled southeast toward Burgundy through Fontainebleau, Sens, Auxerre and Vermenton, he found the people poorly clothed. "I observe the women and children carrying heavy burdens, and laboring with the hoe. This is an unequivocal indication of extreme poverty."[3]

Between Sens and Vermenton he saw the plains of the Yonne River in corn and the hills in vines, but "the wine not good." Although little known today, the areas around Auxerre then produced more red wines than Burgundy's Cote d'Or.[4] Though inferior in quality to the wines of Burgundy, Auxerrois wines were popular in Paris because they were cheaper and more readily available. Located on the Yonne River, Auxerre had become a major wine center largely because transportation of its wines to Paris was easier and far less expensive than the landlocked wines of Burgundy. When Jefferson visited Auxerre, the "finest and most generous" red wine came from the vineyards of Clos de la Chainette.[5] The walled vineyard still exists and is located at the psychiatric hospital in Auxerre and consists of 7.5 acres planted in Pinot Noir and Chardonnay grapes. Because of its small production and local popularity, the wines of Clos de la Chainette are seldom seen outside the Department of Yonne and are so scarce that even locally they must be ordered a year in advance.[6] Another popular 18th century red wine of this area had the unlikely name of Migraine and was owned by the Bishops of Auxerre. It was known for its spirit, body and ability to travel and was popular in England and Italy. Other well-known Auxerrois wines went by such names as Judas and Pied de Rat.[7]

Today the vineyards of Auxerrois are shadows of their former selves: a mere 2,200 acres centered around the communes of Chitry-le-Fort and St. Bris-le-Vineux, noted mainly for their white wines, and Irancy and Coulanges-la-Vineuse, for their reds. The phylloxera epidemic of the 1870's was the first blow to the area's prosperity, and this was followed by the shipment of cheap Languedoc wines via the railroads at the turn of the century.

Twelve miles to the east of Auxerre is the town of Chablis, now world-famous for its dry white wines with their flinty bouquets and acidic bite. Jefferson did not visit Chablis, probably because he was not aware of its wines. Chablis did not have the reputation then that it has since acquired. Duncan M'Bride, a London wine merchant and author, wrote six years after Jefferson's visit: "Vin da Chable [sic] is a light pleasant wine, and not unwholesome to be used at table instead of beer."[8] By the 1820's, the reputation of Chablis as a fine wine had been recognized and was cited by Henderson and Jullien for its finesse and flavor.[9]

As he approached Dijon, Jefferson described the people as being well-fed and well-clothed, but noted that it was Sunday. Jefferson spent three days in Dijon at the Hotel de Conde where he paid a tavern price of four livres for a bottle of the best red Burgundy, "e.g. of Vosne." He determined to travel incognito throughout his trip and planned on having servants who knew nothing of him. To insure his anonymity he intended taking on a new valet at every principal city. But the man he engaged in Dijon, Petitjean, was so adept that he kept him on throughout the trip, engaging an additional local valet whenever he stayed more than a day.[10]

Dijon was the former capital of the Duchy of Burgundy with a population of 20,000. It was and is a handsome city with wide, well-paved streets and charming old houses centered around the Place Royale, now called Place de la Liberation, on which is situated the palace of the former Dukes of Burgundy. The medieval palace now houses the Hotel de Ville (Town Hall), and a museum containing one of the best collections of provincial paintings in France. The museum features a great banquet hall, in the middle of which are the tombs of Philip the Bold and John the Fearless.

Surrounding the former ducal palace are many of Dijon's richest monuments; churches and mansions dating from the period when Dijon was the capital of the Duchy of Burgundy. Jefferson's account book shows that he paid to see the Hotel de Ville and probably visited the nearby Palace of Justice, the churches of St. Michel (16th century) and Notre Dame (13th century) and the half-timbered houses that line the streets just to the northeast of Notre Dame.

Several miles south of Dijon Jefferson entered the heart of Burgundy, the Cote d'Or, a series of low hills home to many of the world's greatest vineyards. He describes the Cote as a solid rock overlaid with "about a foot of soil, and small stone in equal quantities, the soil red and of middling quality. The plains are in corn, the Cote in vines." Of the vineyards nestled along the hillsides, Chambertin was the first in view, followed by "Vougeot, Romanée, Vosne, Nuits, Beaune, Pommard, Volnay, Meursault and end at Montrachet." Jefferson mounted a pony, "put a peasant on another and rambled through their most celebrated vineyards."[11]

In the margin of his notes he drew the following diagram:

			:o:	la baraque
"Chambertin	o	: :	r.	
Vougeau		:o:	r.	
	r.r.	: :		
Romanie	o o	: :		Veaune
	r	:o:		Nuys
Beaune		:o:	r.	
Pommard	o	: :	r.	
Voulenaye	o	: :	r.	
Meursault	o	: :	w.	
Montrachet	o	: :	w.	
		:o:		Chagny"
		: :		

The dotted vertical lines indicate the main route; the locations of villages with respect to it are designated by "o." Red and white wines are shown by "r" and "w."

He noted that the vines "begin to yield good profit at 5 or 6 years old and last 100 or 150 years." In contrast, today the vines of Burgundy do not last more than 40 to 50 years. The late Louis Latour, Sr., one of Burgundy's leading growers and negociants explains: "In 1787 the vines were not grafted on American roots like they are now since the phylloxera crisis. When a vine became too old to produce enough grapes, a branch was curved and covered with soil and a new vine began to grow. So a vineyard could last more than a century but in fact it was regularly revived. Now a grafted vine cannot last more than 40 years."[12]

Phylloxera, a root louse that attacks and kills the vines' roots, was accidentally introduced into France in the early 1860s on vines originating in the eastern United States to replace diseased vines and for hybridization. Within 25 years phylloxera destroyed almost every vineyard in the world except those in Chile, Cyprus and a few other scattered areas.[13]

No successful method of control was found until the origin of the louse became involved in the answer. Certain genera of American root stocks were immune to the louse, so the European vines were grafted onto these stocks, eventually saving the vineyards from extinction. Today, with few exceptions, the wines of the world are produced from vines grafted onto American root stocks.

Jefferson's stay in Burgundy lasted only a few days, but what he learned about the region's wines would last his lifetime. He thought Chambertin the best of the reds, followed by Vougeot [Voujeau] and Vosne [Veaune] because they were the "strongest, and will bear transportation." These vineyards are in the northern section of the Cote d'Or called the Cote de Nuits and were, and are still, the wines of Burgundy that live longer and improve with age, and in so doing reach a degree of perfection that most other Burgundies fail to achieve.[14]

Chambertin, a Grand Cru,[15] still sells for astonishing prices, but its entitlement to the cachet as the best red wine of Burgundy is in serious question. This 32-acre vineyard is now owned by 23 proprietors, resulting in what has been called "wines of enormous differences in quality" with some wines of insipid quality bearing the Chambertin name. There are, of course, a few proprietors who can and do produce in great vintages Chambertins that, when mature, justify its reputation and perhaps even its extraordinary prices.[16]

The tiny village of Vougeot is named after the stream-like river Vouge that runs behind it. In the 12th century land was given to the monks of Citeaux, and by 1336 the monks owned all 124 acres of vineyards, which they surrounded with a stone wall. Over the years the monks built a large Renaissance Château and its wall-enclosed vineyards, cellars and 12th century wine presses make it today one of the principal tourist attractions of the Cote de Nuits. Working with their primitive wine presses, the monks made both red and white wines and became such skilled winemakers that for centuries the wines of Clos de Vougeot were considered the best of all Burgundies.[17]

When Jefferson visited, Clos de Vougeot was still owned by the monks. Its annual production was about 50,000 bottles and the wines had a reputation for excellence.[18] As a result of the French Revolution, Clos de Vougeot was sold in 1790 at public auction and this, in combination with French inheritance laws, resulted in today's chaotic web of nearly 80 persons owning and producing wines from the original 124 acres.[19] An almost immediate loss of quality was reported following its divestiture.[20] With such diverse ownership, there is no one standard for what modern-day Clos de Vougeot should taste like and, therefore, bottles of Clos de Vougeot of the same vintage from different producers will vary in character and quality. It is this unpredictability of so many red Burgundy wines that makes the adage *caveat emptor* sound advice even for the most knowledgeable wine-drinker.

Clos de Vougeot

In recognizing the wines of Vosne for their quality Jefferson did not delineate their order of rank, but it is clear that such an order existed. Alexander Henderson singled out Romanée-Conti, Richebourg, La Tache and Romanée St. Vivant for "their beautiful color and exquisite flavor and aroma, combining ... qualities of lightness and delicacy with richness and fullness of body,"[21] a remarkably accurate description of these wines today.

Amazingly, these four vineyards continue to produce wines of such high quality that Henderson's comments are an understatement. Romanée-Conti and La Tache are owned exclusively by Domaine de la Romanée-Conti and are two of the world's most expensive wines. Richebourg, and especially that made by Domaine de la Romanée-Conti, has many wine enthusiasts who find it the richest, and most concentrated and seductive, of all Burgundies.[22] Romanée St. Vivant, the largest of these four Grands Crus, also has followers who admire its delicacy and finesse and although it does not sell for the astronomical prices of its three neighbors it is extremely expensive.

Jefferson observed that it was "pretended that the adjoining vineyards produce the same qualities but that, belonging to obscure individuals, they have not obtained a name, and therefore sell as other wines."[23] Jefferson apparently did not get a chance to drink wines from some of the adjoining vineyards such as Bonnes Mares, Musigny, and Grand Echezeaux, or he would not have written "pretended." Arriving in the old town of Beaune on March 8, he lodged at Chez Dion a l'Écu de France and promptly hired a guide to the vineyards of Pommard, Volnay and Meursault. It was here that he met Etienne Parent, a cooper and wine merchant, who became his Burgundian wine counselor and friend,[24] guiding him through the tortuous task of selecting the best Burgundian wines in a period before appellation controlee, consumer guides and wine newsletters.

Although the red wines of the Cote de Beaune such as Volnay and Pommard have been famous for centuries, its glory emanates from the white wines of the three communes of Puligny-Montrachet, Chassagne-Montrachet and Meursault, all made exclusively from the Chardonnay grape. The towns of Puligny and Chassagne and certain Grands Crus vineyards surrounding them have affixed to their names that of the area's most famous vineyard-Montrachet. Although Montrachet has retained its charismatic taste over the past two hundred years, there is a difference in its size and production. Jefferson recorded that the vineyard produced 30,000 bottles annually from about 50 acres. At the time Montrachet belonged to only two proprietors, Monsieur Clermont who leased his portion to some wine merchants, and the Marquis Sarsnet from Dijon, whose part was farmed by Monsieur de la Tour.[25] It was at the vineyard of Monsieur de la Tour that Jefferson was introduced to Montrachet, which he called the best white wine of Burgundy, a distinction it retains.[26] Jefferson recorded that it sold for two livres eight sous when new and three livres when fit for drinking,[27] a price that was equivalent to the best Bordeaux, i.e., Lafite, Haut-Brion, Margaux and Latour.

Today there are only 19.76 acres of Le Montrachet producing a scant 15,000 bottles yearly and owned by at least seventeen different persons or organizations.[28] The difference in size and production is explained by the fact that Jefferson did not distinguish between the three vineyards entitled at that time to use the suffix "Montrachet" in their names, i.e., Montrachet (now known as Le Montrachet), Chevalier-Montrachet (18.1 acres) and Bartard Montrachet (29.3 acres).[29] Two other vineyards have since been allowed to use the suffix Montrachet: Bienvenues-Batard-Montrachet (9.11 acres) and Criots-Batard-Montrachet (3.87 acres).[30] As is the case today, Le Montrachet sold then for twice to three times more than its hyphenated neighbors[31] and remains the most expensive dry white wine in the world.

Burgundy Wine Bottles

Other remarkably fine dry white wines are made in the vineyards surrounding the towns of Chassagne-Montrachet and Puligny-Montrachet. Of special note are the sixteen Premiers Crus vineyards of Chassagne-Montrachet and the fourteen Premiers Crus vineyards of Puligny-Montrachet that produce wines of elegance and finesse that are often equal in bouquet and taste to their Grands Crus neighbors. In fact, white Burgundies that carry the names Chassagne-Montrachet and Puligny-Montrachet, without a vineyard designation, are usually wines of breed and quality.

Just to the northwest of the Montrachet vineyards is the quaint town of Meursault, completely surrounded by stone walls. Jefferson thought the best wine of Meursault came from the vineyard of Goutte d'Or (drop of gold), owned by the Bachet [Bache] family. It became one of his favorite table wines during his remaining two and a half years in France. The Bachet family traces its Burgundian roots to the 16th century and, at the time of Jefferson's visit, Goutte d'Or was operated by Jeans Joseph Bachet (1757-1839).[32]

The total vineyard area of Goutte d'Or was just over 13 acres, the same size it is today. By 1855 records show that it had become the property of a number of families, one of which remained Bachet.[33] Today the Goutte d'Or vineyard area has several owners, with the main exporters to the United States being Domaine Des Comtes Lafon, Domaine Francois Gaunoux, Louis Latour and Domaine Rene Manuel. Other Meursaults of equal reputation at the time were Les Perrieres, Les Combettes, Les Charmes and Les Genevrieres,[34] and these five vineyards continue to make outstanding dry white Burgundies. Together with ten other Meursault vineyards they not only enjoy Premiers Crus classification, but are rated by wine experts as the best of this select group of premier Meursaults. Because Meursaults have never been as fashionable as the wines from Puligny-Montrachet and Chassagne-Montrachet, they sell for less. Jefferson noted that a bottle of Le Montrachet cost three times as much as a bottle of Goutte d'Or and, over time, this price difference has significantly widened.

Passing through the Cote de Beaune, he compared a variable beyond the control of man, the stone content of the vineyards at Meursault. "At Pommard and Volnay I observed them eating good wheat bread; at Meursault, rye. I asked the reason of the difference. They told me that the white wines fail in quality much oftener than the red, and remains on hand. The farmer therefore cannot afford to feed his labourers so well. At Meursault, only white wines are made, because there is too much stone for the red. On such slight circumstances depends the condition of man!"[35] Today the quality of white Burgundies is more reliable than the reds.

The town of Volnay and its vineyards, southwest of Beaune and sandwiched between the vineyards of Pommard to the north and Meursault to the south, had the reputation of being the most delicate and the best of the red wines from southern Burgundy,[36] a distinction many wine enthusiasts would argue that it holds to this day. The character of the Volnay wines that Jefferson enjoyed, a light-colored, perfumed wine of cherry flavor and light tannins, resulted from the earliest harvest in Burgundy and quick fermentation.[37]

In flavor he considered Volnay the equal of Chambertin but relegated it to fourth place behind Chambertin, Vougeot and the wines of Vosne because it was lighter in body, lacked the longevity of its more celebrated northern neighbors and did not bear transportation as well. Jefferson discovered, however, that Volnay had two distinct advantages over the wines of Chambertin, Vougeot and Vosne. It cost only one quarter as much and was ready to drink after one year.[38] Volnay became his favorite Burgundy red table wine.

In the 18th century the time for picking grapes in the Cote de Beaune was strictly regulated. About a month before the grapes were picked, a committee of judges from Beaune began the first of three visits to the vineyards to examine the maturity of the grapes. On the third visit the first day for harvesting the grapes was decided. It was the tradition that the vineyards of Volnay were the first to be harvested, followed the next day by Pommard. Thereafter, the other vineyards in the Cote de Beaune were allowed to gather their grapes. Anyone picking even a basket of grapes before the official date was subject to confiscation and a severe fine.[39]

The rapid fermentation of Volnay wines was largely a result of the manner in which the grapes were harvested. The vats were brought into the vineyards and filled to the brim with whole clusters of grapes, which by virtue of their weight caused crushing and brought about the onset of fermentation. This partial carbonic maceration assisted in building up the aromatic content of the wine as well as reducing its tannic content. Sugaring was not generally practiced at this time and, in Volnay, fermentations were finished within 20 to 30 hours.[40]

Jefferson, who was not in Burgundy during the harvest, did not describe the method by which the grapes were crushed but it was accomplished by the bare feet of men who entered the vats naked. An English wine merchant, Thomas George Shaw, who spent over a week in Burgundy some 75 years after Jefferson's visit, reported: "If it injures the sale of burgundies I shall be very sorry but it is my duty as a faithful historian to relate that a very unusual way of procuring juice from the grapes in this district [Cote d'Or] is by men who step into the vats, 'in puris naturalibus', words which I am unable to translate, not having a Latin dictionary by me. I rather think, however, that the meaning may be gathered from what lately occurred to a friend, who, when opening a door, in another department in France, was alarmed by loud screams in a female voice: 'N'entrez pas, N'entrez pas, je suis en sauvage."[41]

Modern production methods in Volnay are in many ways linked with the past and responsible for the character of today's Volnay wines. Early harvesting, retention of whole clusters, relatively short fermentations of four to seven days and early bottling all have combined in recent vintages to produce wines of great charm, soft texture and aromatic flavors that develop sooner than wines from neighboring Pommard or further north.[42]

Although it is clear that Jefferson's favorite white Meursault came from the vineyard of Goutte d'Or owned by Monsieur Bachet, the vineyard origin of his favorite Volnay is less clear. Neither Parent nor Jefferson ever identified a particular vineyard from which Parent purchased the Volnay wines he sold Jefferson. Although the general reputation of the wines then, as now, was very high, the vineyard areas singled out for special recognition were Les Cailleret, En Caillerets, En Cailleret-Dessus and Champans.[43]

Leaving Beaune on March 9 Jefferson traveled south through Chalon, Sennecey, Tournus, St. Albain and Macon. As he approached the old city of Chalon, he observed the work that had gone into digging a canal that would connect the Saone River at Chalon with the Loire at Digoin. When completed Jefferson predicted that it would "reanimate the languishing commerce of Champagne and Burgundy, by furnishing a water transportation for their wines to Nantes . . . "[44] Without this canal Burgundy was landlocked, and, lacking safe and cheap transportation, its wines were seldom known beyond Paris. Consequently, they suffered in foreign markets, especially in England where the wines of Bordeaux had been popular since the 17th century. To reach England the wines of Burgundy were transported to the Yonne River in one-horse carts that carried two casks called *pieces* that held the equivalent of 250 bottles each. The wines were then sent by barge to Paris and then up the Seine to Rouen for transhipment to London. Since the wines were shipped in casks, such a long journey invariably meant a loss of wine through theft or spoilage, and these losses made it almost prohibitively expensive to transport the wine of Burgundy beyond Paris. Nothing could be done to insure that the wines would reach their final destination without the casks having been broached by the wagoners and bargemen transporting them. These men had a well-earned reputation for drinking the wines, and attempts to thwart this deceit by putting the wines in double casks, in casks packed in straw and sewn in canvas, failed.[45] The best method of assuring that you would get what you paid for, and the method employed by Jefferson for the shipment of most of his French wines following this trip, was to have his wines bottled by the producer or some honest merchant such as Parent. Bottling increased the price considerably but it was worth it.

Jefferson stayed the night of March 9 in Tournus at the Hotel du Palais Royal.[46] While in Tournus he probably took time to visit the Burgundian-Romanesque styled church of St. Philibert, dating from 1009 and located in the center of the old town. The nave with its large round rose-colored pillars and transverse or barrel vault ceilings is a rare combination that would have attracted Jefferson's architectural eye.

In the morning Jefferson started for Beaujolais, his route paralleling the Saone River. On his left were the plains of the Saone and on the right undulating hills planted in vines. Many of the hillside vineyards enclosed by stone walls sloped gently to the plains and formed scenic valleys. Jefferson does not mention the wines but today they represent some of the best values available in dry white wines.

Just to the south of St. Aubain is the city of Macon and the surrounding vineyards of Maconnais. Here, as in all of Burgundy, the Chardonnay grape produces white wines and, regardless of the degree of complexity, good wines. Wines from these regions frequently seen on American restaurant wine lists and in wine shops that represent consistent quality and good value are Macon-Villages, Macon-Lugny, Macon-Vire, Macon-Prisse, St. Veran and the somewhat more expensive Pouilly-Fuisse.

South of Macon Jefferson entered Beaujolais and was struck by its beauty, calling it the richest country he had ever beheld "where nature has spread its richest gifts in profusion." He described it as extending from the top of a ridge of mountains running parallel with the Saone with gentle sloping hills "scarcely anywhere too steep for the plough." The hillsides were in vines with some corn and the plains in corn and pasture. Jefferson commented on a method they had of "mixing beautifully the culture of the vines, trees and corn. Rows of fruit trees are planted about 20 feet apart. Between the trees, in the row, they plant vines four feet apart and espalier[47] them. The intervals are sowed alternately in corn, so as to be one year in corn the next in pasture, the third in corn, the fourth in pasture, etc." Here, as everywhere in France, women were paid only half as much as men, but they were not required to do heavy work.[48]

Jefferson spent four days in Beaujolais, staying at the estate of Monsieur and Madame de Laye-Epinaye at their Château de Laye located between St. Georges-de-Reneins and Villefranche-Sur-Saone. The estate of Château de Laye was about 15,000 acres in vines, corn, pasture and wood and in Jefferson's words, "a rich and beautiful scene." Jefferson's friends, Abbes Chalut and Arnoux, had written a letter of introduction to the de Laye-Epinaye family. Monsieur Epinaye was away in Paris but Madame Epinaye entertained him with "'a hospitality, a goodness and an case which was charming."[49]

The owner of the estate, Monsieur de Laye-Epinaye, had a limited jurisdiction over both criminal and civil actions, which extended only to what Jefferson called "the first crude examination." After this examination the accused was referred for a final examination and decision to the regular judges of the country. Since prosecution of a criminal matter to sentence and execution cost Monsieur de Laye about 5,000 livres, he was slack in criminal prosecutions. This, Jefferson called, "a good effect from a bad cause."[50]

A year and a half later when Jefferson's friend, William Short, was on his own grand tour of France and Italy, Short spent eight days at Château de Laye where he was treated by Monsieur and Madame de Laye-Epinaye with kindness. Short reported to Jefferson how much the de Layes desired to see him again and "they frequently drank and made me drink to your health and with an air of so much sincerity that I could not help giving full faith to it, and the more so as we were in a plain kind of dining room as different from a salle a manger in Paris as the table of some of our Albemarle friends is from that of a rich financier in Philadelphia."[51]

The dining room in which Jefferson and Short were entertained is indeed plain in design. Its entrance is off the reception hall and is twenty three feet long and nineteen feet wide. At the far end of the room there are two doors that lead to the kitchen below. On the outside wall are two fifteen-foot windows that look out onto a park. There is no fireplace. Heat is admitted by opening two vents on the inside wall and drawing heat from a fireplace on the other side of the wall. The reception hall floor has a cherry and beech parquet floor identical to the floor that Jefferson later installed in his parlor at Monticello.[52]

The de Laye estate dates from the 14th century, but the present château was built in 1740 and the family chapel in 1770.[53] Château de Laye is no longer owned by the de Laye family, having been purchased in 1832 by the de Fleurieu family that still resides there.[54]

Jefferson did not comment on the wines of Château de Laye or, for that matter, on the wines of Beaujolais. The wines were made then, as they are now, from the Gamay grape. A typically well-made Beaujolais is a light, fruity, easy to drink red wine that should be drunk young and can accompany most foods. The best Beaujolais comes from ten communes just north of Château de Laye. They are called Crus du Beaujolais and are known by their commune names: Brouilly, Cotes de Brouilly, Chenas, Chiroubles, Fleurie, Julienas, Morgon, Moulin a Vent, Regnie and Saint-Amour. These wines are followed in order of rank by wines labeled "Beaujolais-Village." After Beaujolais-Village, the wines are labeled simply "Beaujolais" and carry the Appellation Beaujolais Controlee designation such as the wines that are still made at Château de Laye and distributed by a negociant in St. Georges de Reneins.

CHAPTER SIX

The Rhone Valley and its Wines

ontinuing south through a cold, beating rain Jefferson arrived in Lyons on March 15 and lodged at the Hotel du Palais Royal on the Place de Bellecour, still considered one of the finest squares in Lyons. He found "a good deal to be seen here." As was his habit, he went sightseeing and visited the oldest Roman amphitheater in France but was unimpressed, describing it as a "feeble remains."[1] Nevertheless, Lyons was the starting point of his study of Roman antiquities, remarking that from Lyons to Nimes, he was "nourished with the remains of Roman grandeur" and "immersed in antiquities from morning to night."[2] His sightseeing was probably cut short by the rain, hail, and snow that had pelted him almost from the moment of his departure from Paris, sixteen days earlier.

Taking advantage of the inclement weather, Jefferson caught up on his letter writing. He had carried away from Burgundy the remembrance of great wines—not the "waterish Burgundy" that Shakespeare spoke of in *King Lear* and which still masquerades as red Burgundy in far too many bottles. He wrote Parent ordering 125 bottles of 1782 Montrachet and requested a list of prices and best vintages for the wines of Chambertin, Vougeot, Romanée, Vosne, Nuits, Beaune, Pommard, Volnay, Montrachet and Meursault. Jefferson obviously had hopes of making his own because he requested of Parent a dozen vines from the vineyards of Montrachet, Vougeot and Chambertin.[3]

Leaving Lyons, Jefferson headed down the Rhone. From Paris to Lyons, Jefferson's carriage had been pulled by three horses, but after leaving Lyons and for the rest of the trip, except for his journey into Italy, his carriage was pulled by four or five post horses.[4]

In the Roman city of Vienne, 20 miles south of Lyons, Jefferson was angered when he visited "the Pretorian Palace, [known today as the Temple of Augustus and Livia], as it is called, comparable for its fine proportions to the Maison Carrée, totally defaced by the Barbarians who have converted it to its present purpose; its beautiful, fluted, Corinthian columns cut out in part to make space for Gothic windows, and hewed down in the residue to the plane of the building." It was then being used as a church and schoolroom.[5]

He visited and thought handsome the sepulchral *Pyramide* located a short way out of town. Over the years a legend developed, erroneously, that this pyramid marked the grave of Pontius Pilate. Located in the middle of a deserted side street, it stands about 50 feet high with a square base pierced by four arches. It is believed to have been the domed center of a Roman amphitheatre wall dating from the fourth century.[6]

On March 16, accompanied by guides, Jefferson set out for Cote Rotie, five miles below Vienne. He described the vineyards of Cote Rotie as "a string of broken hills, extending a league [three miles] on the river from the village of Ampuis to the town of Condrieux." The vineyards, terraced up steep granitic hillsides, came in precipices to the river, the same as they do today.[7]

The wines of Cote Rotie (roasted slopes) date back at least to Roman times, and there is some authority that the vineyards were originally planted by the Greeks in the sixth century B.C.[8] Although the vineyards have ancient origins, the popularity of the wines of Cote Rotie developed a little later than those of Burgundy, Bordeaux or Hermitage. At the time of Jefferson's visit, the best quality Cote Roties had an excellent reputation and were prized for their color, strength, bouquet, taste and ability to age[9] but were not yet of such high "estimation as to be produced commonly at the good tables of Paris."[10] Then, as now, Cote Roties were made exclusively from the Syrah grape.

The wines of Cote Rotie Jefferson thought quite good. "There is a quality which keeps well, bears transportation, and cannot be drunk under four years. Another must be drunk a year old. They are equal in flavor and price."[11] This is an interesting comment because the wines of Cote Rotie in the 18th century were often kept in wood for four to seven years and had a reputation for developing in the bottle for as much as 30 years.[12] Today, first quality Cote Rotie wines are aged in the barrel for only 18 to

26 months but still have a remarkable ability to develop and mature in the bottle. Just when a particular bottle of wine is at its best for drinking depends on many circumstances, but certainly the best quality Cote Roties of great vintage years need more bottle age than Jefferson's one to four years. When produced in outstanding vintage years, they have considerable tannin and need somewhere between five to twenty years to round out and develop their full potential of raspberry bouquets and berry flavors. However, these same wines of lesser vintages can be quite enjoyable in two to four years, in line with Jefferson's comments.[13]

Jefferson noted that the best red wines of Cote Rotie were made by Monsieur de la Condamine of Ampuis at his vineyard, Moulis, and by Monsieur de Leusse in his "grand tupin," and by Monsieur de Montjoli, Monsieur du Vivier and Monsieur du Prunel. Monsieur de la Condamine's château was known as Montlys a Saint Cyr Sur Rhone located just outside of Ampuis, but those vineyards have been abandoned. Just below Ampuis is the hamlet of Tupin, also singled out by Jefferson's reference to Monsieur de Leusse's vineyards. The Marquis de Leusse Grand Tupin vineyards have suffered the same fate.[14] The two best known vineyards of Tupin today are Les Prunelles and Le Car. The Les Prunelles vineyards could very well be the vineyard, or a part of the vineyard, owned in Jefferson's time by Monsieur du Prunel. There is a remarkable similarity to the names. Even with the disappearance of these two vineyards, the great wines of Cote Rotie come from the same vineyards that Jefferson saw strung across these granitic hillsides. The winemakers have changed, but the grape and the soil have remained the same.

Jefferson normally ordered his French wines shipped to him in bottles, which increased the price substantially. The best Cote Roties sold for 12 sous a bottle in cask but bottling and shipment to Paris added an additional eight sous, or two-thirds, to the price. Still, at one livre a bottle, they were great bargains.

The wine bottle, as we know it today, had come into being about 40 to 50 years before Jefferson's arrival in France. It evolved from a decanter shape, when it was used primarily to carry wine from the cellar-barrel to the dinner table, to a cylindrical shape with a short neck that could be laid on its side.[15] The popularity of corks as stoppers in wine bottles developed over the first half of the 17th century and paralleled the emergence of the corkscrew.[16] Early corkscrews were made of a steel screw attached to a ring. Jefferson carried with him a small travel case that contained, among other things, such necessities as a toothbrush, dentifrice, toothpicks, combs, pen, ink, paper and a corkscrew.[17]

Where the vineyards of Cote Rotie end at the town of Condrieux, Jefferson observed that the best white wines of the area began, and that "the best of the white are at Château Grillet [Grillé] by Madame la veuve Peyrouse." The name Condrieux comes from the French *Coin du Ruisseau,* or corner of the stream, and the town appropriately sits on a curve in the Rhone River.[18] The wines of Condrieux and Château Grillet have always been made exclusively from the Viognier grape. The exact origin of the Viognier grape is not known but it is certain that wine was made at

Condrieux as early as the Roman occupation.[19] Until recently this was the only area in France where the Viognier grape was planted.[20]

The owner of Château Grillet, Monsieur Neyret-Gachet, writes of his interest "to learn that Thomas Jefferson was to see the local vineyards and even Château Grillet! In our records it seems that Madame Veuve Perouse was the owner at the time—the spelling is different but the sound is right!

"Our wine is still and has *always* been made from only one kind of grape, those of Viognier D'or, or golden Viognier, and vinification tradition is as much as we know the same, the wine being kept in barrels for about two years."[21] Actually, the vinification methods have changed. In Jefferson's time, the wines of Condrieux and Château Grillet were both sweet and dry.[22] The sweet wine was made in much the same way as Sauternes, i.e., Viognier grapes were allowed "to become shrivelled and almost rotten [Botrytis cinerea]" before they were picked, and allowed to ferment only twelve hours and then run off into smaller casks. This sweet wine was essentially a dessert wine and had a reputation for keeping a long time and turning amber with age.[23]

All of the wine produced at Château Grillet today is dry with a lingering floral bouquet of apricots and a delicate, spicy taste, and has the distinction of being the smallest vineyard in France with its own Appellation Contrôlée, consisting of only seven and a half acres. The vines are planted on a succession of terraces that climb to the top of a steep hill 500 feet above the Rhone. The vineyard sets above the château and forms a horseshoe that gives the appearance of an amphitheatre. It has a south-easterly exposure and at the height of summer the grapes are subjected to intense heat. Since the vineyard is small with 1000 cases or so produced annually, this limited production in combination with its popularity makes it expensive.

Between Cote Rotie and Tains the country became more untamed and more pleasing to his eye: "Nature never formed a country of more savage aspect than that on both sides the Rhone. A huge torrent, rushing like an arrow between high precipices often of massive rock, at other times of loose stone with but little earth. Yet has the hand of man subdued this savage scene, by planting corn where there is little fertility, trees where there is still less, and vines where there is none. On the whole, it assumes a romantic, picturesque and pleasing air."[24]

Twenty miles farther south, Jefferson stopped at the village of Tains, located between the river and its "justly celebrated" terraced vineyards. He lodged at the posthouse and suffered a miserable night. He later warned, "do not go to the tavern of the Post House the master of which is a most unconscionable rascal," but he was captivated by the wines of Hermitage, especially the white wines.

"The wine called Hermitage is made on the hills impending over the village of Tains; on one of which is the hermitage which gives its name to the hills for about two miles, and to the wine made on them. There are but three of those hills which produce wine of the 1st. quality, and of these the middle regions only. They are about 300 feet perpendicular height, ¾ of a mile in length and have a Southern aspect... and, in its most precious parts, without any perceptible mixture of earth." Jefferson climbed to the top and recommended the panoramic view. "Go up to the top of the hill [Hermitage], for the sake of the sublime prospect from thence."[25]

Hermitage's name relates to a legend that the first hermit, Gaspard de Sterimberg, returned badly wounded from the crusades around 1225 A.D. with Syrah grape cuttings. He chose solitude, meditation and cultivating vineyards rather than returning to the crusades. Other hermits joined him on the hillside. Jefferson recorded that the last hermit died in 1751, but the wine has made the name immortal. A reconstructed version of the Hermit's Chapel sits near the top of the hill and is owned by the Jaboulet family who have named their best red Hermitage "La Chapelle" and their white Hermitage "Gaspard de Sterimberg."[26]

It is unlikely that the Syrah grape came to Tains as late as the 13th century. There is clear evidence that the Syrah grape was planted on the hills above the village of Tains in Roman times and some evidence that these vines were planted by Phocaeon Greeks somewhere around 500 B.C.[27] In any event, the Syrah grape, and what later became known as Hermitage, has a long and renowned history. The origin of the grapes that make the white wine, the Roussanne and Marsanne, is less clear although they, too, date back long before Jefferson's visit.

The white Hermitage that Jefferson drank was not totally dry; it had a touch of sweetness, a powerful aroma, and a peculiar flinty taste.[28] The wines were fermented in small wooden casks and allowed to remain there for four to six weeks. "When clear they were drawn off, placed in larger casks and periodically racked. They were not put into bottles until about four years old."[29] Because so little white was made, the vintners made the white sell the red. In other words, a purchaser had to "buy two or three times the quantity of the red" to get the white. At three livres a bottle it was as expensive as the best growths of Bordeaux and Burgundy and not ready to drink until four years old.[30] A small quantity of sweet white Hermitage was also made by taking the ripest grapes and spreading them on straw where they remained for six to eight weeks or until they became shriveled. They were called straw wine, *Vin de Paille*, and were sweet in flavor and aroma and were considered to resemble the best Constantia.[31]

Jefferson considered white Hermitage and Champagne the two best white wines of France. He held white Hermitage in such high esteem that he called it "the first wine in the world without a single exception."[32] During his presidency he purchased 550 bottles of white Hermitage from the House of Jourdan. The Jourdan vineyards were eventually inherited by the Monier family who, because of their ancestry, revived the name Chastaing de la Sizeranne. The Jourdan vineyards presently belong to the house of M. Chapoutier who calls his red Hermitage, La Sizeranne and his white Hermitage, Chante-Alouette (Lark's Song).[33] To drink a white Hermitage from the same vineyard, and made from the same grapes that Jefferson shared with dinner guests at the President's House, one need only buy M. Chapoutier's Chante-Alouette. Robert Parker rates Chante-Alouette along with Les Rocoules and Les Muret as the three finest and longest lived white Hermitages.[34]

The red wine, made of Syrah grapes grown on red-tinged earth mixed with small rottenstone, Jefferson said, "cannot be drunk under four years, and improves fastest in a hot situation. There is so little white made in proportion to the red, that it is difficult to buy it separate. They make the white sell the red."[35]

Although Jefferson does not single out the red wines of Hermitage for special praise, they had already acquired a high reputation, when genuine, for their "full body, dark purple color ... exquisite flavor and perfume, which is ... compared to that of the raspberry,"[36] a definition that aptly describes a great red Hermitage today. In fact, they were held in such high esteem in Burgundy and Bordeaux that red Hermitage was often blended with the finest wines of these two regions to add body, strength and power. Nathaniel Johnston, a prominent English Bordeaux wine merchant at the time of Jefferson's visit to Bordeaux said: "The Lafite 1795 which was made up with Hermitage was the best liked wine of any of that year."[37]

Red Hermitage is still known as one of the longest-lived non-fortified wines. George Saintsbury in his *Notes on a Cellar Book* called a 40-year-old Hermitage "the manliest French wine I ever drank..."[38] Hugh Johnson says that red Hermitage "improves for many years until its scent and flavor are almost overwhelming" but laments that it is rarely kept long enough to develop these qualities.[39]

Jefferson was told that the best vineyards were owned by "Monsieur Meus, seigneur of the place, Monsieur de Loche avocat, Monsieur Berger avocat, Monsieur Chanoine Monron, Monsieur Gaillet, Monsieur de Beausace, Monsieur Deure, Monsieur Chalamelle and Monsieur Monnet and two or three others." Forty-seven years later Alexander Henderson identified these same vineyards by their vineyard names as: Le Meal, Les Greffieux, de Bessas [Bessards], Beaumes and Les Rocoules.[40]

Writing 200 years after Jefferson's visit, Robert M. Parker, Jr. rates the vineyards in an almost identical order. "The principle vineyard here is Les Bessards, and the wines produced from its granite soil are the deepest in color, most intense in flavor, and often the richest and fullest in body, with a great deal of tannin. Further down the slope is Le Meal, also a top site for great Hermitage. Meal is reputed to produce very fragrant, supple, intense fruity wines. At the very bottom of the hill is Les Greffieux, which has the richest soil and produces lighter, more perfumed, velvety textured wines with great finesse. Le Greffieux is also one of the best locations for the white wine varietals, Marsanne and Roussanne. These are the three most highly prized vineyards, and traditional thinking has it that the greatest wines of Hermitage must be made from a blend of all three locations. However, there are other notable vineyards. Other recognized vineyard sites are L'Hermite, the highest vineyard; Beaumes, in the middle of the hill and known for its fruity, aromatic, soft red and white wines ..."[41]

Although Jefferson did not discuss the other area wines of Crozes Hermitage, St. Joseph, Cornas, and St. Peray, he did note that their hillsides were covered in vines. The vineyards of St. Joseph, Cornas and St. Peray are all located across the river from Hermitage on the west side of the Rhone. Because Jefferson was traveling on the east side, he may not have had a chance to visit these vineyards. While their reputations were overshadowed by the more highly esteemed white and red wines of Hermitage, these vineyards were known in Jefferson's time for producing quality wines. St. Peray was known for its dry white wines which, when bottled in the spring following the vintage, often produced a sparkle and froth, like the wines of Champagne.[42] The wines of Cornas were known then, and are known now, for their rich, deep color, full-bodied flavor, and aging potential. The vineyards of St. Joseph, just north of Tournon, also produced quality wines.[43]

From Tains south to Montelimar the mountains of the Dauphine and Languedoc were covered with snow and the plains planted in corn, clover, almonds, mulberries, and walnuts. In the neighborhood of Montelimar the vines were planted in rows six, eight or ten feet apart with corn filling the intervals. In this part of the Rhone Valley the people lived mostly in villages and their houses were made of mud or of round stone and mud. Laborers made between 16 to 18 sous per day and were required to feed themselves. Women were paid only half that and often for the same work. A family rarely ate meat. "A single hog salted," Jefferson said, "being the year's stock for a family. But they have plenty of cheese, eggs, potatoes and other vegetables and walnut oil for their salad."[44]

There was a reason why the common people rarely ate meat. It was known as *Capitainerier*—the authority granted by the King to the nobility or "princes of the blood" that gave a particular nobleman all rights to game within a certain locality, even on lands not belonging to him. The people had no rights to kill game for their meals on pain of going to prison and, for second offenders, often death.[45]

Arriving at Orange on March 18th, Jefferson pronounced "sublime" a triumphal arch (64' x 28' x 61½') at the entrance to the city and erected in about 25 A.D. during the period of Marcus Aurelius. He stayed at the Royal Palace Hotel and then went to the arena or Roman theater. He was outraged to find that "in this 18th century, in France, under the reign of Louis XVI, they are at this moment pulling down the circular wall of this superb remains to pave a road. And that too from a hill which is itself an entire mass of stone just as fit and more accessible."[46] In other words, they were demolishing the theater to make a road to it.

Fortunately this desecration stopped, for the Roman theatre still stands in most of its glory. Dating from the second century A.D., the wall composed of massive blocks of brown stone faces the town and serves as the stage backdrop. Entering the theatre from the right one sees the curved tiers of stone and wooden seats climbing the hillside excavated for this purpose. Since 1894 it has been used as a national theatre and today is used for such varied activities as local school plays to professional performances by such artists as Luciano Pavarotti.[47] The theatre seats about 10,000 and its natural acoustics are exceptional.

Curiously, Jefferson said nothing about the red wines of southern Rhone, especially what we know today as Châteauneuf-du-Pape, one of France's most popular wines. At the time of Jefferson's visit, the wines of Châteauneuf-du-Pape were known simply as Châteauneuf, or in the case of three vineyards, by their domain names: La Nerthe

Passions

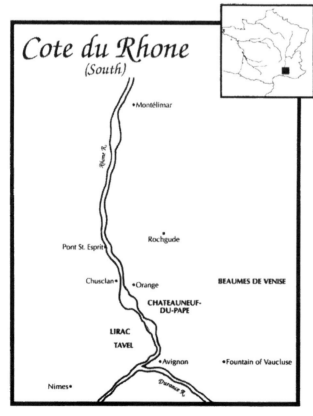

[La Nerte], Saint Patrice and Château Fortia [La Fortiasse]. Although these wines did not enjoy anything like their current popularity, at three and four years old they were considered very good and were sold in England and the United States. They were aged in wood for two years and had a reputation for being long-lived. By 1833 the wines were known by their current name, Châteauneuf-du-Pape.[48]

The vineyards of Châteauneuf-du-Pape lie between Orange and Avignon. The name derives from the summer castle built by Pope John XXII between 1318 and 1333. Except for the tower little remains of

The Rhone Valley and its Wines

the castle. Still, it is worth a special visit. Built on the high ground, there is a sweeping view of the surrounding countryside with its vineyards, silver olive groves and russet villages.[49]

Leaving Orange early the following morning, Jefferson traveled to the fortified town of Pont St. Esprit that takes its name from a bridge spanning one of the swiftest reaches of the Rhone River. He spent the night here and may have drunk with his dinner a rose wine from the vineyards of Chusclan [Chuzclan] located about six miles from Pont St. Esprit. It was a wine esteemed for its delicate bouquet and flavor and ranked in quality with the nearby rose wines of Tavel and Lirac.[50]

Wine is believed to have been produced at Chusclan by the Romans in the 5th century A.D. It was exported to Holland and England at the time of Jefferson's visit.[51] Although some red wine is now made in Chusclan, its reputation is still based on its dry rose wines made primarily from the Grenache and Cinsault grapes that have a fruity, fresh aroma and flavor and should be drunk young.

In the morning on leaving Pont St. Esprit, Jefferson observed from the summit of the first hill "a beautiful view of the bridge at about two miles distance, and a fine landscape of the country both ways from thence an excellent road ... through very romantic scenes. In one part, descending the face of a hill, it is laid out in serpentine, and not zig-zag, to ease the descent. In others it passes through a winding meadow ... the high hills of Languedoc still covered with snow ... mulberry are leafing; apple trees and peas are blossoming; the first butterfly I have seen." But with this natural beauty, he observed an abundance of beggars and people in rags. As for the wines, he found them good and of a strong body and at a cost of only two or three sous a bottle, very inexpensive.[52]

CHAPTER SEVEN

A Peep Into Elysium: Roman Grandeur

Nearing Nîmes Jefferson detoured to Remoulins and stopped to see the Pont du Gard, a magnificent Roman aqueduct built towards the end of the first century B.C. to carry fresh water from the town of Uzés to Nîmes. As he approached through a plain covered with olive trees to his right and mountains on his left, he saw its three-tier arch construction spanning the Gard River, a distance of 295 yards. Built by slave labor using huge blocks of uncemented stone, its six foundation arches support a second tier of eleven arches which in turn support the upper tier of thirty-five arches. When operational the water flowed through a covered concrete channel on the top. Jefferson described it as "a sublime antiquity and well preserved."[1]

After twenty centuries the Pont du Gard remains in superb condition; its huge blocks of stone look as if laid yesterday. An interesting time to visit it is in the morning between six and seven when the sunrise casts a pink glow across the bridge, its reflection shimmering in the river. The water channel is now dry and the visitor can walk its entire length.

Approaching Nîmes on March 20, Jefferson could see the remains of the Roman tower, the Tour Magne, on the summit of a hill overlooking the city. During his three-day stay in Nîmes he lodged at the Hotel du Louvre calling it a "very good" inn.[2] Arthur Young, a fellow agriculturist, who traveled through France at the same time as Jefferson, and who stayed at the

Pont du Gard

Hotel du Louvre two months after Jefferson's visit, described it as "a large, commodious, and excellent inn" with a reasonably priced dining hall accommodating as many as 40 persons.³ The Hotel du Louvre still operates as a hotel and its facade looks as it did when Jefferson's carriage arrived over 200 years ago. The vaulted dining room ceiling is the same as when Jefferson and Young dined there. The hotel sits by the Square de la Courronne, a small and pretty little park; it is within walking distance of all the Roman antiquities.

Jefferson scarcely mentions his meals on the road, but they consisted of mutton, poultry, pork, partridge, rabbit, game, ragouts, and sauces heavily spiced with garlic,⁴ and at Nimes his dinners were accompanied by an "excellent" *vin ordinaire* that cost only two or three sous a bottle. Another bargain was silk stockings, "the cheapest in France."⁵

The *vin ordinaire* was probably a red wine known as Ledenon which he became acquainted with on this trip and later imported during his retirement years. The Ledenon vineyards were located near Nimes and consisted of 800 acres. The best vineyard areas of 450 acres were called Plane de Paza. Ledenon, known for its agreeable bouquet, was the most expensive of the wines of Nimes and was "served pure at tables of the finest rank in France." It was considered the equal in quality and taste to the wines of Châteauneuf-du-Pape and Tavel.⁶

Other well-known red wines in the Nimes region were St. Gilles and Costiere. St. Gilles, considered the better of the two, was called *vin de remede* because it was used to strengthen and color weaker wines. Today the white, red and rose wines of this area are known as Costieres du Gard and have a VDQS *(Vin Delimite de Qualite Superieure)* appellation. The red wines, made principally from the Carignan grape, are popular locally for their light, fruity bouquets and are delicious with the local *boeuf gardiane*. A white wine called Blanquette de Calvisson was also made at Nimes and said to have been "tolerably good."⁷

Nîmes, first settled as a Roman colony about 50 B.C., contains more monuments of Roman antiquity than any other city in France, which attests to its former importance within the Roman Empire. Jefferson wasted no time investigating these treasures. He visited the Maison Carrée [Quarree] (Square House), one of the great Roman remains, gazing at it for "whole hours ... like a lover at his mistress. The stocking-weavers and silk spinners around it consider me an hypochondriac Englishman, about to write with a pistol the last chapter of his history. This is the second time I have been in love since I left Paris. The first was with a Diana at the Château de Laye-Epinaye in the Beaujolais, a delicious morsel of sculpture by Michael Angelo Slodtz."⁸ The Maison Carrée, a Roman temple built in the time of Augustus, is an oblong building with a portico and fluted Corinthian pillars that comprised part of the Forum Complex of ancient Nîmes. Admired through the ages, its architectural proportions and symmetry were later used by Jefferson in designing the State Capitol in Richmond, Virginia and during Napoleon's reign as the model for the Church de la Madeleine in Paris.

During this visit to Nimes he saw the collection of *Objets d'Art* of the well-known antiquarian Jean Francois Seguier (1703-1784) who had supervised the excavations and restorations of the Maison Carrée. One object of antiquity that struck his fancy was a Greek askos (wine pitcher). On returning to Nimes on May 10th, he paid a craftsman named Souche 18 livres to make a model of this "antique vase." At this price the model was made from a material less expensive than silver or bronze—probably wood.

About five blocks from the Maison Carrée, and in the center of Nimes, is the Roman amphitheatres built in the early first century, A.D. Arles has a similar arena built about the same time. Jefferson visited both, and thought the arena in Nimes the best preserved, calling it "a superb remains." It consists of 60 arches that continue around the circumference on two levels. Young saw it as "a prodigious work built without mortar that has withstood the attacks of weather and the worse depredations of the barbarians in the various revolutions of sixteen centuries."[9] In amphitheatre like these throughout the Roman Empire, crowds delighted in seeing all types of spectacles including gladiators fighting gladiators, gladiators fighting lions, domesticated panthers pulling chariots, bulls battling rhinoceroses, and chariot races.[10]

Jefferson's account book shows that he also visited the Jardin de la Fontaine and the Temple of Diana and the Roman baths. The fountain flows from beneath the rocks of Mt. Cavalier into a series of basins constructed in about 1740 together with a series of walks and canals. The Temple of Diana survives only as ruins, and is to the left of the fountain gardens and in front of the Roman baths. Above the fountain gardens at the top of Mt. Cavalier is the Tour Magne. The original function of Tour Magne is unknown but it probably served as a watch or signal tower. From the fountain gardens the Tour Magne is reached by walking up a series of paths that twist through a beautifully landscaped park. Jefferson does not tell us whether he made the climb to the top of Tour Magne but, given his penchant for viewing things from their greatest height, he probably did. The visitor today can reach the top of Tour Magne by climbing its 140 steps and be rewarded with a spectacular view of the Rhone Valley.

Jefferson's next stop was the city of Arles, a Roman colony founded in 46 B.C. At one time Arles competed as an important port with Marseilles. It is here that the Rhone River divides into two branches before emptying into the Mediterranean to the south. Jefferson stayed at a "detestable" tavern located on one of Arles' narrow, winding, cobble-stoned streets. He visited three Roman antiquities that are still of special interest: the Alyscamps, the Graeco-Roman theatre remains and the amphitheatre.

In the suburbs of Arles, at a church,[11] Jefferson viewed "some hundreds of ancient stone coffins along the road side. The ground is thence called les champs elysees." These are the Alyscamps or Elysian Fields, the renowned Roman and early Christian burial grounds of Arles. In the Middle Ages, Alyscamps was considered sacred and it became a pilgrimage Shrine of the Dead. At the request of the dying, friends would place their bodies, after death, in caskets and float them down the Rhone River to Arles. The bodies were then buried in the Elysian Fields in elaborately sculpted limestone coffins and tombs. When Jefferson visited Alyscamps, many of the elaborate sarcophagi had been removed, sold or destroyed. Today virtually all of the decorative sarcophagi are missing.

He saw the Graeco-Roman theatre remains consisting of "two Corinthian columns, and of the pediment with which they were crowned, very rich, having belonged to the ancient Capitol of the place." This theatre is estimated to have been so large that 16,000 people could be seated. But for Jefferson the principal monument was the amphitheatre, which had seated over 20,000 people.[12]

At Arles Jefferson had available a pleasant red *vin d'ordinaire* that was made from grapes grown in the immediate environs and the surrounding towns of Orgon, St. Maries and Tarascon. The wine was similar in style to the wines of St. Gilles, although not quite as good.[13]

The country from Nîmes to Aix-en-Provence waved in vines. As Jefferson "vibrated" along in his carriage, he amused himself with thoughts far removed from wine, architecture, sculpture, paintings, agriculture, politics, or Newton's laws of planetary motion, but with "physical researches" such as why postillions wore such enormous boots encased like an Egyptian mummy, and concluded that it was "because a Frenchman's heels are so light, that without this ballast, he would turn keel up."[14]

Before reaching Aix-en-Provence, Jefferson stayed the night in St. Remy and lodged at the Cheval Blanc, where he found the tavern keeper an intelligent man. The Cheval Blanc continues as a hotel and the room where Jefferson stayed the evening of

Graeco-Roman Theatre

March 25 still exists. It is located on the first floor, just to the left of the hotel's entrance. It appears remarkably well-preserved with a ribbed vault ceiling, a large fireplace and windows that look out to the town's church and its 14th century Gothic belfry. [15]

He visited "some fine ruins" about a half a mile south of the town, a mausoleum and the oldest triumphal arch outside of Italy. It is believed the arch was erected on orders from Julius Caesar to commemorate the Roman capture of the port of Massalia (Marseilles). The date and purpose of the mausoleum, called the *Tomb of the Julis*, are less clear. Jefferson owned a 1777 print of these antiquities which is now at Monticello. [16] Across the road from these two well-preserved antiquities is the excavated remains of the Roman town of *Glanum*. The remains reveal outlines of a forum, baths, temples and the only Greek dwelling unearthed in France.[17]

As Jefferson toured these Roman antiquities, he saw around him the same views that Vincent Van Gogh was to immortalize 100 years later. The *Glanum* ruins have as a backdrop the rugged but beautiful Alpilles Mountains, a view that Van Gogh used for several paintings. The Saint-Paul-de-Mausole Asylum, where Van Gogh confined himself for a year (May 8, 1889 to May 13, 1890) following the self-amputation of his right ear, is located a stone's throw from the *Glanum* ruins and across the road from the Roman Mausoleum and the Triumphal Arch. The asylum is a converted 12th century Augustinian monastery and still operates as a mental hospital. Van Gogh's brother, Theo, in his letter to the asylum director made just two requests: that Vincent be allowed to continue to paint and that he be given a half liter of wine with his meals. It was in this setting that Van Gogh created many of his most vivid and powerful paintings. "Irises," "Olive Orchard" (the first of 15 olive grove pictures), "Mountain [Alpilles] Landscape Seen Across the Walls," "Starry Night," and "Enclosed Wheatfield With Reaper" are just five of the more than one hundred paintings and drawings that Van Gogh created during this time.[18]

The visitor today can literally walk in the footsteps of Jefferson and Van Gogh and, while visiting the Roman antiquities, enjoy the views of the countryside with its olive groves, cypress trees, and orchards surrounded by the Alpilles mountains. In fact, a visit to these Roman ruins can be combined with a walking tour of seven actual scenes that Van Gogh painted, with metal placards holding color reproductions of Van Gogh landscapes.

Jefferson's journey then took him to Aix-en-Provence. As he approached Aix, the valley "rich and beautiful" spread out towards the mouth of the Rhone and the Mediterranean. He arrived in Aix-en-Provence on March 26 and stayed four days at the Hotel St. Jacques. Aix-en-Provence was the *raison d'etre* for his trip. In a letter to his daughter Martha he repeated what he had told several friends before leaving. "My journey hitherto has been a very pleasing one. It was undertaken with the hope that the mineral waters of this place might restore strength to my wrist. Other considerations also concurred. Instruction, amusement and abstraction from business, of which I had too much at Paris."[19]

The mineral waters of Aix-en-Provence had been famous since Roman times for their healing powers. Over the centuries the baths were destroyed and the source of the water lost until accidentally rediscovered in 1704. An account of what the baths looked like and how they worked is given by Tobias Smollett. "The magistrates, with a view to render them more useful and commodious, have raised a plain building, in which there are a couple of private baths with a bed-chamber adjoining to each, where individuals may use them both internally and externally for a moderate expense. These baths are paved with marble, and supplied with water, each by a large brass cock, which you can turn at pleasure. At one end of this edifice, there is an octagon, open at top, having a basin, with a stone pillar in the middle, which discharges water from the same source, all round, by eight small brass cocks; and hither people of all ranks come … with their glasses, to drink the water, or wash the sores, or subject their contracted limbs to the stream. This last operation, called the *douche*, however, is more effectually undergone in the private bath, where the stream is much more powerful.…"[20] Smollett reported that the baths "were found serviceable to the gout, the gravel, scurvy, dropsy, palsy, indigestion, asthama, and consumption; and their fame soon extended itself all over Languedoc, Gascony, Dauphine, and Provence."

Short knew that Jefferson planned on bathing his injured right wrist in these mineral waters. In anticipation that Jefferson would be disappointed in the healing effects of the Aix baths, he wrote Jefferson, "Although I have little faith in the waters of Aix, I have a great deal in its climate. But provided you receive the benefit you wished for, I will not dispute about the cause which may produce so desirable an effect. I hope you will let me know … whether the one or the other has shown any influence on your wrist."[21] And Short was right; the baths failed to improve Jefferson's wrist. Jefferson advised Short: "Having taken 40 douches, without any sensible benefit, I thought it useless to continue them. My wrist strengthens slowly. It is to time I look as the surest remedy, and that I believe will restore it at length."[22] But the Provence sun, that later inspired Van Gogh, Matisse, Cezanne, Monet, Renior, Derain, Picasso and Chagall, did for his spirits what the waters could not do for his wrist. "The man who shoots himself in the climate of Aix must be a bloody minded fellow indeed. I am now in the land of corn, wine, oil, and sunshine. What more can man ask of heaven? If I should happen to die at Paris I will beg of you to send me here, and have me exposed to the sun. I am sure it will bring me to life again. It is wonderful to me that every free being who possesses *cent ecus de rente*, does not remove to the Southward of the Loire. It is true that money will carry to Paris most of the good things of this canton. But it cannot carry thither it's sunshine, nor procure any equivalent for it. This city is one of the cleanest and neatest I have ever seen in any country. The streets are straight, from 20 to 100 feet wide, and as clean as a parlor floor … [with] rows of elms from 100 to 150 years old, which make delicious walks."[23] These handsome elms provided shade to the rich in their carriage rides and walks along the Cours Mirabeau, the main street of Aix-en-Provence, lined with 17th and 18th century mansions, and described by some as the most beautiful street in Europe. The Cours was developed in 1651 after Marie de Medici brought to France from Italy the cratic custom of "taking the air in public," either in carriages or on foot or in chairs instead of walking in one's own garden. The trees died in an elm blight about 1830 were replaced by plane trees.[24] These now line, in double columns, both sides of the Cours Mirabeau.

His second evening in Aix was spent at the Municipal Theatre located a hundred yards east of the Cours. Troubadours, musicians and actors traveling north from Italy, Spain, Portugal and Africa, and traveling south from England, Scandinavia, Paris and Lyons, routinely performed operas, ballets, tragedies and comedies at the Municipal Theatre. At the beginning of the eighteenth century, the theatre had taken over and settled into the Royal Tennis Courts, built in 1660, and had been redecorated just one year before Jefferson's visit.[25] In describing his evening at the theatre, Jefferson wrote: "We were last night treated with Alexis and Justine, and Mazet, in which the most celebrated actresses from Marseilles came to bear a part for the advantage of her friend whose benefit night it was. She is in the style of Mde. Dugazon, has ear, voice, taste and action. She is moreover young and handsome and has an advantage over Mde. Dugazon and some other of the celebrated ones of Paris, in being clear of that dreadful wheeze or rather whistle in respiration which resembles the agonizing struggles for breath in a dying person."[26] The Municipal Theatre continues to be active in the cultural life of Aix.

Jefferson enjoyed Aix. He thought it a "neat town" with bread "the equal to any in the world" and the best olive oil. The many vineyards around Aix at Marseilles, Arles, Orgon and Tarascon produced red wines of good color, body and flavor that improved with some age but required drinking within six to seven years.[27] Today, just to the south of Aix is a vineyard that Robert Parker calls "one of the best kept winemaking secrets of Provence." It is Château Simone with 37 acres of well-landscaped vineyards located in Palette, France's second smallest appellation. The Rougier family has operated Château Simone for over 150 years, and, although white, red and rose wines are made, it is the red wines that achieve the highest distinction.[28] The wines of Château Simone are so popular that they are not always available at Aix's restaurants.

On March 29 he set out in his carriage for Marseilles, a distance of about 20 miles. The road leading to Marseilles, one of the most traveled in France, was described as being in a "scandalous condition ... not wide enough, at places, for two carriages to pass with convenience." The country was hilly and intersected by chains of mountains of rock with vines, corn, mulberries, almonds and willows growing among rows of olive and fig trees that produced the most delicate figs known in Europe. The vineyards around Marseilles produced wines of good color, body, spirit and flavor. Cassis, just fifteen miles east of Marseilles, had the reputation for producing a quality sweet white wine.[29] Many of the vineyards around Marseilles made a *vin cuit* or boiled wine that was compared with Tokay and often sold as such.[30]

Jefferson said that his journey to this point had been a continual feast of new objects and ideas. In order to make the most of the time available, he avoided "good dinners and good company" and "courted the society of gardeners, vignerons, coopers, farmers, etc. and have devoted every moment of every day almost, to the business of enquiry."³¹ Unfortunately, Jefferson's account books, letters and notes reveal little about the people he met along the way, what they thought, or how they acted.

Marseilles

But Arthur Young tells us something of French manners. Young was repeatedly astonished by what he called the "taciturnity" of the French. "I came to the kingdom expecting to have my ears constantly fatigued with the infinite volubility and spirits of the people, of which so many persons have written, sitting, I suppose, by their English firesides." To the contrary, Young found that the French simply would not talk to foreigners or strangers and at dinner they acted like "tongue-tied Quakers" staring into space. At the Hotel du Louvre in Nîmes, he reported that "with a different party at every meal it is the same, not a Frenchman will open his lips."³² Since Jefferson sat at this very dining table just two months before Young's visit, we can assume that he received the same silent treatment.³³

Young was also astounded by the depths of ignorance the French people exhibited of the world around them. And this included not just peasants but merchants and other business people. He tells of an experience with a well-dressed French merchant who "plagued me with abundance of tiresome foolish questions, and then asked for the third or fourth time what country I was of. I told him I was Chinese. How far off is that country?—I replied, 200 leagues [600 miles]. *Deux cents lieus! Diable! C'est un grand chemin!*" On another occasion a Frenchman asked him where he was from. "After telling him I was an Englishman, he wanted to know if we had any trees in England?-I replied, that we had a few. Had we any rivers?—Oh, none at all . . . This incredible ignorance . . . is to be attributed, like everything else, to government."³⁴ Young's observations were made in July 1787, two years before the beginning of the French Revolution.

Jefferson saw Marseilles as an amphitheatre surrounded by mountains of rock and, within that amphitheatre, a mixture of naturally rich valleys and plains that stretched to the mountain bases six to nine miles distant. He found Marseilles "a charming place. All life and activity . . . like London and Philadelphia" with an extensive society and an animated commerce.³⁵ He spent a week in Marseilles staying at the Hotel de la Princesse from March 30 to April 6.

Jefferson's stay in Marseilles was busy with excursions to the Château Borely [Borelli] and a boat ride to the Island Château d'If, and an evening at the theater which was new but not as striking as the theatres he was to attend in Bordeaux and Nantes.[36]

As usual, he took to the high ground and visited the Château Notre Dame de la Gard on a hill with a magnificent view of the city and the Mediterranean that included vine-clad hills, gardens, country houses and clusters of islands, including the Isle d'If, the place of Mirabeau's imprisonment.[37]

He looked up Mazzei's friend Soria and found him not only alive but one of the most successful merchants in Marseilles. However, Soria's wealth had been somewhat diminished a few days before Jefferson's arrival as a result of his son having "eloped with jewels and money to the value of 40,000 livres and ... not yet heard of and famous in the adventures of Count of Monte Cristo."[38]

Through a letter of introduction from Chastellux he made the acquaintance of Henry Bergasse, one of France's great wine merchants. Bergasse had Jefferson to dinner, introduced him to friends, provided him with information and took him to his wine cellars, where Jefferson saw in casks the equivalent of over 1,500,000 bottles of wine. The temperature of Bergasse's wine cellar was a constant 54 degrees.[39] He also learned that the best method of packing wine when bottled was to lay the bottles on their sides and cover them with sand.[40]

While he traveled, he sought not only information, but for products to transplant to America. "I find here [Marseilles] several interesting articles of culture; the best figs, the best grape for drying, a smaller one for the same purpose without a seed, from Smyrna, olives, capers, pistachio nuts, almonds. All these articles may succeed on, or southward of the Chesapeake."[41]

Marseilles was also a great emporium for Italian rice, and it was here that Jefferson hoped to find out "whether it was the use of a different machine for cleaning which brought European rice to market less broken than ours," but in spite of several inquiries no one could explain to him the nature of the machine. Consequently, Jefferson decided to make a detour into the Piedmont area of Italy to find out if, indeed, the Italians had a better rice machine. Rice then, and not wine, took Jefferson into Italy, where he found that "the machine is absolutely the same as ours"[42] and later learned that the rice was inferior in quality.

Jefferson left Marseilles for Toulon on April 7. His route took him northeast to Aubagne and Cuges through a countryside laid up in terraces of vines, olives and corn. From Cuges to Toulon the mountains became higher and as his carriage descended through narrow mountain passes, he could see the Mediterranean in the distance. Near Toulon, the mountains narrowed as he entered the high-walled north gorge of the village of Ollioules, an enclave that had become the haunt of outlaws.[43]

It was into the Ollioules pass that the Bishop of "D" in *Les Miserables,* a few years after Jefferson's visit, went out from the town of Chastelar and brought back the chest of church treasures that had been stolen by the notorious highwayman Cravatte and his brigands. If Jefferson was aware of the dangers of being robbed or murdered by entering this mountain pass, his only comment was, "the mountains then reclining a little from their perpendicular ... has given place to the little village of Ollioules, in the gardens of which are oranges in the open ground."[44] The Ollioules pass is still there. Man has not changed its natural contours, just the surface over which the traffic flows. Today a steady stream of cars passes through its granite boulders and the only danger it presents is a motor vehicle accident.

At Toulon a vineyard named *La Malque* had the reputation for producing a good red wine that improved with age.[45] At Ollioules, Cuers, and Hyeres slightly less robust red wines were made called *Vins de la Cote de Toulon*. Jefferson's stay of two days gave him the opportunity to become acquainted with the local wines.

From Toulon he set out for Nice and his trip across the Alps into Italy. Approaching the village of Hyeres with a population of about 5,000, he entered a plain three miles in diameter bound by the sea to his right and mountains on his left. Hyeres' streets were about eight feet wide and twisted and turned up a steep hillside. Since the streets were so narrow, carriages could not enter the town and the wealthier inhabitants were carried about in chaises. Here he visited a botanical garden kept by King Louis XVI.[46]

From Hyeres the road led through valleys and across mountain ranges with stretches of natural beauty, fishing hamlets and medieval hillside villages. After spending the night of April 9 at Frejus, Jefferson continued his journey through the Esterel Mountains to the Mediterranean sea town of Napoule. The Esterel Mountains were covered with pines, evergreens, laurel, cypress, firs, box, and juniper mingled with marjoran, thyme, lavender and sage. But hidden among its beauty were dangers of which Jefferson seemed unaware. If there was a spot in France more dangerous for the traveler than the Ollioules mountain pass, it was the rugged Esterels where highwaymen, many of whom had escaped from the prison in Toulon, had taken sanctuary in its gorges and ravines. But, since it was the only land route to Italy, it had to be crossed.[47]

The Swiss geologist Horace-Benedict de Saussure explored the Esterel on foot the same year as Jefferson's trip, and his captivation with its natural beauty was tempered by an uneasiness for his safety. "The main road is entirely exposed, and is dominated by salient rocks, on which the brigands plant their sentinels. They suffer travellers to advance to some open space between these points of vantage. Then, from their ambushes in the woods, they swoop down on them and plunder them, whilst the sentinels keep a good look-out, lest the guards should come and surprise them. In the event of any of these appearing, a whistle suffices to warn the robbers, and they dive out of sight into the forest. It is absolutely impossible to reach them. Not only is the undergrowth very dense, but it is encumbered with huge blocks of stone. There are neither by-roads nor paths; and unless one knows the intricacies of the woods as well as do the brigands themselves, no one can penetrate into them, except very slowly. The forest extends to the sea, and the whole district, entirely uncultivated, is a place of refuge for the convicts who have escaped from the g[...] all the robbers of the country."⁴⁸

In the middle of the mountain was the posthouse wh[ere ...] changed horses. Although the road across was steep and bordere[d ...] a good road. As Jefferson's carriage descended the mountain, he cou[ld see] the Mediterranean between the mountain divisions. He obviously did [not have] trouble because he described this part of his trip simply as "18 miles of [a gentle] descent of a very high mountain."⁴⁹

From Napoule, Jefferson traveled to Antibes along a road that passed near [the] Mediterranean and over hills and strings of valleys surrounded by the snow-capped mountains of the Alps.

Reaching Nice on April 10, Jefferson found it a flourishing city with new houses and new streets being built in a section of the city called the New Borough. He lodged at the Hotel York which he described as "a fine English tavern, very agreeably situated, and the mistress a friendly agreeable woman."⁵⁰

Nice was so heavily populated by the English that Jefferson referred to it as "an English colony." He found it a handsome city with good accommodations, a "gay and dissipated society," and a superb climate. It had a magnificent sea view that was appreciated from a terrace that opened onto the sea and was formed from the roofs of a row of low houses on one side of the street, about a quarter of a mile long, covered with a stucco floor.⁵¹ Although today the famous Promenade des Anglais is longer and extends along the sea between the beach and the roadway, the rooftop promenade still exists. It is found on the roofs of the houses and shops in the old town section that face the sea and adjacent to the Château ruins, or castle-hill. Jefferson did not make note of it but he certainly would have climbed to the top of the Château ruins for a view of Nice, the Mediterranean, the Alps and the countryside. Today, from the Château ruins, the visitor can follow a walkway through a landscaped park that leads to a point above the Château that provides an even more spectacular view.

Through his Parisian friend, Abbe Arnoux, Jefferson was introduced to a local wine merchant, Andre Sasserno. At Sasserno's house, he sampled the wines of Bellet—white, red and rosé—which came from vineyards a few miles northeast of Nice. Jefferson found the wines good "though not of the first quality,"⁵² but later changed his opinion and called them "remarkably good."

He felt differently when, in retirement in 1819, he tasted one of 300 bottles of this wine ordered from Sasserno's son. Its sour taste-and the equally souring thought of 299 bottles-provoked a definition of Jefferson's taste in wine: "My taste for the wines of Nice, and for the particular quality of it which I drank at your father's house in Nice [1787], and which M. Spreafico sent me in 1816, will, I fear, become a troublesome circumstance to you; and chiefly perhaps because the expressions characterizing subjects of taste and flavor in one language have not always terms synonymous in another. To remove this difficulty, I will explain to you the particular terms we use to designate particularly different flavor or characters of wine. These are 1. *sweet* wines,

...retti doux of Spain, Calcavallo of Por-
...vins de Grave, du Rhin, de Hochheim,
...r of sweetness or acidity as Madere see,
...which are in truth a compound in their
...ness, barely sensible to the palate. The
...y is made so by putting a small quantity
...another quality which is often found in
...call *rough* or *astringent*, and the French
...nething of this in all the wines of Nice
...e of Oporto as to approach to bitterness
...being thus explained, I will observe that
...o in 1816 was *silky* and a little *astringent*,
...d, and the most esteemed here generally.
That of 1817 was *dry*, ... an excellent wine. That of 1818, last received, has its usual astringency indeed, but is a little acid; so much so as to destroy its
usual good flavor. Had it come in the summer, I should have suspected its having acquired its acidity by fretting in the hold of the ship, or in our hot warehouses, on a
summer passage. But it was shipped at Marseilles in October, the true time for shipping delicate wines for this country. With these explanations of the meaning of our
terms, I will now pray you, Sir, to send me through Mr. Cathalan, 150 bottles of the
wine of Bellet of the *silky* quality sent me in 1816 by Mr. Spreafico, if to be had; and
if that was of an accidental recolte [vintage] not always to be had, then send it of the
dry quality, such as was sent me in 1817."[53]

Were the wines from Sasserno's vineyards white or red? Even though Jefferson refers to white wines in designating the taste and character he expected from Sasserno's
wine, it was the red wine of Bellet that he esteemed. Twenty-five years later Jullien
confirmed that the only wine of repute produced from the Bellet vineyards was a red
wine described as delicate and agreeable.[54]

Attempts to locate the precise vineyards that produced Sasserno's wines were unsuccessful, but the best wines of Bellet are made in the mountains above Nice from
vineyards that are among the oldest in France.[55] Robert M. Parker, Jr. describes the
wines of Bellet as "Nice's best-kept secret." Red, rose and white wines are made in this
small appellation but the white wines are the wines that excel today, and the best
white wines are made principally from a grape called the Rolle.[56] The white wines
seem to acquire an extra dimension when drunk with the seafood served at the many
outdoor restaurants lining the Cours Saleya in Nice's old section. Most of the wines
of Bellet are consumed at the many restaurants along the French Riviera but some
can be found in the United States in major wine markets.[57]

From Nice Jefferson counseled Lafayette to take a similar trip "and to do it most
effectively you must be absolutely incognito, you must ferret the people out of their
hovels as I have done, look into their kettles, eat their bread, loll on their beds under
pretense of resting yourself, but in fact to find if they are soft. You will feel a sublime

pleasure in the course of this investigation, and a sublimer one hereafter when you shall be able to apply your knowledge to the softening of their beds, or the throwing of a morsel of meat into the kettle of vegetables." In this regard Jefferson noted that laborers breakfasted on a piece of bread with an anchovy or an onion, and for dinner "bread, soup and vegetables. Their supper the same." But, overall, Jefferson was pleased to find among the peasants less physical misery than he had expected to find. They were generally "well clothed with plenty of food, not animal indeed, but vegetables, which is as wholesome."[58]

CHAPTER EIGHT

Italy and the Riviera

Because no highway existed along the Mediterranean coast from Nice to Genoa Jefferson's trip into Italy from Nice required him to cross the Maritime Alps, a distance of 93 miles before reaching the town of Coni. In Jefferson's words the road was "probably the greatest work of this kind whichever was executed either in ancient or modern times. It did not cost as much as one year's war." The road was a series of twists and turns up and down the mountains and in good weather wide enough for carriages to pass, but a problem developed when winter snows made the road impassable. Because the snows prevented carriages from passing, Jefferson put his carriage in storage, rented mules, and on April 13, his 44th birthday, started across the Alps on the back of a mule.[1]

Jefferson first crossed Mt. Braus, and on the descent to the town of Sospello (now named Sospel and a part of France) he saw a cluster of mountain peaks on the horizon. Sospel was situated on a torrent abounding with speckled trout and surrounded by olive trees in blossom. Jefferson passed the night here. We do not know where he stayed, whether at the posthouse or a tavern, and what if anything he did to celebrate his birthday. If he drank wine with his dinner, he would have brought it from Nice since there were no vineyards in this mountain region.[2]

He spent the next day crossing Mt. Brois, a more savage and picturesque journey than the day before. Descending Mt. Brois, he passed the village of Saorge [Saorgio] and its castle "where a scene is presented the most singular and picturesque I ever saw. The castle and the village seem hanging to a cloud in front. On the right is a mountain cloven through to let pass a gurgling stream; on the left a river over which is thrown a magnificent bridge. The whole forms a basin, the sides of which are shagged with rocks, olive trees, vines, herbs, etc." This scene has been altered because the castle was destroyed five years after Jefferson's visit, but the village still is seen hanging to a cloud in front.[3] Saorge is built into the mountainside and commands the whole pass. Jefferson did not stop at Saorge, probably because it would have meant a major detour. Even today Saorge can only be reached through a tunnel cut through the mountain.

Before reaching Tende, Jefferson passed by Ciandola [La Giandola] which he described "of only two houses, both taverns." Today, Ciandola is an attractive village that lies in a valley between the mountain ranges with a number of pleasant outdoor cafes. It is a perfect place to stop and admire the surrounding scenery. Jefferson stayed the night at the village of Tende, surrounded by precipitous walls of rock, in an inn, "all black, dirty, stinking, and no glass windows."[4]

Early the next morning he set out to cross the Col de Tende, the mountain range that separates the Maritime from the Ligurian Alps. This was the most dangerous part of his trip. Col de Tende was the highest mountain he had to cross; still covered with ice and snow, the high winds or storms within the mountain passes often created avalanches. Since the wind was "most quiet" in the early morning hours, the routine was to leave Tende at dark "in order to cross Col de Tende as soon after the break of day as possible."[5]

Halfway up were quarters for a detachment of soldiers posted to prevent smuggling and an inn called La Ca (The House). It was here that Jefferson would have hired several men to assist him and his valet in ascending and descending the mountain. These men, called *"coulants"* used a hoe-like device to break the ice and make steps for the mules. Near the top, Jefferson had to get off his mule and climb on foot because even though the mountain mules were sure-footed and frost-shod, the ice was so hard and slippery that they often stumbled and fell. Although the climb to the top was arduous and dangerous in winter months, the way down was the envy of anyone who has ever enjoyed a toboggan or sleigh ride. The traveler descended the mountain in a wooden sleigh called a *Leze*. One of the coulants sat in the front of the sleigh, the traveler in the middle and another coulant stood in the rear. The front coulant used his feet to regulate the speed of the sleigh's descent which was so rapid that the village of Limone was reached in about an hour.[6] Today Col de Tende is the dividing point between France and Italy and is crossed by driving through a tunnel; sleigh rides down its mountain slopes are a thing of the past.

Limone, at the base of Col de Tende, was headquarters for the muleteers and so Jefferson abandoned his mules and rented post-horses and a carriage for the rest of his trip in Italy until reaching Genoa.

Descending the Alps towards the walled town of Coni, Jefferson viewed the plains of Po, a rich carpet of green flecked with clusters of figs, cherries, walnuts, vines, olives, lavender, thyme, chestnuts and corn.[7] The three days that it took to reach Coni had been filled with "many curiosities and enchanting objects." He lodged at the Croce Bianca [Blanche].

He then traveled to Turin through the towns of Centale, Savigliano and Racconigi and along the way he saw vines planted in a manner which he had not seen before. At intervals of about 8.f. they plant from 2. to 6. plants of vine in a cluster. At each cluster they fix a forked staff, the plane of the prongs of the fork at a right angle with the row of vines. Athwart these prongs they lash another staff1like a handspike, about 8.f long, horizontally, 7. or 8. feet from the ground. Of course it crosses the rows at right

Italy and the Riviera

angles. The vines are brought from the foot of the fork up to this cross piece, turned over it, and conducted along over the next, the next, and so on as far as they will extend, the whole forming an arbour 8.f. wide and high, and of the whole length of the row, little interrupted by the stems of the vines, which being close round the fork, pass up thro' hoops, so as to occupy a space only of small diameter."[8]

On reaching the Po River, Jefferson crossed on what he called a swinging batteaux, two boats placed side-by-side with a common platform onto which the horses and carriage were driven.

Arriving in Turin on April 17, he stayed two days at the Hotel d'Angleterre, the best hotel. It was here that Jefferson first tasted the precursor of today's Nebbiolo grape, which makes some of Italy's best wines: Barolo, Barbaresco, Gattinara and Ghemme. He found the "Nebiule" wine singular, melding three contradictory characteristics: "It is about as sweet as the silky Madeira, as astringent on the palate as Bordeaux, and as brisk as Champagne. It is a pleasing wine."[9]

His comments are out of character with the big, full-bodied, dry, tannic Barolos and Barbarescos that are made today in Piedmont from the Nebbiolo grape. Nebbiolo wines are not sweet nor do they effervesce, because the style of making these red wines has changed radically. Throughout the 18th century, and well into the 19th century, fermentation was never allowed to finish, leaving the wines sweet and often unstable. Redding talks of these red wines being "fermented but a short period and the best being *Vin de Liqueur*." It was not until the 1840s that the big, dry wines we know today as Barolos and Barbarescos emerged. The incomplete fermentation also left them *frizzanti* which probably explains the "brisk as Champagne" comment.[10]

At the time of Jefferson's visit Turin was the capital of the little kingdom of Sardinia or what is today Piedmont. Although it was considered by many as one of the most beautiful cities in Europe, Young, who visited Turin two years after Jefferson, was unimpressed with its long, broad, straight streets. He saw the houses as old and dirty and made of an ugly brick with narrow windows and iron balconies. The Strata di Po, Turin's finest street, Young said could not compare with at least fifty streets in London.[11] It is unlikely that Jefferson, who had a low opinion of London's architecture[12] and was used to the rectangular symmetry of American cities, saw Turin in the same light. Certainly the architect in Jefferson allowed him to appreciate Turin's Baroque architecture: the Palazzo Madama, the Palazzo Carignano (Napoleon's residence in

Turin

1794 and the birthplace of Victor Emmanuel II), the Palazzo Reale (the Royal Palace), and the Piazzas San Carlo and Castello.

Jefferson went sightseeing but records only visiting a "Cabinet of Antiquities," which was probably housed in the Museum Lapidario at the University of Turin. While at the university, the bibliophile in Jefferson would have taken him to see the university library, now the *Biblioteca Nazionale*, with its rare collection of incunabula, including Pliny's *Historia Naturalis*.[13]

Later he took an excursion to the Village of Moncaglieri [Moncalieri] and visited the 15th century royal castle that Young called the "Windsor of Piedmont." The castle, on a hill above the village, had a view of the Po and the plains which spread to a ridge of mountains that formed the Dutchy of Montferrat. The castle still offers a panoramic view of the countryside but with the addition of highways and modern buildings a changed perspective. It may have been here that Jefferson first drank the "thick and strong" red wine of Montferrat which he later recommended.[14]

The next day, he rented horses and traveled to Superga, the burial place of the Sardinian kings situated on a hill east of Turin. From the dome of the Basilica of Superga, he looked out on the Alps and Apennines, the valley of the Po and the vine-clad hills of Montferrat. Next he traveled to Stupinigi and saw the royal hunting lodge.[15]

In Turin Jefferson learned that the exportation of rice in the husk from Piedmont was prohibited and punishable by death. He had come a long way to determine the superiority of Piedmont rice, and he was not to be deterred by a death threat. He filled his coat pockets with rice and possibly risked the life of a muleteer, Poggio, to smuggle a bagful to Genoa. He succeeded in getting the rice out of Italy and sent it to the South Carolina Society for Promoting Agriculture. Responding on behalf of the Society, Ralph Izard found the rice inferior to the South Carolina variety and, fearing that the comingling of the rice could lead to an undesirable hybrid, asked Jefferson to send no more.[16]

This was not the first or last time Jefferson was guilty of smuggling to avoid a restrictive law. A year later in Amsterdam he admired some cups for tea, coffee and chocolate made of East India porcelain. When he learned that their importation into France was prohibited, he wrote Andre Limozin in Rouen: "This [the cups] being prohibited, I must leave to you the method of conveying it to my house in Paris, either over the walls of your town or through them as you see best ... If it could pass by payment of duties, I should pay them cheerfully, but I apprehend it is prohibited altogether. Perhaps it could be reported as glass or some other dutied article."[17]

From Turin to Vercelli the plains were cultivated in corn, pasture, vines, mulberries, walnuts and some willows and poplars. The people were poorly clothed compared to the people of France, and the women worked at heavy laboring jobs. Stopping overnight in Vercelli, he lodged at the Hotel of the Three Kings. It was here that he drank "a wine called Gatina [Gattinara] made in the neighborhood of Vercelli, both red and white." Jefferson thought the white Gattinara resembled a Carcavelos, a sweet wine

Italy and the Riviera

from Portugal which he drank throughout his life. Burton Anderson believes that this wine was "probably made from the Erbaluce grape still grown at Caluso (near Vercelli) for a sweet passito."[18] The red wines of Gattinara, made from the Nebbiolo grape, were, like its near neighbors, Barolo and Barbaresco, also on the sweet side. Gattinaras today, although somewhat lighter and less tannic than Barolos, when made by a good vintner and properly aged are dry, rich and silky.

He also drank an "esteemed" light red wine from Salussola.[19] The town of Salussola lies

twelve miles northwest of Vercelli on the edge of the Po plains and La Serra hills. It "must have been 'esteemed' locally," Burton Anderson writes, "since the authoritative *Storia della vite e del vino in Italia* does not refer to wine from Salussola in the 18th century ... No wine of note is made at Salussola today."[20]

From Vercelli to Novara, the fields were in rice and mostly under water. Along this route he found "still another method of planting the vine. The long rows of trees they lash poles from tree to tree. Between the trees are set vines which passing over the pole are carried on to the pole of the next row, whose vines are in like manner are brought to this, and twined together, thus forming the intervals between the rows of trees alternately into arbors, and open space."[21]

Jefferson found Milan on a level plain and so surrounded with vines, corn, pasture, and gardens that it could hardly be seen until "you are in the streets."[22] It was so cold on Jefferson's arrival on April 21 that the rice ponds were frozen over a half inch thick. He stayed at "the best inn," the Albergo Reale [Alberghi Reali], and bought a guide, *Nuova Guida di Milano*.[23]

In Jefferson's eyes, the Cathedral of Milan was not an architectural splendor but "a worthy object of philosophical contemplation to be placed among the rarest instances of the misuse of money. On viewing the churches of Italy it is evident without calculation that the same expense would have sufficed to throw the Appennines into the Adriatic and thereby render it tera firma from Leghorn to Constantinople."[24]

He spent one day, from sunrise to sunset, in the town of Rozzano [Rossano] at a dairy, learning the intricacies of parmesan cheese and examining the local ice houses and the methods of storing snow. With bursts of energy that characterized his trip, he journeyed north to Lake Como, went to Casino and examined another rice-beating machine, visited Villa Simonetta, famous for its echo, and enjoyed an evening at the theater.[25] James Boswell, who visited Simonetta twenty-two years before Jefferson, fired a pistol "from the window of an upper story opposite to a wall" and counted the sound repeat fifty-eight times.[26] If Jefferson visited the 15th Century abbey-church of Santa Maria Delle Grazie and its monastery refectory containing Leonardo da Vinci's fresco of the "Last Supper," he does not mention it.

It was in Milan that Jefferson contemplated going on to Rome, but there just wasn't time. Or as he put it to a friend: "It was cruel . . . not be to able to take the step to Rome. But there are moral slaveries as absolute as the physical ones."[27]

On the 24th he headed south to Genoa, staying in Pavia at the Croce Bianco Inn. He visited the University of Pavia and saw a botanical garden laid out in the Linnaean system.[28] Jefferson did not comment on the local wines but in the environs of Pavia a dry white sparkling wine of no particular quality was produced.[29]

On leaving Pavia the agriculture changed from rice fields to vines and mulberries, with the Apennines in the distance. Passing through the towns of Voghera and Tortoma without comment, he spent the night in Novi at the posthouse. From Novi to Genoa he crossed the Apennines and halfway down near the town of Campomarone he came upon vineyards and olive trees.

Genoa, famous as a seaport and as the birthplace of Christopher Columbus, rose above the Mediterranean and was laid out in a semicircle. During his three days in Genoa, he stayed at the Le Cerf, in what is now the old port section of the city and described by Jefferson as an inn "more in the French style" with its back windows looking onto the Mediterranean.

He made garden tours to some of the country seats of the Genoese nobility at Sestri, Pegli, and Nervi. Prince Lomellino's gardens at Sestri were the finest he had seen outside of England. At Nervi, he was impressed by the gardens of Count Durazzo.[30]

From Genoa Jefferson decided to return to Nice by boat because there were no roads, just paths suitable only for mules and walking that led through the mountains and along the seacoast. Tobias Smollet, a Scottish physician and novelist, who traveled this same route 23 years before Jefferson, had mused: "What a pity it is that they cannot restore the celebrated Via Aurelia . . . which extended from Rome by way of Genoa and through this country as far as Arles upon the Rhone!" The Via Aurelia had been one of the great Roman roads over which the Roman armies marched into Gaul. After the decline of Rome, it fell into decay and disappeared.[31]

Jefferson arranged passage on a felucca, an open boat propelled by one sail and twelve oarsmen.[32] However, because of contrary winds and his own "mortal seasickness," he abandoned his sea journey after two days and set in at the fishing village of Noli.[33] Noli, it seems, had everything: narrow streets, medieval towers, the ruins of a castle, precipices hanging over the sea covered with aloes, vineyards, olive groves—everything except a decent inn. He spent the night in a "miserable tavern" and dined on sardines, fresh anchovies, ortolans, and strawberries accompanied by an "indifferent" white wine.[34]

As with other villages along the Riviera, warm weather now brings an invasion of sunbathers and vacationers to Noli, but it has retained much of its essential character. The castle ruins still overlook its narrow streets and the Mediterranean, but the beach where Jefferson landed is covered with beach umbrellas and chaise longues and its cobble-stoned streets house the usual seaside resort shops, small hotels and bistros. Some white wine is made locally but for private consumption, and it is probable that the white wine Jefferson drank was from a local vintner.[35]

The next morning he hired a guide and three mules and for the next two days clambered across the precipices of the Apennines. Once across, the change of scenery was as abrupt as it was exhilarating. To the horizon extended the blue Mediterranean, white sand beaches, orange and lemon groves and the silver green of olive trees gilded by the sun. The lure of a life of anonymity in harmony with nature pervaded his thoughts as he passed through sleepy Mediterranean fishing villages, where "if any person wished to retire from their acquaintance, to live absolutely unknown, and yet in the midst of physical enjoyments, it should be in some of the little villages of this coast, where air, earth and water concur to offer what each has most precious. Here are nightingales, beccaficas, ortolans, pheasants, partridges, quails, a superb climate, and the power of changing it from summer to winter at any moment by ascending the mountains. The earth furnishes wine, oil, figs, oranges and every production of the garden in every season. The sea yields lobsters, crabs, oysters, thunny, sardines, anchovies, etc."[36] The uninterrupted vistas that evoked Jefferson's thoughts of getting away from it all have for the most part been paved with highways, hotels, marinas, golf courses, pizza parlors, leaving in their wake eroded beaches, tunneled mountains, leveled dunes, razed pine forests, and mutilated remnants of olive, orange and lemon groves.

Descending to the coast of what is now known as the Italian Riviera, Jefferson walked along the shore from Louano [Loano] to Albenga, spending another unpleasant night in "the most detestable gite, called a tavern, that I ever saw in any part of the earth, and the dearest too."[37] But despite physical discomforts, he was taken by Albenga's natural beauty, "a rich plain opening from between two ridges of mountains triangularly to the sea" abounding in olives, figs, mulberries and wine. Albenga, like so many of its coastal neighbors, has become a seaside resort but without any evidence of its past. There are a few vineyards in the plains but the best wine is made from the Pigato grape that grows on the coastal hills around Albenga. It makes a white wine that is "rich and velvety with a sunny yellow color, a hint of wild fennel in its ample aroma."[38]

Jefferson stopped at the seaside towns of Oneglia and Port Maurice, a mile apart, that he called "considerable places and in a rich country" surrounded by vines and olive groves.[39] He spent the night in San Remo. The old section of town, with its narrow streets, flights of steps, archways and crowded houses, occupied a steep hill that sat between two valleys, planted with orange and lemon groves. His room at the Auberge de la Postea looked into a handsome garden with palm trees under the windows. He also had available a very good *vin d'ordinaire* that was made in the environs.[40]

The following morning Jefferson continued along the Italian Riviera coastline to Nice. At Bordighera he observed extensive plantations of palms on the hills and in the plains, and noted that supplying of palm branches to the Catholic churches for Palm Sunday was a source of commerce for the town. From Menton to Monaco he was surrounded by groves of oranges and lemons, and he mused along the way that "a superb road might be made along the margin of the sea from Laspeze ... to Nice," by which travellers could enter Italy without crossing the Alps.[41] Jefferson's idea of a coastal highway took almost a century to come about. The first road that opened travel between Italy and France was built by Napoleon along the mountaintops from Nice to Menton. Begun in 1805 and completed seven years later it became known as the Grande Corniche. The Grand Corniche looks down on a series of spectacular panoramic views: the Mediterranean, the mountain range of the Esterel, Nice, Villefranche, Cannes, Cap d'Antibes and other seaside towns.

CHAPTER NINE

Provence and Languedoc

Although exhausted and weary, Jefferson stayed only one night in Nice before retrieving his carriage, renting post horses and heading back through southern France by way of Antibes, Napoules, and again through the Esterel Mountains.

Leaving Frejus on May 3, he took a different route for his return to Aix-en-Provence traveling along the lower slopes of the Maures Mountains and through the towns of Luc, Brignoles and La Galiniere. Along the way he noted olive groves and vineyards. This stretch of country is known today as the Cotes-de-Provence. The vineyards in this area now produce robust red wines that go well with the rich, strong flavors of Provencal food.[1]

Arriving in Aix on May 4, he returned to the Hotel St. Jacques and the next morning set out for Marseilles for three days of rest and recuperation. Rested and ready for

Avignon

the final leg of his trip, he left Marseilles for Avignon stopping the night in the town of Orgon [Olgon] on the Durance River.[2]

Avignon traces its roots to the Romans and thereafter successive masters: the Burgundians, Franks, the kingdom of Arles, the counts of Provence and the sovereigns of Naples. In the 14th century, Avignon was sold to Pope Clement V, and from 1309 to 1377 it was the residence of seven popes. When Jefferson arrived in Avignon early on May 9, it was still under the aegis of the Papacy.

He took lodgings at the Hotel de St. Omer. Apparently Jefferson was not pleased with his accommodations at the St. Omer because, when later recommending where to stay in Avignon to his friends Shippin and Rutledge, he recommended the posthouse over the St. Omer, describing the St. Omer as disagreeably situated.[3] Shortly after his arrival, he went to see Laura's Tomb in the Church of the Cordeliers and what he saw was "nothing but a stone in the pavement, with an engraved figure partly effaced, surrounded by an inscription of Gothic letters, and another in the wall adjoining, with the armorial of the family of Sade."[4] The church was destroyed in the French Revolution.

Jefferson rented horses and made a "charming" excursion to Petrarch's retreat at the Fountain of Vaucluse, about twenty miles east of Avignon. Petrarch (1304-1374) was an Italian poet raised in Avignon who entered the church during the pontificate of John XXII. At the age of twenty-three he is supposed to have met Laura, a simple country girl, and to have fallen in love with her. Legend has it that they often met at Laura's birthplace near the Fountain of Vaucluse. His religion and her virtue made their love hopeless and Laura died in 1348, a virgin. Petrarch immortalized her through his poetry. Arthur Young on seeing Laura's tomb mused: "How many millions of women, fair as Laura, have been beloved as tenderly but, wanting a Petrarch to illustrate the passion, have lived and died in oblivion!"[5]

Jefferson arrived at the fountain "somewhat fatigued, and sat down by the fountain to repose myself. It gushes, of the size of a river, from a secluded valley of the mountain, the ruins of Petrarch's château being perched on a rock 200 feet perpendicular above. To add to the enchantment of the scene, every tree and bush was filled with nightingales in full song."[6]

The village of Vaucluse with its assemblage of cafes, hotels, billboards, trinket shops and food carts gives the visitor the initial impression that one has arrived two hundred years too late. However, a ten minute walk along a shaded path following the banks of the Sorgue River leads to the mouth of a huge cave at the foot of a mountain.

The gushing fountain can now only be experienced in late March and early April, being fed by melting mountain snows. Still, the Fountain of Vaucluse is a sight to see with mountain boulders filling the mouth of the stream bed and water rushing from the surrounding rocks. Near the fountain-cave is a restaurant straddling the rushing water with trout darting beneath the sunlit surface-the perfect place for tired travelers to "repose" themselves with a glass of local wine and lunch.

Fountain of Vaucluse

Actually the château on top of the hill was not Petrarch's but the ruined castle of the Bishops of Cavaillon. Petrarch lived in a cottage near the fountain. From the top of this hillside Jefferson looked out on a view of the Rhone Valley, the mountains of Provence and the Dauphine covered with snow.

At Avignon Jefferson discovered a white wine he thought the equal of Montrachet and Sauternes—"vin blanc de Rochegude." Produced in the rich, reddish countryside near Avignon, Jefferson thought it so good he ordered a quantity for his Paris residence. Two years later he shared his discovery with President Washington and John Jay, describing it as one of the best white wines of France.

The vintner from whom Jefferson bought this wine, Robert d'Aqueria, took his title "Marquis de Rochegude" from the tiny village of Rochegude that he owned. His properties and vineyards extended beyond the village of Rochegude and included vineyards at Bedoin, Rieres and the Marquis' château near Avignon.[7]

Jefferson said this wine resembled a dry Lisbon and reminded him of Madeira. Lisbon wines were fortified, having had their fermentation stopped by the addition of brandy, and even the dry Lisbons were sweet to some degree.[8] Jefferson's comments make for an interesting comparison because the Marquis said that his wine was of "Cheres" (Sherry), which has an affinity in taste with Madeira, or with a fortified wine. The Rochegude wine was aged six years in cask and at 22 sous a bottle it was not expensive. By 1825 it was not available at any price because production ceased following the Marquis' death.[9]

Although the Marquis' records do not tell us what grape varietal made his *Vin Blanc de Rochegude,* Jefferson's description strongly suggests that it was a sweet fortified white wine. With only one exception, the wines produced today in these same vineyard areas are wines made primarily from red grapes such as Grenache, Syrah, Mourvedre, Cinsault and Carignan and sold as Cotes-du-Rhone-Villages. The exception is a sweet lightly fortified white wine made from the Muscat grape that is grown in the vicinity of the valley town of Beaumes-de-Venise lying between Rochegude and Avignon and dating to Roman times. It is unknown when the Muscat grape was first planted here, but it is the only place in the southern Cotes du Rhone where it is planted—evidence that the Marquis' *Vin Blanc de Rochegude* was the ancestor of today's Beaumes-de-Venise.[10]

Muscat de Beaumes-de-Venise is a first class wine with its own AOC designation, and though called a *vins doux nature/*, it is a lightly fortified sweet wine having had its fermentation arrested by the addition of brandy. As an aperitif or dessert wine it has been gaining in popularity. Many consider it France's best sweet Muscat wine and several excellent Beaumes-de-Venise wines are available in the United States.[11]

Although Jefferson fails to mention the Palace of the Popes, he could not have missed its fortress-like battlements and parapets dominating Avignon's skyline. Built over thirty years (1335-65) it served as the home of several popes and is considered a magnificent specimen of 14th century military architecture.

Across the Rhone River at the village of Villeneuve-les-Avignon, he visited the Chartreuse du Val-de-Benediction founded in 1356 by Innocent VI and at one time one of the most prosperous monasteries in France. It is now a group of ruins that includes a 14th century church, the papal chapel, the refectory and the great cloister.[12]

On May 10 Jefferson left Avignon and returned to Nimes, staying this time at the Hotel de Luxembourg which was located next door to the Hotel du Louvre on Square de la Courrone. In preparing his travel notes he recommended the Louvre over the Luxembourg, but that comparison can no longer be made because German soldiers blew up the Luxembourg during the Second World War. He again visited the Roman Amphitheatre and Maison Carrée.[13] The next day he headed south to ancient Languedoc. This part of his trip would take him to Lunel, Montpelier, Frontignan and along the Canal-du-Midi (also known as the Languedoc Canal), Sète, Agde, Bezier, Narbonne, Carcassonne and ending at Toulouse, the former capital.

As Jefferson traveled from Nimes to Lunel, the hills to his right and the plains on his left were covered with vines. Jefferson found Lunel remarkable for its fine sweet white Muscat wines. A small amount of red Muscat was made, but the best were white. Years later Jefferson compared the sweet fortified white wines of Lunel and Frontignan, noting that though similar in taste, Lunel "is not quite so rich."[14] Other travelers of that era found the bright yellow colored wines of Lunel to be more delicate and less cloying with a less distinct flavor of the Muscat grape.[15] Not more than 12,500 to 25,000 bottles a year of first quality white Vin Muscat de Lunel was made, and consumed so rapidly that it was impossible to buy aged bottles.[16]

On May 11 he was in Montpelier. Although Jefferson dismisses Montpelier with "this place is soon seen" it was, in fact, a prosperous city with clean, well-built villas and a handsome town square called Promenade du Peyrou from which there was a panoramic view of the countryside. "To the south, the eye wanders with delight over a rich vale, spread with villas, and terminated by the sea. To the north, a series of cultivated hills. On one side, the vast range of the Pyrenees tend away until lost in remoteness. On the other, the eternal snows of the Alps pierce the clouds. The whole view one of the most stupendous to be seen, when a clear sky approximates these distant objects."[17] Jefferson attended the theatre and paid one livre four sous for a bottle of Lunel wine.[18]

Le Square Peyrou is still the place to visit for a great view of the surrounding countryside, and a starting point to the city's principal places of interest. They include the Square's triumphal arch erected in 1691 in honor of Louis XIV, the *Place de la Comedie* (Theatre and the Fountain of the Three Graces), *The Jardin des Plantes* (France's oldest botanical gardens), the Fabre Museum (containing over 800 paintings), the Cathedral of St. Pierre, the university and the 18th century Esplande Promenade.

At Montpelier Jefferson discovered a wine that he later imported and drank with friends at Monticello and the President's House—St. George d'Orques. The vineyards of St. George d'Orques, located a few miles west of Montpelier, consisted of about 1,250 acres with the best wines coming from vineyards called Serres, Poujols, Cabrides and Celleneuve. St. George d'Orques had a reputation as a quality red wine with a good bouquet. Aged in cask for three years, it would keep after bottling for five or six years.[19] The vineyards of St. George d'Orques still produce red and rose wines which have AOC status and while popular locally are rarely seen in the United States.

On his way to Sète [Cette], he stopped at the small Mediterranean town of Frontignan where he made the acquaintance of Monsieur Lambert, a physician and vintner. Jefferson liked Lambert and described him as a very sensible man with "a considerable income in addition to the revenue from his vineyard and is thus enabled to practice his profession with ease." Over dinner at Lambert's home Jefferson sampled Lambert's sweet white and red Frontignan wines and immediately ordered 250 bottles of the "best" to be shipped to his Paris home. This was the first of several orders of Lambert's Frontignan which Jefferson considered best when drunk young. "It is potable the April after it is made, is best that year, and after ten years it begins to have a pitchy taste resembling it to Malaga. It is not permitted to ferment more than a half day, because it would not be so liquorish [sweet]. The best color, and its natural one, is amber." The fermentation was stopped by the addition of a neutral alcohol or brandy, so when the alcohol was added determined the sweetness of the wine. Jefferson learned from Lambert that although about 250,000 bottles of sweet Frontignan was produced annually, only 150,000 bottles were wines of first quality. or about 15,000 bottles.[20]

A month after their meeting, Dr. Lambert wrote to Jefferson expressing thanks for the convivial time they had shared and reporting that he had filled Jefferson's order for 250 bottles of his 1786 wine. Lambert added 33 bottles of his red Muscat "from a little barrel" that Jefferson had seen in his cellar and expressed a desire of having. The wines were shipped in six cases and marked J.M.P. (Jefferson Minister Plenipotentiary). Lambert was of the opinion that his wines of the 1786 vintage were of an outstanding quality and extremely sweet as a result of the previous summer's drought. He suggested that Jefferson place them in his cellar and allow them to improve with bottle age.[21]

At the time of Jefferson's trip the white wine of Frontignan had already earned a reputation as a high quality sweet desert wine made from the white Muscat grape.[22]

The vines grown on the hills surrounding this hamlet of about 2,000 inhabitants faced southeast into the sun and were sheltered by the mountains to the north and west. Most of the vines were very old and the sweetness was achieved by allowing the grapes to remain on the vines until they had become shriveled, even raisin-like, and then stopping their fermentation after "half a day."[23] The resulting wine was luscious, with a marked flavor of the Muscat grape. Small amounts of sweet red Frontignan wines were made in a similar manner from black Muscat grapes.[24]

The principal market for the best quality Frontignan was Paris, where over half the production was sold. The inferior quality wines of Frontignan were bought by the wine merchants in Sète and then "sold by them for Frontignan of first quality. They sell 30,000 pieces a year [7,500,000 bottles] under that name." Although some of the vintners of Frontignan attempted to avoid such deception by marking their casks with a hot iron, these empty casks were often sold to Sète wine merchants for a premium, thus giving the deception the seal of authenticity.[25]

The sweet Muscat wines of Frontignan and Lunel were enjoying their greatest popularity at the time of Jefferson's visit, and this popularity extended into the early part of the 19th century. Andre Simon finds evidence of Frontignan's popularity from the number of silver wine labels extant bearing its name, i.e., Frontignan, Frontignac, Frontiniac, Frontigniac, Frontignia, Frontenac, Frontaniac, Frontiniac.[26] Their popularity faded in the 19th century and by 1872 the vineyards of Frontignan were reduced to about 570 acres and those of Lunel to about 125 acres.[27] This loss of popularity was directly attributable to cheap imitations that were concocted in the Sète laboratories and shipped throughout the world and which bore little resemblance to the genuine wines of Frontignan and Lunel. Wine recipe books, giving precise directions and details on how to make imitation Frontignac wine, became commonplace.[28] In 1864 the London wine merchant, Thomas George Shaw, reported that "in Frontignan and Lunel, so noted for their few casks of delicious sweet wine, much of the land is now used for the common dark kind."[29]

Sweet Muscat wines are still produced on the coast of the Mediterranean at Lunel and Frontignan but, sadly, the quality of these wines exported to the United States is not the same today. The Lamberts of the past have been replaced by cooperatives that often turn out aromatic brown wines lacking finesse in bouquet and flavor. However, a glass of Frontignan drunk after lunch while visiting Frontignan was first rate with an excellent balance of sweetness and acidity and a fine apricot taste and aftertaste, proof that quality Frontignan is still made.

Leaving Lambert, Jefferson set off to Sète [Cette], a town of about 10,000, located a few miles from Frontignan. He lodged at the Au Grand Gaillon, located in what is now the old section lying at the foot of Mont Saint Clair, between the Mediterranean and a saltwater lake, the Etang de Thau. After Marseilles, Sète was the most important French seaport on the Mediterranean and the principal seaport for the Canal-du-Midi. Jefferson noted that Sète was a city of growing commerce, principally relating to wine. The wine trade consisted mainly of the wines of Frontignan, Lunel and the wines from around Beziers that were often sold as Frontignan. In later years Sète became a great manufacturer of wine. Because of its excellent port facilities, wines were regularly shipped to Sète from Spain, Portugal, and Italy. From these wines and the local wines, Sète wine chemists were able to manufacture in their laboratories any type, kind, or style of wine. Sète gained the reputation of being able to concoct any of the world's wines, from Falernian of ancient Rome to new claret or old Burgundy. These imitation wines described as Malaga, Alicant, Madiera, etc. were shipped all over the world, but primarily to Germany, England and the Scandanavian countries.[30]

Agoston Haraszthy, on visiting Sète in 1861, remarked: "Cette is the great manufacturing place for spurious wines, millions of gallons of imitations being here made, of every brand in existence, and sold to all parts of the world, a few drops of the genuine being used to give the taste of the different qualities. So perfect are some of these imitations, that it is with difficulty you can distinguish the spurious wines from the genuine. The country around being flat and the soil sandy, the wine is very poor, and, as the vines yield largely, the wine is almost as cheap as water. The manufacturers buy up these wines and by their chemical preparations, fix them up, and sell them, mostly to the American market, for good prices. Such are the wines we drink as Château Margaux, Lafitte, Chambertin, etc., etc.,"[31]

From Sète Jefferson took passage on a boat through the Etang de Thau to the town of Agde. As he traveled the Etang, he observed: "On the right of the Etang de Thau are plains that are sun whipped, then hills [the Cevennes], in olives, vines, mulberry, corn and pasture. On the left a narrow sandbar separating the Etang from the sea along which it is proposed to make a road from Sète to Agde."[32]

Jefferson spent two days at Agde, a town of about 8,000 dominated by an old castle-like cathedral. Here he continued his trip along the Canal-du-Midi (also called the Languedoc Canal) to Toulouse. The normal passage on the Canal-du-Midi from Agde to Toulouse by post boats was four days. Jefferson decided, however, to hire a boat, a horse and driver, and travel at his leisure. His passage took nine days. He always lodged at the town where he tied up for the night.[33] It was on this trip that he became acquainted with the wines of Roussillon, Rivesaltes and Limoux that he later imported and drank with friends at Monticello and the White House.

The Canal-du-Midi ran from Agde in the south to Toulouse in the west and by

CETTE.
Entrée du Port.

connecting with the Garrone River at Toulouse and the Etang de Thau to Sète, it linked the Atlantic and the Mediterranean coasts. The Canal-du-Midi was one of the great engineering achievements of the 17th century. Pierre Paul Riquet, the genius who designed and built it, died in 1681, six months short of seeing his life's ambition fulfilled. Its opening in 1681 provided impetus to viticultural activity, general trade and prosperity in Languedoc. Its locks still work but, though the canal is used today, the railway and road systems are now the principal means of transportation along this route.

The next two weeks of his travels left such an impression on him that he would tell his young friend John Rutledge that "there is nothing in France so well worth seeing as the Canal and country of Languedoc, and the wine country of Bordeaux."[34]

As he traveled the Canal-du-Midi, Jefferson examined everything. "I have passed through the Canal from its' entrance into the Mediterranean at Cette to this place [on the canal], and shall be immediately at Toulouse, in the whole 200 American miles, by water; having employed in examining all its details nine days, one of which was spent in making a tour of 40 miles on horseback, among the Montagnes noires, to see the manner in which water has been collected to supply the canal; the other eight on the canal itself. I dismounted my carriage from its' wheels, placed it on the deck of a light bark, and was thus towed on the canal instead of the post road. That I might be perfectly master of all the delays necessary, I hired a bark to myself by the day, and have made from 20 to 35 miles a day, according to circumstance, always sleeping ashore. Of all the methods of travelling I have ever tried this is the pleasantest. I walk the greater part of the day along the banks of the canal, level, and lined with a double row of trees which furnish shade. When fatigued I take seat in my carriage where, as much at ease as if in my study, I read, write, or observe. My carriage being of glass all round, admits a full view of all the varying scenes thro' which I am shifted, olives, figs, mulberries, vines, corn and pasture, villages and farms. I have had some days of superb weather, enjoying two parts of the Indian's wish, cloudless skies and limpid waters serenaded along the way with nightingales in full chorus."[35]

Occupations were included in his hunger for information as he observed that canal locks were generally kept by women but could not be operated by them because of the heavy labor. "The encroachments by the men on the offices proper for the women is a great derangement in the order of things. Men are shoemakers, tailors, upholsterers, staymakers, mantua makers, cooks, doorkeepers, housekeepers, housecleaners, bedmakers. They coeffe the ladies, and bring them to bed: the women therefore, to live are obliged to undertake the offices which they abandon. They become porters, carters, reapers, wood cutters, sailors, lock keepers, smiters on the anvil, cultivators of the earth &c. Can we wonder if such of them as have a little beauty prefer easier courses to get their livelihood, as long as that beauty lasts? Ladies who employ men in the offices which should be reserved for their sex, are they not bawds in effect? For every man whom they thus employ, some girl, whose place he has taken, is driven to whoredom."[36]

Approaching the city of Beziers he could see the Gothic Cathedral of St. Nazaire standing above the bridge spanning the Orb River and dominating the town's reel roofs. Here he made the simple observation, "A wine country." He does not tell us where he stayed or what he saw but noted that vast amounts of Frontignan-style wines were made from grapes grown in the country around Beziers, but of a quality inferior to the first quality wines of Lunel and Frontignan. If honestly labeled, Beziers wines were sold under the designation of Picardan de la Montagne and Picardan de la Marine, the name of the grape and area where they were grown.[37] However, most of these wines were sold to merchants in Sète and re-sold to the world as Frontignan.

From Beziers Jefferson sailed the canal staying overnight at the towns of Argiles, La Saumal, and Marseillestte, before arriving at the fairytale-like city of Carcassonne. From Argiles to La Saumal, the hills to his right were heavily planted with vines which, Jefferson was told, made good wine. Actually, the wines produced from vineyards in the immediate vicinity of Narbonne, Carcassonne, and Castelnaudary did not have a reputation for quality. The wines were known for being sour and were nearly always used for distillation.[38] But good wines were made not far away in the hills around Limoux and Rivesaltes and Jefferson managed to find them.

Passing the city of Narbonne, colonized by the Romans in about 118 B.C., he saw on his left three mountain ranges, the Pyrenees, Corbieres, and the Alberes. Within these ranges is France's oldest and southern-most wine producing region—the Roussillon. Vines are believed to have been originally planted in the 7th Century B.C. by Greek seafarers. Since the Middle Ages the sweet wines have enjoyed a fine reputation and, at the time of Jefferson's visit, they were enjoying their greatest popularity, especially those from Rivesaltes.

A variety of wines were produced in Roussillon, but those Jefferson liked best were the sweet white wines of Muscat de Rivesaltes. These came from vineyards around the town of Rivesaltes, about five miles north of Perpignan, and were considered "lighter on the stomach than Frontignan" and thought by many the best fortified sweet wine in all of France.[39] Just where Jefferson first drank Muscat de Rivesaltes is unclear but it was probably at Narbonne, Argiles, La Saumal or Marseillette. Its taste obviously remained on his palate because he continued to import it until the last year of his life.

The vintage in the Rivesaltes vineyards normally began at the end of September or the first week in October. After the grapes were picked they were left in containers for five or six days until dried or shriveled, concentrating their sugar content. When mature they took on a bright golden color, developed a fragrant bouquet and the delicate flavor of quince which distinguished them from other sweet wines. According to Henderson they were known to keep for more than a century.[40]

The red wines of Roussillon were made from a variety of grapes but principally the Mataro, the Carignan and the Grenache. The red wines were stored in wood ten to fifteen years before bottling and developed a golden tinge and a rancid taste. They had a reputation for keeping for long periods but were never considered rivals of the best Bordeaux, Burgundies or Hermitages. However, because of their dark color and strength, they were often bought by vintners in the northern parts of France to add body and flavor to their wines. This was especially true during poor vintages in Burgundy and Bordeaux.[41]

From La Saumal to Carcassonne the canal paralleled the Aude River. Passing at points into and above the hills created by the river, it provided Jefferson a view of the surrounding plains impastoed with vines, corn, mulberries, olives, willows and extensive fields of St. Foin in bloom.

Approaching Carcassonne by way of the canal, Jefferson discovered that it was two distinct towns: the ancient fortress and the lower part. Although Jefferson's arrival at Carcassonne on May 18 brought him into the *ville basse* or lower part, he could see from his boat the crenellated walled medieval section of *El Cite* high on a hill to his

Vintage in the South of France

left. He stayed in Carcassonne, but we are not told where. Given his penchant for seeing the sights from the highest point, he surely walked the ramparts of the old fortress town that commanded the main road to Spain with magnificent views of the Languedoc in every direction.

El Cite is a medieval city with two walls at different heights, surmounted by 54 towers surrounding the town. The walls enclose centuries of history, beginning with the Romans and followed by a succession of conquerors including the Franks, Visigoths, Moors, Viscounts of Bezier and, finally, the Kings of France. *El Cite* is entered by crossing an old wooden drawbridge that spans a dry moat.[42] The medieval buildings lining its cobble-stoned narrow streets now house souvenir shops and little restaurants, but it is still the closest thing one can experience to a time warp. When Jefferson walked its streets the inhabitants mainly moved about on horseback or on foot.[43]

It was probably here that Jefferson became acquainted with the wines of Limoux that he imported in retirement. The vineyards of Limoux, located a short distance from Carcassonne, produced sweet and sparkling wines. The sparkling wine lost its sweetness with age, and at its best, ranked with sparkling St. Peray, but never with Champagne.[44]

From Carcassonne he stopped in Castelnaudary lodging at the Hotel de Notre Dame. Here he rented horses and went into the Noire Mountains to St. Ferroel [St. Feriol] les Cammazes [Escamaze] and Lampy to visit the source of the canal's water.[45]

From Castelnaudary the country continued hilly but richly cultivated. Passing Naurouze he noted that this marked the highest ground which the canal had to pass between the Mediterranean and the Atlantic Ocean. On the night of May 20 he stayed at Baziege.

At Toulouse the Canal-du-Midi ended. He could have gone on by boat along the Garonne River but decided to travel to Bordeaux using the post roads. That night he stayed at the Hotel du Griffon d'Or. Jefferson left unrecorded what he observed of Toulouse's many attractions. The church of St. Sernin was an easy walk from his hotel and he could have visited and climbed its octagonal tower for a view of the town.

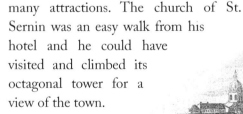

CHAPTER TEN

Bordeaux: its Wines and Vineyards

Jefferson's journey from Toulouse to Bordeaux took five days by the post roads through Montauban, Moissac, Malause, Tonneins, Marmande, La Reole and Langon. Montauban, where he spent the night, is located a short distance from Gaillac, the home of Cahuzac red wines. Jefferson's Parisian friend, the Duke of Rochefoucault, was the Seignor of Cahuzac, and Jefferson had been introduced to Cahuzac wines early in his Parisian stay.[1] He had purchased a barrel of Cahuzac before beginning this trip. Eighteenth century Cahuzac was aged in wood six to eight years before bottling and was said to gain in quality with additional bottle age.[2] The wine was known for "being very full in color, stout, and spirituous" and was used as a blending wine in Bordeaux.[3] During his presidency Jefferson imported Cahuzac wine in 68 gallon casks. Today it carries an Appellation Galliac Controllee designation, although by some accounts the wines are not what they once were.[4]

At Langon he entered a different world—Bordeaux country. Crossing the Garonne River at Langon by ferry he passed by the villages of Sauternes, Preignac and Barsac, "where the best white wines of Bordeaux are made." He noted that the plains were entirely of sand and gravel and that vines were planted in rows five to six feet apart, a practice that continued in Bordeaux. He stayed the evening of May 24 in Castres, leaving the next morning for Bordeaux.

In Bordeaux he resided four days at the Hotel de Richlieu. He inspected a third-century Roman arena, taking time to measure its bricks. He visited Château Haut-Brion and walked through its vineyards, describing the soil as sand mixed with round gravel or small stone and very little loam. Although Haut-Brion is located in the Graves region at Pessac, southwest of Bordeaux, and not in the Medoc, he accurately observed that "this is the general soil of Medoc."[5]

Following his visit to Château Haut-Brion he wrote his brother-in-law, Francis Eppes: " . . . meeting at this place with Capt. Gregory, just sailing for Portsmouth, I cannot deny myself the pleasure of asking you to participate of a parcel of wine I have been chusing for myself I do it the rather as it will furnish you a specimen of what is the very best Bordeaux wine. It is of the vineyard of Haut-Brion [Obrian], one of the four established as the very best, and it is of the vintage of 1784, the only very fine one since the year 1779. Six dozen bottles of it will be packed separately addressed to you and delivered to Capt. Gregory, who will take care to send it to you, and perhaps call on you himself."⁶

The origins of Haut-Brion go back approximately 300 years before Jefferson's visit, to a family with the name of Pontac. As early as 1505, Arnoud de Pontac, the Mayor of Bordeaux, had become wealthy by exporting wine and importing cloth. For the next 150 years the Pontac family thrived as merchants, lawyers, and landowners. By 1660 another Arnoud de Pontac had become one of the most powerful men in Bordeaux, and the vineyards of his ancestral house, Château Haut-Brion, had the reputation for producing outstanding wines.

Samuel Pepys' diary reveals that by 1663 Pontac's wine of Haut-Brion was already being exported to London. Pepys records that he "drank a sort of French wine, called Ho Bryan, that hath a good and most particular taste that I ever met with." Haut-Brion's reception was so extraordinary that in 1666 Pontac sent his son-in-law to London to open a tavern under the sign of "Pontack's Head." From all accounts it was

Chateau Haut-Brion

a great success and remained in business until about 1780.[7] Its fame spread, and eleven years after the opening of Pontac's tavern the English philosopher, John Locke, visited Haut-Brion and observed, "a tun of the best wine of Bordeaux, which is that of Medoc or Pontac, is worth . . . 80 or 100 crowns."[8]

Arnaud de Pontac's death in 1682 did not slow the family's influence on the Bordeaux trade. Over time the Pontac family established vineyards in Blanqueford, located six miles northeast of Bordeaux. More than half of the wines produced were red but Blanqueford became known for its dry white wines with a clove-like bouquet and flinty taste. The Pontac Blanqueford vineyards were later acquired by the Dulamon family and became known as Château Dulamon, later to be known as Dariste.[9] When Jefferson examined the Pontac vineyards in Blanqueford they were owned by Monsieur Dulamon [du Lamont].

Although technically not located in the Graves region, the Pontac Blanqueford wines were listed as Graves, and Jefferson rated Pontac the best of the dry white wines. Unfortunately, these wines can no longer be tasted because the vineyards have become a casualty of urban development.[10]

At the time of Jefferson's visit, Bordeaux was a big, rich city with about one-third of its export business in wine. The Gironde was crowded with ships and the city had an air of opulence. Many of the foreign wine merchants were of English, Irish, German and Dutch heritage. These strangers had become wealthy and turned the *Quai Des Chartrons* into one of the most exciting commercial and fashionable residential areas in the world, their mansions bordering the wide curving quays lined with elm trees. Although this area is still home to the wine trade, the elegant 18th century mansions now serve as offices and warehouses.

Jefferson recorded the principal Bordeaux English wine merchants as "Jernon, Barton, Johnston, Foster, Skinner, Copinger and MacCartey," and the chief French wine merchants, "Feger, Nerac, Brunneau, Jauge, and du Verger." These Chartrons merchants had contracts with the great châteaux (such as Jernon and Feger with Château Margaux and Barton with Château Lafite) and controlled the supply and prices of the wines.[11] Jefferson visited the wine merchant house of Ferger, Gramont and Cie, and ordered 252 bottles of Château Margaux: fifteen dozen for himself and six dozen for his brother-in-law, Francis Eppes.

The French Revolution had the effect of strengthening the position and hold of the foreign wine merchants. To escape the guillotine many French wine merchants and vineyard owners fled the country. Others were not so fortunate, such as the owners of Châteaux Lafite and Margaux who were guillotined and their estates confiscated.[12]

On May 27 Jefferson saw a comedy at the new Grand Theater designed by Victor Lewis and considered among the finest in France. The front portico consisted of twelve Corinthian columns above a balustrade with twelve statues of the muses and graces. Above the huge vestibule was a concert hall with a staircase ascending two flights to a circular auditorium.

THEATRE AT BORDEAUX.

Although Jefferson's trip through the Bordeaux wine country was 68 years before the 1855 classification of the vineyards, his selection of Bordeaux's best Medocs and Sauternes was an extremely accurate projection of their later official rankings. He categorized only four vineyards of "first quality": Châteaux Margaux [Margau], Latour [La Tour de Segur], Lafite [la Fite] and Haut-Brion [Hautbrion]. In 1855 the vineyards of the Medoc were classified as first, second, third, fourth and fifth growths and these same four vineyards were named as the only first growths. Of the more than one thousand vineyards only one outside the Medoc, Château Haut-Brion, was chosen to join the other 60 elite Medoc vineyards given this distinction. They were chosen not by taste, but by the prices they had brought over many years.[13]

Jefferson's comments suggest that the maturation of Bordeaux wines was more rapid than today. Jefferson said Châteaux Latour, Margaux and Haut-Brion were ready to drink after four years, and Lafite, because it was a lighter wine, after three years. In fact, Jefferson was of the opinion that "all red wines decline after a certain age, losing color, flavor and body. Those of Bordeaux begin to decline after seven years old."

To drink classified Bordeaux of outstanding vintages in less than seven years would be considered infanticide today; ten or more years bottle age would be preferable. Jefferson's opinion is puzzling since present-day vinification methods are designed to bring more rapid maturation than earlier, primitive systems.

Was Jefferson drinking the great clarets too soon? An owner and former managing director of Château Lafite-Rothschild, Elie de Rothschild, thinks he was, and doubts the propriety of Jefferson drinking the Grands Crus after only three or four years. "From my experience and tasting and hearsay, I think that on the contrary the [1787] vinification methods were much cruder and the wine much harder. They often left the wine on the grapes for two or three months and that is one of the reasons I have drunk 1811 Lafite that was not dead.

"I do not think . . . it was right to drink Grands Crus that early. Maybe what Jefferson meant was that the wines were bottled after four years and they could be drunk if you wished, as before [then] they were in the cask and not on the market."[14]

Jean Delmas, manager of Château Haut-Brion, believes necessity, rather than maturity, motivated Jefferson. "As far as the vinification methods are concerned, we can almost assume that it has not been radically changed; on the contrary the length of time that the wines remain in vats with the skins on has sensibly diminished since the 18th century rather than increased."[15]

Another explanation is offered by Jean-Paul Gardere, the former manager of Château Latour, who wrote that because of the 18th century vinification practice

Chateau Latour

"of fermenting the grapes with the stalks on or with the stalks only partially removed, you could say that the wines were clearly stronger then, than at present, and a longer fermentation period was necessary then. Consequently, we think that Mr. Jefferson was drinking his Château Latour before it was ready to give complete satisfaction."[16]

What did these four great wines taste like when served at Jefferson's dining tables in Paris, Monticello and Washington? Lafite was known for its "silky softness on the palate and its charming perfume... Latour has a fuller body, and, at the same time, a considerable aroma, that wants the softness of Lafite. Châteaux Margaux, on the other hand, is lighter, and possesses all the delicate qualities of Lafite except that it has not quite so high a flavor. Haut-Brion, again, has more spirit and body than any of the preceding, but is rough, when new, and requires to be kept six or seven years in wood; while the others benefit from bottling in much less time." Alexander Henderson's description, made over 170 years ago, is, for the most part, an accurate comparison of their styles today.[17]

The number of bottles produced by these four vineyards over the past two hundred years has increased but their reputations for greatness have remained amazingly consistent. Jefferson reported that Château Margaux produced about 150,000 bottles a year, Latour 125,000 bottles, Haut-Brion 75,000 bottles and Château Lafite 175,000 bottles. Today, in an average vintage, Château Margaux makes about 390,000 bottles per year, Latour 240,000 bottles, Haut-Brion 180,000 bottles and Lafite 350,000 bottles.[18]

Behind the four first growths Jefferson listed "Rozan, Dabbadie, ou Lionville, la Rose, Quirouen, Durfort," followed by a "third class" of wines consisting of "Calons, Mouton, Gassie, Arboete, Pontette, de Terme and Candale. After these they are reckoned common wines."

All twelve of the wines he named were later listed in the Classification of 1855. Rozan or Rausan is now known as Château Rausan-Segla, a second growth from Margaux; Larose is Château Gruard-Larose, a second growth from St. Julien;[19] Durfort is Château Durfort-Vivens, a second growth from Margaux; Calons is Château Calon-Segur, a third growth from Saint Estephe; Mouton is Château Mouton-Rothschild, now a first growth from Pauillac; Gassies is Château Rauzan-Gassies, a second growth from Margaux; Pontette is Château Pontet-Canet, a fifth growth from Pauillac; De Terme is Château Marquis-de-Terme, a fourth growth from Cantenac.

Henri Martin, the late proprietor of Château Gloria, researched the names mentioned by Jefferson and concluded that "Dabbadie ou Leoville in St. Julien-Beychevelle, then belonged only to Monsieir d'Abadie." It has since been divided into three châteaux: Leoville-Las-Cases, Leoville-Poyferre, Leoville-Barton, all of which are now second growths from St. Julien. "Quirouen is the phonetic translation of Kirwan, a third growth which still exists at Cantenac. Arboete, or Château LaGrange, is a third growth in St. Julien-Beychevelle, and Candale, is Château d'Issan, a third growth at Cantenac."[20]

Sauternes comes from an area of five small communities located some twenty miles south of Bordeaux: Barsac, Bommes, Fargues, Preignac and Sauternes. Other than Medoc, it was the only region classified in 1855. Three quarters of a century before the French classification, Jefferson had chosen Château d'Yquem the "best" of the Sauternes.[21] Château d'Yquem was designated a "First Great Growth" in the 1855 classification to distinguish it from 24 other Sauternes vineyards which were classified first or second growths.

Château Yquem, which pleased many of Jefferson's dinner guests, is said to have changed in taste 60 years after Jefferson's visit because of *botrytis cinerea* (the noble rot), a parasite that lives on grapes. The happy circumstance that brought the noble rot to the vines of Yquem was an accident. The story goes that in 1847 the Marquis de Lur-Saluces, the owner of the Château d'Yquem, returned from Russia to his estate where they were waiting his return in order to begin the harvest. His return was so late in the year that most of the grapes were overripe and completely contaminated with botrytis. Nevertheless,

Chateau Yquem

the order was given to harvest them and the wine made from these grapes was of such a high quality that its fame quickly spread.

Count Alexandre de Lur-Saluces, the current proprietor of Château d'Yquem, adds, "This accident, according to my interpretation, gave birth to a harvest which was quite out of the ordinary. During the 1860's the Grand Duke Constantine, the Czar of Russia's brother, on a visit to Yquem tasted the extraordinary harvest of 1847 which, by the way, they did not dare commercialize for fear of astonishing the consumers. The Grand Duke found this wine so good that he offered an exorbitant price for a barrel of it.

"This chance incident was without doubt the catalyst that changed the thinking of the period and led them to consider the grape rot as particularly desirable and to seek it rather than avoid it at the time of the grape harvest, thus obtaining a systematically sweet wine. Of course, the risk is infinitely greater and the yield much less but the effort leads one to a truly outstanding wine, unique of its type and that is the true expression of this Sa uternais soil."[22]

Today Château d'Yquem produces an average of 75,000 bottles annually. Jefferson records that in 1787 the production was 150,000 bottles.[23] The decrease may be attributed to the methods employed in harvesting the grapes since 1847. The crop is often picked grape by grape-sometimes requiring as many as ten or eleven pickings to achieve the final product and limiting the gallons of wine per acre to less than one-fifth of that produced if normal methods were followed.

Jefferson mentioned other Sauternes of distinction. From the Commune of Preignac he recorded the best was made at President du Roy's vineyards, now known as Château de Suduiraut and classified a first growth. He thought the best wine from the Commune of Barsac belonged to President Pichard, who also owned Château Lafite. The late Henri Martin thought Jefferson mistaken about the location of Pichard's vineyard. "The Departmental Archives of the Gironde show his properties at Sauternes, Bommes, etc. . . . . President de Pichard possessed Château Peyraguey at Bommes, now two vineyards: Château Lafaurie Peyraguey and Château Haut-Peyraguey." Jefferson found the wines of Sauternes the "pleasantest" and those of Barsac the "strongest."[24]

Were the wines of Sauternes and its surrounding communes of Barsac, Preignac, Bommes, and Fargues dry or sweet in Jefferson's time? The overwhelming evidence is that they were sweet but not so sweet as they are today. Henderson records that the wines from these communes "all have a sweetish taste, at least when new," but adds, "these wines, also, keep very well acquiring an amber color, and a very dry taste, as they get old."[25] The increased sweetness of today's Sauternes probably results from careful picking and crushing of the grapes after they have become fully *botrytizied*.

In Graves Jefferson describes how they successfully grafted the vine: "When the graft has taken they bend it into the earth and let it take root above the scar. They begin to yield an indifferent wine at 3 years old, but not a good one till 25 years, nor after 80, when they begin to yield less, and worse, and must be renewed . . . They

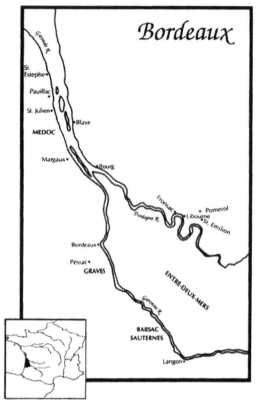

dung a little in Medoc and Grave, because of the poverty of the soil, but very little; as more would affect the wine."[26]

Of the dry white wines of Graves, Jefferson found the best to be "Pontac, which formerly belonged to M. de Pontac, but now to M. de Lamont." Henri Martin notes that it was renamed Château Delamon, but the vineyard has since been lost to urban development. Jefferson thought St. Bries second best, belonging also to M. de Pontac. This may have been Château Pontac Monplaisir in the commune of Villenave d'Ornon. Third best was Château Carbonnieux [Carbonius], a property of the Benedictine monks, and the wine was not sold until it had acquired three or four years bottle age.[27]

Unlike today's white wines which are generally preferred young, Jefferson records that the whites aged better than the reds, needing 15 or 20 years. The best vintage available was 1784, there having been no other good year since 1779.[28]

The relation of prices the first, second and third growth red Bordeaux wines brought has not changed significantly over the past 200 years. Jefferson's notes reveal that Lafite, Latour, Margaux and Haut-Brion, depending on the vintage, quality and the age of the wine, sold for as much as two-and-a-half times the price of the second and third growth wines. A dramatic price difference existed between first growth Medoc red wines and the sweet wines of Sauternes and Barsac. Again, depending on the vintage, quality and the age of the wine, Lafite, Latour, Margaux and Haut-Brion sold for three to eight times more than the best vintages of Château d'Yquem. This price difference no longer exists and Château d'Yquem now sells at a premium to the first growth Medocs.

As Jefferson traveled through the Bordeaux countryside talking to vignerons, workers and wine merchants, he learned that only by purchasing directly from the vineyard owners could he avoid the deception of blending-in of other wines, and this is how he subsequently ordered his wines.[29] By ordering directly from the winemaker, he in effect received his wines château bottled, a bottling method that did not become standardized with Medoc châteaux until the 1930s. Although he was told by a wine broker named Desgrands "they never mix the wines of first quality but they mix the inferior wines to improve them," the evidence indicates that even the four first growths were often blended before being sold. Blending of one year with another is attested to by Elie de Rothschild: "First, in those days there were no laws and quite often the owners used to blend various years ... and sell them under a different year. Example: blend 1787 plus 1786 plus 1762 equals 178? The very old books also give accounts of cases where 'a touch of angostura,' as one says for cocktails, could have been added in the form of Portugese wine or Spanish wine."[30]

Redding records the mixing of Grands Crus for exportation. "The first growths of Medoc are never sent to England in a perfect state, but are, when destined for that market, mingled with other wines and with spirit of wine. The taste of the pure wine is not spirituous enough for the English palate, and *more* body is given by the mixture of Hermitage, Beni Carlos from Spain, and alcohol, ordinarily to the extent of three or four twentieths percent."[31]

On May 29 Jefferson left Bordeaux by boat from the Quai de Chartrons.[32] Sailing up the Gironde he passed on the left many of Medoc's famous vineyards: Châteaux Kirwan, Rausan-Segla, Palmer, Marquis de Terme, and Margaux. To his right the hilly countryside was planted chiefly in vines. At Lamarque his ferry crossed to the east side of the Gironde and docked at the town of Blaye.

The vineyards surrounding Blaye and those of Bourg, Canon, Pomerol and Saint-Emilion to the southeast, though then second in rank behind the wines of Medoc and Graves, were still, in the words of Henderson, "deserving of notice."[33] Indeed the wines of Bourg were "in former times ... in greater demand than those of Medoc," and though Jefferson does not mention these wines, they were only a step down in quality from the red wines of Graves.[34]

Jefferson left the sandy, gravelly loam of Medoc behind without mentioning the wines of St-Emilion or Pomerol, although St. Emilion is perhaps the oldest wine town in France.[35] There are perhaps two explanations for this omission. First, Jefferson was in Bordeaux and receiving advice from Bordeaux wine merchants. It is unlikely that they would have told him about wines other than their own. There was a second reason. The wines of St. Emilion and Pomerol were shipped out of Libourne and not Bordeaux. The Dutch and the English had established their presence in Bordeaux, and since the only method of reaching Libourne was by boat (there were no bridges across the Garonne), there was little commerce between the two cities. As a consequence, the fine reputations that St. Emilions and Pomerols enjoy today had not emerged.

Jefferson's journey now took him north over hilly, barren terrain and through Etauliers, Mirambeau and St. Genis. Approaching the Charente River near Pons he found the countryside heavily planted with vines that continued until he reached Rochefort.[36]

From Rochefort to La Rochelle he observed little cultivation except for some corn, pasture and clover. Leaving La Rochelle and heading northeast to Usseau and Marans, he stopped for the night in St. Hermines. In the morning he continued on to Nantes through a barren countryside.

Nantes, near the mouth of the Loire, was already a large city of 150,000 when Jefferson arrived on June 1. He stayed the evening but early the next morning was off to Lorient. There were no vineyards along this stretch of countryside. The ragged people lived mostly in villages with the women employed in heavy laboring jobs, a sure sign to Jefferson of extreme poverty, but he found Lorient a prosperous, modern city with broad paved streets and a seaport that carried on a busy trade with the West Indies. After climbing 120 feet to the top of the Discovery Tower with its view of the city's harbor, he stayed at the Hotel de l'Epee Royale. Eight years earlier the Hotel del Epee Royale had hosted John Adams, John Paul Jones and the officers of the *Poor Richard* at an elegant dinner where was "practiced the old American custom of drinking to each other" which, Adams confessed, "is always agreeable to me." Adams recorded that their conversation covered "some hints about language, and glances about women, [and] produced this observation, that there were two ways of learning French commonly recommended—take a mistress and go to the comedy." Following dinner and a review of Captain Jones' Marines, Adams recorded in his diary his impressions of John Paul Jones:

"This is the most ambitious and intriguing Officer in the American Navy. Jones has Art, and Secrecy, and aspires very high. You see the Character of the Man in his uniform, and that of his officers and Marines, variant from the Uniforms established by Congress. Golden Button holes, for himself–two Epauletts–Marines in red and white instead of Green.

Excentricities, and Irregularities are to be expected from him—they are in his Character, they are visible in his Eyes. His Voice is soft and still and small, his Eye has keenness, and Wildness and Softness in it." [37]

From Lorient Jefferson traveled to Rennes, the capital of Brittany. He discovered that only a few traces of its medieval heritage remained as nearly the entire town burned in 1720. The country and the living conditions of the people from Rennes back to Nantes he described as "precisely similar to that from Nantes to Lorient."[38]

Returning to Nantes on June 6, Jefferson stayed at the St. Julien Inn. The theater at Nantes was a majestic structure, built of white stone with a portico front of eight elegant Corinthian pillars and a grand vestibule. Young said that it was "twice as large as Drury-Lane, and five times as magnificent."[39] The city had the marks of prosperity: new buildings, large mansions lining the waterfront, a handsome inn called the Hotel de Henri IV, and a book club.

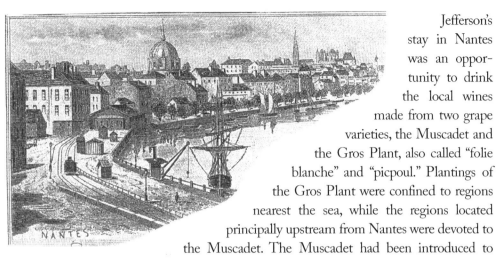

Jefferson's stay in Nantes was an opportunity to drink the local wines made from two grape varieties, the Muscadet and the Gros Plant, also called "folie blanche" and "picpoul." Plantings of the Gros Plant were confined to regions nearest the sea, while the regions located principally upstream from Nantes were devoted to the Muscadet. The Muscadet had been introduced to Nantes from Burgundy (where it had been known as the Melon grape) during the Middle Ages. Of the wines produced from these two grapes the Muscadet yielded the best quality. At the time of Jefferson's visit the vineyard areas around the villages of Vallet, Mouzillon, and Monnieres reputedly produced the best Muscadets.[40] These vineyard areas now lie within the region of Sevre-et-Maine known for producing the best Muscadets.[41]

He stayed the night of June 7 at the Hotel de Brethene in the old town of Ancenis.[42]

On June 8 he left for Tours and followed the river through a countryside dotted with steeples, windmills and hillsides covered with vines.

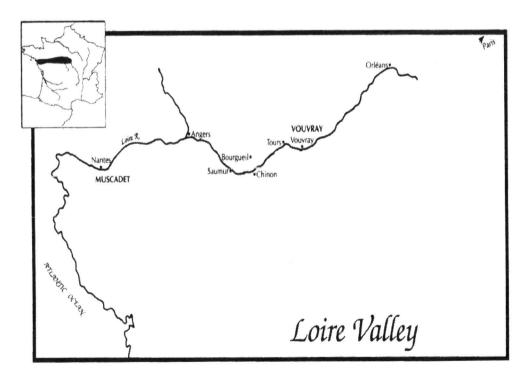

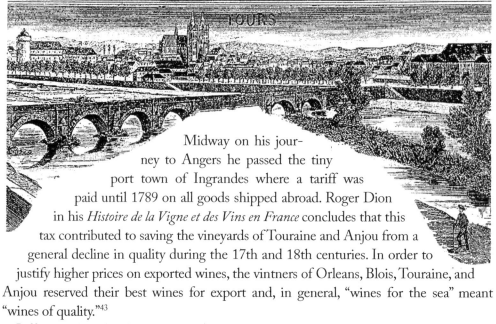

Midway on his journey to Angers he passed the tiny port town of Ingrandes where a tariff was paid until 1789 on all goods shipped abroad. Roger Dion in his *Histoire de la Vigne et des Vins en France* concludes that this tax contributed to saving the vineyards of Touraine and Anjou from a general decline in quality during the 17th and 18th centuries. In order to justify higher prices on exported wines, the vintners of Orleans, Blois, Touraine, and Anjou reserved their best wines for export and, in general, "wines for the sea" meant "wines of quality."[43]

Jefferson thought the wines of Angers were good, "not equal, indeed to the Bordeaux of the best quality, but to that of good quality, and like it." Both red and white wines were made in the districts of Anjou and Touraine. The white wines of this region are made from the Chenin Blanc grape, and it is not until you reach Sancerre and Pouilly-sur-Loire, further to the east, that Sauvignon Blanc, a white grape of Bordeaux, is grown. The red wines of Anjou and Touraine have, however, been made for centuries from the Cabernet Franc, a principal red grape of Bordeaux, so it is likely that Jefferson was referring to the red wines of Angers.

As he approached Tours he observed that the hills on both sides of the Loire were a white soft limestone into which people had cut out partitions, chimneys, doors, and made into homes. He likened the scene to rabbit burrows full of people. Jefferson's only comment about the numerous noble castles and châteaux lining the Loire and its nearby hillsides was "many châteaux."[44]

He lodged in Tours at the Hotel a la Gadere and he took time to call on a Monsieur Gentil to inquire about Voltaire's theory concerning the spontaneous growth of shells.

Shortly after leaving Tours he visited Château Chanteloup where he heard a nightingale, saw "an ingenious contrivance to hide the projecting steps of a staircase in the Boudoir" and was interested in how three pumps in the kitchen garden worked.

Chanteloup had been the château of the Duke of Choiseul, one of Louis XV's ministers, and the first floor consisted of seven rooms including a large library containing Gobelin tapestries. Surrounded by the Amboise Forest, the château gardens included a 144-foot-high Chinese pagoda that the Duke had built as a memorial.[45]

From Blois to Orleans there were extensive vineyards along flat, sandy plains, but Jefferson makes no mention of the wines. Five miles northeast of Blois, on the road to

Orleans, Jefferson stopped to see Menars, the former residence of Madame de Pompadour, who had been Louis XV's mistress. He lodged the last night of his trip at the post-house in Orleans.[46]

Returning to Paris on June 10, he regarded his trip a personal triumph. "I . . . never passed three months and a half more delightfully."[47]

CHAPTER ELEVEN

The Wine Connoisseur

Following his return to Paris in June of 1787, Jefferson wrote Parent and ordered one feuillette (the barrel equivalent of 125 bottles) each of Volnay and Goutte d'Or of the best vintage available for drinking. Jefferson asked Parent to bottle the wines before shipment and deliver them to the gate at the Champs-Elysées which "my house touches."[1] His wine supply was so low he urged Parent to ship them in the warm weather.

Parent purchased two feuillettes of 1784 Meursault, Goutte d'Or, from the vineyard of Monsieur Bachet, and a 1785 red wine of the name "la Comarenne." Parent did not tell Jefferson that this was a wine from neighboring Pommard, and not a Volnay, just that it was of the "best element." It was considered one of the three best wines of Pommard along with Les Rugiens (now divided into two sections, called Haut and Bas) and Les Epenots,[2] and at 21 sous per bottle, it cost only a third as much as its more celebrated northern neighbors.[3]

Parent's "la Comarenne" is known today as Clos de la Commaraine and consists of 9.23 acres of vineyards enclosed by a stone wall and adjacent to the town of Pommard. The château was built in 1112 and is one of the oldest houses in France. Surrounded by vineyards, the château is the private home and wine headquarters of the Jaboutlet-Vercherre family who have occupied it since 1834.[4]

Jefferson was impressed by Clos de la Commaraine because its taste lingered on his palate. He recorded in his Garden Book on April 20, 1810, "planted in the 11. uppermost terrasses of the E. vineyard 165. cuttings of a native winegrape rec'd. from Major Adlum of Maryland. This grape was first discovered by a gardener of Governor John Penn's & transplanted into his garden in or near Philadelphia. I have drank of the wine. It resembles the Comartin [sic] Burgundy."[5]

Parent advised Jefferson that he had also ordered for him a feuillette of Monsieur Latour's Montrachet for 339 livres "to wit, 279 for the feuillette, 30 for the bottles, 6 for the baskets, for the packing 8, bottling 4, string and corks and straw 3, and to have the bottles shipped to the wine store and returned filled 3, for a total of 339 livres. In

CHATEAU MARGAUX.

connection with the vine plants you wanted, I immediately went to Clos Vougeot and Chambertin to get them, but all were out but I was assured that I could get some in late October."[6] Having the wine bottled added to the cost (in this case 17%), but Jefferson considered bottling necessary to assure its authenticity, to keep it from being pilfered by the wagoners, and, of course, to keep it longer and in better condition. Late 18th century Burgundy wine bottles were broader at the shoulder than at the base and had tall graceful thin necks. Just below the lip was a band of glass called a "string rim." As a method of keeping the corks in, a string went over the cork and was tied round the glass rim.[7] Straw was used as packing material and placed between the bottles to keep them from breaking.

The wine merchants, Feger, Gramont and Cie, whom he had visited in Bordeaux, had written to advise that his order of 180 bottles of 1784 Château Margaux was on its way to Paris, and another six dozen had been shipped to Francis Eppes in Virginia. The invoice cost of 747.11 livres was about three livres per bottle, the same price per bottle he paid Parent for the Montrachet.[8] Jefferson notified R & A Garvey, merchants in Rouen, that the wine would be arriving there shortly, and requested that it be sent to him by land as "conveyance by water is slow and uncertain."[9]

His trip also served as a personal eye-opener into the daily lives of the common people, and it was an ugly sight. Poverty, servitude and discontent met him at every turn and stop on his journey. The repression of the French peasant was perpetuated by a feudal law known as *Capitaineries*, the right of the King to grant the nobility exclusive possession and control of all game, even on lands that did not belong to them. Peasants who defied this authority and killed game were subject to imprisonment, and second offenders were often put to death.

The plight of the common vintner was made worse by an over-supply of wine, and Jefferson came away convinced that the culture of the grape was not a desirable occupation "in lands capable of producing anything else.[10] It is a species of gambling, and of desperate gambling too, wherein, whether you make much or nothing, you are equally ruined. The middling crop alone is the saving point, and that the seasons seldom hit. Accordingly we see much wretchedness amidst this class of cultivators. Wine too is so cheap in these countries that a laborer with us, employed in the culture of any other article, may exchange it for wine, more and better than he could raise himself. It is a resource for a country, the whole of whose good soil is otherwise employed, and which still has some barren spots and a surplus of population to employ on them. There the vine is good, because it is something in the place of nothing. It may become a resource to us at a still earlier period: when the increase of population shall increase our productions beyond the demand for them both at home and abroad. Instead of going on to make a useless surplus of them, we may employ our supernumerary hands on the vine. But that period is not yet arrived."[11]

By early August Jefferson sensed a change in the political atmosphere. "You remember," he wrote John Jay, "that the nation was in a delirium of joy on the convocation of the Notables and on the various reformations agreed on between them and the government. The picture of the distress of their finances was indeed frightful, but the intentions to reduce them to order seemed serious . . . . Despair has seized every mind, and they have passed from an extreme of joy to one of discontent. The Parliament, therefore, oppose the registering of any new tax, and insists on an assembly of the States-General. The object of this is to limit expenses and dictate a constitution . . . ."[12] With his hand still withered and the fingers swollen and crooked, he wrote Madison: "This country is really supposed on the eve of a bankruptcy. Such a spirit has risen within a few weeks as could not have been believed. They see the deficit in the revenues, and the hopes of economy lessen daily . . . . the King's passion for drink is divesting him of all respect. The Queen is detested and an explosion of some sort is not impossible."[13]

A member of the Royal Court with whom Jefferson became friendly, and who later proved an embarrassment to him, was Count de Moustier, the newly appointed French Ambassador to the United States. A month after his return to Paris, Jefferson sent Moustier a bottle of Lambert's Frontignan wine explaining that while hundreds of thousands of bottles of imitation wine were sold as Frontignan, only Lambert and five other vintners made genuine "first quality" Frontignan.[14] By return mail Moustier asked Jefferson to order for him sixty bottles of Lambert's Frontignan so that he might distribute it in America to new acquaintances "to whom I wish to be accepted."[15] Moustier was accompanied on his American assignment by his sister-in-law, Madame de la Marquise de Brehan and her son. Before their departure Jefferson sent letters of introduction extolling the personal and public character of both Moustier and Madame de Brehan and saying of her: "I think it impossible to find a better woman, more amiable, more modest, more simple in her manners, dress, and the way of thinking."

Jefferson ordered a hundred bottles of Lambert's Frontignan and had it shipped to Moustier in America.[16] It would appear, however, that Moustier ended up drinking all or most of the wine himself. His pompous and condescending attitude, in combination with the obvious sexual liaison that existed between him and Madame de Brehan, left him friendless in American social and diplomatic circles. John Jay reported "that an improper connection subsists between him and the Marchioness and that Moustier's pompous, arrogant and unsocial behavior had simply fueled the scandal."

Madison was even more blunt in his assessment. "Moustier proves a most unlucky appointment. He is unsocial, proud and niggardly and betrays a sort of fastidiousness toward this country. He suffers also from illicit connection with the Madame de Brehan which is universally known and offensive to American manners. She is perfectly soured toward this country. The ladies of New York (a few within the official circle excepted) have for some time withdrawn their attentions from her. She knows the cause, is deeply stunned by it, views everything thro the medium of rancor and conveys her impressions to her paramour over whom she exercises despotic sway... both the Count and the Marchioness are particularly unpopular among their countrymen here. Such of them as are not under restraint make very free remarks and are anxious for a new diplomatic arrangement."[17]

In August he received a letter from his friend, and Albermarle County neighbor, Wilson Miles Cary (an original subscriber to the Philip Mazzei "Agricultural Company") asking if Jefferson could recommend a merchant in Bordeaux for the consignment of tobacco. Sensing a chance to convert Virginia tobacco into French wines, Jefferson was quick to respond. "There is a Mr. John Bondfield of whom I have a good opinion. He is an American, and is Agent there [Bordeaux] for the United States. If wine is your object, he is a good judge of that. He supplies me, as he had before done Dr. Franklin, with very good. They cost 30 sous a bottle and two livres when 3. years old, which is the age before which they should not be drank. If you like white wines, ask for Sauterne which is the best in that country, and indeed is excellent."[18]

A month later he was offering to procure for his merchant friend in Richmond, Alexander Donald, "any wines of this country which you desire. I have visited all the most celebrated wine cantons, have informed myself with the best vignobles and can assure you that it is from them alone that genuine wine is to be got, and not from any wine merchant whatever."[19]

Donald accepted his offer and asked Jefferson to purchase for him a gross of the best French claret. As a guideline to what he expected, Donald added: "I tasted some that you sent Mr. Eppes. It was good, but I have drank better."[20] Jefferson's response was to immediately send Donald 124 bottles of 1784 Château Margaux from his own cellar with the explanation: "You say you have tasted at Mr. Eppes's some wine I had sent him, which was good, but not equal to what you have seen. I have sent him twice; and what you say would correspond to the first batch. The second was of Château Margaux of the year 1784 bought by myself on the spot, and a part of the very purchase from which I now send you. It is the best vintage which has happened in nine years, and is one of the four vineyards which are admitted to possess exclusively the first reputation. I may safely assure you therefore that, according to the taste of this country and of England there cannot be a bottle of better Bordeaux produced in France. Its cost to me at Bordeaux three livres a bottle, ready bottled and packed. This is very dear; but you say you do not limit me in price."[21]

The first batch of wines Jefferson sent Eppes consisted of 144 bottles ordered through Bondfield in December 1784. When ordering this wine Jefferson had simply identified it as a wine he had drunk at Benjamin Franklin's house. In filling the order, Bondfield did not identify the wine but said that it was a "first growth." Jefferson's quick reaction to Donald's criticism of the Eppes claret is proof that his palate had sent him a similar signal, that Bondfield's unidentified "first growth" did not measure up in quality to the first growth wines he had drunk during his visit to the Bordeaux wine country. Jefferson returned from his trip convinced that only by buying directly from the vineyard owner could he get unadulterated wine. "The vigneron never adulterates his wine, but on the contrary gives it the most perfect and pure possible. But when once a wine has been into a merchant's hands, it never comes out unmixed. This being the basis of their trade, no degree of honesty, of personal friendship or of kindred prevents it."[22]

One crisp morning in October, with "the sky clearing," Jefferson mounted his horse and rode toward the Bois de Boulogne. On this occasion he did not stop to "survey its beautiful verdure" or "to retire to its umbrage from the heats of the season.[23] Instead, he was "away to my Hermitage." His Hermitage was the communal retreat of a group of lay brothers known as the "Hermites." To reach the Hermitage, Jefferson traveled through the Bois de Boulogne to Longchamps where he took the ferry across the river to the village of Suresnes, and then climbed to the top of Mont Valerien, known also as Mont Calvaire, where the monastery stood.

The Hermites supported themselves by providing accommodations to paying guests like Jefferson, selling wood, honey and silk stockings from their manufactory, and wine from their vineyards-known locally as *vin de Suresnes*. Their vineyards were located on the lower slopes of Mont Valerien and faced southeast toward Paris. Vineyards had flourished on these hillsides for over 900 years and the wine had the reputation of a good quality *vin ordinaire*. It was especially popular with Parisians who by leaving the city could eat and drink for only a fraction of what it cost in Paris because of taxes levied on everything entering the city.[24]

The Hermitage was an idyllic retreat for the American minister who often felt a compelling need to be alone.[25] Housed in a stately old monastery on top of Mont Valerien, it provided a sweeping view of the countryside: the villages of Suresnes, Puteaux, Longchamps, the Bois de Boulogne, Paris, Sevres, Saint-Cloud, Bellevue, all connected by the winding Seine. With silence enjoined, except at dinner, Jefferson could relax and use his time for working, reading, walking, thinking or simply resting. At dinner, conversation among guests, who usually knew one another, was a welcome addition to meals accompanied by *vin de Suresnes*.[26] The food was good if the Hermites knew guests were expected, but as one habitue warned upon learning that Jefferson was planning a visit: "If you plan to go to Hermit brothers tomorrow, please pay my respects to the gentlemen of our table . . . tell good Brother Joseph to tell the cook to have something good for you. If they're not forewarned, the cuisine lacks variety and is very lean."[27]

Passions

VUE DU MONT VALÉRIEN ET DE L'ÉGLISE DES HERMITES, PRÈS PARIS

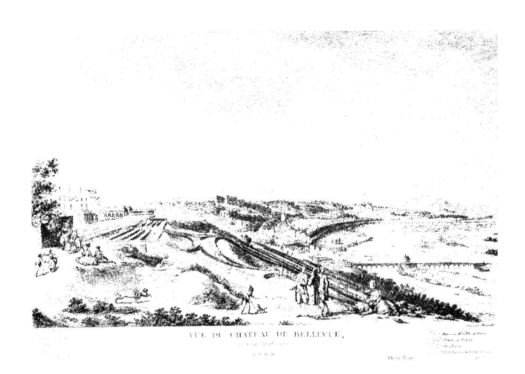
VUE DU CHÂTEAU DE BELLEVUE.

Another available retreat was in the comfort of a warm bath aboard one of the boats that plied the Seine for this purpose. John Adams tells of boarding such a boat near the Pont Royal and taking a bath in "a little room, which has a large window looking out over the river into The Tuileries. There is a table, a glass and two chairs, and you are furnished with hot linens, towels, etc. There is a bell which you ring when you want anything."[28]

In September Maria Cosway returned to Paris for a three month visit, but their spark of romance was dead. They saw almost nothing of each other and Jefferson's lame excuse that "from the meer effect of chance, she is happened to be from home several times when I have called on her, and I, when she has called on me"[29] does not explain their failure to renew a relationship that had inspired his "My Head and My Heart" letter. Still, for whatever reason, as an excuse to see her, as an attempt to rejuvenate a sagging friendship or as a farewell, Jefferson planned a "great dinner" in Maria's honor in early December and left the selection of some of the guests to Maria. What happened that night between the fiery Italian artist and the American minister is not known, but Maria's cold, impersonal, jealous note to him a week later says it all. "I cannot breakfast with you tomorrow; I bid you adieu. Once is sufficiently painful, for I leave you with very melancholy ideas. You have given my, dear sir, all of your commissions to Mr. Trumbull, and I have the reflection that I cannot be useful to you."[30]

A few days after Maria's sudden departure, Trumbull returned to Paris and stayed with Jefferson. He brought with him the original small "Declaration of Independence" and the "Surrender of Lord Cornwallis at Yorktown" and hoped to paint Jefferson's portrait and the portraits of the French officers who were at Yorktown directly onto the canvases. Jefferson managed to get the cooperation of the principal French officers, and Generals Rochambeau, Lafayette, Chastellux and Admirals De Grasse and De Barras among others "were painted from life in Jefferson's house."[31]

If the dinner party and Maria's abrupt departure for England upset Jefferson, he did not allow it to interfere with purchasing wine. As Christmas approached he was concerned with his depleted wine cellar. Remembering that Bachet's 1784 Goutte d'Or was "so good," and Parent had advised that four feuillettes remained, Jefferson wrote Parent, "I will take another 3 feuillettes, if they are still available. If he ran out, be good enough to supply me with one feuillette of the same Goutte d'Or, where you find it best, and ship it to me in bottles as soon as possible. Send also a feuillette of red Volnay wines, also in bottles." He also inquired whether Monsieur Latour still had any of the four feuillettes of 1784 Montrachet he had seen in his cellar, "one of which I bought."[32]

Parent reported that Bachet had two feuillettes of 1784 Goutte d'Or for sale at 100 livres per feuillette, or he could purchase a feuillette of first quality Meursault for 84 or 86 livres but it "would not be as good." As for Latour's 1784 Montrachet, it was all gone but he had some 1785 available at 300 livres a feuillette, and a farmer Dent of Clermont and Chagny had for sale at 300 livres each six feuillettes of '84 Montrachet.

Passions

Parent also promised to send the vines if Jefferson still wanted them. By return mail Jefferson ordered Bachet's two feuillettes of Goutte d'Or, and one feuillette of a "first quality" 1784 Volnay but passed on the Montrachet, leaving open the option to order it later. And, of course, he wanted the vine cuttings.

Within three weeks Parent purchased, bottled and packaged Jefferson's wine order but delayed sending it because "I believe it would not do at all to ship them to you in this very cold weather. It might break the bottles and the wine would be lost."[33] Early in February Parent shipped the wines along with "a small bunch of vine plants, 12 Montrachet, including 6 from Monsieur de Clermont's vineyard, 10 from Clos Vougeot, 9 from Chambertin, and 8 from Romanée . . . ."[34] Jefferson acknowledged receipt of the vines and the wine in good condition except for "one broken bottle."[35]

A week before Christmas Jefferson wrote to Monsieur d'Yquem for 250 bottles of his 1784 vintage. It is clear from this letter, and a companion letter to John Bondfield, that Jefferson had not visited Château d'Yquem during his tour through Bordeaux. Fearing that Monsieur d'Yquem "does not know either my name or character public or private . . . I must ask you also to add on the letter the address of M. Diquem with which I am unacquainted . . . . Perhaps I should have addressed myself to Monsr. Salus his son-in-law, as I am not certain whether he is not either jointly or solely interested at present in the vineyards." [36]

Within a month Bondfield advised that 250 bottles of Yquem were on their way "by water carriage which is equally expeditious, less subject to breakage and considerable less charge." Bondfield enclosed a letter from Count Lur Saluce, M. d'Yquem's son-in-law, advising that he was now the owner of the estate and that he had drawn and bottled Jefferson's wine with the greatest care.[37]

Chateau Lafite

Before leaving for America the well-connected Moustier had written his cousin Madame de Pichard, the wife of the owner of Château Lafite, telling her that his friend "Mr. Jefferson, Minister of the United States of America, desires, dear cousin, to have your good wine" and requesting that Jefferson be treated "as you would treat us."[38] Knowing that Moustier had contacted the estate, Jefferson wrote to Pichard in February, reminding him that "as I passed through Bordeaux in May of last year, I did myself the honor of introducing myself to you to pay my respects and to thank you for the kindness you extended to Mr. Barclay our counsel, in the very unpleasant business he was involved in in Bordeaux.[39] I hasten to renew my thanks and I take the liberty of asking for a favor. The excellent wines called La Fite are produced by your people. If you have some of the 1784 vintage, and if you could accommodate me with 250 bottles, I would be infinitely grateful. If it is possible to have them bottled at your place, this would be a guarantee that the wine is natural and well drawn . . . . Will you then allow me sir, during my stay in this country, and perhaps even after my return in America, to call on you directly anytime I need wines produced by your house?"[40]

CHAPTER TWELVE

Holland, The Rhine Valley and Champagne

Toward the end of 1787 John Adams learned that his request to return home had been granted. Adams had represented the United States at The Hague in securing loans and other financial matters, and he decided that it was important that he return to Holland in order to tie up any loose ends that existed in financial arrangements between Holland and the United States.[1] Three days after her husband had left for Holland, Abigail wrote Jefferson advising that John "would be delighted to meet you there" but that he would have to leave immediately after completing his business.[2] Jefferson, who had no experience in the United States' financial dealings with the Dutch, and knowing that as the sole minister he might be called upon to conduct future financial negotiations, found the prospect of such a get-together exciting. He immediately wrote Adams: "Our affairs at Amsterdam press on my mind like a mountain ... I am so anxious to confer with you on this ... I will set out the moment some repairs are made to my carriage ... I hope to shake you by the hand within 24 hours after you receive this."[3]

On March 4, 1788, Jefferson left Paris in his carriage for Amsterdam following the postroads northeast through France and Belgium. Traveling with him was his valet, Espagnol. That evening he stayed in the town of Peronne at the Hotel Grand Cerf and the following night at the town of Braine-le-Comte. In the morning he had breakfast in Brussels, and lodged that night in Antwerp.[4] Two hundred years earlier Antwerp was the home of such great Flemish masters as Van Dyck and Massys. It had enjoyed great prosperity and had been one of the richest commercial cities in Europe. But it had been in decline and its streets now were deserted after dark. It was, as one visitor said, "A city for the lover of solitude and the dweller with silence."[5]

Two days later he arrived in Rotterdam. He drank tea and a bottle of wine with dinner and then joined a happy crowd in celebration of the prince's birthday.[6] Jefferson described the fireworks as the "most splendid I had ever seen & the roar of the joy the most universal I had ever heard. My journey had been little entertaining. A country of corn and pasture affords little interest to an American who has seen in his own country so much of that, and who travels to see the country and not its towns. I am as yet totally undecided as to the time and route of my return."[7]

The following day he reached The Hague and much to his relief Adams was still there. From The Hague the two ministers left for Amsterdam.[8]

At the time of their arrival in Amsterdam on March 10, 1788, there were over 250,000 residents and it was the most important financial and commercial city in Europe. Its busy harbor was filled with ships; its streets, traversed with canals and quays, were crowded with merchants, sailors, and beautifully appointed shops and inns. Visitors could see the city from a strange conveyance called a *sleepkoets,* a coach nailed to a wooden sleigh drawn by a horse. A main task of the driver was to oil the runners in order to prevent them from catching fire.[9]

Adams and Jefferson lodged at the best hotel, *Het Wapen van Amsterdam* (The Amsterdam Arms) where Jefferson stayed until March 30. Jefferson participated with Adams in negotiations with the Dutch bankers. The results of their negotiations led to the execution of bonds that, when later ratified by Congress, assured adequate financing for the United States for the next two years.[10]

Adams left Amsterdam on March 11 for London, and that evening Jefferson dined alone at the Amsterdam Arms. With his meal he drank chocolate and a bottle of Moselle wine. His hotel receipts do not reveal where he dined on the 12th and 13th but on March 14 he again dined alone at the Amsterdam Arms. He drank a half bottle of Graves wine and ate 50 oysters! The following night he and a dinner companion consumed another 50 oysters and one and a half-bottles of wine.[11] Who his dinner guest was is not recorded, but a likely candidate was his old friend and mountain-top neighbor, General Frederick Riedesel who was then living in Amsterdam.[12]

During the next two weeks, Jefferson had dinner at the Amsterdam Arms on nine occasions. His wine consumption varied from no wine with his dinner on three occasions to sharing a bottle or two when dining with companions. The four other evenings when he dined alone he ordered either a bottle of Moselle or Graves wine.[13]

Jefferson's selection of the wines of Moselle and Graves to accompany his dinners was probably dictated more by necessity than preference. As a wealthy nation without vineyards of its own, Holland had a long affinity with the wines of Moselle and Graves. Moselle wines, shipped up the Rhine from Coblenz, a relatively short and easy journey to Amsterdam, were popular and plentiful. The Dutch connection with the Bordeaux wine trade dated from the early 17th century.[14]

Jefferson's three weeks in Amsterdam were filled with sight-seeing, attending concerts, the study of Dutch architecture, and the manner of fixing a flagstaff. He made notes on dining tables with single or double leaves, a machine for drawing empty boats over a dam, a bridge on a canal turning on a swivel, a lantern over street doors which gave light equally into the antechamber and the street, and a

Dutch wheelbarrow. He even set out details of coops and avaries for pigeons, partridges and pheasants.[15]

On March 20 he made a ten mile excursion to Haarlem whose chief attractions were its world-renowned organ in the Church of St. Bavon and its tulips and hyacinths.[16] Its old houses of hewn stone and brick surely caught Jefferson's architectural eye. Here he visited the house of the Amsterdam banker, Henry Hope, that had been built by Jean-Baptiste DuBois, a famous Flemish architect.[17] Two days later he visited Zaandam, famous for its hundreds of windmills and as the place where Peter the Great of Russia learned ship-building in 1696. He may have arrived in Zaandam on a yacht of one of the rich and friendly Dutch bankers with whom he and Adams had negotiated the loans. He dined in Zaandam and returned that evening to Amsterdam.[18]

Leaving Amsterdam on March 30 the peripatetic diplomat decided to travel down the Rhine as far as Strasbourg "in order to see what I have not yet seen."[19] Before leaving he wrote to his old friend Baron de Geismar, whom he had befriended when Geismar was an interned Hessian prisoner in the Charlottesville area in 1779. Jefferson asked Geismar to meet him, if possible, in Frankfurt at the Rothen House Tavern where he would be staying.[20]

Jefferson traveled by boat to Utrecht and along the way saw nothing but plains covered with grass, a few farms and canals lined with country houses. He lodged in Utrecht at Aubelette's, "the best tavern," and had a bottle of Rhine wine with his dinner.[21]

From Utrecht to Nijmegen his carriage followed the post roads, and the hills of the Rhine served as the backdrop to windmills, hedgerows, canals, boats, cornfields and farmhouses built of brick and covered with tile or thatch, but only a few châteaux. He crossed the Waal River (known as the Rhine in Germany) into ancient Nijmegen. The streets were wide and clean and the ramparts were laid out as gardens. From a hill (Bellevue) near the Chez un Anglois Inn on Place Royale, where he stayed the night, he took in a view up and down the Waal. He was told that the nearby Château of Valkhof (Falcon's Castle) had lodged Julius Ceasar. "This is giving it an antiquity of at least 18 centuries, which must be apocryphal."[22]

Actually Charlemagne resided there for a time and later his son, Louis the Pious, so his guide may have simply confused the two emperors. Jefferson later recommended the château as a place to see.

Somewhere along the way he was advised that at Nijmegen "you must bribe your horse hirer to put as few horses to your carriage as you think you can travel with. Because with whatever number of horses you arrive at the first posthouse in Germany, with that they will oblige you to go on through the whole empire." In a rare moment of frugality, Jefferson "paid the price of four horses on the condition they would put but three to my chariot."[23]

Early the next morning he left the Netherlands and entered Germany on what he called a vibrating boat—a ferry large enough to hold carriages and horses. No sooner had he crossed into Germany than he noted a "transition from ease and opulence to extreme poverty. The soil and climate are the same. The governments alone differ."[24]

In the late 18th century Germany was a collection of small electorates, principalities and free cities with custom barriers at every border. The quality of the roads varied from good to bad depending on the political subdivision through which one traveled. Another hardship that Jefferson encountered was the condition of the inns and taverns. Except for a few along the Rhine, they were execrable, known mainly for their dirt, bad food, and the indifference of the landlords. "When your carriage stops at the inn, you will perhaps perceive, instead of the alacrity of an English waiter, or the civility of an English landlord, a huge figure wrapt in a great coat, with a red worsted cap on his head and a pipe in his mouth, stalking before the door. This is the landlord. He makes no alteration in his pace on perceiving you, or, if he stops, it is to eye you with curiosity; he seldom speaks, never bows, or assists you to alight; and perhaps stands surrounded by a troop of slovenly girls, his daughters, whom the sound of wheels has brought to the door, and who, as they lean indolently against it, gaze at you with rude curiosity and surprise."[25] German travel conditions had the reputation of being at least 100 years behind the rest of Europe.

The bleakness of the village of Kleve, where he spent the night of April 1 at the posthouse, seemed to epitomize Germany's general poverty, with no shops or other signs of commerce or wealth.[26]

At Duisberg [Duysberg], a walled village, Jefferson wanted to locate the "remains of the encampment of Varus, in which he and his legions fell by the arms of Arminius but there was not a person to be found at Duysberg who could understand either English, French, Italian or Latin. So I could make no inquiry."[27] His journey continued southeast through Germany and the bumpy, dusty road to Dusseldorf led over hills and through the plains of the Rhine planted almost entirely in corn. At Essenberg he crossed the Rhine in a scow with sails, a distance of about 500 yards.

Arriving in Dusseldorf on April 2, Jefferson stayed at the Chez Zimmerman, "the best tavern I ever saw in my whole journey." He visited the gallery of paintings in the Palace of the Palatinate Elector. He called the collection sublime and "equal in merit to anything in the world" not because of the "old faded red things" of Rubens, but because of the room devoted to the paintings of Adriaen Wanderwerff. That evening Jefferson dined alone and drank "one old bottle of Rhine wine."[28]

Following the post roads along the valley of the Rhine from Dusseldorf to Cologne, he stopped to see Schlossbernath, the elector's summer palace built by Nicolas de Pigage. He crossed the Rhine at Cologne on a pendulum boat.[29]

Cologne, the birthplace of Rubens, was a sovereign city of about 60,000 inhabitants with more than a 100 churches, including a cathedral considered one of the

world's most magnificent Gothic edifices.³⁰ Jefferson stayed at the Holy Ghost, Chez lngel, "a good tavern." His tavern bill reveals that with his dinner he again had a bottle of Rhine wine and was charged for three cups of chocolate.³¹ He recorded that "Here the vines begin, and it is the most Northern spot on the earth on which wine is made.³² Their first grapes came from Orleans, since that from Alsace, Champagne, etc." "It is 32 years only since the first vines were sent from Cassel, near Mayence, to the Cape of Good Hope, of which the Cape wine is now made ... That I suppose is the most Southern spot on the globe where wine is made and it is singular that the same vine should have furnished two wines as much opposed to each other in quality as in situation."³³ Jefferson had long been familiar with wines from the Cape, recording in 1779 payment of 24 pounds for Cape wines.³⁴

Wine is known to have been made at the Cape in 1659, and by the early part of 1700 vineyards flourished. Cheapness compensated for quality (with the exception of Constantia, which was highly prized) as the wines were distributed around the world by visiting ships.³⁵

Made from the Muscat grape, Constantia had established its reputation in Europe as a quality South African wine as early as 1722. There were two growths of Constantia: Great (a sweet red wine) and Little (a sweet white wine) made at the eastern base of what was called Table Mountain on two contiguous farms located about nine miles from Cape Town.³⁶ Both red and white Constantia were fortified.³⁷

The next part of his journey, the plains of Cologne, Bonn and Andernach "yielded much wine, but bad. The good is furnished from the hills. There are no châteaux, nor houses that bespeak the existence even of a middle class. Universal and equal poverty overspread the whole." In Bonn he stopped to see the Electoral Palace (1717-1730), and further up stream at Andernach he saw a large collection of millstones but could not figure out from where they were quarried.³⁸

On April 5 he reached Coblenz at the confluence of the Moselle and the Rhine and an important wine trade center. He lodged at "The Wildman au l'Homme Sauvage a very good tavern." A year later Jefferson recommended this tavern to his friends Rutledge and Shippen. Jefferson had purchased a map of the German post roads from the owner but, when its cost was not included in his bill, he failed to pay for it. Later, in going over his accounts, he noticed this omission and asked Rutledge and Shippen to pay for the map. When Shippen paid for the map, the Wildman was pleased to learn that Jefferson remembered him. He recalled Jefferson as the man who examined the vineyards or "at least the man who was instructed about them."[39]

The Wildman introduced Jefferson to a "gentleman well acquainted with the vineyards and wines of the Moselle." Jefferson did not visit the Moselle, and it was through this acquaintance that he acquired much of his information about the relative merits of that area's wines.

He learned that the best Moselle wines were made in mountainous country about 45 miles away and recorded "the first quality (without any comparison) is that made on the mountain of Brownberg adjoining to the village of Dusmond . . ."[40]

Dusmond can no longer be found on a map because in 1920 it took the name of its famous wine Brauneberg, the Brown Hill.

Brauneberg is still a wine of great distinction. "Brauneberg has more spiciness and richness than any other Moselle," writes Hugh Johnson. "It is the most hock-like wine of the river, and perhaps, for this reason, used to be considered easily the best in the last century."[41] Jefferson's classifying Brauneberg as the best Moselle was based on his drinking a 1783 Brauneberg and comparing it with a Graach of the same year. "Brownberg is quite clear of acid, stronger, and very sensibly the best." Brauneberg was followed in quality by Wehlen [Vialen], Graach [Crach] and Piesport, then Zelting [Selting] and, surprisingly, Bernkastel, last. "After this there is a graduation of qualities . . ." These ratings were based on the prices at which the wines sold per foudre, a foudre being the equivalent of 1100 bottles.[42]

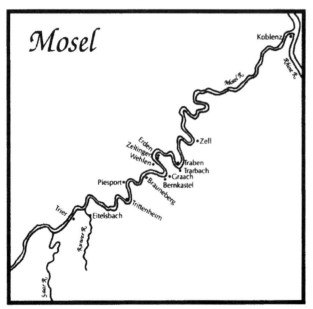

Although present-day wine experts might quibble over the precise rankings of the best wines from these famous vineyards, most would concede that the vineyards of Bernkastel, Brauneberg, Graach, Piesport, Wehlen and Zelting still pro-

Holland, The Rhine Valley and Champagne

duce wines of remarkable quality. Jefferson cautioned that "these wines must be five or six years old before they are quite ripe for drinking." Today, with the exception of Ausleses, Beerenausleses and Trockenbeerenausleses most Moselle's can and should be drunk sooner than Jefferson's recommendation. Following his afternoon wine tasting of the Moselle's best wines, he chose for his evening meal what was probably The Wildman's house wine, a "½ pot of wine" with his soup and a "½ pot of wine" with his dinner. [43]

At Coblenz he crossed the Rhine and journeyed over hills planted in corn, some vines and forests of beach and oak. At Nassau, crowned by a ruined castle, the road to Schwelbach climbed over steep mountains that reminded Jefferson of his passage over the Alps. He decided that if he were to travel this route again he would eliminate the mountain passage by following the Rhine as far as possible and travel by barge until the road resumed, a distance of only six to twelve miles. He was told that along this route "are the most picturesque scenes in the world," a fact which is attested to by anyone who has traveled the Rhine by boat.

He arrived in Frankfurt on April 6 and resided four days at the Rothen House or The Great Red House owned by John Adam Dick and Son. Dick, who Jefferson called a great wine merchant, had between three and four hundred tuns of wine in his cellar, the equivalent of 375,000 to 500,000 bottles.[44] "You may taste at their tavern genuine Hock, and of the oldest." Dick's son had lived in London and spoke both English and French. Here Jefferson met Arnaud, a "sensible, active and obliging" *valet de place* who became his guide to the vineyards of Hochheim, Johannisberg and Rudesheim where Jefferson found that wines of the "very first quality" were made. Dick's wine list included vintages from 1726 to 1783 of Hochheim, Rudesheim, Johannisberg, Marcobrunn, Nierstein, Laubenheim and Bodenheim. Johannisberg was the most expensive with Hochheim, Rudesheim and Marcobrunn, selling for the same prices. Nierstein, Laubenheim and Bodenheim were the least expensive and equal in price.[45]

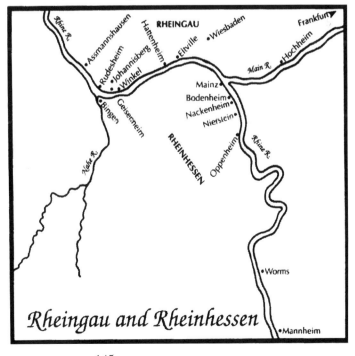
Rheingau and Rheinhessen

Jefferson's Rothen House tavern receipts reveal he did not have wine with his supper on his first night in Frankfurt, but the next day he drank with his dinner a 1726 bottle of

Hochheim! At supper he was joined by his old Albemarle friend, Baron de Geismar and they shared a second bottle of the 62-year-old Hochheim.[46] After supper they attended the theatre and saw a comedy.

On the 8th Jefferson and Geismar visited Geismar's army garrison in Hanau ten miles from Frankfurt. Jefferson compared Frankfurt's throbbing vitality to Hanau's "quiet . . . mansions of the dead. Nobody is seen moving in the streets; . . . every door is shut; no sound of the saw, the hammer, or other utensil of industry. The drum and fife is all that is heard. The streets are cleaner than a German floor, because nobody passes them."[47] That evening he saw another comedy.

The next day he advised Short: "My old friend the Baron de Geismar met me here, on a letter I had written him from Amsterdam, and has been my cicerone. It happens to be the moment of the fair of Frankfurt which is very great. Yesterday we made an excursion up the Maine to Hanau, passing the ground where the Battle of Bergen was fought in the war before last. Tomorrow we shall go to the vineyards of Hochheim, and perhaps of Rudesheim and Johannisberg, where the most celebrated wines are made. I met in Hanau with many acquaintances, the officers who had been stationed in Albemarle while in captivity. I have seen much good country on the Rhine, and bad whenever I got a little off of it. The neighborhood of this place has been to us a second mother country. It is from the Palatinate on this part of the Rhine that those swarms of Germans have gone who, next to the descendants of the English, form the greatest body of our people. I have been continually amused by seeing here the origin of whatever is not English among us. I have fancied myself often in the upper parts of Maryland and Pennsylvania."[48] Geismar and Jefferson had dinner that evening at the Red House Tavern, and shared two bottles: a 1781 Johannisberg at a cost of two florins and a Rudesheim at one and a half florins.

In the morning (April 10) Jefferson paid his bill at the Red House Tavern, rented horses and traveled with Geismar to Hochheim. Jefferson described the vineyards on a "gentle slope of about ¼ of a mile wide, extending ½ mile toward Mayence. It is of a southwestern aspect, very poor, sometimes gray, sometimes mulatto, with moderate mixture of broken stones. The vines are 3 feet apart and stuck with sticks about 6 feet high . . . They are dunged once in 3 or 4 years. One thousand plants yield from one to two aumes [170 to 340 bottles] a year. They begin to yield a little at three years old, and continue to 100 years, unless sooner killed by a cold winter."[49] He was told that the best vineyard owners kept their wines fifteen years before selling them. Before leaving Hochheim Jefferson purchased 100 vines for his Paris garden.

From Hochheim Jefferson and Geismar traveled to Mainz [Mayence] on the left bank of the Rhine. Riding through its narrow, crooked streets his carriage stopped at the Hotel Mayence where he found the accommodations "good and reasonable." He and Geismar shared a bottle of Rudesheim with their dinner.[50]

Up early and accompanied by his valet, Arnaud, Jefferson traveled down the

Rhine in a "small but dull kind of batteau, with two hands rowing with a kind of large paddle, and a square sail but scarcely a breath of wind." Traveling at only five miles an hour it took three and a half hours to reach Rudeshcim. He noted that the vineyards at Rudesheim were terraced up the hillsides and the soil consisted of slate, rottenstone and clay. As for the wines they were "not at all acid, and to my taste much preferable to Hochheim, tho' but of the same price."[51] The best Rudesheim vineyards, Jefferson observed, were located a mile from the village and faced south along terraced hillsides. Today the word "Berg" appears before the names of these vineyards, i.e., Rottland, Roseneck and Schlossberg to distinguish them from the parrish vineyards. These Berg vineyards still produce outstanding wines, but as Hugh Johnson has observed, "not always in the hottest years."[52] Jefferson also commented on the vineyards just behind the village, noting there "is a little spot, called hinderhouse belonging to the counts of Sicken and Oschstein wherein each makes about a tun [1,270 bottles] of wine of the first quality. This spot extends from the bottom to the top of the hill."[53]

Leaving Rudesheim he traveled back toward Mainz stopping to taste the wines of Schloss Johannisberg. He described them as "the best made on the Rhine without comparison and [is] about double the price of the oldest Hock." He thought a thirteen-year-old bottle of 1775 Johannisberg the best. Jefferson noted that Schloss Johannisberg was owned by the Bishop of Fulda "who improved its culture so as to render it stronger, and since the year 1775 it sells at double the price" of Hochheim and Rudesheim.[54] Schloss Johannisberg, remarkable for its bouquet and flavor, rather than strength, remains the most famous vineyard in Germany and its name epitomizes quality.

Further up the Rhine Jefferson's little boat stopped at the vineyard of Marcobrunn on the water's edge between Hattenheim and Erbach. To Jefferson's palate Marcobrunn was slightly inferior to the wines of Rudesheim, Johannisberg and Hochheim. He recorded that Marcobrunn's mulatto, and stone hillside "yields wine of the 2nd quality." Certainly, if price were the sole criterion, it deserved this rating because it sold for substantially less than its more famous neighbors.[55]

Jefferson bought four bottles of wine and fifty vine shoots that he planted in his Paris garden. He obviously planned on transplanting them to Monticello for he wrote Geismar: "I take the first moment to inform you that my journey was prosperous: that the vines which I took from Hochheim and Rudesheim are now growing luxuriously in my garden here, and will cross the Atlantic next winter, and that probably, if you ever revisit Monticello, I shall be able to give you there a glass of Hock or Rudesheim of my own making."[56] The vines probably were still growing in his Paris garden when he left France in September 1789 to return to America for a six-month leave of absence-a "temporary stay" that became permanent with history's turn of events.[57]

At Marcobrunn Jefferson abandoned his batteau and returned by carriage to Mainz. With dinner he drank a bottle of Johannisberg Riesling.[58]

Jefferson recorded that there were "three kinds of grapes in use for making white wine: 1. The Klemperien, of which the inferior qualities of Rhenish wines are made, and is cultivated because of its hardness... 2. The Riesling [Rhysslin] grape which grows only from Hochheim down to Rudesheim. This is small and delicate, and therefore succeeds only in this chosen spot. Even at Rudesheim below the village being of the 3d kind of grape, which is called the Orleans grape."[59]

The Klemperien grape is a misnomer according to two wine experts who believe Jefferson was referring to the Kleinberger or White Elbling grape. Fritz (S.F.) Hallgarten wrote: "I am now quite sure that Jefferson meant 'Kleinberger' grape."[60]

Harold P. Olmo, Professor Emeritus of Viticulture at the University of California at Davis, was unable "to find this name [Klemperien] in early publications on grape vines in Germany. It is likely a misspelling and probably refers to the White Elbling. In parts of the Moselle, at least in the early 1800's, the White Elbling was sometimes called Kalmmer or Klemmer, with Kleinberger as another synonym.

"The White Elbling was the most widely planted variety in the Rhine Valley in the early 18th century, occupying over 75 per cent of the acreage, but has since lost its position to other varieties of better quality."[61]

Jefferson was told that Moselles "must be 5 or 6 years old before they are quite ripe for drinking" and the Rheingaus not before at least five years. Moselles are usually not aged five or six years today, except great vintage years such as 1983, 1989, and 1990 or the sweeter wines such as Auslese, Beerenauslese, and Trockenbeerenauslese. But compared to John Dick, whose most expensive wines were 62 years old, Jefferson recommended early drinking.[62]

The Moselle and Rheingau wines that Jefferson drank 200 years ago, although made from the same grape, the Riesling, were far different than today's sweet wines. Their dryness exceeded the French white wines, and they were aged for long periods of time, often not being served until fifty years old.[63] Age increased the expense, although Dr. Hans Ambrosi, a leading German oenologist, points out that the practice of drinking German wines old was based on necessity. Dr. Ambrosi reports that "vinification methods have changed to the extent that:

"a) With today's modern presses, less tannic acid goes into the must.
"b) A too-high acid content in the must can be reduced by adding lime.
"c) The young wines can be cleaned up through filtration and beautification products much faster than before. While years ago, a high-acid content could only be reduced to an acceptable taste by years of storage, the same can be achieved in weeks with today's methods."

Dr. Ambrosi believes that even the Rheingau wines could use more aging than they are generally allowed. "What Mr. Jefferson wrote about the Moselle and Rheingau wines, namely, that they should not be drunk before 5-6 years, is still true today for the Rheingau wines. The Moselle wines have changed of late toward a lighter, fresher and more spirited taste; that is, the youngness suits these wines very well.

"The Rheingau wines in their form are still hardy, with a high extract content. The youngness and freshness is not of such importance as with the Moselles. That is why we recommend to our customers, as Mr. Jefferson already wrote, to age the Rheingau wines at least 5 to 10 years."[64] The Riesling, which originated in the Rhine Valley, is still nurtured in all the great vineyards of the Moselle and Rheingau districts.

The third variety Jefferson mentions, the Orleans grape, was, according to legend, planted on the hills of Rudesheim by Charlemagne. "The Orleans grapes were still there," observed the late Fritz Hallgarten "when I left Germany in 1933. I have drunk Rudesheimer Berg Orleans, a wine of the then Prussian Domain in the Rheingau. Orleans ripened even later than Riesling, and was therefore replaced by Riesling. It was a pinot (Burgundy) type and had a reputation for longevity.

"I remember the taste well. It was a wine which had more body than the Riesling, a type of white Burgundy, but with a higher acidity content than Burgundy wine, say from Macon or Pouilly Fuisse which we drink today. It was the acidity of the wine which reminded you that it was of the Rheingau origin. It was a good wine, but not a great wine."[65]

Jefferson dismissed the German red wines calling them "absolutely worthless." German red wines were and are still made principally from the Spatburgunder grape (the German name for Pinot Noir) that was grown near Assmanshausen, around the river's bend from the Rheingau vineyards. The Spatburgunder is the grape varietal from which red Burgundies and the increasingly popular Pinot Noirs from California and Oregon are made. But in the colder climates of the Rhine, the Pinot Noir does not thrive as well and produces a light colored, light bodied wine of no distinction to the connoisseur, but popular and appreciated in Germany.[66]

On April 12 Jefferson was on the road to Oppenheim, traveling through the wine region known today as the Rheinhessen. He recorded that the cantons of Laubenheim, Bodenheim, and Nierstein were esteemed for producing wines of a quality just below that of the vineyards of Rudesheim, and he remembered that they had been prominently displayed on John Dick's wine list.[67] The wines of Laudenheim, a village about six miles from Mainz, were produced from grapes that grew on a steep hillside facing southeasterly into the sun. The vineyards between Laubenheim and Nierstein were planted on hillsides so steep that they were almost perpendicular to the Rhine. "It is to be observed that these are the only cantons on the south side of the river which yield good wine, the hills on this side being generally exposed to the cold winds, and turned from the sun." Today vineyards on these same hillsides continue to produce the best quality wines of the Rheinhessen with Nierstein being singled out for making some of the very best.[68]

Approaching Oppenheim, situated on a hill above the river and dominated by the Church of St. Catharine, he saw "the commencement of the berg-strasse, or mountains which separate at first the plains of the Rhine and Maine, then cross the Neckar at Heidelberg, and from thence forms a separation between the plains of the Neckar and Rhine..."⁶⁹ Late that evening his carriage arrived at The Cour du Palatin, a "good tavern" in Mannheim.

In the morning he purchased a guidebook and spent the day, his forty-fifth birthday, "seeing things." He visited the Elector's Palace, a huge stone quadrangular building with an art gallery that he thought "more considerable than at Dusseldorf but has not so many precious things." That evening he went to the theatre.

From Mannheim he took several side trips. He visited Kaeferthall and saw a herd of wild boar and a field of rhubarb. On an excursion to Dossenheim he saw Angora goats, and at Schwetzinger he thought the gardens behind the Elector's Castle among the best in Germany though "not to be compared to the English gardens."⁷⁰

At Heidelberg he made the long, steep ascent to the castle and thought it the "most noble ruin" he had ever seen. Among the ruins was a round tower and the remains of a chapel with statues of saints and warriors looking down from niches along massive walls covered with ivy. These "noble" ruins were the handiwork of man and nature. A hundred years before Jefferson's visit, the Heidelberg Castle had been ravaged by wars, but the final insult was delivered by nature in the form of a series of lightning strikes in 1764 that reduced the castle to the ruinous condition that Jefferson found. He made precise measurements of the Great Tun of Heidelberg, which had been built in 1751 to replace an older vat. Although the tun was empty, Jefferson calculated that it was capable of holding 283,000 bottles. From the edge of a precipice looking down on the Neckar River and across a green valley to the Black Forest, Jefferson was reminded of the view from Petrarch's château at Vaucluse and in majesty thought it "would stand well alongside the pyramids of Egypt."⁷¹ His notes do not tell us at what time of day he witnessed this scene, but

Heidelberg

at sunset with the river and mountains bathed in a pink glow, the view is unforgettable.

The road from Heidelberg to Karlsruhe was one of the best of his journey with the hills above the Neckar on one side and the plains sloping down to the Rhine on the other. He stopped in Karlsruhe on April 15. Based on "the appearance of his dominions" Jefferson declared the Margrave of Baden an excellent sovereign. He stayed at the Prince Hereditair tavern which he found "good and reasonable." Jefferson recommended visiting the Margrave's Palace, the central point from which the town's streets diverge in the form of a fan. In the gardens behind the Palace, he saw deer, Angora goats, beavers and a fine collection of pheasants.[72]

In Strasbourg he stayed at the Hotel a L'Esprit for three days, April 16, 17 and 18. He discovered Amand Koenig's bookstore, "the best shop for classical books I ever saw."[73] Jefferson continued to buy books from Koenig while living in Paris through Prevost, a Left Bank bookseller. He visited the cathedral and went to the top of its spire, 465 feet, calling it the "highest in the world, and the handsomest." But even for the superbly conditioned Jefferson, it was not an easy climb, and a year later in his notes to Shippen and Rutledge he qualified his recommendation by saying, "But let it be the last operation of the day, as you will need a long rest after it."[74]

Of the local Alsatian wines he commented on only one. "The vin de paille [straw] is made in the neighborhood of Colmar in Alsace ... It takes its name from the circumstance of spreading the grapes on straw where they are preserved till spring, and then made into wine. The little juice then remaining in them makes a rich sweet wine, but the dearest in the world without being the best by any means. They charge 9 livres the bottle for it in the taverns of Strasbourg. It is the caprice of wealth alone which continues so losing an operation. This wine is sought because dear, while the better wine of Frontignan is rarely seen at a good table because it is cheap."[75]

The late Jean Hugel, one of Alsace's leading producers and shippers, explained the method by which it was made: *"Vin de Paille* has not been made since the end of the 19th century, although we do have in our cellars a few rare bottles of an 1884 *Vin de Paille,* almost certainly one of the last made.

"The process of vinification was relatively simple although of long duration. Noble grapes, having been harvested in the normal way, during late October or early November, were placed on straw mats and left until about Christmas. By this time, most of the water in the grapes had evaporated, leaving behind a concentrated juice. The shrivelled grapes, looking like raisins, were then pressed in special small presses.

"Because of the high sugar content, the juice was extremely difficult to ferment, but on the occasion when it was achieved, it produced a succulent, rich, naturally sweet dessert wine, fully justifying its fabulous price by the months of careful work that went into its preparation.

"Although, as Mr. Jefferson noted, it was at this time available in the taverns of Strasbourg, it was not a wine for general consumption. It was considered more of an elixir, a concentrate of the goodness of the wines of the region, and its habitual usage was to be administered by the teaspoonful to persons acutely ill or in danger of dying, bearing in mind the primitive state of medical science at that time."[76]

Actually, two types of straw wine were made in Alsace. The method described by Jefferson and Mr. Hugel produced a wine that in taste and color resembled Malaga. Some winemakers, however, employed vinification methods that allowed the juice to ferment a second time, and when bottled the wine was luscious and sparkling and, according to Redding, "very agreeable to the palate."[77] It is surprising that with a three-day stay in Strasbourg Jefferson did not comment on other Alsatian wines. At the time, Alsace, now the easternmost province of France between the Vosges Mountains to the west and the Rhine to the east, produced wines from the Riesling, Gentil, Traminer, Elbling and Burger grapes. His bill for lodging at the Hotel a L'Esprit shows that in addition to the nine livres he spent for the bottle of straw wine, he was charged twelve livres for two bottles of Rhine wine.[78] At six livres a bottle they were twice as expensive as the best wines of Bordeaux or Burgundy. They might have been German wines from the Rhine Valley but were probably Alsatian, made from the Riesling grape, and highly esteemed in the late 18th century. Not only were Alsatian Rieslings considered the equal to the best wines of Germany, they also had great staying power. Redding mentions that "the Riesling wine at Strasbourg will keep 100 years."[79]

From Strasbourg his route led west across France. Jefferson comments on vineyards around Nancy "where a bad wine is made." He had hardly recorded the intricate design of an oxen plough before he turned again to women at work. "The women here, as in Germany do all sorts of work. While one considers them as useful and rational companions, one cannot forget that they are also objects of our pleasures. Nor can they ever forget it. While employed in dirt and drudgery, some tag of a ribbon, some ring or bit of bracelet, earbob or necklace, or something of that kind will show that the desire of pleasing is never suspended in them. How valuable is that state of society which allots to them internal employments only, and external to the men. They are formed by nature for attentions and not for hard labour."

Before returning to Paris he traveled to Champagne staying in Épernay at the Aubergiste de l'hotel de Rohan. Monsieur Cousin, the owner and a vintner, was his guide to the Champagne vineyards. Jefferson noted that "the hills from Ay to Cumiercs are generally about 250 feet high. The good wine is made only in the middle region. The lower region however is better than the upper because this last is exposed to cold winds and a colder atmosphere."[80]

Jefferson made the following "topographical sketch of the position of the wine villages, the course of the hills, and consequently the aspect of the vineyards."[81]

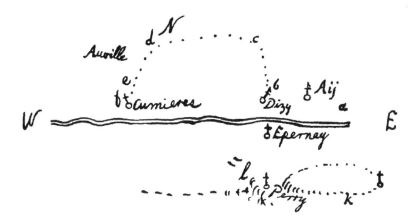

Virtually all Champagne today is sparkling, but in the 18th century most French wine drinkers, and Jefferson himself, preferred the non-sparkling variety. Foreign demand favored sparkling Champagne, and because it sold for a higher price, the vintners made increasing amounts of it. Jefferson recorded that "The sparkling are little drank in France but are alone known and drank in foreign countries. This makes so great a demand and so certain a one that it is dearest by about an eighth and therefore they endeavor to make all sparkling if they can. This is done by bottling in the spring from the beginning of March to June. If it succeeds they lose an abundance of bottles from ⅒ to ⅓. This is another cause increasing the price."[82] But, because the vinification methods were far cruder than they are today, nonsparkling Champagne could only be made "when they know from some circumstance that the wine will not be brisk. So if the spring bottling fails to make a brisk wine, they decant it into other bottles in the fall and it then makes the very best still wine. They let it stand in the bottles in this case 48 hours with only a napkin spread over their mouths, but no cork. The best sparkling wine decanted in this manner makes the best still wine and which will keep much longer than the originally made still by being bottled in September."[83]

Jefferson was of the opinion that the white "Pinot" grape (Chardonnay) did not make as fine a Champagne as the red Pinot Noir, noting that "the bulk of their grapes are purple, which they prefer for making even white wine. They press them very lightly (without treading them or permitting them to ferment at all) for about an hour so, that it is the beginning of the running only which makes the bright wine. What follows the beginning is of a straw color and therefore not placed on a level with the first; the last part of the juice produced by a strong pressure is red and ordinary. They choose the bunches with as much care to make wine of the very 1st quality as if to eat. Not above 1/8 of the whole grapes will do for this purpose. The white grape, tho not so fine for wine as the red, when the red can be produced, and more liable to rot in a moist season, yet grows better if the soil be excessively poor, and therefore in such a soil it is preferred: because there indeed the red would not grow at all."[84]

Contrary to the opinion of some contemporary wine drinkers, who claim that Champagne does not improve with age and must be drunk young, Jefferson thought that sparkling Champagne improved with a certain amount of age. "The brisk wines lose their briskness the older they are, but they gain in quality with age to a certain length. These wines are in perfection from two to ten years old, and will even be very good to fifteen. 1766 was the best year ever known. 1755 and 1776 next to that. 1783 is the last good year, and that not to be compared with those. These wines stand icing very well."[85] A modern-day expert, Hugh Johnson, is in essential agreement with Jefferson. "Most important of all it should be mature. Very young champagne makes enemies. Time finds in it inimitable glorious flavours."[86]

Jefferson describes the cellar of a Champagne house as being "admirably made, being about 6. 8. or 10 f. wide vaulted and extending into the ground in a kind of labryinth to a prodigious distance, with an air hole of 2.f. diameter about every 50. feet. From the top of the vault to the surface of the earth is from 15. to 30. f. I have no where seen cellars comparable to these. In packing their bottles they lay a row on their side, then across them at each end they lay laths, and on these another row of bottles, heads and points on the others. By this means they can take out a bottle from the bottom or where they will."[87]

Jefferson discovered in Ay a still Champagne that was to become his favorite—that of Monsieur Dorsay. Dorsay was a prosperous merchant who resided in Paris and owned many vineyards in and around Ay. His cellars in Ay were surrounded by a one and one-half acre walled vineyard located between what is now Rue Jules Lobet (formerly Rue 1' Huilerie) and Rues de la Chartre and de la Brache.[88] Of all the Champagnes Jefferson tasted during this visit, he found Dorsay's the best. The Benedictine monks at Hautvillers [Auvillij] produced first quality Champagnes that supplied the King's table but on tasting them Jefferson said: "Their white is hardly as good as Dorsay's." In the little town of Pierrij he tasted the 1782 wine of Monsieur de Failli which he thought "really very good, though not equal to that of M. Dorsay of 1783." He bought of all Monsieur Dorsay's remaining supply of nonsparkling Champagne of the year 1783-sixty bottles at three and a half livres a bottle, a little more than he paid for Margaux, Haut-Brion, Lafite and Latour.[89]

Jefferson observed that the best winemakers bought most of their grapes from small proprietors who could have made first quality wines if they had been able to cull their grapes, but being poor they could not afford this luxury. Consequently, small vineyard owners entered into contracts with established proprietors who bought only their best grapes or "about ⅓ of the grapes fit to make wine of the 1st quality." By blending the grapes from his Ay vineyard with grapes from his other vineyards and from the small producers who could not afford to make their own wines, Dorsay became Ay's largest Champagne producer.[90] The practice of large Champagne houses buying most of their grapes under contracts from small vineyard owners continues to this day, and most of the grapes crushed and made into Champagne are not from vineyards owned by a particular Champagne house.

After two days of tasting the wines from the vineyards of Épernay and the surrounding villages of Dizy, Ay, Hautviller, Cumieres, and Pierrij [Pierry], Jefferson left, convinced that he had learned just enough to know that there was more to learn about the intricacies and nuances of Champagne. He planned a return visit at harvest time, but now his duties in Paris required his return. On April 23 he headed back to Paris noting along the way that the plains of the Marne and Seine were very picturesque.[91]

CHAPTER THIRTEEN

The French Revolution Begins

The poverty and suffering that Jefferson witnessed on this trip increased his mounting hatred of monarchies. Two days after his return he wrote George Washington: "I was much an enemy of monarchies before I came to Europe. I am 10,000 times more so, since I have seen what they are. There is scarcely an evil known in these countries, which may not be traced to their king, as its source, nor a good, which is not derived from the small fibers of republicanism existing among them. I can further say, with safety, there is not a crowned head in Europe, whose talents or merits would entitle him to be elected a vestry man by the people of any parish in America."[1]

In his mail was a letter from Bondfield explaining that Lafite's owner, Pichard, had sold all of his 1784 vintage, and though some 1786 Lafite was available, it was not ready to drink. Bondfield attempted to assuage Jefferson's disappointment by suggesting that a few hogsheads of 1784 Haut-Brion, the next best red wine of that vintage, were still available. Jefferson promptly notified Bondfield to send 125 bottles of the 1784 Haut-Brion and acknowledged the safe receipt of his 250 bottles of Yquem.[2]

Bondfield purchased the Haut-Brion and advised that it was being sent by ship to either Rouen or Havre. But after more than five months of "a constant expectation of hearing that the wine of Haut-Brion was on its way," Jefferson wrote: "If the wine has been forwarded, I will thank you for information of the conveyance by which it came. The Sauterne sent me by the Marquis de Saluces turns out very fine. I shall be glad to receive your draught for both these objects."[3] A chagrined Bondfield confessed that his coopers had misdirected the wine and, having been caught up in the vintage and a family wedding, he had forgotten to follow up on it. But Bondfield expressed confidence that he could fill Jefferson's order.[4] A disappointed Jefferson, expecting to return to America in a few months, and not knowing when the wine might reach him, replied: "The accident of the wine of Haut Brion is of no consequence; and if you should not already have received or engaged for more to replace it, I can do without it." Asking again to be billed for the Yquem, he gave it high praise, telling

Bondfield, "This proves a most excellent wine, and seems to have hit the palate of the Americans more than any wine I have ever seen in France."[5]

Jefferson extended his assistance to all Americans visiting Paris who asked for it. Two who fell into his sphere of strong attention were Thomas Lee Shippen, son of Dr. William Shippen, Jr. of Philadelphia and the nephew of Arthur Lee, and John Rutledge, Jr., son of Governor Edward Rutledge of South Carolina. When these two young men arrived in Paris in early 1788, preparatory to starting out on a grand tour of Europe, Jefferson was quick to extend his friendship and advice. Rutledge had arrived in Paris in November short of funds and Jefferson loaned him 600 livres. Rutledge then went to England and returned to Paris in March. Shippen arrived at Jefferson's house in January. Jefferson invited him to dinner twice a week, presented him to court and introduced him to his social and political friends.

Shippen and Rutledge had waited for Jefferson's return before beginning their grand tour of Europe. Jefferson, swamped by official duties, was unable to furnish them with letters of introduction and copies of his travel notes of France, Italy and Germany before they left on May 7. However, on June 19, he mailed them letters of introduction and a detailed outline of his travel notes with recommendations of routes to follow, places to stay, and the wines to drink, but with the admonition, "They have been scribbled so hastily and so unformally that I would not send them, did not a desire of accommodating yourself and Mr. Rutledge get the better of my self love."[6]

"We still punctually followed your directions," Shippen wrote from Germany. "At Coblenz [Coblentz] we found the Wildman a very civil one to us, and having no true Brownberg in the house, he sent out and got some for us. It is the best Moselle I ever drank."[7] From Coblentz they followed Jefferson's advice and took a boat up the Rhine to Mainz. Along the way they lodged in Rudesheim and breakfasted on samples of Schloss Johannisberg wine.[8] "What a delicious liqueur sir it is! But I found it too expensive for us to think of importing it. The price on the spot is between 5 and 6 shillings sterling a bottle by the stuck which holds about 4 pipes." Rutledge shared Shippen's sentiments regarding the Johannisberg wine and reported that Geismar had been a hospitable guide and presented them at court.

In Dusseldorf Shippen followed Jefferson's suggestion and visited the gallery of paintings, but he also went beyond the town's walls to visit the Society of La Trappe, something Jefferson had not mentioned. Having heard so many strange stories of their rigid abstinence from worldly enjoyments and their employing "so many minutes in every day in scratching up their own grave with their fingers," Shippen was surprised to find them "a fat jolly, wicked set of rogues who when not praying were allowed to work in the gardens, to walk into town, . . . to talk, eat and drink as much as they pleased, and to indulge themselves in all licentiousness."[9]

America's first wine connoisseur had planned on witnessing the vintage in Champagne, but the gathering storm of the French Revolution had created "squalls" of work that prevented his return.[10] Instead, Short left on his own grand tour, with plans to meet up with Rutledge and Shippen. He was accompanied as far as Lyon by John and Lucy Paradise. In Beaune, the first thing he did "was to go to Parent's. Unfortunately, he was gone some distance from home. A heavy rain was falling, but still his wife insisted on sending for him. On our return to the tavern we found Mrs. Paradise in a fever to be gone. We dined and finding that Parent did not arrive and that her fever increased we ordered the posthorses, after being assured by two Benedictins, who were at the tavern and who had come there to superintend the making of their wine, that even if Parent should arrive he would not be able to shew us what we wished to see, as the vintage was finished, and there were no considerable cellars in Beaune. These Benedictins themselves were setting off for Chalons because the business of wine making was finished. After the posthorses were put to and we in the carriage Parent arrived. He assured us the contrary and said he should have been able to have shewn us several cellars where the wine was still making. It was now too late and we were obliged to go on. I saw with a great deal of pleasure Volnay [Volnais], Meursault and Montrachet [Montrache]. I paid with sincerity my tribute of gratitude to the two last for the many glasses of fine wine they have given me, by gazing at them as we passed and by never quitting them with my eyes as long as we remained within sight of them. They made us pay at the tavern at Beaune three livres for a bottle of Volnais. I did not however think it equal to a wine we had at Auxerre for the same price and which I think was made in the neighbourhood. It was of the year 84, and that at Beaune much newer. I learned with pleasure from Parent that this year would be still better for wine than that of 84 . . . . I ate of the grape of which the Volnais is made. I was struck by its resemblance to some of our wild grapes in Virginia and particularly some that grow in Surrey on my father's estate. The shape of the bunch, the size and color, and still more the taste of the grape, so absolutely the same, that I think it would be impossible to distinguish one from the other . . . . I recollect my father made one year by way of experiment some wine, of what grapes however I know not. The wine was very sweet and very agreeable to my taste, but not at all resembling the Volnais."[11]

When Jefferson visited Nimes in 1787, he saw the antiquarian collection of Jean Francois Seguier (1703-1784) who had supervised the excavation and restoration of the Maison Carrée a few years earlier. Struck by the unique beauty of a bronze askos (wine pitcher) excavated from ruins in the vicinity of the Maison Carrée, Jefferson thought it would make the perfect gift to show his appreciation for Clerriseau's assistance in designing the Virginia State Capitol.[12] Jefferson engaged a local artisan, Souche, to craft a wooden model. Souche made the model but, for some unexplained reason, it was never delivered to Jefferson.

Short, whose itinerary took him to Nimes, contacted Souche with the idea of obtaining a copy of the askos for Jefferson. Short learned that Souche had retained a model of the askos, or perhaps still had the missing model, and made arrangements for a wooden copy to be sent to Jefferson. However, when Jefferson received it, he kept it for himself and gave Clerriseau a gift of a silver coffee urn. Jefferson, while

President, had a silver askos made from Souche's wooden model. Both askoses are now at Monticello.[13]

Another personal errand Short accomplished for Jefferson occurred in Avignon. Here he visited the estate of the Marquis de Rochegude and, because he was unable to meet the Marquis' wine manager, Short was obliged to execute Jefferson's wine commission by "tasting and choosing six dozen bottles of Rochegude's white wine at his hotel . . . and leaving a memorandum for it to be sent to you to Paris. The wine is kept in the country where it is made. That which I tasted of which kind you are to have is six years old. It cost 21 sous instead of 24 sous as you imagined the bottle included. It is to be paid when received at Paris together with the price of carriage and duty. It should arrive in a short time from this and will be sent to your address. They told me that they often send it to Paris and that you might be sure of being well served. You may be the more sure still as it is considered only as a trial and they have hopes of continuing to supply you."[14]

Throughout his nine-month European tour Short continued to pay attention to viticulture and wine. From Milan he reported to Jefferson: "You must have observed the vines were cultivated differently here from France. I have also found a little treatise on that subject which perhaps may be useful. I have no doubt we shall find it proper to cultivate the vine in America, at least for a part of our own consumption."[15]

While Jefferson and his friends were shivering through one of the coldest winters in the history of Paris, he received word that Rutledge and Short had decided to leave the snow and cold of northern Italy for the warm sunshine of Rome.[16] The winter of 1788-89 was so severe in Paris that "All communications, almost, were cut off. Dinners and suppers were suppressed, and the money laid out in feeding and warming the poor, whose labours were suspended by the rigor of the season. Loaded carriages passed the Seine on the ice, and it was covered with thousands of people from morning to night, skating and sliding. Such sights were never seen before."[17]

The weather had caused Jefferson to delay ordering his favorite dry white wine and he explained to Parent, "I have been meaning to ask you for a shipment of Meursault wine. But this season was so rough that I thought it best to wait until it relents. It was long in coming so now I have an urgent need for it. Therefore, I would appreciate your shipping me 250 bottles of Goutte d'Or de Meursault. I got so used to Mr. Bachet's 1784 that if he still has some, I would prefer it. If he is out of it, be kind enough to supply the best available in this class of wine. I always trust you for quality, and let the price whatever it should be, while still considering quality rather than price."

Parent purchased the wine and shipped it in four baskets containing "248 or 249 bottles" at a total cost of only 272 livres. Jefferson's discerning palate noticed a difference in the quality of this wine and he pointed it out to Parent. "The Bachet wine you sent has made me a bit demanding. The shipment I just received from you was not as perfect. I would have thought it was a year other than 1784, if you hadn't told me it was that year. I am told that last year [1788] was excellent for wine quality. Therefore, I will order this vintage from you next fall."[18]

For the masses the brutally cold winter had consequences far more serious than an interruption to the pleasures of wine drinking. The price of bread, which even in normal times accounted for half the household budget, nearly doubled in price. This meant that the peasant or laborer had to spend four-fifths of his earnings on bread alone! But hunger was not the only catalyst to the gathering storm of revolution. By convening the States-General the King had allowed hope to creep into the peasants lives.[19]

In January Gouverneur Morris whose pen, according to Madison, had "styled" the Constitution, arrived in Paris on private business and immediately contacted Jefferson. Though they were political opposites, Morris and Jefferson held an intellectual respect for one another that transcended their political differences and, during the eight months that Jefferson remained in Paris, they were social companions. Morris, a frequent dinner guest at the Hotel de Langeac, wrote in his diary, "Mr. Jefferson lives well, keeps a good table and excellent wines which he distributes freely and by his hospitality to his countrymen here possesses very much their good will."

Gouverneur Morris

Jefferson, with Gouverneur Morris, witnessed from his balcony the annual Parisian rite of Spring, known as the *Promenade a Longchamps*.[20] Each year on Wednesday, Thursday and Friday in the week before Easter, Parisians paraded along the Champs-Elysées and across the Bois de Boulogne to the little church at Longchamps. The origin of this rite had been to enjoy the music of the Tenebrae services at the Abbaye de Longchamps church, but over time it evolved into a parade featuring Parisians from every walk of life dressed in their Sunday best, on foot and riding in ornate carriages. "Everybody that has got a splendid carriage, a fine set of horses, or an elegant mistress, send them out on these days to make a show at Longchamps."[21]

John Adams, who witnessed the fete on a number of occasions, said that its popularity evolved from boredom and tells an anecdote about a prostitute whose carriage was so superior to any other that it brought on the wrath of Marie Antoinette. "For some years, the ladies who were not acknowledged to have established reputations, were observed to appear in unusual splendor in these processions, and all indecency increased from year to year till one of the most beautiful but one of the most infamous Prostitutes in Paris had sold her charms to such profit that she appeared in the most costly and splendid equipage in the whole row, six of the finest horses in the Kingdom, the most costly coach that could be built, more numerous servants and richer liveries than any of the Nobility or Princes. Her own dress in proportion. It was generally agreed to be finest show that had ever been exhibited. This was so audacious an insult to all modest women and indeed to the national morality and religion, that the Queen to her honor sent her a message the next morning, that if she ever appeared again, any where, in that equipage she should find herself in Bicetre the next morning."[22]

By the end of March a peasant insurrection was spreading throughout France. The people began to hunt and kill game, tithes and other forms of taxation were ignored, and such feudal rights as *banalite du moulin* and *droit du four*-the obligation of the peasantry to have their corn ground in the seigneur's mills and their bread baked in the seigneur's ovens—were disregarded. This seething disobedience developed into attacks on the nobility and clergy and their property, especially their archives and feudal title-deeds.[23]

A month before the storming of the Bastille Jefferson told Madison that the third estate (the common people) requested the nobles and clergy to eliminate the distinction of orders "and to do the business of the nation. This was on the 10th—on the 15th they moved to declare themselves the National Assembly.... The Commons have in their chamber almost all the talents of the nation; they are firm and bold, yet moderate. There is indeed among them a number of very hot headed members; but those of most influence are cool, temperate, and sagacious. Every step of this house has been marked with caution and wisdom. The Noblesse on the contrary are absolutely out of their senses. They are so furious they can seldom debate at all. They have few men of moderate talents, and not one of great in the majority. Their proceedings have been very injudicious. The clergy are waiting to profit of every incident to secure themselves and have no other object in view. Among the Commons there is an entire unanimity on the great question of voting by persons."[24]

On June 20 the representatives of the third estate were locked out of their meeting hall by order of the King. They promptly reassembled on the tennis court at Versailles and in the words of Jefferson, "They there bound themselves to each other by an oath never to separate of their own accord til they had settled a constitution for the nation on a solid basis, and if separated by force, that they would reassemble in some other place."[25]

On the Fourth of July Jefferson hosted a large dinner party that included, among others, Lafayette, Gouverneur Morris, Philip Mazzei and John Paradise. After dinner Morris, whose sentiments were clearly on the side of the nobles, urged Lafayette "to preserve if possible some constitutional authority to the Body of the Nobles as the only means of preserving any Liberty for the People. The current is setting so strongly against the Noblesse that I apprehend their destruction."[26]

Four days later a concerned Jefferson advised the French foreign minister, Montmarin: "My hotel having been lately robbed, for the third time, I take the liberty of uniting my wish with that of the inhabitants of this quarter, that it may coincide with the arrangements of the police to extend to us the protection of a guard." Jefferson was concerned enough to have bars and bells put on the windows of his house.[27]

The spark that seems to have set off the insurrection in Paris was the King's dismissal of his popular finance minister, Necker. News of Necker's exile to Geneva reached Paris at noon on July 12. Thousands of Parisians flooded the Palais Royal (the owner, the Duke of Chartres had joined the third estate), where orators, such as Camille des Moulins, gave the call to arms. That night and the next day crowds swarmed throughout Paris looking for arms. Jefferson told Thomas Paine that on the morning of July 14th "the mobs immediately shut up all the playhouses. The foreign troops were advanced into the city. Engagements took place between some of them and the people. The first was at the Place Louis XV where a body of German cavalry being drawn up, the people posted themselves upon and behind the piles of stone collected there for the bridge, and attacked and drove off the cavalry with stones." Having won the first skirmish, a crowd of over 7,000 crossed the river and moved on to the Invalides[28] in search of arms and ammunition, "and being refused the people forced the place and got here a large supply of arms. They then went to the Bastille and made the same demand. The Governor after hoisting a flag of truce and deploying a hundred or two within the outer draw bridge and fired on them. The people without then forced the place, took and beheaded the Governor and Lt. Governor, and here compleated arming themselves ... the Marquis de la Fayette was made commander in chief of the men raised."[29] Gouverneur Morris, on seeing the Governor of the Bastille's head paraded through the streets, called it "the Liberty Pole of France."

Jefferson was not an eyewitness to the seige of the Bastille but he was privy to eyewitness accounts. His words of what happened on that fatal day are probably as

The Bastille

trustworthy as can be found, and show that his sympathies were with the people. "The tumults in Paris which took place on the change of the ministry, the slaughter of the people in the assault of the Bastille, the beheading of the Governor and Lieutenant Governor of it, and the Prevost de Marchands, excited in the King so much concern, that bursting from the shackles of his ministers and advisors, he went yesterday morning to the States-General with only his two brothers, opened his heart to them, asked them what he could do to restore peace and happiness to his people, and showed himself ready to do everything for that purpose, promising : particularly to send away the troops."[30]

The King ordered away all the troops and came to Paris "in procession, having in his coach the most popular characters, the States-General walking on foot in two ranks on each side of it, and the Marquis de la Fayette on horseback at their head. There were probably 60 or 80,000 armed Bourgeois lining the streets thro' which he was to pass. Today or tomorrow the residue of his new ministers are to retire, and probably they will think it prudent to get out of the way for a while. The pallor of the States is now I think out of all danger. This is the sum of this astonishing train of events . . ."[31] Sensing the tumult over, Jefferson felt privileged to have witnessed "the wonders which have taken place here."[32] "My fortune has been singular, to see in the course of fourteen years two such revolutions as were never before seen."[33]

Jefferson's involvement in the French Revolution changed from spectator to participant when in August he allowed his home to become a secret meeting place for Lafayette and six others attempting to forge a coalition "as being the only means to prevent a total dissolution and civil war."[34] Jefferson recalled the meeting: "The cloth being removed, and wine set on the table, after the American manner, the Marquis introduced the objects of the conference . . . The discussions began at the hour of 4 and were continued to ten o'clock in the evening; during which time I was a silent witness to a coolness and candor of argument unusual in the conflicts of political opinion-to a logical reasoning and chaste eloquence disfigured by no gaudy tinsel of rhetoric or declamation, and truly worthy of being placed parallel with the finest dialogues of antiquity, as handed to us by Xenophon, by Plato and Cicero."[35]

On September 26, 1789, after five years in France, and with two years of his appointment as minister remaining, Jefferson, his two daughters and slave-servants, Sally and James Hemings, left Paris for what he thought would be a six-month leave of absence. Before leaving he wrote John Jay: "I have sent from this place [Paris], together with my own baggage, two hampers and two boxes, which when arrived at Havre I have taken the liberty to order to be separated from my baggage and sent by the first vessel to New York to your address. The marks and contents are as follows:

Tl. No. 30. Tl. No. 31. These are hampers containing samples of the best wines of this country, which I beg leave to present to the President and yourself, in order that you may decide whether you would wish to have any, and which of them for your own tables hereafter, and offer my service in procuring them for you. The kinds are 1. Montrachet (the best kind of white Burgundy) 2. Champagne non mousseux (i.e. still) much preferred here to the sparkling, which goes all to foreign countries. 3. Sauterne (a white Bordeaux) 4. Rochegude (from the neighborhood of Avignon, somewhat of the Madeira quality) 5. Frontignan. I have bought all of these from the Vignerons who made them, the 1st, 2nd and 5th when on the spots myself, and 3rd and 4th by writing to them."[36]

Two days later he arrived at Le Havre and lodged at the same inn where his French adventure had begun five years earlier, the Aigle d'Or. Due to bad weather he was unable to sail out of Le Havre for ten days. When the coastal storms cleared, the Jefferson party made their way to the Isle of Wright but were prevented from sailing by contrary winds. *After* two weeks of further delay the future president went aboard the *Clermont* leaving behind everything-everything except wine hampers containing 38 bottles of Meursault, 60 bottles of Sauternes, 36 bottles of Montrachet, 36 bottles of Champagne, 60 bottles of Rochegude and 58 bottles of Frontignan. Finally, on October 23, the *Clermont* sailed for Norfolk "in company with upwards of thirty vessels . . . ."[37]

CHAPTER FOURTEEN

Wine Consultant and Secretary of State

On October 29 the *Clermont* sailed from Yarmouth, carrying the forty-six-year-old minister who expected he would in time return to France. Except for a little seasickness their twenty-six day voyage was uneventful, and they enjoyed some "of the finest autumn weather it was possible to have." After landing at Norfolk Jefferson learned by reading a newspaper that the President had nominated him, and the Senate had confirmed him, as America's first Secretary of State. Jefferson was flattered but troubled by the appointment because he preferred returning to France. Conversations with Madison and an exchange of letters with George Washington made it clear that the President felt he needed him. "I found it better in the end to sacrifice my own inclinations to those of others."[1] On February 14, 1790, he accepted the new appointment.[2]

After visiting with the Eppeses and friends in Norfolk, Jefferson and his daughters arrived at Monticello on December 23. The slaves were readying the mansion for Christmas: draping the doors with holly, stuffing geese and ducks and decorating the Duncan Phyfe expanses of mahogany with boxwood arrangements. Almost immediately plans took shape for the marriage of Martha to her second cousin, Thomas Mann Randolph, Jr. On February 23 they were married at Monticello. Jefferson was pleased with the match saying that Randolph's "talents, temper, family and fortune ... are all I could have desired."[3]

Two days after the new year Jefferson wrote Richmond merchant James Brown complaining that a delivery of provisions that arrived before Christmas was short one box of wine. Expressing the hope that it was omitted in error, Jefferson ordered six gallons of good French brandy and twelve wine glasses.[4] One of the owners of the business, Alexander Donald, and a friend of Jefferson's, promptly wrote expressing regret about the mix-up with the box of wine and sent along a ten-gallon cask of "very fine French brandy," adding, "I will venture to sport an opinion that you will find use for it."[5]

A week after Martha's marriage Jefferson prepared for his new appointment. He again left Polly under the "motherly care" of Elizabeth Eppes.[6] His trip to New York was "as laborious a journey . . . as I ever went through . . . a snow of eighteen inches deep falling . . . the roads through the whole were so bad that we could never go more than three miles an hour, sometimes not more than two, and in the night but one."[7]

He stopped in Philadelphia to visit Benjamin Franklin. Franklin was eighty-three, bedridden, in pain, emaciated but in good spirits, and Jefferson reported this to their mutual friends in France. Franklin died the next month.[8]

When he arrived in New York on March 21, it was a city of 33,000 spread along the tip of Manhattan. He took temporary quarters at the City Tavern, an inn that occupied the full block between Thames and Cedar Streets on Broadway. Two months later he moved into more permanent quarters at 57 Maiden Lane.[9]

Throughout his life Jefferson suffered incapacitating migraine headaches. Before being stricken by a series of headaches so severe that he was unable to work for the entire month of May, he wrote to his friends in France reporting his new appointment and sadly adding that he would not be seeing them again.[10] To his new son-in-law, Thomas Mann Randolph, Jr., he hinted on the dangers of marital infidelity: "Judge Bedford of Delaware the other day wounded dangerously his wife and killed her adulterer with the same shot."[11]

Within a month of assuming his new duties he received a troubling letter from his old friend and revolutionary colleague, George Mason—troubling not only in what it told him but what it asked of him. Mason reported that John Bondfield, the American consul at Bordeaux, and Jefferson's original Bordeaux wine consultant, had fallen hopelessly in debt, had lawsuits pending against him for large amounts of money and that, if he had any property, he was hiding it from his creditors. Mason urged Jefferson to investigate the accuracy of his charges and if he found them correct, as he would, that he recommend Mason's son's partner, Joseph Fenwick, as the new consul to Bordeaux.[12] What, if anything, Jefferson did to determine the accuracy of George Mason's allegations is not clear, but on June 16 Jefferson wrote Mason "that Bordeaux was given to Mr. Fenwick according to your desire."[13] In a letter advising Bonfield that he had not been reappointed consul, Jefferson explained it on the basis that "the Senate refused in every instance, where there was a *native citizen* in any port, to consent to the nomination of any other."[14]

Bondfield's reply was short and sad. "It is in common practice before an old servant is dismist to assign to him some mark of disapprobation or to thank him for his past attentive services, also to discharge the sums due him, or to provide for him a descent retreat."[15]

During the less than six months the new Secretary of State lived in New York he dined frequently with President and Mrs. Washington. In fact, it was at a presidential dinner party that Washington gave for his Secretary of State shortly after his arrival that Jefferson first met Alexander Hamilton, Secretary of the Treasury.[16] Edmund Randolph, the heir to Jefferson's law practice and now Washington's personal lawyer, and Henry Knox, Secretary of War, were also there. He dined with John and Abigail

GEN. WASHINGTON'S CARRIAGE.

Published by A. O. CRANE, Boston, Mass.

Adams at their manor house in Richmond Hill, now Greenwich Village, and visited with his best friend and fellow Virginian, James Madison, who was serving in Congress.

Shortly after his arrival Jefferson learned that his stay in New York was temporary; Congress had passed a bill transferring the capital to Philadelphia for ten years, and, thereafter, permanently to the new capital, Washington, D.C.[17] Under these circumstances wine purchases for his immediate consumption were confined to Madeira, a case of Italian wine and some porter. However, in preparation for his coming stay at Monticello before reestablishing his government residence in Philadelphia, Jefferson was busy ordering wines. As with everything in his life quality was more important than price, and in a letter to James Brown ordering a quarter cask of wine he added: "I would prefer good Lisbon; next to that Sherry, next to that Carcavelos [Calcavelo]; but still a good quality of the latter would be preferable to an indifferent quality of the former. If none of these, then claret. Whatever kind you can procure me, be so good as to have it bottled before sent ... If the wine you send me be either Lisbon, Sherry or Calcavelo, then I would be glad of 3 or 4 dozen in addition, of any sound weak wine, either red or white, which would be good for mixing with water, the kinds specified not being proper for that."[18] Brown sent a first quality sherry that had been imported from Cadiz eighteen months earlier. When bottled it increased Jefferson's Monticello inventory by one hundred and forty-four bottles. Brown also included forty-two bottles of Port.[19]

As Washington's Secretary of State, Jefferson was guiding the chief executive through other perilous foreign waters-ordering French wines. Three days before leaving in August on a six day trip through Rhode Island with the President, Jefferson wrote Short: "Being just now informed that a vessel sails this afternoon for a port in

Normandy, and knowing that the President wished to have some Champagne, and that this is the season to write for it, I have been to him, and he desires 40 dozen bottles. The execution of this commission I must put upon you, begging the favor of you to procure it of the growth of M. Dorsay's vineyard at Ay opposite to Épernay in Champagne, and of the best year he has, for present drinking. His *hommes d'Affaires* when I was there was a M. Louis, and if the same be in place it will perhaps be best to write to him, and it may give him the idea of a more standing customer if he knows that the application comes through the person who bought the remains of his wine of 1783 in April 1788 being in the company with a M. Cousin. It is to be *Non-mousseux*. M. Dorsay himself lives in Paris. We have not time to procure a bill to enclose you herein, but I will take care to forward one immediately by some other conveyance. I am anxious this wine should not move from Champagne til the heats are over and that it should arrive at Philadelphia before the spring comes on. It will of course be in bottles ... Call for the best possible, and they may be sure of a continuance of such an annual demand as long as it comes of the best."[20]

On September 1 Jefferson and Madison left New York in Jefferson's phaeton for their homes in Virginia. During a stopover in Philadelphia, where Jefferson made arrangements for his new residence, he remembered that in addition to the Champagne, the President had also asked him to order "30. dozen of Sauterne [Yquem], 20. dozen of Bordeaux de Segur [Latour] and 10. doz. of Frontignan." Intending to pay Jefferson for the wine in advance, Washington, too entangled in matters of state forgot to pay him. Jefferson worked payment out in his letter to Short. "In the multiplicity of his business before his departure he has forgot to do this: and it remains that we do not permit him to be disappointed of his wine by his omission. But how to do it? For the amount of the whole I suppose will be 3000 livres[21] and the being obliged to set up a house in New York, then to abandon it and remove here, has really put me out of condition to advance such a sum here. I think however it can be done, without incommoding you, by your drawing on the bankers in Amsterdam. On the President's return here (about the 1st of December) bills shall be remitted you, and by using these for your own purposes instead of making new draughts for your salary on the bankers, all will stand right without any special mention in the public accounts. I will make any necessary explanations at the Treasury, should any be necessary."[22]

Jefferson's letter to Short was accompanied by a letter to Joseph Fenwick, the new U.S. Counsel in Bordeaux, asking that Fenwick "forward to me some wines for the President and myself. They are written for in the inclosed letters to the respective owners of the vineyards and are as follows:

M. la comte de Lur Saluce	30. doz., Sauterne for the President
	10. doz. do. for myself
M. de Miromenil	20. doz. vin de Segur for the President
Madame de Rozan	10. doz. vin de Rozan for myself
Monsieur Lambert at Frontignan	10. doz. Frontignan for the President
	5. doz. do. for myself

To these I must beg you to add 10. dozen for me of a good white vin ordinaire, or indeed something better, that is to say of such quality as will do to mix with water, and also be drinkable alone. Such I suppose may be obtained at Bordeaux for ten sous the bottle. I would wish you to buy it of the person who makes it, and give me his name and address, that, if it suits me, I may always be sure of the same quality. This letter will go under cover to Mr. Short, who will furnish you with the means of payment. Be so good as to have the wines delivered immediately and forward them by the first safe vessel bound from Bordeaux to Philadelphia. I have directed those for the President to be packed separately and marked G.W and mine T. I. You will receive them ready packed. Those from Frontignan cannot probably be forwarded so soon as the others. You need only send the letter to Dr. Lambert at Frontignan, with a note of your address, and he will forward them to Bordeaux and draw on you for the amount of the wine and expenses."[23]

Adding a personal touch, he enclosed individual letters. To Madame de Rausan he advised that "I had the opportunity on a tour I made during my stay in Paris of visiting the canton of best Bordeaux wines, among which was de Rozan, your cru, of excellent quality. Would you please send me 10. dozen bottles of the best for drinking now, bottled and packed at the vineyard."[24] To Count Miromenil, owner of Château Latour, he wrote: "I have had the opportunity of visiting the canton of the best wines of Bordeaux and of having seen your vineyard which produces the wine known as Segur and know that it is one of the best cru of this canton. I am writing for our President General Washington...."[25] Count de Lur Saluce at Château d'Yquem was told that "The white wine of Sauterne, of your cru, that you have been kind enough to send me in Paris early in 1788 has been so well accepted by Americans who know good wines that I am sure that now that I am back in the United States my countrymen here will admire them. Our President, General Washington would like to try a sample. He would like for you to send him 30. dozen, sir, and for myself I would like to have 10. dozen, to be bottled, packed separately, and marked as indicated above, shipping in a way that will insure their protection against breakage."[26] He reminisced to his friend Dr. Lambert, "I still remember your excellent wines. Could you kindly send me as soon as possible ten dozen bottles for our President General Washington, and five dozen for me, of white and red, but the last in proportion.... Decide the best way for a rough voyage, for me, the five dozen should be put in half bottles if you have them...."

Count Miromenil acknowledged Jefferson's letter and advised that Château Latour was now owned by his two sons-in-law and managed by Seigneur Domenger "to whom I am going to send your letter and ask him to fill this order which to me is important because I wish to please General Washington."[27] Later, however, Jefferson heard through Joseph Fenwick that the President's order for Château Latour could not be filled because the estate manager reported that there was no wine "on hand that would do justice to his estate." Using good judgment, Fenwick substituted 1786 Lafite and added "we hope [it] will prove perfect and give entire satisfaction."[28]

Dr. Lambert's letter recalled the day he had the pleasure of visiting Jefferson at his home in Paris and went on to express the hope that General Washington would find his wines good. Based on what Count Moustier had told him about American wine tastes, Dr. Lambert chose a less sweet (liquoreux) wine than his previous shipment but he had no red Muscat to send Jefferson.[29]

From the d'Yquem estate Jefferson received a letter from the Countess de Lur Saluce reporting that because of the death of her husband she was now "in charge of Château d'Yquem and its white Sauternes... I hope you will be satisfied with the shipment I am sending you which consists of 10 cases of 50 bottles each, 150 bottles for you and 350 bottles for General Washington...."[30]

Fenwick thought the cost of the Yquem at thirty sous per bottle extraordinarily high. Actually, relative to the prices he paid for the other wines, and certainly by today's prices, the Yquem was not expensive. The 1786 Lafite cost three livres, or twice as much as the Yquem, and Dorsay's Champagne at almost three and a half livres a bottle was even more expensive.[31]

Madame Rausan's reply was highly encouraging. She advised that his order for ten dozen bottles of her Margaux wine had been shipped "four cases of 25 bottles each of the 1785 vintage in French glass at two and a half livres per bottle and a fifth case of 25 bottles of 1786 in English glass at three livres per bottle ... bottled expressly for you" and that all of the bottles were hallmarked with her personal seal because she never engages in "fraud or the mixing of my wine." She went on to point out that her 1786 wine would improve with some bottle age and that though the 1785 was good there were better years. Sensing in Jefferson a good future customer, Madame Rausan advised that she still had in stock two or three thousand bottles of 1785, three barriques of 1786 and a barrique each of 1788 and 1790.[32]

Leaving Philadelphia on September 8, Madison and Jefferson stayed in Wilmington, Delaware, and the next night at Chestertown on the Eastern Shore of Maryland. The following morning they were at Rock Hall, about twelve miles from Chestertown, waiting for the ferry to cross the Chesapeake Bay to Annapolis. They were joined by Jefferson's young friend from Paris, Thomas Lee Shippen, who reported to his father: "I never knew two men more agreeable than they were. We talked and dined, and strolled, and rowed ourselves in boats, and feasted upon delicious crabs." When they landed in Annapolis, Shippen met his friend Shaaff, who became their guide. Shaaff took them to the top of the State House dome and for three hours Shaaff opened "the roofs of the houses" and told them all the local gossip.[33] Many of these handsome houses are still part of the Annapolis landscape: William Paca House (1765), James Brice House (1767), Maryland Inn (circa 1770), John Shaw House (circa 1725), Maryland State House (1772), Chase-Lloyd House (1769), Hammond-Harwood House (1774), Middleton Tavern (1740) and others.

The magnificent dome from which Jefferson and Madison walked the widows walk and viewed "the finest prospect in the world, if extent, variety of wood and water in all their happiest forms can make one so," still crowns the Maryland State House.[34] The exact source of the design is undetermined but it is believed to be based on the Schlossturm, the free-standing tower on the north side of the palace in Karlsruhe, Germany.[35] Jefferson surely saw that dome when he visited the Karlsruhe palace on April 15, 1788, the same year that the dome was finished and placed on the Annapolis State House. Given Jefferson's sense of architectural form, he would have remembered the striking similarities of these two beautiful domes.

A Front View of the State-House &c. at ANNAPOLIS the Capital of MARYLAND.

A modern view of Annapolis from the State House Dome

They remained in Annapolis two days, lodging at Mann's Tavern. The well-traveled Shippen called Mann's "the most excellent in the world." Since George Washington's stay there eight years earlier Mann had put on two additions, one of which Shippen called magnificent. Before leaving for Georgetown on September 12, they feasted on turtles seasoned with a fine old Madeira, still a Maryland tradition. After dinner they set out for Georgetown and lodged in Queen Anne's at a place that was "a most perfect contrast to Mann's—mosquitoes, gnats, fleas and bugs contended with each other for preference, and we had nothing decent to eat or drink. You may imagine how much we slept from the company we were in."[36]

Leaving early, they had breakfast in Bladensburg at the home of Mrs. Margaret Adams, a black woman, who kept the best house in town. They reached Georgetown by nightfall. After breakfast the three travelers were joined by a "cavalcade of thirteen" local gentry for viewing the flat farm land and wooded areas adjacent to Georgetown, then the first choice on the Potomac for the location of the new federal city. Later they went by boat to the Great Falls of the Potomac, four miles above the town, and described by Shippen as a "romantic scene."[37]

Two days later the Virginians were seated at the dinner table at Mt. Vernon where their fireside conversations were probably enlivened by some of the President's best Madeira. From Fredericksburg Jefferson sent merchant James Brown a note requesting a "half a gross of good porter. Should you not be able to get good, I would then be glad of good ale." Brown's prompt reply confirmed the availability of the porter and added, "I have just received a few Butts of Lisbon of a good quality." The porter along with a cask containing thirty three and a half gallons of Lisbon wine were delivered at Monticello shortly after Jefferson's arrival on September 18.[38]

Jefferson was never happier than when at home with family and friends. During the next month and a half an intrusion into his happiness was his disappointment on learning that a cask of French brandy and the cask of Lisbon wine sent by Brown had "both been tapped by the waggoners tho' the latter was in a double cask. They knocked out the head of the outer one."[39] Just before setting out for Philadelphia on November 8, Jefferson sent Brown a note ordering two gross of bottles and six gross of corks.

When Jefferson arrived in Philadelphia on November 20, 1790, it was America's largest and most sophisticated city, with a population of over 45,000. Although Jefferson publicly criticized Federalist aristocratic pomp, he rented a house from Thomas Leiper on High Street that he had remodeled with stabling for six horses, room for three carriages, a veranda and a garden house.

Eighty-six packing cases arrived from Paris to fill the rooms with six gold leaf sofas, forty-four gold-leaf chairs with damask coverings, tables, commodes, mirrors, blue and crimson draperies, wallpaper, statuary, and twelve cases containing 680 bottles of wine, all French. Alexander Hamilton, Secretary of the Treasury, allowed all of Jefferson's French imports to enter duty free except for the twelve cases of wine and one hundred and forty-five rolls of wallpaper.[40]

One of the principal tasks that Jefferson left Short, who remained in Paris as the American *charge d'affairs,* was the packing and shipping of his household effects, discharging his servants, selling his carriage and horses, terminating the lease on the Hotel de Langeac and seeing to it that the Cahuzac, Graves and other wines still in casks were bottled before being shipped. His French house servant Petit at first refused to join him in America. It was only after a personal letter from Jefferson explaining how much he needed Petit that Petit relented and arrived in Philadelphia a year later, bringing with him a stock of foods and condiments that Jefferson missed most: maccaroni (spaghetti), parmesan cheese, figs, raisins, almonds, mustard, vinaigre d'estragon, olive oil, and anchovies.[41]

With his Philadelphia wine cellar stocked with French wines America's first Secretary of State ordered a long-time favorite, Madeira. From Henry Sheaff, a grocer and wine merchant at 223 Market Street, he purchased twelve bottles of Madeira, and from another merchant, John Nanearrow, a twenty-three gallon cask of Madeira which when bottled increased his cellar inventory by 111 bottles. In March he received from John Bulkeley & Son in Lisbon a wine sampler consisting of 36 bottles of six different types of Portuguese wines. Jefferson preferred the oldest, Termo, and ordered a pipe of it.[42]

In the spring Jefferson made plans for a vacation trip through the Hudson Valley with James Madison, but before leaving he set about putting in order some personal matters. Alexander Donald, then in London, asked Jefferson his opinion of the best Bordeaux wines and their prices with the obvious intention of importing them. Jefferson's reply essentially reiterated the opinions he had expressed in his travel notes and letters following his trip through southern France with the further suggestion that Donald "add to all prices 5 sous for bottles and bottling ... If you should apply to Madame de Rausan or Monsieur de Lur-Saluce, if their stock of good wine should be low, it may add an inducement to them to name me. In all cases the owner is the person to apply to. He will either send you none, or good. He never adulterates, because he would be *afelo de se* to do it."[43] But he emphasized to Donald that, regardless of what he ordered, the only means of guaranteeing the genuineness of the wines was to order them directly from the owner.

He advised Gouverneur Morris, the new U.S. Minister to France, that a bill had passed the House of Representatives "for raising monies for the support of the Indian War, while the duties on every other species of wine are raised from one to three-fourths more than they were, the best wines of France will pay little more than the worst of any other country, to wit between 6 and 7 cents a bottle and where this exceeds 40 percent of their cost, they will pay but the 40 percent. I consider this latter provision as likely to introduce an abundance of cheaper wines of France, and the more so as the tax on ardent spirits is considerably raised." Jefferson added that he hoped that this friendly gesture would induce the French National Assembly to repeal some obnoxious laws it had passed with regard to commerce with the United States.[44]

Fearing that some of the wines he had ordered might arrive while he was away and be placed in a warehouse and spoil, Jefferson instructed his clerk, Henry Remsen, Jr. to watch for them. It is well that he did because, during his absence, Remsen received notice that four boxes and four baskets covered in oil cloth had arrived from France. Presuming correctly that they contained wine (they were President Washington's 40 dozen bottles of Champagne), Remsen placed them in Jefferson's cellar. A few days later fourteen cases of wine from Charleston arrived, which Remsen also cellared.[45]

Shortly before beginning his trip Jefferson received a letter from Pierre Guide, the brother of Jean Baptiste Guide, whom Jefferson had met in Nice.[46] Guide had arrived in Baltimore with a shipload of Mediterranean products with the intention of setting up trade between the United States and Sardinia. Guide sent Jefferson a list of articles that he had brought to America. Jefferson looked over the list "with eagerness in hopes of finding in it some of the kind of wine which I drank at Turin under the name of Nebiule." Not finding the wine that he remembered "as sweet as the silky Madeira, as stringent on the palate as Bordeaux and as brisk as Champagne," he gave Guide a standing order for five or six dozen of the best Nebbiolo wine should it become available. Seeing on the list *Vin Vieux Rouge de Nice* and remembering its high quality and fine taste, he ordered three dozen bottles. He intended to distribute them "in the best houses" of Philadelphia as samples of a wine that he liked and thought deserved to be better known and, in anticipation of taking some with him on his trip, he instructed Guide to dispatch a dozen to him by return stage.[47] A day before leaving on his trip a disappointed Jefferson wrote Guide, "on repeated inquiries at the different stage-offices, I find that it has never arrived...."[48]

Jefferson was aware that colonial tavern accommodations were far less comfortable and convenient than those in France and England. Colonial America did not have posting inns or houses. One traveled by either the public stage or by private carriage. There was no such thing as hiring a carriage or horses from post to post as in England and France.[49]

American taverns had a well-deserved reputation for lacking basic amenities. One traveler described them as being "indifferent for bed and table but good for horses." Sleeping quarters were usually crowded and communal. Beds were placed in the public rooms of taverns. The Marquis de Chastellux, staying in a Virginia tavern, described the sleeping quarters as consisting of "one large room for the whole company, with a blanket for each individual." An Englishman staying in Norfolk in 1785 reported sleeping on straw bedding "with blankets and no sheets" in a room with 20 other men.[50] Bathing facilities and toilets were primitive; taverns kept chamber pots in the bedrooms and had outside privies.[51]

Tavern entertainment consisted of backgammon, cards, chess, billiards and dice. In rural areas horse racing and cockfighting were popular. Many states had laws against gambling but these laws were rarely enforced. Other forms of entertainment consisted of shows and curiosities that regularly toured towns and cities, and tickets to these events were sold by tavern-keepers.[52] Since much of the social life of a town or city centered around its taverns they were natural settings for political gatherings.

Tavern food varied from bad to good with chances for a good meal better in the cities or, as an English traveler put it, "Instead of wishing it was better, I thanked God it was not worse."

Rum and homemade brandies were the most popular drinks and were drunk either straight, in punch, or in a toddy—rum mixed with sugar and water. Wine was not a staple. In fact, except for some indifferent sherry or Madeira, wine was usually not to be had.

Given these conditions, the length of the trip and the two travelers' love of wine, the corkscrew Jefferson always carried was probably put to daily use opening the variety of bottled wines he brought with him.[53] Wines that Jefferson stored in barrels or casks such as Madeira, sherry or Termo were carried in what was called "case bottles." Case bottles derived their name from the portable wooden chest or case in which they were carried. The case usually contained ten compartments for holding eight large and two small mold-blown bottles with spherical stoppers. Jefferson owned such a portable chest and bottles, and it was used for carrying wines and other beverages.[54]

On May 17, 1791, Jefferson left Philadelphia and joined James Madison in New York City for their tour of upstate New York and parts of New England. The itinerary for this vacation was put together by Jefferson and the purpose, as expressed by Madison, was "health, recreation and curiosity." They spent four weeks walking over battlefields, fishing, killing rattlesnakes, shooting squirrels, studying botanical curiosities and visiting friends.[55] Not everyone, however, saw their trip in the same light. One of Hamilton's supporters reported to him that "they scouted silently through the country, shunning the gentry... and quarreling with the eatables; nothing good enough for them."[56]

Jefferson and Madison departed New York on May 21. James Hemings, who had accompanied Jefferson to France, was along and took Jefferson's phaeton and horses on to Poughkeepsie while the future presidents traveled up the Hudson by boat. On the twenty-third they reached Poughkeepsie and stayed at Hendrickson's Tavern, where Lafayette stayed during his triumphal revisit to America thirty-three years later. In the morning they headed north and were in Albany on May 26, and the following day visited Cohoes Falls on the Mohawk River near its confluence with the Hudson River. Jefferson estimated its height at 70 feet. Chastellux called these falls, presently in Cohoes, Albany County, "one of the wonders of America."[57] At Bemis Heights (formerly Stillwater} they explored the battlegrounds which were "the principal scenes of Bourgoyne's misfortunes" and "which cost so much blood to both parties."[58]

Three miles north of Bemis Heights they stopped at the home of Doctor Elias Willard (1756-1827) to discuss the Hessian Fly. After breakfast at Ezekiel Ensign's Tavern, they traveled eleven miles north to Schylerville (formerly Saratoga) where they "viewed the campments and ground where the British piled their arms." Today a monument commemorates the place where General John Burgoyne surrendered his army of British and Hessian troops to General Horatio Gates on October 17, 1777. Burgoyne's surrender was America's first major victory. It caught the world by surprise and convinced a growing number of Englishmen that England could not win the war. In France Louis XVI signed a Treaty of Alliance with America within two days of hearing the news.

After dining at Archibald McNeil's tavern, three miles north of Schylerville, they traveled to the French and Indian War outposts at Fort Edward. The following day they reached Lake George, and after visiting Fort George and Fort William Henry, they sailed its entire length. Jefferson thought Lake George "without comparison the most beautiful water I ever saw; formed by a contour of mountains into a basin thirty-five miles long, and from two to four miles broad, finely interspersed with islands, its water limpid as crystal, and the mountain sides covered with rich groves of thuja, silver fir, white pine, aspen, and paper birch down to the water-edge; here and there precipices of rock to checker the scene and save it from monotony. An abundance of speckled trout, salmon trout, bass and other fish, with which it is stored, have added, to our other amusements, the sport of taking them."[59] Time has not changed Lake George's beauty.

Their thirteen-mile journey from Lake George to Fort Ticonderoga was through a verdant valley enclosed by the Adirondack Mountains. Built by the French as Fort Carillon in 1755, Fort Ticonderoga's strategic location on the southern tip of Lake Champlain had been considered important from the time of the French and Indian Wars. As Jefferson walked the fort's ramparts and looked out on Lake Champlain and the distant Green Mountains he must have had mixed emotions, realizing that the fort's contribution to winning the war had been made possible in part by the heroism of America's most infamous traitor, Benedict Arnold, who had embarrassed Jefferson with his surprise attack on Richmond ten years earlier, causing Jefferson and the Virginia Assembly to flee.

Fort Ticonderoga was captured from the British on May 10, 1775, in a surprise attack by Ethan Allen and his Green Mountain Boys and a Massachusetts unit led by Benedict Arnold. The significance of its capture lies in what General Washington did with the fort's artillery. Washington designated Colonel Henry Knox, a former Boston bookseller, to organize and carry out the transporting of the fort's cannons to Boston. Lashing forty-two artillery pieces weighing over sixty tons to fifty sleds pulled by oxen, Knox and his men started in late December, 1775, through a snow storm, and covered the three hundred miles to Boston in just two months. The cannons were placed near Dorchester Heights and were used to bombard the British who occupied Boston. Knox's feat, called the "noble train of artillery," resulted in the American army's recapture of Boston.

Following the war Fort Ticonderoga was totally neglected and fell into ruins. The fort has now been completely restored. The visitor can follow Jefferson's footsteps

Ruins of Fort Ticonderoga

and view from its ramparts the beauty of Lake Champlain and Vermont's Green Mountains.[60]

After dinner at Ticonderoga the Virginians sailed fifteen miles up Lake Champlain to Crown Point, "which have been scenes of blood from a very early part of our war history."[61] They lodged at Chimney Point in Vermont, directly across the lake from Crown Point. Crown Point, at Lake Champlain's narrowest point, is now a historical national park displaying the ruins of the old English and French forts, a view of Lake Champlain and a display of excavated wine glasses, wine bottles and other 17th and 18th century artifacts. On May 31 the pair sailed halfway to Split Rock but, because of rough water and headwinds, their voyage was cut short. Jefferson found Lake Champlain "much larger" but "far less pleasant water than Lake George."[62]

Retracing their steps, they visited, on June 2, "two very remarkable cataracts" on the Hudson River, Wing's Falls (now Glens Falls) and Sandy Hill Falls (now Bakers Falls)[63] and later crossed the Hudson at Saratoga. They lodged at Colvin's Tavern in the town of Cambridge near the Vermont border and headed the next day for Bennington, Vermont, through mountains covered with sugar maple, white oak and beach.[64]

Before reaching Bennington, they visited the Bennington battle sites in Hoosick Falls, New York. Standing on top of the hill where Colonel Baum and his Hessian troops had camped before being routed, they were told how it came about: As General Burgoyne's army pursued the American army, following its retreat from Forts Ticonderoga and Mt. Independence, the British learned that an American cache of food and ammunition was stored at Bennington. Burgoyne ordered a detachment of Hessian troops under Colonel Baum to seize it. What the British didn't know was that a tough New Hampshire Indian fighter, John Stark, was assembling a colonial force of New Hampshire, Vermont, and Massachusetts volunteers to defend Bennington. Perhaps it is apocryphal, but tradition has it that Colonel Stark (he was made a brigadier general after this battle), before giving the order to fire the first shot, is said to have looked over at the Hessian positions and said to his battalion commanders: "The British will be ours or Molly Stark will sleep a widow tonight."

On August 16 the fighting, which Stark described as "one continuous clap of thunder," began. Within two hours Baum and over two hundred of his troops had been killed and the rest captured. Later that evening Stark's troops, with the help of Colonel Seth Warner and the Green Mountain Boys, engaged and defeated a British reinforcement detachment led by a Colonel Breymann. What started out as a routine foray turned into a stunning defeat for Bourgoyne's invading army and laid the groundwork for his surrender at Saratoga two months later.

The battle sites are now within a historic state park located two miles beyond the Vermont border just off Route 67 in New York State. At the top of the hill where Baum and his troops were routed, the visitor has a sweeping view of the surrounding hillsides. A bronze memorial depicting the battle sites and three large placards facing north, south and east with photographs are displayed and outline the countryside with descriptions of how the troops maneuvered before and during the battles. In Bennington an obelisk marks the site of the American storehouses which Baum had expected to capture.

Arriving in Bennington on June 4 Madison and Jefferson lodged at Captain Elijah Dewey's (1744–1818) tavern, later known as the Walloomsac Inn.[65] Dewey had been an active revolutionary, serving as a captain in the battles at Bennington and Saratoga and hosting many revolutionary meetings at his inn. They remained in Bennington two days, probably one day longer than they had anticipated, because a Sunday blue law prohibited traveling on the Sabbath. Saturday evening was spent with a political ally and friend, Moses Robinson, the former governor and the newly elected Senator from Vermont.

Early on Monday morning they continued their journey southwest across Connecticut, breakfasting at Killock's in Williamstown, now the site of Williams College and the Clark Museum, and staying at Sarah Williams Marsh's public house in Dalton. The following day they dined at Smith's Inn in Worthington and lodged at Pomeroy's in North Hampton. On June 8, although "with cavalry in part disabled,"[66] they arrived in Hartford where they stayed for two days at the town's most prominent tavern, Frederick Bull's, at the sign of the bunch of grapes on Main Street, opposite the court house.[67]

A few days later they reached Guilford on the Long Island Sound, had dinner at Medab Stone's tavern and "sailed for Long Island and was on the Sound all night."

"Bennington, 1793"

Landing on the northeastern tip of Long Island at Oyster Pond Point (now Orient Point) they breakfasted at The Tupple's Inn.

Their journey from Greenport to Palmer, a distance of about twenty miles, took them through a countryside that today is planted in vines and produces some of New York's best wines from the wineries of Bedell, Pindar, Lenz, Peconic Bay, Hargrave, Bidwell, Pugliese, Mattituck Hills, Paumanok, Jamesport, and Palmer.

On June 13 they dined at Griffin's in Riverhead and lodged at Downs in Morichies. In the morning they breakfasted with Jefferson's old friend and fellow Congressional delegate, William Floyd, at his home on the Forge River in Brookhaven Township and visited the Unquachog Indians, a tribe of about "twenty souls." Jefferson, who had a lifelong interest in Indian languages, compiled a vocabulary of Unquachog words.[68] They then traveled to Flushing, Long Island, where they stopped at the Prince Nursery, the most famous nursery in America. The man from whom Jefferson attempted to buy the nursery's entire stock of sugar maple trees, William Prince, was the third proprietor. On returning to Philadelphia he ordered from the Prince catalogue thirty-one additional items including a variety of roses.[69] When Prince filled the order he sent sixty sugar maple trees, six cranberry trees and ten different kinds of roses. Although the nursery had a wide variety of native and hybridized grapes, Jefferson's order did not include grapevines.[70]

They spent that night in Jamaica. The following day, June 16, they returned to the mainland via the Brooklyn ferry and ended their trip in New York City. Their journey of over 700 miles had been, in the words of Madison, "a very agreeable one, and carried us thro an interesting country new to us both."[71] Three days later Jefferson arrived in Philadelphia tired, but pleased, and in an age before credit cards, almost broke, with only $8.60 "cash in hand."[72]

Five days after his return Jefferson sent Tobias Lear, Washington's private secretary, a note suggesting that because the day was cloudy it would be a favorable time to pick up the President's four hampers of Champagne. Always thoughtful as to when a wine would be at its best for drinking, he suggested that Lear open a case of each and place the bottles on the shelves so "that they may be settled before the President's return."[73]

Gray's Gardens, on the west bank of the Schuykill River at Gray's Lower Ferry, was one of his favorite recreational spots. It was modeled after the public gardens of London and provided food, drinks, and other refreshments in a setting of "alcoves, arbours, and shady walks."[74] Although Jefferson was not one for observing holidays, he placed the Fourth of July in a special category. He always celebrated it, so he probably attended the Fourth of July celebration at Gray's Gardens that included fireworks and other festivities from six a.m. to ten p.m.[75] His account book shows that the next day he purchased wine from John Swanwick (1740-1798), a Philadelphia merchant, and paid Pierre Guide for the three dozen Bellet wines that finally found their way to Philadelphia.[76]

In September Jefferson wrote Madame Rausan expressing his pleasure with the wine she had sent him and placed another order for "500 bottles of the year 1785 in *bottles* and two barrels of 250 bottles each, of the harvest 1790, *in casks* . . ."[77] President Washington must have felt the same about M. Dorsay's Champagne because five months after receiving it he had Jefferson order another three hundred and sixty bottles of Dorsay's "best still Champagne" fit for present use.[78]

Later he received a letter from Fenwick advising that the political situation in France had created obstacles to commerce with the United States, and that the problems in the wine trade were exacerbated by the prior year's "bad crop of wine" which had increased the price of brandy, a principle export to America.[79] A month or so later Humphreys reported that a long drought had produced a shortage of wine in Portugal.[80]

On December 4 Jefferson noted in his account book a payment of $68.65 to Philadelphia merchant Henry Sheaff for wine.[81] It was at about this time that Sheaff asked Jefferson for guidance on the quality, prices and sources of the best European wines. Jefferson's "Notes to Henry Sheaff"[82] with a few exceptions has left a legacy of wine advice that has, for those wines that still exist, stood the tests of time.

Notes to Henry Sheaff:

Lisbon wines. The best quality of the dry kind is called Termo, and costs 79 Dollars the pipe at about 2 years old. At 5 years old it is becoming a fine wine; at 7 years old it is preferable to any but the very best Madeira. Bulkeley and son furnish it from Lisbon.

Sherry. The best dry Sherry costs at Cadiz, from 80 to 90 Dollars the pipe. But when old and fine, such as is sent to the London market it costs £30 sterling the pipe. Mr. Yznardi, the son, Consul of the US. at Cadiz, at this time in Philadelphia, furnishes it.

The following facts are from my own enquiries in going thro' the different wine cantons of France, examining the identical vineyards producing the first quality of wines, conversing with their owners, and other persons on the spot minutely acquainted with the vineyards, and the wines made on them, and tasting them myself

Burgundy. The best wines of Burgundy are Montrachet, a white wine. It is made but by two persons, to wit Monsieur de Clermont, and Monsieur de Sarsnet. The latter rents to Monsieur de la Tour. This costs 48 sous the bottle, new, and 3 livres when fit for drinking.

Meursault. A white wine. The best quality of it is called Goutte d'or. It costs 6 sous the bottle new. I do not believe this will bear transportation. But the Montrachet will in a proper season.[83]

Chambertin, Vougeau, veaune, are red wines, of the first quality, and are the only fine red wines of Burgundy which will bear transportation, and even these required to be moved in the best season, and not to be exposed to great heat or great cold. These cost 48 sous the bottle, new and 3 livres old. I think it next to impossible to have any of the Burgundy wines brought here in a sound state.

Champagne. The Mousseux or Sparkling Champagne is never brought to a good table in France. The still, or non-mousseaux, is alone drunk by connoisseurs.

Aij [Ay]. The best is made at Ai;: by Monsieur d'Orsay, who makes more than all the other proprietors of the first quality put together. It costs 3 livres the bottle when of the proper age to drink_, which is at 5 years old. The Red Champagne is not a fine wine. The best is made by the Benedictine monks at Auvillaij [Hautvillers].

The wines of Burgundy and Champagne being made at the head of the Seine, are brought down that river to Havre from whence they are shipped. They should come down in the month of November, so that they may be brought over sea in the winter and arrive here before our warm spring days. They should be bottled on the spot where they are made. The bottle, bottling, corking, and packing costs 5 sous a bottle. Capt. Cuttery Consul of the U.S. at Havre a good person and well informed, to supply the wines of Burgundy and Champagne.

Bordeaux red wines. There are four crops of them more famous than all the rest. These are Château-Margau [Margaux], Tour de Segur [Latour], HautBrion [Haut-Brion], and de la Fite [Lafite]. They cost 3 livres a bottle, old: but are so engaged beforehand that it is impossible to get them. The merchants, if you desire it, will send you a wine by any of those names, and may you pay 3 livres a bottle: But I will venture to affirm that there never was a bottle of those wines sent to America by a merchant. Nor is it worth while to seek for them; for I will defy any person to distinguish them from the wines of the next quality, to wit.

Rohan-Margau [Rausan-Margaux now known as Rausan-Segla}, which is made by Madame de Rohan. This is what I import for myself, and consider as equal to any of the four crops. There are also the wines of Dabbadie [the three Leovilles], la Rose [Gruaud-Larose], Quirouen [Cuiteau Kirwan], and Durfort [Durfort-Vivens] which are reckoned as good as Madame de Rozan's. Yet I have preferred hers. These wines cost 40 sous the bottle, when of the proper age for drinking.

Bordeaux white wines. Grave. The best is called Pontac, and is made by Monsieur de Lamont. It costs 18 sous a bottle.

Lamont. It costs 18 sous a bottle.

Sauterne. This is the best white wine of France (except Champagne and Hermitage) the best of it is made by Monsieur de Lur-Salus, and costs at 4 years old (when fit to drink) from 20 to 24 sous the bottle. There are two other white wines made in the same neighborhood called Prignac and Barsac, esteemed by some. But the Sauterne is that preferred at Paris, and much the best in my judgment. They cost the same. A great advantage of the Sauterne is that it becomes higher flavored the day after the bottle has been opened, than it is at first.

Mr. Fenwick, Consul of the US. at Bordeaux, is well informed on the subject of these wines, and has supplied the President and myself with them genuine and good. He would be a proper person to endeavor to get from the South of France some of the wines made there which are most excellent and very cheap, say 10 or 12 sous the bottle. Those of Roussillon are the best. I was not in Roussillon myself, and therefore can give no particular directions about them.

At Nimes I drank a good wine, stronger than claret, well flavored. The tavern price of which was 2 sous the quart. Mr. Fenwick might perhaps be able to get these brought through the Canal of Lanquedoc. A good correspondent at Amsterdam might furnish the following wines.

Moselle. The best of these is called Brownberg, being made on a mountain of that name adjoining the village of Dusmond, 15 leagues from Coblentz, to which last place it is brought and stored for sale. The best crop of Brownberg is that of Baron Breidbach Burreasheim. It costs 22 sous the bottle when old enough to drink. It is really a good wine.

Hock. There has been discovered within these 30 years, a finer wine of this quality called Johannisberg, now decidedly preferred to Hock. They both cost 5 sterl. a bottle when of the oldest and best quality. It is to be observed of the Hock wines that no body can drink them but Germans, or the English who have learnt it from their German kings. Compared with the wines of more Southern climates they are as an olive compared with a pine-apple.

Observe that whenever the price of wine by the bottle is mentioned, it means to include the price of the bottle, which is 5 sous deduct that sum therefore, and it leaves always the price of the wine."

With his wine cellars at Monticello and Philadelphia well supplied, Jefferson's wine purchases in 1792 were kept to a minimum. His account book entries show expenditures for wine from July 7, 1791 to January 13, 1792, costing $412.84. But for the succeeding nine months he spent only $98.20 for wine that included a quarter cask of Lisbon and a cask of claret and portage for a pipe of Termo.[84] His major wine interest during this period seems to have been tracking down the whereabouts of the thousand bottles of Madame Rausan's wine he had ordered and prepaid in September. Having not heard from either Fenwick or Short regarding this order, Jefferson wrote to both of them in April expressing the fear that his order had miscarried.[85] As it turned out, his apprehensions were justified. His letters never reached Short or Fenwick and he never received these wines.[86]

In the middle of July Jefferson left Philadelphia for his annual summer vacation at Monticello. While "indulging in reverie and rural occupations, scarcely permitting anything to occupy my mind seriously,"[87] his reverie was interrupted by a letter from his servant, Petit, claiming that the wife of Jefferson's coachman, Frances, had accused Petit, among other things, "of sodomy and the lover of men," Petit told Jefferson that if he did not discharge Frances, he would leave for France.[88] Jefferson's response was swift. Writing to his clerk, John Taylor, Jefferson instructed Taylor to attempt to work out a resolution of the dispute, but if it could not be resolved, to decide the matter in Petit's favor. The bachelor Petit refused any compromise and insisted on Frances' and his wife's immediate expulsion from the household; Frances was discharged.[89]

Jefferson left Monticello on September 27, and four days later was having breakfast with President Washington at Mt. Vernon. Before breakfast they had a discussion that covered Jefferson's contemplated retirement as Secretary of State, whether Washington should stand for re-election and Jefferson's concern that a group around the President "had monarchy in contemplation." Jefferson pointed out that Alexander Hamilton was one of the principals and, "that I had heard him say that this Constitution was a shilly shally thing, of mere milk and water, which could not last, and was only good as a step to something better." Washington attempted to talk Jefferson out of his retirement plans and their conversation ended with Washington exhorting Jefferson "not to decide too positively on retirement."[90]

Shortly after returning to Philadelphia on October 5, 1792, Jefferson received a letter from David Humphreys advising that the Portuguese agricultural minister was considering discriminating against American corn by prohibiting trade in corn with America and giving that trade exclusively to Naples.[91] Jefferson immediately wrote Humphreys telling him to "interpose your opposition with the Minister, developing to him all the consequences which such a measure would have on the happiness of the two nations." In an unveiled threat an irritated Jefferson said: "What would he say should we give our wine trade exclusively to France and Spain? It is well known that far the greatest proportion of the wine we consume is from Portugal and its dependencies ... he should reflect that nothing but habit has produced in this country a preference of their wines over the superior wines of France, and that if once that habit is interrupted by an absolute prohibition it will never be recovered."[92]

During the closing years of the 18th century Portuguese wines were popular in the United States and any threat to ban their importation certainly should have raised serious concern to the Portuguese agricultural ministry. Madeira, long a colonial staple and a lifetime Jefferson wine, remained popular. Bucelas was a popular white wine which came from vineyards in the Tagus Valley near Lisbon. It had a deep golden color and was made chiefly from the Arinto grape, said to be the same

Wine Consultant and Secretary of State

as the Riesling.[93] Jullien compared it in style, when pure, with Barsac, but stronger.[94] One of Jefferson's personal favorites, which he imported in casks, was Termo, a white wine grown in vineyards located west of Lisbon. It was drier than Bucelas and, when not spoiled with the addition of brandy, had an excellent reputation. Another wine that was represented in the earliest inventory of Jefferson's wine cellar was Lisbon. Made from the Muscatel grape, it came in a variety of styles: dry, semi-sweet or sweet. There were red and white Lisbon wines, but white Lisbon was the most popular.

Carcavelos, or Carcavella as it was sometimes called, came from an area surrounding the village of Oeiras, ten miles west of Lisbon. Genuine Carcavelos had a nutty taste and was richer and sweeter than Lisbon wines and sold for higher prices. With age it took on an almondy flavor and many of the characteristics of a fine, old Madeira. The sweetness was achieved by checking the fermentation with the addition of brandy. Because of its popularity, sweet Lisbon wines were often indiscriminately sold as Carcavelos. The invasion of oidium and later phylloxera devastated the Carcavelos vineyards to such an extent that by 1867 production had dwindled from 500,000 liters to 6,000 liters.[95] But more destructive than oidium or phylloxera to the Carcavelos vineyards was urban growth.[96]

Jefferson's Portuguese wine purchases at this time were through John Bulkeley, an American merchant in Lisbon and a member of a prominent New England family that had sided with the British during the war. Bulkeley had sent a note expressing his pleasure that Jefferson approved of the quality of the Termo and thanked him for his order of three additional pipes.[97] Jefferson continued to buy wine from Bulkeley, but he blocked Bulkeley's application for appointment as the American Consul in Lisbon by reminding George Washington that "his birth and sentiments seem to set him aside."[98]

Jefferson continued to follow, as best he could, the convulsions of the French Revolution. Although he had warned Lafayette "we are not to expect to be translated from despotism to liberty, in a feather-bed,"[99] the sickening news that he received toward the end of the year from Gouverneur Morris in Paris dashed any remaining hopes he had of a peaceful resolution to France's Revolution. "We have had one week of unchek'd murders in which some thousands have perished in this City. It began with between two and three hundred of the Clergy who had been shut up because they would not take the

Oaths prescrib'd by Law, and which they said was contrary to their Conscience. Thence *these Executors* of speedy Justice went to the Abbaye where the persons were confined who were at court on the tenth. These were dispatch'd also and afterwards they visited the other Prisons. All those who were confined either on the Accusation or Suspicion of Crimes were destroyed. Madame de Lamballe was (I believe) the woman kill'd, and she was beheaded and embowelled, the Head and Entrails were paraded on pikes thro the Street and the Body dragged after them. They continued I am told at the Temple till the Queen look'd out at this horrible Spectacle. Yesterday the Prisoners from Orleans were put to Death at Versailles." He then learned of the murder of his friend, the Duke of Rochefoucault. "A guard had been sent a few Days since to make the Duke de la Rochefoucault prisoner. He was on his Way to Paris, under their Escort, with his Wife and Mother when he was taken out of his Carriage and killed [stoned to death]. The Ladies were taken back to la Roche Guyonne [the Duke's country estate] where they are now in a State of Arrestation. Monsieur de Montmorin [Minister of Foreign Affairs] was among those slain at the Abbaye."[100]

Though politics and concern for his friends in France occupied his thoughts, Jefferson continued to share his knowledge of wines. Charles Coatsworth Pinckney had undertaken the importation of olive trees into his native state of South Carolina. Jefferson helped coordinate this effort through Stephen Cathalan in Marseilles and Joseph Fenwick in Bordeaux. In a letter to Pinckney on December 2 Jefferson enclosed copies of his letters to Cathalan and Fenwick soliciting their help for the "olive scheme," and then pointing out "that you cannot better address yourself for certain wines of that country, then to these two gentlemen; that is to say, to Mr. Cathalan for Cote Rotie, Hermitage, Frontignan and Lunel, and to Mr. Fenwick for Claret of the *four crops*, that next in quality, Sauterne, Pontac, Barsac, and Grave. I took much pains myself to visit the best vineyards and learn the names of the best winemakers, of which I gave a list to Fenwick, and have been perfectly satisfied with the wines he has sent to different persons in consequence of it."[101]

With retirement on his mind Jefferson set about replenishing his wine cellar at Monticello ordering from Fenwick 500 bottles of the best quality red vin ordinaire, "such as is drunk at the best tables" for delivery to James Brown in Richmond so "that it may arrive before the warm weather of the ensuing spring."[102]

When John Trumbull returned to America he resided in Philadelphia and aligned himself politically with Hamilton. He became critical of Jefferson's support of the French Revolution. Toward the end of his term as Secretary of State Jefferson had a dinner party that was attended by, among others, Trumbull and William Branch Giles, a Virginia Congressman and political and social friend of Jefferson's. The events of that evening marked the end of the Trumbull-Jefferson friendship. Trumbull claims that no sooner had he taken his seat in the drawing room than Giles began to berate him because of his puritanical New England ancestry. Throughout dinner Giles continued to attack Trumbull's Christian beliefs and Jefferson, "in nodding and smiling assent to all the virulence of his friend, Mr. Giles, he appeared to me to avow most distinctly, his entire approbation. From this time my acquaintance with Mr. Jefferson became cold and distant."[103]

At another Jefferson dinner party a conversation between Hamilton and Jefferson highlighted the political and philosophical differences that existed between these two brilliant men. At the request of President Washington, Jefferson had convened the heads of the departments along with Vice President Adams. "I invited them to dine with me, and after dinner, sitting at our wine" in a room hung "with a collection of the portraits of remarkable men, among them were those of Bacon, Newton, and Locke, Hamilton asked me who they were. I told him they were my trinity of the three greatest men the world had ever produced naming them. He paused for some time: 'The greatest man,' he said, 'that ever lived, was Julius Ceasar.' Mr. Adams was honest as a politician, as well as a man; Hamilton honest as a man, but, not as a politician, believing in the necessity of either force or corruption to govern men."[104]

On the morning of January 9, 1793, Jefferson joined President Washington and a huge crowd to watch Jean Pierre Blanchard make the first successful American balloon ascension from the courtyard of the Philadelphia Walnut Street Prison.[105] Two weeks later, Peter Legaux (1748-1827), an adventurous Frenchman who had planted a vineyard on his 206 acre estate just outside of Philadelphia, called on Jefferson to find out why Mazzei's vineyard at Colle had failed. Jefferson explained to Legaux that Mazzei had "planted a considerable vineyard and attended to it with great diligence for three years and then the war carne on." Some of the laborers whom Mazzei had brought with him from Italy enlisted, and others got jobs as gardeners or went to farming for themselves. Mazzei went to Europe as an agent of the State of Virginia and rented Colle to General Riedesel "whose horses in one week destroyed the whole labor of three or four years, and thus ended an experiment, which, from every appearance, would in a year or two more have established the practicability of that branch of culture in Arnerica."[106]

An Englishman, Isaac Weld, visited Monticello a few years later and had other thoughts on why Mazzei's vineyards had failed. "Several attempts have been made in this neighborhood to bring the manufacture of wine to perfection; none of them however have succeeded to the wish of the parties . . . . The vines which the Italians found growing here were different, as well as the soil, from what they had been in the habit of cultivating, and they were not much more successful in the business than the people of the country. We must not, however, from hence conclude that good wine can never be manufactured upon these mountains. It is well known that the vines, and the mode of cultivating them, vary as much in different parts of Europe as the soil in one country differs from that in another. It will require some time, therefore and different experiments, to ascertain the particular kind of vine, and the mode of cultivating it, best adapted to the soil of these mountains."[107]

In February Jefferson had his friend Congressman Elbridge Gerry, to dinner and, shortly thereafter, received a note from Gerry inquiring about the name of the delicious dessert wine Jefferson had served and how he might buy it. By return courier Jefferson advised Gerry that it was "Sauterne, and costs 1/sterling the bottle, (included) at 3 years old, earlier than which it should not be tasted, and still much better not to drink it till 4 years old, one year then makes great odds in the flavor. The best crop is that of the Countess de Luz-Saluce . . . . Let it be bottled by the maker and packed. No other introduction will be needed than to mention my having advised you to apply to Mr. Fenwick. From this circumstance he will know exactly the quality of the wine wanted."[108]

In the spring, Jefferson moved from his residence in town to a three room cottage on the east bank of the Schuykill River, near Gray's Ferry "entirely embosomed in high plane-trees, with good grass below; and under them I breakfast, dine, write, read, and receive my company."[109]

It was about this time that the personal enmity and political differences that had developed between Hamilton and Jefferson accelerated. Hamilton, more than a decade younger, became the symbol of Federalist efforts to concentrate power in the national government rather than in the states rights that Jefferson favored. Jefferson became convinced that Hamilton and his followers were opposed to democratic principles. "I had left France in the first year of her revolution, in the fervor of natural rights and zeal for reformation. My conscientious devotion to these rights could not be heightened, but it had been aroused and excited by daily exercise . . . An apostate I could not be, not yet a hypocrite; and I found myself for the most part the only advocate on the republican side of the question." Jefferson saw it as a losing battle and decided to step aside. He informed Washington that he intended to serve only through the end of September, but allowed the President to persuade him to remain until the end of the year.[110]

Preparations for his retirement saw him making arrangements for wines to be shipped to Monticello. Three pipes of Termo, vintage 1788, ordered in April, 1793, from John Bulkeley were earmarked for delivery to James Brown in Richmond.[111] In August, when he received word that his order for 540 bottles of 1788 Medoc of the best quality red *vin ordinaire* had arrived in Baltimore, he had it sent to Robert Gamble in Richmond for reshipment to Monticello. He sent a note to Fenwick acknowledging the wine and promising, "I shall trouble you annually."[112]

That same month saw the spread of the yellow fever epidemic in Philadelphia. President and Mrs. Washington were among the first to evacuate Philadelphia. On September 17th Jefferson and his daughter Polly departed. After crossing into Maryland their journey took them over some of the worst roads in the nation. The road from Elkton to Baltimore was so bad that the stage driver called upon the passengers to lean from one side to the other to balance the stage and keep it from turning over from deep ruts and pot-holes.[113]

On January 1, 1794, George Washington acknowledged with "sincere regret" Jefferson's resignation as Secretary of State. Almost fifty-one, after up-close encounters with the snakebites of politics, Jefferson retired happily to Monticello. He said he hated politics and swore his departure from it forever[114] and, on January 5, he was on his way home.[115]

He was to learn that during his long absences Monticello and his other farms had fallen into ruinous conditions. "I find, on a more minute examination of my lands in the short visits heretofore made to them permitted, that a ten year's abandonment of them to the ravages of overseers has brought on them a degree of degradation far beyond what I had expected."[116] But he seemed ready for the challenge, writing John Adams, "I return to farming with an ardor which I scarcely knew in my youth, and which has got the better entirely of my love of study."[117] Maria, who was unmarried, and Martha with her two children and husband joined him. Jefferson turned his attentions to Monticello, making architectural changes that would never end. He was tearing down and rebuilding; reaching for perfection in his home until his death.

He devised a crop-rotation system to restore the land, strung across central and western Virginia, that had been exhausted by soil-depleting crops. It was part of his plan to put his financial affairs in order and Monticello on a paying basis. He hoped that a nailery with John Hemings at the helm would bring in funds to support his plantation standard of living. He also installed Petit in a new role, that of overseer.

But if his lands were depleted, his wine cellar was still adequate. By actual count on May 24, 1794, he noted: "Stacked the following empty bottles. Short English 261 long [bottles] 160. French 670 = 1091. These are besides about 500 full bottles in ye house—509 + 1600." Two months later he received the last of his wines from Philadelphia—46 bottles. Jefferson's care in accounting for empty bottles might seem strange today, but much of the wine he imported arrived in casks and was later bottled. Since bottles were an additional item of expense, they were retained and reused.

After being home just more than a month Jefferson entered in his memorandum book, "The 1st one case of Claret of 36 bottles is finished this day. It has lasted 30 days exactly, there being no other wine in use at the same time." Jefferson and his family obviously enjoyed this claret because with help from a neighbor, B. Calvert, they consumed an additional 108 bottles over the next three months.[118]

His retirement years from 1794 to 1797 saw little in the way of new wines or travel. In November he paid $73.14 to Philip Wyckin & Co. for freight and duty for a pipe of "good dry Sherry, ready for drinking" that he had sampled at the residence of the Spanish agents in Philadelphia and had ordered through Joseph Yznardy in September of the previous year.[119] He continued to import Spanish wines through Yznardy for many years. The following spring he again paid for a pipe and a keg of wine from Yznardy and, in a letter to Philip Mazzei, almost as an aside, he mentions "were a ship coming from Leghorn direct to Richmond and the captain would bring, as a venture of his own, some good Vendi wine,... I should always like it."[120] Jefferson's "vendi" was probably Verdea, a white wine with a green tinge produced in the vicinity of Florence.[121]

Despite his protestations of happiness this was the most boring period of his life. In a letter to his daughter Maria, in whom he detected a willingness to withdraw from society, he confessed: "From 1793 to 1797 I remained closely at home, saw none but those who came there, and at length became very sensible to the ill effect it had upon my mind, and of its direct and irresistible tendency to render me unfit for society and uneasy when necessarily engaged in it. I felt enough of the effect of withdrawing from the world then, to see that it led to an anti-social and misanthropic state of mind, which severely punishes him who gives in to it; and it will be a lesson I shall never forget."[122]

Although he told Madison that his youthful "spice of ambition" was gone, letters were coming up the mountaintop filled with politics and requests for advice. When Washington refused a third term and Jefferson's political party voted him their support for president, he acquiesced and became the standard-bearer for the Republican (now the Democratic) party. Elections were not then decided by popular vote, but by the number of Congressional votes. When Adams received the majority (71 votes to Jefferson's 68), he became president, and Jefferson, although not his political ally, became vice-president.[123]

Ignored by Adams, Jefferson presided over the Senate and spent the remainder of his time on private interests, such as American Philosophical Society activities (he had been appointed President of the Society the day before his inauguration as vice-president), or at Monticello.[124] He and Adams had their political differences, and Jefferson viewed Adams as the aristocratic personification of the Federalist party he had grown to abhor.

Congress adjourned for the summer recess in 1797, and Jefferson left for Monticello where he could "exchange the roar and tumult of bulls and bears, for the prattle of my grand-children and senile rest." He also looked forward to the marriage of Polly to her cousin John Wayles Eppes. They were married at Monticello on October 13, 1797.

When Jefferson was two years into his vice presidency, a young Swiss citizen, John James Dufour, visited Monticello. The 33-year-old Dufour had come to America from Switzerland in 1796 to grow grapes and make wine. Before starting his vineyard efforts, Dufour did an inspection tour of all the known vineyards in what then constituted the United States. Having heard of Jefferson's efforts to grow grapes, Dufour naturally traveled to Monticello to inspect the vineyards firsthand. He found that the vineyards "had been abandoned, or left without any care for three or four years before which proved, evidently, that it had not been profitable."[125]

After serving four years as vice-president, an office he found "honorable and easy," this time Jefferson accepted his party's nomination with alacrity. Unlike today's politicians, Jefferson did not take to the hustings but remained at Monticello until the end of November, 1800, when he returned to Washington (the new Capital since June) and awaited the election results. Adams' sixty-five votes were not enough, and his hope for a second term was defeated. Jefferson and Aaron Burr tied with seventy-three votes each. After thirty-six ballots the House of Representatives voted in favor of Jefferson. Looking back on the political events that took place in 1800, the author of the Declaration of Independence saw it "as real a revolution in the principles of our government as that of 1776 was in its form."[126]

CHAPTER FIFTEEN

Wines in the White House

The roads leading to the raw, new capital were dirt when Thomas Jefferson became President in 1801. When it rained the dirt became rivulets, melding into the mud-colored landscape lined by a few taverns with impossibly wretched accommodations. There were no hotels, restaurants or coffee houses. No sidewalks or lamps interrupted the darkness along the few roads in the Federal City.

The Federal City, a noble concept on paper, was in reality a cluster of about 15 boarding houses grouped around the still-unfinished Capitol building and encircled by a forest. The boarding houses had as their residents a transient society, for virtually none of the members of Congress had built homes in Washington or brought their wives with them. They spent only the winter months there when Congress was in session. Houses were so isolated that numbers were not necessary; instead, they were identified as "near the President's house, west of the War Office, opposite the Treasury or whatever."

For public entertainment the residents had their choice of a race track[1] or a theatre that was "astonishingly dirty and void of decoration." "One must love the drama very much to consent to pass three hours amidst tobacco smoke, whiskey breaths and other stenches mixed up with effluvia of stables," wrote one resident, "and miasmas of the canal, which the theatre is exactly placed and constructed to receive." Gouverneur Morris may have described the city best when he wrote, in 1803, "All we lack here are good houses, wine cellars, decent food, learned men, attractive women and other such trifles to make our city perfect . . . it is the best city to live in—in the future."[2]

Jefferson arrived in the new capital on November 27, 1800, while vice president and took rooms at Conrad and McMunn's boarding house on the south side of Capitol Hill. Jefferson's only concession to rank at Conrad's was that his bedroom had a separate drawing-room for visitors, but he dined with his fellow boarders at a common table that seated about thirty.[3]

Most accounts of Jefferson's inauguration, on March 1, 1801, have the president-elect walking from Conrad and McMunn's to the still unfinished Capitol, reading his inaugural address in the crowded Senate Chamber and returning to his boarding house on foot. One eyewitness, however, remembers Jefferson riding on horseback from Conrad and McMunn's "without a single guard or even a servant in his train, dismounted without assistance, and hitched the bridle of his horse to the palisades."[4]

On returning to Conrad's the new President took his usual place at the far end of the table and dined on boarding house fare.[5] This first presidential dinner was in sharp contrast to the White House dinners that he would host during the next eight years for congressmen, diplomats, scientists, and friends.[6]

Shortly after his inauguration he received a letter of congratulations from Peter Legaux, the French immigrant who was growing grapes and making wines in his vineyard at Spring Mills, 13 miles northwest of Philadelphia. Legaux, who had formed the Pennsylvania Vine Company, offered to send Jefferson thousands of vines from his nursery for planting in Virginia. In a follow-up letter Legaux invited the President to become a subscriber, and although Jefferson's name does not appear on Legaux's subscription list, the names of Alexander Hamilton, Aaron Burr, Benjamin Rush, and Citizen Genet[7] do. Three weeks after his inauguration the new President wrote to Legaux thanking him for the offer of the vines but noting "it is too late this season but will want them for next." A year later, Jefferson had Anthony Giannini plant in his southwest vineyard grapevines sent to him by Legaux.[8]

Legaux claimed that his vineyard contained "... from France 300 plants from three kinds of grapes in the highest estimation, of which are made Burgundy, Champagne and the Bordeaux wines." Legaux is credited with popularizing a grape he said was from the Cape of Good Hope, but which was later determined to be the native Alexander grape. Whether Legaux deliberately promoted and sold under the name of Cape vines the native Alexander grape is not known, but when confronted with evidence that his Cape grape was the Alexander, he insisted that he had obtained it from the Cape of Good Hope. Perhaps because of its mislabeled origin the Cape, or Alexander grape became popular and was planted throughout the United States. It did poorly in New England and New York but seemed to thrive in the west (now the mid-west) especially around Cincinnati, Ohio.[9] Speaking about the Alexander grape eight years later, Jefferson suggested to John Adlum that "it will be well to push the culture of that grape without losing time and effort in search of foreign vines, which it will take centuries to adapt to our soil and climate." Although Jefferson pronounced Adlum's version "worthy of the best vineyards of France"—perhaps to encourage Adlum—the Alexander grape was known to have a pronounced foxy flavor and is no longer grown commercially.[10]

The camping-out quality of the makeshift Federal City was reinforced by the President's House, an unlikely predecessor to today's White House with its manicured hedges, rose gardens and lawns. Although over $300,000 had been spent, the structure was unfinished not only in frame but in furnishings. Abigail Adams, who endured eight months there, remembers "bells wanting, fires wanting, not a single

Wines in the White House

The President's House

apartment finished. The half-finished audience room was used as a drying room in which to hang up clothes." Irish architect James Hoban, who designed the President's House, complained that the workmen had left out the upper story and had not "built cellars which President Jefferson, after experiencing great losses in wines, had been obliged to add at a depth of sixteen feet under ground. These are so cold that the thermometer stood two degrees lower in them than it did in a vacant spot in the icehouse early in July, when in the shade out of doors it was ninety-six."[11]

The bachelor President accepted the social leadership expected of him, turning his home into the most interesting social center in the city. With the help of Philipe Letombe, the French envoy in Philadelphia, Jefferson assembled a staff of eight with the most important slots going to two Frenchmen. To administer the White House, Jefferson hired Etienne Lemaire, and as his chef 42 year old Honore Julien.[12] The pomp that had been associated with the levees of Presidents Washington and Adams came to an end.[13] "You drink as you please," one Senator described a Jefferson evening, "and converse at your ease." Or as Jefferson put it, "The principle with us, as well as our political constitution is the equal rights of all, and if there be an occasion where this equality ought to prevail preeminently, it is in social circles collected for conviviality. Nobody shall be above you, nor you above anybody, pele mele is our law." His open-handed hospitality encompassed political friend and enemy. The two political parties were not mixed but entertained separately.

The Georgetown market stalls, with produce picked only hours before, were shopped daily for meats, eggs and vegetables including lettuce, asparagus, peas, tomatoes, squash, eggplant, shad, sturgeon, rockfish, oysters, wild game, venison, duck, pigeon, squirrel, poultry, and a variety of fruits, including local currants, strawberries and watermelons.[14] When Monticello's overseer, Edmund Bacon, visited the White House, he shopped with Lemaire. Bacon recalls the social demands of the presidency: "Mr. Jefferson often told me that the office of vice-president was

Passions

far preferable to that of president. He was perfectly tired out with company. He had a very long dining-room, and his table was chock-full every one of the sixteen days I was there. There were congressmen, foreigners, and all sorts of people, to dine with him. He dined at four o'clock, and they generally sat and talked until night. It used to worry me to sit so long; and I finally quit when I got through eating, and went off and left them. The first thing in the morning there was to go to market. Mr. Jefferson's steward was a very smart man, well educated, and as much of a gentleman in his appearance as any man. His carriage-driver would get out the wagon early in the morning, and Lemaire would go with him to Georgetown to market...."[15]

By the time the members of the Seventh Congress arrived in Washington, invitations for dinner written by the President were waiting. When Federalist Senator William Plumer received his first dinner invitation he was struck by the fact that "his favor" was "requested" by Thomas Jefferson and not the President of the United States. "Having a curiosity to know what induced Mr. Jefferson to adopt such a form," Plumer asked Jefferson's friend, Senator Giles the reason. The ever blunt Giles told him "that the President meant it should be considered more as the invitation of a private gentleman, than that of President. For if he invited as President he must take the list and invite all the members of the Houses of Congress ... But his present mode will not oblige him, either to invite gentleman of different politics at the same table; or to invite at any time those members who for the hour together abuse him in speeches in Congress, as some gentlemen do."[16]

Dinners were lavish and prepared by Chef Julien on a large coal-burning stove in the basement below the north entrance hall.[17] Diplomats and politicians, hungry for presidential favors, were treated at the President's House to menus that included "rice, soup, round of beef, turkey, mutton, ham, loin of veal, cutlets of mutton, fried eggs, fried beef, a pie called macaroni which appeared to be a rich brown

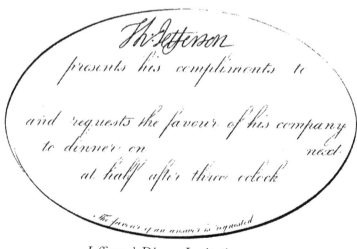

Jefferson's Dinner Invitation

crust . . . a great variety of fruit, plenty of wines and good," according to Federalist Senator Cutler.[18]

Jefferson's White House had two dining rooms, one large and one smaller. The formal dining room on the northwest corner (now the private dining room) was used sparingly for more elaborate functions, and probably when ladies dined at the White House. It had a dumbwaiter built into the doorway that rotated into a service area near the basement stairs where the food was brought up. Jefferson had a similar arrangement for food service at Monticello.[19]

Jefferson's favorite place for dining was the smaller room, today's Green Room. Dinners here were usually stag, and to eliminate any perception of rank, Jefferson used an oval dining table that seated twelve. Dinner began at four and, in the colonial tradition, beer, porter or cider were served during the meal. Jefferson, who was obsessed with privacy, had the dining room equipped with a number of tiered dumbwaiters shaped like vertical lazy susans from which guests served themselves when not actually served by the President himself. "You see we are alone," he would announce, "and our walls have no ears."[20] When the cloth was removed after dinner, wine was served, accompanied by dried fruits, nuts and confections.

Dinner conversations almost always centered around Jefferson's passions: gardening, architecture, wine and his years in France. He loved to reminisce about his time in France and the men and women who had effected historical events. He was fond of telling about the contrasting personalities of Necker and Mirabeau, two of the most important personalities in France. Necker, Jefferson recalled, started the evening in high spirits but faded after nine o'clock. Mirabeau, however, started out brooding until the wine "warmed him into life." For an hour or two he became the life of the party, pouring out gossip, poetry, and anecdotes, but as the night passed on and the wine "heated him," his eyes became dilated, his voice choked, and with his black hair shaking wildly about his face, he would burst into political prophecies. In a more sober moment, Mirabeau suggested to Jefferson that if France was to become another America, France would need another Washington, to which Jefferson replied: "Pardon me, Count, but I consider such is the striking originality of your character, you would deign to imitate any man."[21] Jefferson also told the story of Marie Antoinette's wondering how it was possible for the people of America to be happy without a court. "Surely," she said to Jefferson, "your great deliverer [George Washington] intends to create nobility?" To which Jefferson remembers replying, "Your Majesty, the influence of your own is so powerful that it is the general impression that we can do without them."[22]

In one period of less than four months, 207 bottles of Champagne were served to 651 dinner guests. Jefferson calculated this was "a bottle to $3^1/_7$ persons hence the annual stock necessary may be calculated at four hundred and fifteen bottles a year or, say, five hundred." This Champagne consumption was a mere smidgen of the wines available and served to Jefferson's guests during this period. The President's wine cellar was bulging with barrels of Brazilian Madeira, Pedro Ximenes, sweet and dry Pacharetti, Tent, and bottles of claret and Sauternes. The influence of wine on the dinner conversation is attested to by Senator Plumer who noted in his diary: "My usual course, when invited to dine with him, is to converse very little with him, except on the weather and such common topics, until I come to the dining table, nor even then until after the more substantial dishes are disposed of—and we have drank a glass or two. I do *not* mean, that the President is under the influence of wine for he is very *temperate*. But as I am generally placed next to him—and at that time the company is generally engaged in little parties eagerly talking-and thereby gives him and me more freedom in conversation—and even two glasses of wine oft times renders a temperate man communicate."[23]

In a community starved for social amenities the President's dinners took preference over everything. Jefferson, who seldom dined alone, discovered that fine wines and food were a great way to meet informally with his political friends and foes, never talking politics, but dropping a hint here and there of how he felt on a subject. And he used these almost nightly dinners as a form of legislative lobbying. He did not mix Republicans and Federalists, and he thought out his guest lists so thoroughly that politicians from his own party came from different boarding houses while Federalists were invited by boarding house bloc. The political effect of the dinners is perhaps best summed up by Vermont Federalist Senator Stephen Bradley who snapped over an unpopular executive appointment and the lack of Senatorial opposition, "The President's dinners have silenced them."[24] It would have been less expensive to lobby for votes. The presidential annual salary of $25,000[25] was generous and covered his expenses, but made no contribution toward his retirement. An egalitarian in public life, in private he spared no expenses for pleasure. Food totalled over $6,000 one year; wine $7,597 the first term; less the second term with his stock well in hand. Household and entertainment funds did not come out of the public coffers as they do today but from Jefferson's pocket. His expenditures for food and wine ran a footrace with his income. Income usually lost.

His account books reveal purchases during his eight years as President of over 20,000 bottles of wine from European countries.[26] From Bordeaux he served Rausan Margaux, now Château Rausan-Segla; Châteaux d'Yquem and Filhot; Chambertin from Burgundy; white Hermitage from the Rhone; and Champagne.

Chambertin was the only red Burgundy wine that appeared during his presidential years. The lack of Burgundy wines in the presidential cellars had nothing to do with his tastes or preferences, but was based upon his experience of the high risk of their being spoiled in transportation. "The wines of Burgundy would be very desirable and there are three kinds, Chambertin, Voujeau & Veaune, & one of their wines, Montrachet which, under favorable circumstances, will bear transportation, but always with risk of being spoiled on the way, to either great heat or cold, as I have known by experience since I returned to America. Unless the Champagnes have risen in price more than I am informed, there may be something left of my bill, which I should like to receive in Chambertin & Montrachet in equal & even so

English wine bottle *Burgundy wine bottle* *Bordeaux wine bottle*

small quantities, if you can take the trouble of getting it for me, merely as an experiment. If it succeeds I may ask a quantity the next year. It should leave its cellars in Chambertin & Montrachet about the beginning of October & come through without delay at either Paris or Havre. There was living at Beaune, near Chambertin & Montrachet, a tonnelier named Parent, who being a taster & bottler of wines by trade, was my conductor through the vineyards & cellars of the Cote, & ever after my wine-broker & correspondent. If living, he will execute for me faithfully any order you may be so good as to send him. The only wines of first quality made at Montrachet were in the vineyards of M. de Chermont, & of the Marquis de Sarsnet of Dijon."[27]

The lesser wines of southern France were not ignored: red wine from the vineyards of Bellet near Nice, St. George d'Orgues from Languedoc and Cahuzac from Galliac. St. George d'Orgues, a quality red wine was and is produced north of Montpelier near the Mediterranean coast. The vineyards of about 1,480 acres produced a quality wine that ages well but is rarely seen in the United States today.

While President, Jefferson developed a strong preference for dry sherry. During his first term he purchased large amounts of Spanish wines, through Yznardi, the American Consul in Cadiz, including dry and sweet Paxarete [Pacharetti], Pedro Ximenes, Malaga, Tent, and three pipes of old (10 to 15 years) dry, pale sherry which "has most particularly attached my taste to it. I now drink nothing else, and am apprehensive that if I should fail in the means of getting it, it will be a privation which I shall feel sensibly once a day." Wanting to know the source of this dry sherry, he asked Yznardi to send him the name of the vineyard owner "where the best crop is made so that I may have it purchased directly on the spot where its quality is sure."[28] His taste in Spanish wines ran from Malaga and Pedro Ximenes, both sweet, to pale and dry sherries and dry and sweet Paxarete. Paxarete, was made at an ancient monastery about fifteen miles from Jerez of three-quarter Pedro Ximenes grapes. Jefferson also tried a red, sweet wine called Tinto di Rota, which was known in England as Tent, and was made near the village of Rota north of Cadiz.

Jefferson's first exposure to Italian wines had been during his trip into northern Italy in 1787, and he was particularly impressed with those made from the Nebbiolo grape. He served 250 bottles of Nebbiolo while President, but his favorite Italian wine was Montepulciano from the hilltop town of Montepulciano located about 40 miles south of Siena in southern Tuscany. He also brought in small amounts of wines produced around Florence: Chianti, Aleatico, Artimino, Santo and Lacryma Christi, a highly regarded red wine from vineyards south of Naples.

In the 18th century Portugal exported large quantities of wines produced around Lisbon. Jefferson's favorites were Carcavelos, from vineyards near the village of Oeiras east of Lisbon, and a light country wine called Termo from the province of Estremadura. He was familiar with Bucelas, a sweet wine from vineyards northeast of Lisbon, which was often "sophisticated" and spoiled by the addition of brandy.

Other purchases included Port and large amounts of wines called generically "dry Lisbon" and "Lisbon Malmsey," Marsala (sweet), Syracuse from Sicily and Hungarian Tokay.[29] During his eight years as President he imported eight pipes (about 4,400 bottles) of "Brazil Madeira." Brazil Madeira was a quality wine from the Island of Madeira and at $350 per pipe, it was expensive when compared to a pipe of sherry for $195. The term Brazil Madeira probably got its name from the wooden casks or barrels in which it was aged. Brazilian Satinwood and Baltic oak were the two principal woods used for aging better quality Madeiras.[30]

Senator Plumer, in spite of his politics, was obviously one of Jefferson's favorites and was often invited to dinner. On one occasion he described the dinner as "elegant and rich-his wines very good, there were eight different kinds" including a rich Hungarian wine and a still richer Tokay. At another presidential dinner Plumer noted that after a couple of glasses of wine, Jefferson told him that he was astonished at the extent of "the falsehood and licentiousness of the press ... and he *darkly* intimated that some restraint ought to be by law imposed upon them."[31] Plumer replied that he thought it impossible to pass a law that effectively restrained licentiousness and at the same time did not impair constitutional freedoms and Jefferson agreed. During their conversations Plumer noticed that Jefferson bent his head to hear, and several times asked Plumer to repeat what he had said, leading Plumer to conclude that, at age sixty, Jefferson was becoming hard of hearing. As for his wines, except for the Madeira and Hermitage, Plumer, on this occasion, thought them "not good," which may be more a reflection of Plumer's palate than Jefferson's wines.[32]

At a dinner in the fall of 1804, Senator John Quincy Adams and ten other guests heard Jefferson express annoyance with the new French Minister who presented himself dressed in too much gold lace. Jefferson also admitted his disappointment on how the French Revolution had turned out, calling it a shipwreck. He held forth on the necessity of French and Spanish being a requisite in every young man's education, telling John Quincy that Spanish was so easy that "he had learned it, with the help of a Don Quixote . . . and a grammar, in the course of a passage to Europe, on which he was but nineteen days at sea." To which John Quincy skeptically noted in his diary, "But Mr. Jefferson tells large stories." At dinner Jefferson told how the famous wine merchant, Bergasse of Marseilles, could so perfectly imitate the taste of any kind wine by blending a variety of wines that even the most experienced wine connoisseur could not tell the difference.[33] Years later Jefferson was to learn from his friend Stephen Cathalan that Bergasse's wine prices in combination with the high price of bread, beef and mutton, caused the populace of Marseilles to riot on April 23, 1789, and threaten to destroy his wine cellars. Cathalan called this riot "the first spark which set on fire the revolution all over France."[34]

During his presidency Jefferson took two vacations a year to Monticello, a short one in early spring and, because of the capital's stifling heat and humidity, a longer one in late July or early August that normally extended through September. Before leaving for his summer vacation in 1803 a note from his daughter Martha at Monticello reminded him that "when you send the groceries on, will you remember glasses, tumblers and wine glasses both are much wanting here."[35]

During one such vacation, James Madison and his wife Dolly, and Anna Thornton, the wife of William Thornton,[36] and her mother, arrived at Monticello during a thunderstorm. When they entered the house, Mrs. Thornton was appalled by its dilapidated condition. The reception hall was unfinished with "loose plank forming the floor," and when they went to bed, they had to mount "a little ladder of a staircase about two feet wide and very steep, into rooms of the beds fixed up in recesses in the walls."[37] When Jefferson explained that he intended to complete the construction of Monticello by the next summer, Mrs. Thornton harbored her doubts observing that "he is altered his plans so frequently, pulled down and rebuilt, that in many parts without side it looks like a house going to decay from the length of time it has been erected."[38]

The next morning at breakfast guests were served tea, coffee, muffins, hot wheat, cornbread and ham.[39] Jefferson's routine after breakfast was to retire to his chambers. Guests were left to their own devices, reading, walking, riding, or resting.

Dinner was served at four and to ensure his guests privacy he employed two kinds of "silent butlers." He devised a system of revolving shelves on which foods were placed from outside the room and when ready for service rotated into the dining room. His wines were carried directly from the wine cellar to the dining room via dumbwaiters located on each side of the fireplace. At dinner that evening Mrs. Thornton met William Short "lately from France." She noted that no wine was served until the cloth was removed, meaning until after dinner.

Short had returned to America in 1802, set up residence in Philadelphia and became wealthy as a land speculator. Jefferson and Short's friendship continued. On another occasion Jefferson invited Short to Washington to learn firsthand "an intimate knowledge of our political machine" and to the White House to "take your soup with us everyday, when not otherwise engaged."[40]

William Short

As Jefferson approached the end of his first term as President, Augustus Foster, Secretary of the British Legation, described him as "a tall man, with a very red freckled face, and gray neglected hair; his manners good-natured, frank, and rather friendly, though he had somewhat of a cynical expression of countenance. He wore a blue coat, a thick gray-colored hairy waistcoat, with a red under-waistcoat lapped over it, green velveteen breeches with pearl buttons, yarn stockings, and slippered down at the heels,—his appearance being very much like that of a tall, large-boned farmer." But his farmer's attire was not his only style of dress as Senator Plumer noted in his diary after attending a presidential dinner. "He was well dressed—A new suit of black-silk hose-shoes-clean linnen, & his hair highly powdered. His dinner was elegant & rich—his wines very good—there were eight different kinds of which there were rich Hungary, & still richer Tokay."

Toward the end of his presidency Jefferson became convinced that 'We could in the United States, make as great a variety of wines as are made in Europe, not exactly of the same kinds, but doubtless as good. Yet I have ever observed to my countrymen, who think its introduction important, that a laborer cultivating wheat, rice, tobacco, or cotton here, will be able with the proceeds, to purchase double the quantity of the wine he could make.... In general, it is a truth that if every nation will employ itself in what it is fittest to produce, a greater quantity will be raised of the things contributing to human happiness, than if every nation attempts to raise everything it wants within itself."[41]

To encourage the drinking of foreign wines, Jefferson assigned his Secretary of Treasury, Albert Gallatin, the project of developing a more equal tariff on wines. "I am persuaded, that were the duty on the cheap wines put on the same ratio with the dear, it would wonderfully enlarge the field of those who use wine, to the expulsion of whiskey. The introduction of very cheap wine (St. George) into my neighborhood, within two years past, has quadrupled in that time the number of those who keep wine, and will ere long increase them tenfold. This would be a great gain to the treasury, and to the sobriety of our country. I will here add my tariff, wherein you will be able to choose any rate of duty you please, and to decide whether it will not, on a fit occasion, be proper for legislative attention."[42]

Jefferson at the start of his second term as President

The St. George d'Orgues wine to which Jefferson referred came from vineyards near the city of Montpelier in southern France. Two years after his retirement Jefferson bypassed his friend Stephen Cathalan in Marseilles and wrote directly to a Peter Walsh in Cette advising that he had received "some St. George wine which was much approved. The object of the present letter is to ask the favor of you to send me annually a supply of a pipe (about 120 gallons) of the same quality." Although Jefferson's letter was delivered to Walsh by the American Counsel General to Paris, there is no evidence that he was successful in receiving a yearly pipe.[43]

While Minister to France, Jefferson had become friendly with the Duchess of Rochefoucauld and her liberal and popular son, the Duke of Rochefoucauld. The family was enormously wealthy and owned a number of substantial properties throughout France. In April of 1806 Jefferson wrote William Lee, American

Counsel in Bordeaux, "I hear you've received Hermitage from Cathalan and Cahuzac from Madame de la Rochefoucauld's *homme d'affaires.*" Jefferson placed an order for a cask of Rochefoucauld's dry red Cahuzac, and went on to explain: "I became familiaat the Duchess d'Anville's, during her life, to whom the estate of Cahuzac belonged, with the wines of that name, both *doux* and *see,* made on her estate. The latter is what I admire extremely. The sweet is not to our taste."[44] When the wine arrived a year later it had turned to vinegar and Jefferson was nonplused as to why, because he knew "the superior excellence of Cahuzac see, and that it is a wine of as much body as those of Lisbon, and *Château de la Rochefoucauld* will consequently bear transportation."[45]

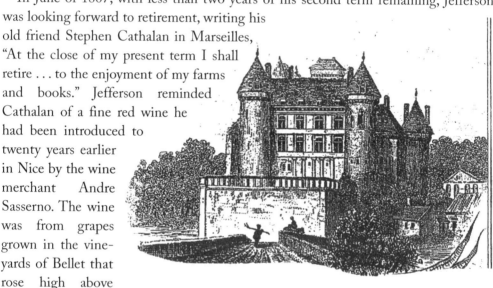

In June of 1807, with less than two years of his second term remaining, Jefferson was looking forward to retirement, writing his old friend Stephen Cathalan in Marseilles, "At the close of my present term I shall retire ... to the enjoyment of my farms and books." Jefferson reminded Cathalan of a fine red wine he had been introduced to twenty years earlier in Nice by the wine merchant Andre Sasserno. The wine was from grapes grown in the vineyards of Bellet that rose high above Nice and faced the Mediterranean. Jefferson asked Cathalan to try to get him a hundred bottles of Sasserno's wine if still available.[46] Three weeks later Jefferson again wrote Cathalan complaining that the white Hermitage which had just arrived from his favorite vintner, Jourdan, was "dry and hard." Still, he ordered another hundred bottles, but only if it is like the last two shipments, "soft or silky."[47]

Within four months Cathalan reported that he had purchased a hundred bottles of Jourdan's white Hermitage "to the exact quality you like." As for Sasserno, he was alive and flattered that Jefferson remembered his wines and was delighted to fill Jefferson's order for a hundred bottles of "that same quality."[48]

As his second term as President drew to an end, and his decision not to seek another term became known, he felt "with infinite grief a contest arising between" his two best friends, Madison and Monroe. To Monroe he wrote, "I have ever viewed Mr. Madison and yourself as two principal pillars of my happiness and were either to be withdrawn, I should consider it among the greatest calamities which could assail my further peace of mind. I have great confidence that the candor of high understanding of both will guard me against this misfortune, the bare possibility of which has so far weighed on my mind that I could not be easy without unburdening it."[49] Fortunately, their political ambitions were accommodated with Madison succeeding Jefferson as President and Monroe serving as Madison's Secretary of State. Eight years later Monroe became America's fifth President.

CHAPTER SIXTEEN

The Vintage Years

Jefferson left the presidency with a feeling of profound relief. "Never did a prisoner, released from his chains, feel such relief as I shall on shaking off the shackles of power. Nature intended me for the tranquil pursuits of science, by rendering them my supreme delight."[1] He was free to return to Monticello where he could indulge without interruption his interests in family, farming, books, gardening, architecture, and wine.

Retirement from the presidency marked the end of Jefferson's political career and resulted in a substantial reduction in income, mainly the loss of his $25,000-a-year presidential salary. His way of life changed. Instead of the hectic pace of "turning the

Monticello

White House into a general tavern" with nightly entertainment, his daily routine found him "in the bosom of my family and surrounded by my books, I enjoy a repose to which I have been long a stranger. My mornings are devoted to correspondence. From breakfast to dinner, I am in my shops, my garden, or on horseback among my farms; from dinner to dark, I give to society and recreation with my neighbors and friends; and from candle light to early bedtime, I read. My health is perfect; and my strength considerably re-enforced by the activity of the course I pursue. Perhaps it is as great as usually falls to the lot of near sixty-seven years of age. I talk of plows and harrows, of seeding and harvesting, with my neighbors, and of politics, too, if they choose, with as little reserve as the rest of my fellow citizens, and feel at length the blessing of being free to say and do what I please, without being responsible for it to any mortal."[2]

In his parlor Jefferson surrounded himself with portraits of the men he most admired in history and in his own life. His "trinity of the three greatest" men, Newton, Bacon and Locke, shared wallspace with Columbus, Sir Walter Raleigh, Americo Vespucci, his fellow ministers John Adams and Benjamin Franklin, and, of course, Washington and Lafayette, as well as busts of Washington, Franklin and Lafayette.[3]

Without his presidential salary, Jefferson knew that he could not maintain his White House staff in retirement. Two of his slaves, Edy and Fanny, had trained under Chef Julian, and in an attempt to maintain the presidential culinary standards in retirement, he had Julian visit Monticello in 1809 to organize his kitchen and give cooking instructions. Apparently his attempts to replicate French cooking, without a

Parlor

French chef, fell short of his hopes for he later wrote, "I envy M. Chaumont nothing but his French cook and cuisine. These are luxuries which can neither be forgotten or possessed in our country."[4]

Dinner was served at about four o'clock "in half Virginian, half French style, in good taste and abundance." At the mahogany table in the dining room wine was sent up by a double dumb-waiter located on each side of the fireplace. The dinner beverages were beer and cider. Wine was not served until after dinner or when "the cloth was removed." One guest remembered sitting until near sundown at the table, where the dessert was succeeded by "agreeable and instructive conversation in which everyone seemed to wish and expect Mr. J. to take the chief part." According to Daniel Webster, Jefferson was an easy conversationalist who regaled his dinner guests with "early anecdotes of revolutionary times; French society, politics . . . and general literature; and the Virginia university. On these general topics he has much to say, and he

Monticello Dining Room

says it all well." Webster also observed that Jefferson had "a strong preference for the wines of the continent."[5]

Six months into his retirement, one visitor reported that instead of a costly variety of French and Italian wines, Jefferson served "Madeira and a sweet ladies' wine" and noted that Jefferson "seems to relish his wine the better for being accompanied with conversation and during the four days I spent there these were the most social hours."[6] His wine tastes were changing with the world around him. Monticello's troubled economy was a factor in Jefferson's shift to lesser-known wines particularly from southern France. His obvious favorites were from Languedoc in southern France: Claret de Bergasse, Limoux, Ledenon and Muscat de Rivesaltes. Jefferson cut back on the quality of his wines—but not on quantity—and his dinner guests continued to eat heartily—duck, oysters, cheese, lamb, beef, turkey, chicken and herring were standard dinner foods.[7]

Jefferson's Claret de Bergasse was not from the Bordeaux area. In 1787 when he toured the French vineyards, he visited Monsieur de Bergasse in Marseilles who had a wine cellar containing in cask the equivalent of over 1,500,000 bottles of wine. Jefferson was fond of telling how Bergasse could duplicate the taste of any wine by blending the wines of Languedoc, an art that was now continued by Bergasse's son. Jefferson called Bergasse's wines perfect imitations and not containing a "drop of anything but the pure juice of the grape."[8]

The wines of Limoux were and are produced from vineyards around the town of that name located 17 miles from Carcassonne. Jefferson became acquainted with them when he traveled through Languedoc along the Canal-Du-Midi. The wine for which Limoux was best known was Blanquette de Limoux. Its name came from the grape from which it was made. Vizetelly described it as a pale, sweet white sparkling wine which lost its sweetness with age and became dry and spirituous. At its best, he said, it might rank with sparkling St. Peray but never with Champagne.[9] Jefferson, not a fan of sparkling wines, ordered his Limoux *non-mousseaux*.[10]

Jefferson's "Ledanon" came from the vineyards of Ledenon near Nimes. He first drank this red wine at Stephen Cathalan's house in Marseilles in 1787.[11] A description of Ledenon cannot be found in current wine books, but it had the reputation of producing the best red wine of the area with a bouquet and taste that pleased the palates of "the first rank in France." Jullien places the Ledenon vineyards in the immediate area of Lirac, St. Genies-de-Comolas, and St. Laurent-des-Arbes and described it as having "a good color, body, spirit, and flavor." Henderson said its red wines were "deservedly esteemed for their delicate flavor and aroma. They vary somewhat in color; but the best of them ... have a bright rose tint."[12] To Jefferson's practiced palate, it had "something of the port character but higher flavored, more delicate, less rough ..."[13]

In a letter to President James Monroe, he recommended "Vin de Roussillon. The best is that of Rivesalte."[14] Jefferson's travels did not take him into Roussillon, but he had seen its rugged mountains in the distance and he remembered its taste. During his retirement years, Muscat de Rivesaltes, large quantities of which he purchased in casks, became his favorite sweet white wine.[15] Its sweetness was achieved by placing the gathered grapes in containers which were exposed to the sun, causing the water to evaporate and concentrate the sugar. When the grapes became almost raisin-like, they were pressed. He compared it in style with dry Paxarete and dry Madeira and said he "used to meet with it at the best tables of Paris, where it was drunk after the repast, as a vin de liqueur. It was a little higher colored than Madeira, near as strong and dry, and of fine flavor. I am not certain of the particular name, but that of Rivesalte runs in my head."[16] The vineyards of Roussillon still produce a variety of wines, white, red and rose—some dry and some sweet, and those of Muscat de Rivesaltes, Cote du Roussillon and Cote du Roussillon-Villages carry AOC designation.

His neighbors and friends thought so highly of his wines, and the reasonableness of the prices, that they were thinking of forming a company with an agent in Richmond to import them once a year. Occasionally he ordered white Hermitage which he referred to as a *bonne bouche* [good taste]. White Hermitage from the vineyards of M. Jourdan, which he considered one of the best wines of France, had on his palate a *un peu de la liqueur*, "silky, soft, smooth in contradistinction to the dry, hard or rough ... barely a little sweetish, so as to be sensible and no more, and this is exactly the quality I esteem."[17]

Jefferson's annual wine order through Stephen Cathalan in Marseilles was for about 600 bottles divided among Bergasse's claret, Ledenon, Limoux, Roussillon and Bellet.[18] Sometimes his household wine consumption outpaced his orders and reorders were necessary. In January, 1818, he wrote Cathalan: "I find from the consumption of the stock sent in 1816 that that asked in 1817 will not carry me thro' the present year. I must therefore request you to send me without delay, say by the 1st vessel bound to the Chesapeake ... 200 bottles of the Vin rouge de M. Bergasse of the Bordeaux quality."[19]

On one occasion Jefferson learned "with much mortification (of the palate at least)" that his annual wine order had gone astray,[20] but when it arrived he assured Cathalan that all of the wines were good, with the wines from Nice, Ledenon, and Roussillon "particularly esteemed."

Jefferson's tastes in wines were Gallic, but his spirit was American, interested in new horizons, experiences and wines. While President, he became acquainted with John Adlum, who has been called the "Father of American Viticulture" for his early efforts with grape cultivation and wine-making. It was a career arrived at after serving in the Revolutionary War, being wounded, captured and released, followed by years as a successful surveyor. At the age of 40, Adlum took a totally different tack and began experimenting with winemaking. His vineyards began their existence in the less than ideal soil of Wilton Farm near Havre de Grace, Maryland.[21] Later he moved his viticultural efforts to Georgetown and purchased 200 acres.

Jefferson came to know Adlum when "a member of Congress from your state (I do not recollect which) presented me two bottles of wine made by you, one of which, of

Madeira colour... the other, a dark red wine was made from a wild or native grape, called in Maryland the Fox grape, but was very different from what is called by that name in Virginia. This was a very fine wine, & so exactly resembling the red Burgundy of Chambertin (one of the best crops) that on fair comparison with that, of which I had very good on the same table imported by myself from the place where made, the company could not distinguish the one from the other. I think it would be well to push the culture of that grape without losing time & efforts in search of foreign vines, which it will take centuries to adapt to our soil & climate. The object of the present letter is so far to trespass on your kindness, & your disposition to promote a culture so useful, as to request you, at the proper season to send me some cuttings of that vine. They should be taken off in February with 5 buds to each cutting, and if done up first in strong linen & then covered with paper & addressed to me at Monticello near Milton, after committed to the post, they will come safely & so speedily as to render their success probable."[22]

Adlum explained that the Madeira-like wine had been made entirely from currants and not grapes, and that when other good judges of wine had tasted it they too thought it had a Madeira-like quality. When, however, Adlum disclosed that it had been made from currants, no one wanted anything to do with it. The other bottle, which Jefferson compared in taste and quality to Chambertin, had been made from a native American black grape, the Alexander, that had been discovered by John Penn's gardner.[23]

Adlum shipped the vines in March and enclosed a bottle of red wine and apologized for making "it too rich by adding sugar."[24] Because of a postal mix-up the vines arrived dried-out and subsequently died. Jefferson admonished Adlum for adding sugar to his wines. "The quality of the bottle you sent before satisfies me that we have at length found one native grape, inured to all accidents of our climate, which will give us a wine worthy of the best vineyards of France. When you did me the favor of sending me the former bottle I placed it on the table with some of the best Burgundy of Chambertin which I had imported myself from the maker of it, and desiring the company to point out which was the American bottle, it was acknowledged they could discover no sensible difference. I noted Cooper's recipe for making wine which you mention in your letter, and regretted it because it will have a tendency to continue the general error in this country that brandy always, & sugar some times, are necessary for wine. This idea will retard & discourage our progress in making good wine, be assured that there is never one atom of anything whatever put into any of the good wines made in France. I name that country because I can vouch the fact from the assurance to myself of the vignerons of all the best wine cantons of that country which I visited myself. It is never done but by the exporting merchants & then only for the English & American markets where by a inhaled taste the intoxicating quality of wine, more that it's flavor, is required by the palate."[25]

Two and a half years into retirement, and with Europe at war, Jefferson changed his opinion that "it was best for every country to make what it could make to best advantage, and to exchange it with others, with those articles which it could not so well make" and came over to believe "that, abandoning to a certain degree those agricultural pursuits, which best suited our situation, we must endeavor to make everything we want within ourselves, and have as little intercourse as possible with Europe in its present demoralised state. Wine being among the earliest luxuries in which we indulge ourselves, it is desirable it should be made here and we have every soil, aspect & climate of the best wine countries, and I have myself drank wines made in this state and in Maryland, of the quality of the best Burgundy."[26]

Through Thomas Appleton, the American Consul in Leghorn, he imported from Tuscany Chianti and other wines produced in the hills around Florence, such as Artimino and Pomino, both regarded as good country wines, and Montepulciano. Eighteenth century Chianti was made from essentially the same grapes as it is today: "Sangiovese, Canaiols rosso, white Trebbiano and white Malvasia."[27]

Henderson called Artimino an "excellent claret" type wine. The wines of Artimino took their name from the hamlet of Artimino, located 20 miles west of Florence. Facing Artimino from another hill about a quarter of a mile away is the Medici Villa Ferdinanda with its 100 chimneys. Jefferson may have first heard of these wines from his friend Mazzei who was born at Poggio a Caiano, three miles from Artimino.

The red wines of Artimino are still made from a blend of four or five grapes from vineyards facing south along hills surrounding the hamlet. The predominant grape is the Sangiovese (70%), the principal grape of all Chiantis. It is sold under a Carmignano DOC as Riserva Villa Medici and Riserva Del Granduca, Fattoria, Artimino and resembles in bouquet and taste a quality Chianti.[28]

In 1716 the Grand Duke of Tuscany singled out four wine zones for special recognition: Carmignano, Chianti, Val d'Arno di Sopra and Pomino.[29] In retirement, Jefferson received an order of Italian wines that included 91 bottles (only 40 of which arrived unbroken) of red Pomino[30] from vineyards located in the hill country surrounding the village of Pomino, 25 miles east of Florence. Jefferson's "very favorite" Tuscan wine, which he sometimes referred to as a Florence wine, was Montepulciano.[31] Appleton was a good judge of Tuscan wines and usually selected Jefferson's Montepulciano from "a particular very best crop of it known to him,"[32] which Jefferson described as being light in body with a taste equal to the best Burgundy.

The Montepulciano vintage of 1815 was so poor that Appleton decided not to purchase any, advising that in other parts of Tuscany "we have, however, many other wines equally light, and very nearly as well flavour'd, at about one half the price" as Montepulciano. Without waiting for Jefferson's response, Appleton purchased a barrel (57 bottles) of Carmignano "which though not equal to that of Montepulciano, is nevertheless one of the best flavour'd of Tuscany." Later that summer he shipped Jefferson 57 bottles each of Artimino and Chianti describing it "of a very high flavor." In September he shipped Jefferson 87 bottles of Arno wine "to which none is superior, except Montepulciano; and in the estimation of many, they are on a level.... These

The Port of Leghorn

Artimino

wines can always be procured, at a much less price than that of Montepulciano, as they are conveyed by the Arno [river], while the latter is transported 150 miles over land."[33] After drinking the wines Jefferson advised Appleton that they were "exactly as you described them. The Arno was the best, but still not equal to Montepulciano...."[34]

Jefferson's description of Montepulciano as a high flavored, light bodied wine "equal to the best Burgundy" is difficult to reconcile with descriptions left us by writers of that era. The 18th century wines of Montepulciano were made from the Aleatico grape, a species of black Muscat that made a sweet wine, though not as sweet as Frontignan and Muscat de Rivesaltes. In a shipment of Italian wines received while President, Jefferson made a distinction between Aleatico and Montepulciano by noting receipt of "38 bottles of Aleatico ... 10 bottles of Montepulciano." Redding called Montepulciano a wine of "great excellence, luscious, with a rich perfume." Its sweetness was achieved by picking the ripest grapes and then drying them indoors for six or seven weeks before they were crushed. A second type of Montepulciano was made by adding water to the pomice, which, after a short fermentation, produced a dry but weak wine. This "second class" Montepulciano was normally served to visitors to the region who reported that it tasted like a weak claret.

Sadly, the Montepulciano, which the poet Franceso Redi called the "king of all wine," no longer exists. Today's dry red wines, labeled Vino Nobile di Montepulciano, are not made from the same grape. Somewhere in the space of 200 years, the vintners of the Etruscan Hills shed the Aleatico grape in favor of a blend of grapes. The "manna of Montepulciano"[35] is thus lost to posterity.

Five years into retirement Jefferson learned, along with the rest of the nation, that the British had captured and burned much of Washington, including the White House and the Capitol, which contained the nation's library. As the possessor of the nation's largest private book collection, he offered to sell the United States Government his library. In offering his books, he noted: "While residing in Paris, I devoted every afternoon I was disengaged, for a summer or two, in examining all the principal bookstores, turning over every book with my own hand, and putting by everything which related to America, and indeed whatever was rare and valuable in every science. Besides this, I had standing orders during the whole time I was in Europe, on its principal book-marts, particularly Amsterdam, Frankfurt, Madrid and London, for such works relating to America as could not be found in Paris."[36]

The government's acceptance of Jefferson's offer served both: the sale price of $23,950 gave him a much needed infusion of cash, and his books became the nucleus for the Library of Congress.[37]

Wine was a preferred drink and a lifetime intellectual interest, but beer had always been one of his favorite dinner drinks, and he now had time to experiment with brewing his own. In a letter to Coppinger, a brewer, he wrote: "I have no doubt, either in a moral or economical view, of the desirableness to introduce a taste for malt liquors instead of that for ardent spirits, the difficulty is in changing the public taste and habit. The business of brewing is now so much introduced in every

Bedroom and Study

state, that it appears to me to need no other encouragement than to increase the number of customers ... I am lately become a brewer for family use, having had the benefit of instruction to one of my people by an English brewer of the first order." The man Jefferson considered the best brewer in America was Joseph Miller, an English sea captain, who stayed at Monticello several months and taught a slave, Peter Hemings, the art of brewing. Hemings became so skillful that many who drank beer at Monticello asked for the recipe.[38] Jefferson's reply to James Madison's request for brewing advice illustrates his pride in Hemings and his beer: "I will give you notice in the fall when we are to commence malting and our malter and brewer is uncommonly intelligent and capable of giving instruction if your pupil is as ready at comprehending it."[39]

In November 1815, Jefferson received a letter from John David, a young man who had come to Albemarle County to plant a vineyard for one of Jefferson's neighbors.[40] David's letter posed a series of questions "on the subject of the vine and wine." Jefferson confessed that when younger he had been "ardent for the introduction of new objects of culture suited to our climate," but now at the age of 72 he was leaving those pursuits to younger men. He went on to tell David that "there is in our woods a native grape which of my own knowledge produces a wine so nearly the quality of the Caumartin of Burgundy, that I have seen at my own table a large company acknowledge they could not distinguish between them ... but there is a gentleman on the Potomak [Adlum] who cultivates it."[41] When David expressed an interest in examining Adlum's vines, Jefferson, not knowing if Adlum was still alive, told David that he would write Adlum "and would even ask him to send me some cuttings of his vines."

After a hiatus of almost six years, Jefferson reminded Adlum that "While I lived in Washington you were so kind as to send me two bottles of wine made by yourself, the one from Currants, the other from a native grape called by you a fox-grape, discovered by Mr. Penn's gardener. The wine of this was as good as the best Burgundy and resembling it. In 1810 you added the great favor of sending me my cuttings. These were committed to the stage Mar. 13. On the 27th of that month I set out on a journey. The cuttings arrived at our post office a day or two after I was detained there till my return. They were received April 19 and immediately planted but having been 6 weeks in a dry situation not a single one lives. Disenchanted by this failure and not having anyone skilled in the culture, I never troubled you again on the subject, but I have now an opportunity of renewing the trial under a person brought up to the culture of the vine and making wine from his nativity. Am I too unreasonable in asking once more a few cuttings of the same vine? I am so convinced that our first success will be from a native grape, that I would buy no other. A few cuttings as short as you think will do, put into a light box, an mixed well with light moss."[42]

Having sold his farm in Havre de Grace, Maryland, Jefferson's letter found Adlum living in Georgetown, but Adlum arranged through the son of a former neighbor, Levin Gale, to supply Jefferson with the vines and promised to send an additional number of cuttings from his new Georgetown vineyards.[43]

While President, Jefferson had sent James Monroe to France and Spain on a special peace assignment, and when Monroe returned to the United States, he "selected and brought with him from France with a view to making wine" a fine collection of vines.[44] Sensing the opportunity to have his vineyards planted with French vinifera vines, Jefferson wrote Monroe and explained, "I have an opportunity of getting some vines planted next month ... will you permit me to take the trimmings of your vines, it shall be done by him [John David] so as to insure no injury to them?"[45]

During the Christmas holidays, 1816, he drank a white wine made from the native Muscadine grape called Scuppernong. Jefferson thought it exquisite and ordered a cask from the vintner, Colonel G. Hutchins Burton of Halifax, North Carolina. Shortly after receiving Burton's two-year old Scuppernong, he wrote: "I am not without hope that thro' your efforts and example, we shall yet see it a country abounding in wine and oil. North Carolina has the merit of taking the lead in the former culture, of giving the first specimen of an exquisite wine, produced in quantity.... Her Scuppernon wine, made on the southside of the Sound would be distinguished on the best tables of Europe for its fine aroma and chrystalline transparence. Unhappily that aroma, in most of the examples I have seen, has been entirely submerged in brandy. This coarse taste and practice is the peculiarity of Englishmen, and of their apes Americans. I hope it will be discontinued, and that this fortunate example will encourage our country to go forward in this culture...."[46]

Six years later Jefferson received a gift of 20 bottles of Scuppernong from a Thomas Cox in North Carolina. In an accompanying note Cox claimed that the casks of Scuppernong Jefferson had purchased from Colonel Burton had actually been made by him, and solicited an order from Jefferson. Jefferson's earlier experience with unadulterated Scuppernong had convinced him that the Scuppernong was proof "that as good wines will be made in America as in Europe ... The vine is congenial to every climate in Europe from Hungary to the Mediterranean, and will be bound to succeed in the same temperatures here wherever tried by intelligent vignerons. The culture however is more desirable for domestic use than profitable as an occupation for market. In countries which use ardent spirits drunkeness is the mortal vice; but in those which make wine for common use you never see a drunkard."[47] Jefferson declined Cox's offer, pointing out that all but two samples of Scuppernong that he had tasted over the years had "been so adulterated with brandy and sugar as to be mere juleps, and not wine; and candor obliges me to say that the 20 bottles now received are so charged with brandy, perhaps too with sugar, as that the vinous flavor is lost and absorbed. There will never be a drinkable wine made in this country until this barbarous practice is discontinued of adulterating with brandy."[48]

When James Monroe was elected to the "splendid misery" of the presidency in 1817, the sage of Monticello spent all but five lines of his letter of congratulations discussing the wines he recommended for the new President's wine cellar.

"I shall not waste your time in idle congratulations. You know my joy on the commitment of the helm of our government to your hands. I promised you, when I should have received and tried the wines that I ordered from France and Italy to give you a note of the kinds which I should think worthy of your procurement; and this being the season for ordering them, so that they may come in the mild temperature of autumn, I now fulfil my promise.

"They are the following:

"Vin Blanc, Liqoureux d'Hermitage de M. Jourdan a Tains. This costs about 82½cents a bottle put on ship-board. "Vin de Ledanon (in Languedoc) something of the port character but higher flavored, more delicate, less rough. I do not know its price, but probably about 25 cents a bottle. "Vin de Roussillon. The best is that of Perpignan or Rivesalte of the crop of M. Durand. It costs 72 cents a gallon, bears bringing in the cask. If put into bottles then it costs 11 cents a bottle more than if bottled here by an inexplicable and pernicious arrangement of our tariff.

"Vin de Nice. The crop called Bellet, of M. Sasserno, is the best. This is the most elegant everyday wine in the world and cost 31 cents the bottle. Not much being made it is little known at the general markets.

"Mr. Cathalan of Marseilles is the best channel for getting the first three of these wines and a good one for the Nice, being in their neighborhood and knowing well who makes the crops of best quality. The Nice being a wine foreign to France occasion some troublesome forms. If you could get that direct from Sasserno himself at Nice, it would be better. And by the bye, he is very anxious for the appointment of consul for the United States at that place. I knew his father well, one of the most respectable merchants and men of the place. I hear a good character of the son, who has succeeded to his business. He understands English well, having passed some time in a counting house in London for improvement. I believe we have not many vessels going to that port annually and yet as the appointment brings no expense to the United States, and is sometimes salutary to our merchants and seamen, I see no objection to naming one there. There is still another wine to be named to you, which is the wine of Florence called Montepulciano, with which Appleton can best furnish you. There is a particular very best crop of it known to him and which he has usually sent to me. This cost 25 cents per bottle. He knows too from experience how to have it so bottled and packed as to ensure it bearing the passage which in the ordinary way it does not. I have imported it

through him annually 10 or 12 years and do not think I have lost one bottle in 100. I salute you with all my wishes for a prosperous and splendid voyage over the ocean on which you are embarked, and with sincere prayers for the continuance of your life and health."[49]

Five months later, from his secluded retreat at Poplar Forest, Jefferson wrote a tavern-owner friend, Samuel I. Harrison, an even more detailed account of the tastes, qualities, sources and prices of his favorite wines.

"As you expressed a wish to have a note of the wines I mentioned to you yesterday, I make one on the back hereof I can assure you that they are esteemed on the continent of Europe among the best wines of Europe, and, with Champagne, Burgundy, Tokay are used at the best tables there. I think Roussillon of Rivesaltt's that which will be most used in this country, because strength & flauor are qualities uhich plcase here, as weakness & flavor do there, a first importation will enable you to judge for yourself, and should you select any on trial & wish to import them hereafter yourself either for the tavern or your own table, I will give you letters to Mr. Cathalan our Consul at Marseilles & Mr. Appleton our Consul at Leghorn, both of them my friends & correspondents of 30. years standing. I salute you with friendship & respect.

"Roussillon wine. This resembles Madeira in colour & strength. With age it is higher flavored, it is considered on a footing with Madeira & dry Pacharetti, and is equally used at the best tables of the continent of Europe. There are many kinds of wine made in Roussillon, but that here meant is the Roussillon of Rivesalt. it cost 74. cents a gallon there, & the duty here is 25. cents the gallon if brought in cask as should be.

"Hermitage. This is one of the first wines of France. The white is much the best, costs 83 1h cents a bottle there, bottle included. it is a pretty strong wine, & high flavored. duty 15. cents a bottle.

"Florence wine. There are several crops under different names but that of Montepulciano is the only good, and that is equal to the best Burgundy. it must come in strong bottles well cemented. When sent in the flask, much of it spoils. cost there 25 cents a bottle, duty here 15. cents requires a good cellar, being a very light wine.

"Claret of Marseilles. made there by a Mr. Bergasse by putting together different grapes, so that it is the genuine juice of the grape, and so perfect an imitation of the finest Bordeaux, as not to be distinguishable. The Bordeaux merchants get it from Bergasse paying one franc u bottle, bottle included, & send it to the US. as of the growth of Bordeauxs, charging 4 francs a bottle.

"Capt. Bernard Peyton, of the Commission business in Richmond, will import there on commission, the cost of being advance him here & a reasonable commission allowed him. The Florence is imported from Leghorn. the others from Marseilles. I give him letters to my correspondents there which will insure him faithful supplies both as to quality & price."

Overall he was very satisfied with the quality of the wines Cathalan sent from southern France, calling them "particularly esteemed," and raising his opinion of Sasserno's Bellet from "indeed very fine" to "superlatively fine."[50] But now and then a slight note of disappointment crept in. In his annual order in 1817 he observed that Sasserno's Bellet from Nice "is good, but it is not exactly that of the preceding year, which was a little silky, just enough to be sensible, and to please the palate of our friends beyond any wine I have ever seen. That now received is dry, but well flavored."

The next year this slight disappointment turned to grief when he opened one of 300 bottles of Sasserno's Bellet wine; its sour taste provoked from Jefferson a definition of the "terms by which we characterize different qualities of wine."[51] In a letter to Cathalan, he reiterated his thoughts on how various wines should taste and then explained why he went into "these details with you. In the first place you are not to conclude that I am become a *buveur* [drinker]. My measure is a perfectly sober one of 3 or 4 glasses at dinner, and not a drop at any other time. But as to these 3 or 4 glasses *Je suis bien friand* [I am very fond of]. I go however into these details because in the art, by mixing genuine wines, of producing any flavor desired, which Mr. Bergasse possesses so perfectly, I think it probable he has prepared wines of this character also; that is to say of a compound flavor of the rough. dry, and sweet, or rather of the rough and silky; or if he has not, I am sure he can. The Ledanon, for example, which is dry and astringent, with a proper proportion of a wine which is sweet and astringent, would resemble the wine of Bellct sent me in 1816 by Mr. Spreafico. If he has any wines of this quality, I would thank you to add samples of 2 or 3 bottles of each of those he thinks approaches this description nearest. The vin rouge qualite de Bordeaux which he sent me the last year is much approved; and it was best not to send it in casks. We know nothing of bottling wines here: and there is the less reason for doing it now, as Congress at their last session, still continuing the fixed duties on certain enumerated wines, reduced that on all non-enumerated from 15 to 6 cents the bottle. Mr. Bergasse should only take care that his wines be not invoiced or shipped under any of the enumerated names, and particularly his claret, or red wine qualite de Bordeaux. I think it would be worth his while to send it an adventure of some dozens of boxes of his Bordeaux to Richmond to make it known . . . . I have labored long and hard to procure the reduction of duties on the lighter wines, which is now effected to a certain degree. I have labored hard also in persuading others to use those wines. Habit yields with difficulty. Perhaps the last diminution of duties may have a good effect. I have added to my list of wines this year 50 bottles of vin Muscat Blanc de Lunel. I should much prefer a wine which should be *sweet* and *astringent,* but I know of none. If you know of any, not too high priced I would thank you to substitute it instead of the Lunel."[52]

Using the wine glasses that have survived at Monticello as a guide, Jefferson's consumption of three or four glasses of wine amounted to about nine to twelve ounces of wine daily. This is less wine than he drank thirty years earlier when he traveled through the vineyards of France and Germany. His travel receipts then show that he drank between a half to a bottle of wine with his dinners and usually after he had been tasting wines at the vineyards.[53]

Later that year Jefferson received a letter from a Julius Oliver bringing him the sad news that his friend Stephen Cathalan had died, and that he, Oliver, would fill his annual wine order. Oliver added a note that Bergasse had some "old vin cuit" that

Jefferson Wine Glasses, 1970–1810

could serve in place of Muscat.[54] Two weeks later another letter from Oliver explained that most of his annual order had been shipped, and included 144 bottles of Bergasse's red wine, vintage 1815; a double cask of M. Chevalier's Muscat de Rivesaltes, 1811; 150 bottles of Ledenon, 20 bottles of old Muscat wine, 18 bottles of vin cuit of Provence, 1809; four bottles of a local vin cuit and six bottles of Clairette of Limoux.

Jefferson had mixed reactions to Oliver's wine selections. Chevalier's six bottles of clairette de Limoux were so good he ordered 150 bottles of "exactly of the same quality." Chevalier's Muscat of Rivesaltes was "an excellent wine" but a little too sweet and Jefferson deferred reordering it. Instead he asked Dodge to purchase 30 gallons of M. Durand's dry Rivesaltes noting that Durand would recollect and furnish the "particular quality" that he liked. He thought Chevalier's Ledenon "also good" but preferred M. Tourneron's who had supplied Cathalan. And as usual, his order included anchovies, macaroni (those of Naples preferred), and virgin olive oil from Aix-en-Provence.[55]

Vin cuit (boiled wine) was common at the time in France, Spain and Italy, and was made by a method originated by the Romans. The vigneron gathered the ripest grapes and exposed them to the sun for five or six days. After the shriveled grapes were pressed, the juice was boiled until the wine was reduced to about one-third of its original volume and poured into wooden casks to cool before the barrel was closed. It was often mistaken for and sold as Malmsey or Malaga.[56] Jefferson obviously did not like the vin cuit selected by Oliver because two years later his cellar inventory showed that only one of the 22 bottles had been opened, and he never reordered it.

A year and a half after advising President Monroe of the wines he should stock for the White House wine cellar, Jefferson took up his pen in passionate advocacy of wine as the beverage of temperance and health. Writing to William H. Crawford,

Secretary of the Treasury, Jefferson observed that among the proposed tariff reforms being considered by Congress, "none was proposed on the most exceptionable article... I mean that of wines. I think it a great error to consider a heavy tax on wines, as a tax on luxury. On the contrary it is a tax on the health of our citizens. It is a legislative declaration that none but the richest of them shall be permitted to drink wine, and in effect a condemnation of all the middling & lower conditions of society to the poison of whisky, which is destroying them by wholesale, and ruining their families. Whereas were the duties on the cheap wines proportioned to their first cost the whole middling class of this country could have the gratification of that milder stimulus, and a great proportion of them would go into it's use and banish the baneful whiskey. Surely it is not from the necessities of our treasury that we thus undertake to debar the mass of our citizens the use of not only an innocent gratification, but a healthy substitute instead of a bewitching poison. This aggression on the public taste and effort has been ever deemed among the most arbitrary & oppressive abuses of the English government. It is one which I hope we shall never copy. But the truth is that the treasury would gain in the long run by the vast extension of the use of the article. I should therefore be for encouraging the use of wine by placing it among the articles of lightest duty. But be this as it may, take what rate of duty is thought proper, but carry it evenly thro' the cheap as well as the highest priced wines."[57]

Apparently Jefferson's letter had its impact because he was elated to learn a month later that Congress was considering a reduction of the duties on wine. To the French Ambassador in Washington he wrote: "I rejoice, as a moralist, at the prospect of a reduction of the duties on wine, by our national legislature. It is an error to view a tax on that liquor as merely a tax on the rich. It is a prohibition of its use to the middling class of our citizens, and a condemnation of them to the poison of whiskey, which is desolating their houses. No nation is drunken where wine is cheap; and none sober, where the dearness of wine substitutes ardent spirits as the common beverage. It is, in truth, the only antidote to the bane of whiskey. Fix but the duty at the rate of other merchandise, and we can drink wine here as cheap as we do grog; and who will not prefer it? Its extended use will carry health and comfort to a much enlarged circle."[58]

At the age of 75, Jefferson undertook his last great project, the founding of the University of Virginia. Five and a half years into the project, with a crippled wrist and fingers, he wrote John Adams, "I am fortunately mounted on a Hobby, which indeed I should have better managed some 30 or 40 years ago, but whose easy amble is still sufficient to give exercise and amusement to an Octogenary rider. This is the establishment of the University, on a scale more comprehensive, and in a country more healthy and central than our old William and Mary."[59] He was the architect who breathed life into every detail of its planning, construction and organization, and he lived to see his dream come true. Lafayette was its first official guest at a dinner given there on November 5, 1824 and five months later, March 7, 1825, the University of Virginia opened. The Rotunda and five pavilions connected by colonnaded walkways still remain the heart of the campus and have been extolled by an architecture critic, the New York Times' Paul Goldberger, as "possibly the greatest piece of architecture in America."[60]

As he approached his 76th birthday, his retirement routine had changed little and his health remained excellent. "I live so much like other people, that I might refer to ordinary life as the history of my own. Like my friend, the Doctor [Rush], I have lived temperately, eating little animal food, and that not as an aliment, so much as a condiment for the vegetables, which constitute my principal diet. I double, however, the Doctor's glass and a half of wine, and even treble it with a friend; but halve its effects by drinking the weak wines only. The ardent wines I cannot drink, nor do I use ardent spirits in any form. Malt liquors and cider are my table drinks, and my breakfast, like that also of my friend, is tea and coffee. I have been blest with organs of digestion which accept and concoct, without ever murmuring, whatever the palate choose to consign to them, and I have not yet lost a tooth by age. I was a hard student until I entered on the business of life, the duties of which leave no idle time to those disposed to fulfil them; and now, retired, and at the age of 76, I am again a hard student ... But whether I retire to bed early or late, I rise with the sun. I use spectacles at night, but not necessarily in the day, unless in reading small print. My hearing is distinct in particular conversation, but confused when several voices cross each other, which unfits me for the society of the table."[61] Jefferson's near perfect health may have been a dividend of his daily disciplines, the habit of bathing his feet in cold water every morning, correspondence, riding horseback among his farms, visiting the plantation shops and gardening until dusk. Three years later, he reported that walking to his garden caused some fatigue but he still rode daily and his health remained good.[62]

Old age did not dim Jefferson's ardor for drinking and serving wine. Between January 1822 and February 1824, Jefferson and his guests consumed 1203 bottles of wine with Claret de Bergasse, Ledenon and Limoux the great favorites.[63] Jefferson also remained a staunch believer in the curative powers of wine, and in a letter to Madison he explained how a cup of rice and a glass of Madeira every two hours had cured his two daughters of a type of typhus fever that they contacted in Paris. According to Jefferson, his youngest daughter, Maria, "took a pint of Madeira a day without feeling it, and that for many weeks." Jefferson went on to boast that by varying this prescription and using a toddy of French brandy about as strong as Madeira he had "carried between twenty and thirty patients through it without losing a single one."[64]

In June 1822 Adlum wrote Jefferson from Georgetown that he had "about four acres of vines now planted—about two of which are in bearing, and the other two acres I expect will bear fruit next year."[65] Jefferson was delighted to hear that Adlum was still pushing the culture of the Alexander grape because "its wine resembles so exactly that of the Caumartin Burgundy." He went on, however, to lecture Adlum on one of his favorite causes—the evils of brandying wine. He gave as an example "a wine of remarkable merit made in considerable quantities in a district of N. Carolina on Scuppernong [Scuppernon] Creek. This wine, when it can be obtained unbrandied would be drank at the first tables of Europe in competition with their best wines. What of it, however, is sent to the general market at Norfolk is so brandied as to be unworthy of being called wine. To get it without brandy requires a troublesome correspondence and special agent. Until this fatal error is corrected, the character of our wines will stand low."[66]

Early the next year, Adlum authored and published a serious work on grape culture titled *Memoir on the Cultivation of the Vine in America and the best Mode of Making Wine*, and shortly before his 80th birthday Jefferson received a copy along with two bottles of wine. Jefferson thanked Adlum for "the two bottles of wine

you were so kind as to send me. The first called Tokay is truly a fine wine of high flavour, and, as you assure me there was not a drop of brandy or other spirit in it. I say it is a wine of good body of its own. The 2d bottle, a red wine, I tried when I had good judges at the table. We agreed it was a wine one might always drink with satisfaction, but of no peculiar excellence. Of your book on the culture of the vine, it would be presumption in me to give my opinion, because it is a culture of which I have no knowledge either from practice or reading." The wine that Jefferson called Tokay was made from the native Catawba grape, which Adlum thought made the best wine. The Catawba became so successful that it eventually replaced the Alexander grape and is still grown as a wine grape in the eastern United States.[67]

In the summer of 1824 Lafayette arrived in the United States for a triumphal tour. His presence was celebrated wherever he went, but the highlight of his trip was his eleven-day stay at Monticello. It had been 35 years since Jefferson had seen his French friend. Except for two visits to the University of Virginia, the two former revolutionaries spent their time together at Monticello. Between themselves and their dinner companions so much red wine was drunk that when Lafayette and his party departed on November 15, Jefferson's stock was almost depleted. Although expecting any day the arrival of his annual wine supply from southern France, Jefferson became fearful of running out and placed an emergency order explaining: "In the meantime I must buy from hand to mouth in the country, and for the present must pray you to send me a box of Claret of about two dozen by the first wagon. I would refer for its quality to your own taste rather than to price, which is no test at all, and generally a mere imposition."[68]

The Vintage Years

Eleven days before his death, Jefferson wrote his last letter, declining an invitation to attend a celebration in Washington of the 50th Anniversary of American Independence. With a knowledge of what freedom meant then, and a prescience of what it would mean to future generations, he left this prophecy: "May it be to the world, what I believe it will be (to some parts sooner, to others later, but finally to all), the signal of arousing men to burst the chains under which monkish ignorance and superstition had persuaded them to bind themselves, and to assume the blessings and security of self-government . . . all eyes are opened, or opening, to the rights of man. The general spread of the light of science has already laid open to every view the palpable truth, that the mass of mankind has not been born with saddles on their backs, nor a favored few booted and spurred, ready to ride them legitimately, by the grace of God. These are grounds of hope for others. For ourselves let the annual return of this day forever refresh our recollections of these rights, and an undiminished devotion to them."[69]

Although Jefferson remained remarkably active during the seventeen years of his retirement, along the way he felt that old age was depriving him of some of the sensual enjoyments of life. To Abigail Adams he wrote: "To see what we have seen, to taste the tasted, and at each return, less tasteful; o'er our palates to decant, another vintage." In 1826 on the Fourth of July, the 50th Anniversary of The Declaration of Independence, Thomas Jefferson died.[70]

Chapter Notes

CHAPTER ONE

1. Julian P. Boyd was the first editor of *The Papers of Thomas Jefferson*, Princeton, N.J.: 1950. [Hereafter cited as *Papers*, followed by volume number and pagination.] The first twenty-one volumes of *The Papers of Thomas Jefferson* were published under the editorship of Julian P. Boyd. Charles T. Cullen was editor of Volumes 22 and 23. The current editor is John Catanzariti whose stewardship began with volume 24 in 1990.
2. Randolph, Sarah N. *The Domestic Life of Thomas Jefferson*, Charlottesville: 1978, 31. [Hereafter, cited as Randolph, S.N.]
3. Malone, Dumas. *Jefferson The Virginian*, Boston: 1948; 66-74. [Hereafter cited as Malone, *The Virginian*.]
4. Lipscomb, Andrew A., ed. *The Writings of Thomas Jefferson*, Vol. 1: 4. [Hereafter cited as T.J., *Autobiography*.] Jefferson said that Henry's talents as an orator were "great indeed, ... such as he had never heard from any other man."
5. Bear, James A., Jr. and Stanton, Lucia, C. *Jefferson's Memorandum Books*, Monticello: annotated, unpublished. All citations of *Jefferson's Memorandum Books* are referenced to the Bear-Stanton work. Page citations are not given because the pagination will change when this work is published. Because Jefferson's entries are annotated, it was an invaluable source of information.
6. *Jefferson's Memorandum Books*; Betts, Edwin Morris. *Thomas Jefferson's Garden Book*, Philadelphia: 1944, 12-16. [Hereafter cited as Betts.]
7. *Jefferson's Memorandum Books*.
8. Malone, *The Virginian*, 157-58. Martha's son, John, died the summer before her marriage to Jefferson.
9. Randolph, Sarah N. *The Domestic Life of Thomas Jefferson*, New York: 1871, 45; Malone, *The Virginian*, 159-60; Betts, 35.
10. *Jefferson's Memorandum Books*; Jefferson recorded in his garden book: "Mrs. Wythe puts 1/10 very rich superfine Malmsey to a dry Madeira and makes a fine wine." Betts, 39-40.

11. Marraro, Howard R. [trans.]. *Memoirs of the Life and Peregrinations of the Florentine Philip Mazzei, 1730-1816*, New York: 1942, L91. [Hereafter cited as Mazzei-*Memoirs.*]
12. T.J. to John Dortie, October 1, 1811.
13. T.J. to John Dortie, October I, 1811.
14. Mazzei, *Memoirs*, 192-93.
15. Garlick, Richard Cecil, Jr. *Philip Mazzei, Friend of Jefferson: His Life and Letters*, Baltimore: 1933, 14-22; [hereafter cited as Garlick.]
16. Garlick, 26.
17. Garlick, 27-29.
18. Mazzei, *Memoirs*, 118.
19. Carmignano was one of four elite wine zones singled out for special recognition in 1716 by the Grand Duke of Tuscany; the other three were Chianti, Pomino and Val d'Arno di Sopra. Carmignano is directly to the west of Florence.
20. Mazzei, *Memoirs*, 124.
21. Mazzei, *Memoirs*, 206-07. Mazzei's enthusiasm for the vineyard project caused Jefferson to plant in April, 1774, "thirty vines just below where the new garden wall will run, towards the westernmost end. Eight of them at the westernmost end of the row were Spanish raisins ... and at the easternmost end were six native vines of Monticello. They were planted by some Tuscan vignerons who came over with Mr. Mazzei." Betts, 52-54, 64.
22. T. J. to Albert Galatin, January 25, 1793; Library of Congress, Manuscript Collections, T.J. Papers, Reel 49. [Hereafter cited L.C. and reel number.]
23. Weld, Isaac, Jr. *Travels through the States of North America during the years 1795, 1796 and 1797*, 2nd ed., London: 1799, 206-09. [Hereafter cited as Weld.]
24. Wine making in Virginia is flourishing today with over forty wineries producing quality wines made from Vitis vinifera grapes-Cabernet Sauvignon, Merlot, Chardonnay, Sauvignon Blanc, Riesling and others. Jefferson would be proud of the support his native state has given to these modern-day Philip Mazzeis. If Jefferson were to set out today from Monticello to Washington, he could drink a variety of local wines at wineries, restaurants, and inns along the way.
25. "If a pipe of Madeira yields 30 doz. bottles, we drink it at 7. years old for 3/ a bottle, which includes the 7. years interest. Such a bottle holds 15 common wine glasses .... A pipe of new Madeira will yield 40. dozen, which brings the price (there being no interest) to 20/ a doz. or 20d. the bottle when drank new." *Jefferson's Memorandum Books*, February 7, 1775.
26. Eberlein, Harold Donaldson and Cortlandt, Van Dyke Hubbard. *Diary of Independence Hall*, Philadelphia: 1948, 144. [Hereafter cited as *Diary of Independence Hall.*] John Adams to Abigail Adams, June 23, 1775; Malone, *The Virginian*, 202-03. Washington, though commissioned by Congress as Commander-in Chief, had no army in waiting.
27. Donaldson, Thomas. *The House in Which Thomas Jefferson Wrote the Declaration of*

Independence, Philadelphia: 1898. The house was located on the southwest corner and was first known as No. 230 High Street and later No. 700 Market Street.

28. Butterfield, L.H., ed. *Diary and Autobiography of John Adams*, 4 Vols., Cambridge, Mass.: 1961, 393-398. [Hereafter cited as *Diary of John Adams.*]
29. *Papers*, I: 413-33; *Diary of Independence Hall*, 171-75.
30. *Jefferson's Memorandum Books; Diary of Independence Hall*, 173-75.
31. Garlick, 51. Mazzei to John Adams, September 5, 1785; *Papers*, VIII: 475-76.
32. Hessian troops were a part of the English army fighting in America as a result of a contract King George III had made through the Duke of Brunswick to furnish 4,300 troops for service in America. General Frederick Riedesel was the commander of the first contingent of 2,282 Hessian troops that reached Quebec in June of 1776. He was later joined by his wife and three young daughters. Riedesel's troops were a major part of General Burgoyne's army.
33. T.J. to Doctor Gordon, July 16, 1788; T.J. to Alexander McCaul, April 19, 1786. Parton, James. *The Atlantic Monthly*, Volume 30, August, 1872, "Jefferson Governor of Virginia," 174-192.
34. Francois-Jean, Marquis de Chastellux (1734-1788) was a Major General and the third ranking officer with the French Expeditionary Forces in America.
35. Chastellux, Marquis de. *Travels in North America in The Years 1780, 1781 and 1782*, 2 Vols., Chapel Hill, NC: 1963 Vol. II, 390-91. [Hereafter cited as Chastellux.]
36. Chastellux, Vol. II, 392-94.
37. Chastellux, Vol. II, 394.
38. T.J. to Chastellux, November 26, 1782. *Papers*, VI: 199-200.
39. T.J. to Benjamin Franklin, January 3, 1783; T.J. to John Jay, January 3, 1783.
40. *Jefferson's Memorandum Books; Maryland Historical Magazine*, Vol. 41, 1946, "Thomas Jefferson in Annapolis," 115-123.
41. The records show that Mann provided and was paid for supplying with dinner forty-nine gallons of claret, thirty-five gallons of port, thirty-two gallons of Madeira, and six gallons of spirits. *Maryland Historical Magazine*, Vol. 10, 55-57.
42. *Maryland Gazette*, June 25, 1812. Lloyd Dulany's house was converted into Mann's Tavern and was a substantial, elegantly-finished house built about 1735 and stood on the corner of Church (now Main Street) and Conduit Streets. In 1790 Mann constructed an impressive brick residence on Conduit Street which eventually was integrated into the tavern. The tavern later became a local theatre, and in the early morning hours of January 17, 1919, the theatre was entirely destroyed by fire. Mann's residence still exists and is now occupied by the Masonic Lodge Number 89. An inventory of the tavern dated 1796 shows "beds 20, linen, 48 chairs, 27 tables, pewter tableware, wine, cider, etc., amenities: carpets, clock, card table, prints, flower pots, Franklin stove." From a paper entitled, "Some Notes on Taverns in Annapolis, Maryland During the Colonial Period," by Nancy T. Baker, Director of Research, Historic Annapolis, Inc., November 1981. Mary-

land Archives Building, Annapolis, Maryland.
43. *Maryland Gazette,* December 21, 1783.
44. James McHenry to Margaret Caldwell, December 23, 1783; Papers,VI:402-14.
45. Wells, William Vincent. *Life of Samuel Adams,* Reprint: 1969, III: 372.

CHAPTER TWO

1. Martha Jefferson to Eliza House Trist, August 24, 1785. See Kimball, Marie. *Jefferson the Scene of Europe,* New York: 1950, 8. [Hereafter cited as Kimball.]
2. Young, Arthur. *Travels During the Years 1787, 1788 and 1789,* London: 1792. [Hereafter cited as Young.] Biographical Note: Arthur Young (1741-1820) was a prolific writer in the field of agriculture. He authored nine volumes on his three agricultural tours of England in 1768 to 1771. In 1784 he began a periodical, *Annals of Agriculture,* which appeared until1809 and ran to 45 volumes. In 1787, 1788 and 1789, Young traveled throughout France and published his notes in 1792, titled *Travels During the Years 1787, 1788, and 1789.* He carried on a wide correspondence with many famous people including George Washington and the Marquis de Lafayette. Although Jefferson and Young were traveling through France at the same time, there is no evidence that they met, then or later. Jefferson's *Farm Book* reveals that he became aware of Arthur Young's agricultural interests and activities through George Washington.
3. Young, 76--96.
4. Nineteenth century "modernism" swept away most of this rich medieval architecture, and the old town walls and ramparts were converted into boulevards.
5. Martha Jefferson to Eliza House Trist, August 24, 1785.
6. Martha Jefferson to Eliza House Trist, August 24, 1785.
7. Taylor, Robert J., ed. *Diary of John Quincy Adams,* 2 vols., Cambridge, Mass: 1981, Vol. 1: 263n. [Hereafter cited as *Diary of John Quincy Adams.*] By the time Jefferson left Paris five years later, the barriers had increased in number to fifty-two. These hated barrier gates were operated by men appointed by the King and known as Farmers-General (tax collectors). Jefferson contemptuously referred to them as "the palaces by which we are to be let in and let out." T.J. to David Humphreys, August 14, 1787.
8. *Papers,* VII: 443; Chastellux to T.J., August 24, 1784. The convent school at Panthemont, founded in 1643, was located on the Left Bank at Rue de Grenelle. It was considered the best private school for young women in Paris. Writing to a friend, Martha said "I was placed in a convent at my arrival and I leave you to judge my situation. I did not speak a word of French ... there are fifty or sixty pensioners in the house, so that speaking as much as I could with them I learnt the language very soon. At present I am charmed with my situation." *Papers,* 8: 436-439; Martha Jefferson to Eliza House Trist, August 24, 1785. Mme. de Beauharnais, later the Empress Josephine, lived at this convent for several years

following the birth of her daughter Hortense. The Panthemont (or Pentemont) buildings are still standing at 106 Rue de Grenelle and 37 Rue de Ballechasse and are now occupied by the Veterans' Administration. Rice, Howard C., Jr., *Thomas Jefferson's Paris*, Princeton: 1976, 64-8. [Hereafter cited as Rice.]

9. Jefferson paid Thomas Barclay (1728-1793), the American Consul General in France and commissioner for settling public accounts of American officials in Europe, 123 livres for the sixty bottles of Madeira, Frontignac and Muscat wines. He paid 2.5livres per bottle for 216 bottles of Bordeaux wine which, he would learn, was too expensive for a nondescript Bordeaux wine.

10. Lararee, Leonard W, ed. *The Papers of Benjamin Franklin*, New Haven: 1959X:XVIII: 455; Stinchcomb, William. *The American Revolution and The French Alliance*, Syracuse: 1969, 7-13.

11. The Adams family arrived at Calais on August 10th and in Paris on the 13th. On the 17th they moved to Auteuil. *Diary of John Adams*, III: 171; *Diary of John Quincy Adams*, Vol. 1: 208-09.

12. Thomas Barclay (1728-1793) as the American Consul General and a commissioner had full powers to settle the financial accounts of the United States in Europe.

13. Adams, C.F., ed. *Letters of Mrs. Adams, The Wife of John Adams*, Boston: 1848, 240-41. [Hereafter cited as *Letters of Mrs. Adams.*]

14. Dumbauld, Edward. *Thomas Jefferson American Tourist*, Norman, Oklahoma: 1946, 62-63. In 1799 the Cul-de-Sac was extended into the boulevard and given its present name, Rue du Helder. The house where Jefferson lived no longer exists. *Papers*, VII: 452; Rice, 37-42.

15. Thomas Barclay to T.J., November 17, 1784.

16. An expression used by Abigail Adams.

17. Rice, 39-41.

18. David Humphreys (1753-1818) was born in Derby, Connecticut and graduated from Yale in 1771. He joined the Continental army, and in 1778 was an aide-decamp to General Putnam, and two years later an aide-de-camp to George Washington. He became a close friend of George Washington and resided with the Washingtons at Mt. Vernon following his return from France. In 1790 President Washington appointed him Minister to Portugal. Four years later he was appointed Minister Plenipotentiary to Spain and in 1797 he married John Bulkeley's daughter in Lisbon. One of the first acts that Jefferson performed as President was to recall Humphreys and replace him because of his Federalist leanings. His literary accomplishments included poetry and the biography of General Putnam.

19. G.W to T.J., June 2, 1784. David Humphreys served in Washington's military family as Washington's aide-de-camp from early 1780 until Washington's resignation in Annapolis as Commander-in-Chief of the Continental Armies on December 23, 1783. Humphreys and Washington remained close friends. See al-

so the *Life and Times of David Humphreys* by Frank Landon Humphreys.
20. John Adams to T.J., January 22, 1825.
21. *Diary of John Quincy Adams*, Vol. 1: 233.
22. William Short (1758-1849) and Jefferson remained friends until Jefferson's death 42 years later. Short eventually returned to America and resided in Philadelphia where he acquired considerable wealth speculating in land and lending money. He never married.
23. T. J. to Short, April 30, 1784; Short to T.J., May 14, 1784; *Papers*, VII, 148-49, 253-55. Short stayed with a middle class family by the name of Royers and there is some evidence that he became romantically involved with the Royers' thirteen year old daughter, Hipolite. See Bizardel, Yvon and Rice, Howard C., Jr. "Poor in Love Mr. Short," *William and Mary Quarterly*, 1964, 5-16.
24. *Papers*, VIII: 270-73.
25. *Letters of Mrs. Adams*, 208.
26. Butterfield, L.H., ed. *Diary and Autobiography of John Adams*, Cambridge, Mass.: 1961, II: 292. [Hereafter cited as *Diary of John Adams*.] Adams arrived in Bordeaux, March 30, 1778.
27. *Diary of John Adams*, II: 293-94.
28. Henderson, Alexander. *The History of Ancient and Modern Wines*, London: 1824, 193. [Hereafter cited as Henderson.]
29. Roof, Katherine Metcalf *Colonel William Smith and Lady: Romance of Washington's Aide and Young Abigail Adams*, 1929, 61. [Hereafter cited as *Journal of Miss Adams*].
30. *Journal of Miss Adams*, 61.
31. T.J. to Charles Bellini, September 30, 1785.
32. Chastellux, II: 392.
33. The Hotel de Salm is located opposite the entrance to the Musee D'Orsay and is open to the public daily except Monday and holidays.
34. The palace passed into the hands of Louis-Philippe-Joseph d'Orleans (1747-1793) who became Due D'Orleans in 1785. Rice, 14-15.
35. T.J. to James Currie, January 14, 1785.
36. *Diary of John Quincy Adams*, Vol. I, 230-31.
37. Rice, 13-18.
38. T.J. to David Humphreys, 14 August 1787; *Papers*, 12:32-33. Gouverneur Morris in his diary recorded on April 8, 1789: "Go to the Palais Royal to walk a little. Take a view of the Circus, which is said to have cost The Duke of Orleans 3,000,000 livres and which he rents for 80,000 livres. It is a vast and elegant building underground, about 120 to 130 yards long and 30 to 40 wide." Davenport, Beatrix Cary, ed. *A Diary of the French Revolution by Gouverneur Morris*, 2 vols., Boston: 1939, I: 34. [Hereafter cited as Morris.]
39. *Diary of John Quincy Adams*, Vol. I, 238.
40. Rice, 18.

41. T.J. to James Currie, January 14, 1785.
42. T.J. to John Bondfield, December 19, 1784; Bondfield to T.J., April 19, 1785.
43. T.J. to Frances Eppes, December 19, 1784; *Papers*, VII: 578.
44. Bondfield to T.J., April 19, 1785.
45. *Journal of Miss Adams*, 73; *Diary of John Quincy Adams*, Vol. I, 218.
46. *Diary of John Quincy Adams*, Vol. 1: 220-21.
47. *Journal of Miss Adams*, 74. John Quincy recorded in his diary that he attempted to obtain a ticket to the theatre that evening but it was sold out. *Diary of John Quincy Adams*, Vol. 1: 221.
48. *Journal of Miss Adams*, 81.
49. *Diary of John Quincy Adams*, Vol. I: 241. It was well known that the Queen had carried on an affair for over two years with Count Axel de Fersen, Colonel Commandant of the Royal Swedish Regiment in the French Army, but there is no positive proof that Fersen was the father of the new Duke. See Huisman, Philippe and Jallut, Marguerite. *Marie Antoinette*, London: 1971, 156-57.
50. T.J. to Short, April I, 1785. *Diary of John Quincy Adams*, Vol. I, 235, 242-44.
51. Jefferson received Gerry's letter of February 25, 1785 on April 26, advising that John Adams had been appointed minister to the English Court of St. James's, that Dr. Franklin's resignation had been accepted by Congress and that Jefferson had been appointed Minister Plenipotentiary to the Court of Versailles. Elbridge Gerry to T.J., February 25, 1785; T.J. to Gerry, May 11, 1785. Jefferson was very pleased with his appointment, writing Monroe, "I have received the appointment of Congress to succeed Dr. Franklin here. I give them my sincere thanks for this mark of their favour. I wish I were as able to render services which would justify their choice as I am zealous to do it." T.J. to James Monroe, May 11, 1785.
52. The Adamses' residence, Hotel Antier on Rue d'Auteuil, looks much the same from the outside as it did when John Adams moved there in 1784, although the surrounding environment including his beautiful garden, have disappeared. A plaque on the front of the *hotel* commemorates the Adamses' residence there. Rice, 94. In July 1785 Benjamin Franklin left France for America, and Jefferson was often asked whether he had replaced Franklin to which he would reply, "No one can replace him, sir, I am only his successor."
53. *Diary of John Quincy Adams*, Vol. 1: 265.
54. T.J. to Madame de Tesse, March 20, 1787; *Papers*, XI: 226.
55. J. Adams to T.J., May 27, 1785.
56. J. Adams to T.J., June 7, 1785.
57. T.J. to J. Adams, June 2, 1785; T.J. to Anthony Garvey, June 2, 1785; *Papers*, VIII: 175; Anthony Garvey to T.J., June 5, 1785.
58. T.J. to Abigail Adams, June 21 and July 7, 1785; J.A. to T.J., August 7, 1785; T.J. to A.A., September 25, 1785; A.A. to T.J., November 24, 1785; *Papers*, IX: 25. The cask of wine was from Gaillac and ordered by Adams from Bondfield at a cost of 319 livres. It held 215 bottles of wine.

59. *Papers*, VIII: J75. Anthony Garvey to T.J., June 5, 1785; J.A. to T.J., June 7, 1785; T.J. to A.A., June 21, 1785; J.A. to T.J., July 16, 1785.
60. T.J. to Charles Bellini, September 30, 1785.
61. T.J. to Charles Bellini, September 30, 1785.
62. Young, *276-77*.
63. T.J. to Charles Thomson, November 11, 1784; *Papers*, VII: 519.
64. Parton, J. *The Life and Times of Aaron Burr,* New York: 1858, 568; Young, 70.
65. Mazzei, *Memoirs*, 291-93; Garlick, 98. Mazzei arrived in France on July 9, 1785 and the next day went to Nantes. On reaching Paris, he went immediately to see Jefferson who lived "in a beautiful *villetta* with a charming garden, at the end of the Champs-Elysées, within gunshot of the stockade through which one must pass on the way to Versailles." Mazzei is obviously mistaken about when he first visited Jefferson at his Champs-Elysées villa. He wrote Jefferson and advised, "I cannot get to Paris before the 21st or 22nd of this [July] month." *Papers*, VIII: 277-78. Jefferson did not move into the Hotel de Langeac on the Champs-Elysées until October 17, 1785. Mazzei was in Paris before Jefferson moved into the Hotel de Langeac. See T.J. to St. John de Crevecoeur, August 22, 1785, and T.J. to Edmund Randolph, September 20, 1785.
66. Using the Grillé de Chaillot as the starting point, he recorded the distance from his residence to the Pont de Neuilly three times greater (2,430 double steps) than to the Place de la Concorde (820 double steps). *Papers*, XI: 484.
67. T.J. to Thomas Mann Randolph, August 27, 1786.
68. T.J. to Chastellux, October, 1786, undated. *Papers*, X: 498.
69. *Diary of John Adams,* Vol. III: 145.
70. *Papers*, VIII: 269-273. Abigail described Williamos as "this curious adventurer, who possessed benevolence, without conduct, and learning without sense," who had borrowed from every American in Paris "until he could get no further credit." Abigail Adams to John Quincy Adams, February 16, 1786. Williamos died four months later.
71. The Hotel de Langeac no longer exists although there is a placard on the Champs-Elysées west of Rue de Berri that commemorates where it stood.
72. T.J. to Abigail Adams, September 4, 1785.
73. T.J. to Nicholas Lewis, September 17, 1787.
74. Stein, Susan R. *The Worlds of Thomas Jefferson at Monticello,* New York: Harry N. Abrams, 1993, 337, 340.
75. T.J. to James Madison, October 28, 1785. Lamoignon de Malesherbes was a nobleman who had a magnificent estate near Fontainebleau and a country-like Paris residence in what is now known as the Montmartre section. He was a great lover of trees and plants. Jefferson supplied him with a number of American seeds and they became friends. Malesherbes became an active participant in the French Revolution and a defender of Louis XVI, only to follow the King to the guillotine. Rice, 44.

Chapter Notes

76. Redding, Cyrus. *A History and Description of Modern Wines,* London: 1833, 231-32. [Hereafter cited as Redding.]
77. T.J. to Francis Lewis, February 9, 1786.
78. Francis Lewis to T.J., May 9 and May 11, 1786.
79. Francis Lewis to T.J., May 11, *1786; Jefferson's Memorandum Books,* August 1, 1786. For the curious who wish to follow the trail of this pipe of Madeira, see Louis Guillaume Otto to T.J., May 11, 1786; T.J. to Jean Jacques Berard & Cie, August 9, 1786; T.J. to Francis Lewis, August 9, 1786; Jean Jacques Berard & Cie to T.J., August 23, 1786. A pipe of Madeira held 110 gallons.
80. T.J. to A. Donald, September 17, 1787; A. Donald to T.J., November 24, 1788.
81. Buffon to T.J., December 31, 1785. In June Jefferson had asked Chastellux to deliver a copy of his *Notes on the State of Virginia* to Buffon. T.J. to Chastellux, June 7, 1785. Georges-Louis Leclerc, Comte de Buffon (1707-1788) had become world famous as the *Intendant* of the Kings natural history collection that encompassed the whole range of nature: animal, vegetable and mineral. The collections were housed in a series of buildings to the east of the Latin Quarter on the left bank known as the Jardin du Roi. When Jefferson was six years old, Buffon's monumental treatise *Histoire Naturelle, generate et particuliere, avec la Descnption du Cabinet du Roi* was published. By the time of Jefferson's arrival in France, Buffon had already served 45 years as the Director and his reputation was world famous. In fact, in compiling his *Notes on The State of Virginia,* Jefferson had studied Buffon's *Histoire Naturelle* and called the author "The best informed of any Naturalist who has ever written."
82. T.J. to Buffon, December 31, 1785; Buffon to T.J., March 27, 1787; Rice, 85-86.
83. T.J. to Bondfield, January 24, 1786.
84. Thomas Barclay to T.J., February 24, 1786.
85. Bondfield to T.J., June 24, 1786; T.J. to Bondfield, August 8, 1786.
86. Bondfield's bill for the purchase of wine for T.J., June 5, 1786, L.C. reel.
87. T.J. to Antonio Giannini, February 5, 1786. Jefferson had originally hired Giannini on November 2, 1788 for "£50 and find him 15 bushels of wheat and 480 lb. meat i.e. bacon when we have it" *Jefferson's Memorandum Books.*
88. Antonio Giannini to T.J., June 9, 1786; *Papers,* IX: 624.
89. Giannini does not appear in Jefferson's records again until four years later, when apparently successful but anxious to return to the vineyards, he offered to buy Mazzei's land at Colle for 70 pounds. "Jefferson's Diary of Philip Mazzei's Affairs," *Papers,* XVI: 308-309.

CHAPTER THREE

1. T.J. to John Adams, November 19, 1785; T.J. to Abigail Adams, November 20, 1785; T.J. to John Adams, November 27, 1785; John Adams to T.J., February 21, 1786.

2. Abigail Adams to Mary Smith Cranch, February 26, 1786. Jefferson had met Smith as early as August, 1785 when Smith came to Paris. They hit it off and immediately became friends. T.J. to Abigail Adams, September 4, 1785.
3. *Jefferson's Memorandum Books.*
4. William Short to William Smith, 23 June 1887; Smith to Short, 30 July 1887.
5. Lawrence Stern was one of Jefferson's favorite popular writers. Jefferson was acquainted with Pierre Dressin and the Hotel d'Angleterre's involvement in Stern's *A Sentimental Journey.* Shortly before his wife Martha's death, Jefferson and Martha exchanged lines from Lawrence Stern's *The Life and Opinions of Tristram Shandy Gentlemen:* "Time wastes too fast: every letter I trace tells me with what rapidity life follows my pen. The days and hours of it are flying over our heads like clouds of windy day never to return-more everything presses on-and every time I kiss thy hand to bid adieu, every absence which follows it, are preludes to that eternal separation which we are shortly to make!" *Papers,* VI: 196-97.
6. Lambert, R.S. *Grand Tour,* New York: 1937, 41.
7. For a detailed account of Golden Square during the 18th century see Chancellor, Beresford E. *The History of the Squares of London,* "Golden Square," 129-140.
8. Mather Brown (1761-1831) painted Jefferson's portrait during his stay in London, probably at his studio at No. 1 Wells Street rather than at his residence on Cavendish Square. *Papers,* IX: 364.
9. Three and a half months earlier Jefferson had suggested to Adams that Portuguese wines be a subject for discussion and negotiation with de Pinto. Jefferson's idea was that the combination of an expanding American population with the popularity of Portuguese wines would inevitably lead to Portugal's wine trade independence from England. See T.J. to John Adams, November 27, 1785.
10. T.J. to John Adams, July 11, 1786.
11. T.J., *Autobiography,* Vol. I: 94.
12. Adams, C.F. *The Works of John Adams,* Vol. I, 420.
13. *Papers,* IX: 399. The king's conduct was in sharp contrast to his cordial reception of John Adams on June 1, 1785. *Diary of John Adams,* III: 180-81.
14. T.J. to Madison, April 25, 1786; T.J. to Richard Henry Lee, April II, 1786.
15. *Jefferson's Memorandum Books;* T.J. to William Smith, September 13, 1786.
16. Peters had served during the Revolutionary War as Secretary for the Board of War and later as a judge on the U.S. Court in Pennsylvania. Dolly's was a favorite haunt of James Boswell (Samuel Johnson's biographer) who described it as "a most excellent place to dine at. You come in there to a warm, comfortable, large room, where a number of people are sitting at table. You take whatever place you find empty; call for what you like, which you get well and cleverly dressed. You may either chat or not as you like. Nobody minds you, and you pay very reasonably. My dinner (beef, bread and beer and waiter) was only a shilling." *Boswell's London Journal 1762-1763,* New York: 1950, p. 86.
17. John Trumbull (1756-1843) was the youngest son of Governor Jonathan Trum-

bull of Connecticut. Educated at Harvard, young Trumbull joined the war effort as one of George Washington's aides and saw action at Dorchester Heights. He later served as General Horatio Gate's deputy adjutant and in 1778 as an aide to General John Sullivan in the Rhode Island campaign. At an early age Trumbull had shown a precocious ability in painting and in 1780 (while The Revolutionary War still raged) he went to London to study painting from Benjamin West. When America executed Major Andres as a spy, in retaliation Trumbull was briefly imprisoned by the British authorities on suspicion of treason but released. On his return to America he assisted his brother Joseph in supplying the American Army. In 1783 he returned to London to resume his studies under West's supervision and spent the next five years painting the major events of The American Revolution.

18. Trumbull, John. *Autobiography, Reminiscences and Letters of John Trumbull, from 1756 to 1841*, New York and London: 1841,92-93,118 [hereafter cited as Trumbull, Autobiography.] T.J. to Humphreys August 14, 1786; T.J. to Thevenard, May 5, 1786. Jefferson met in London three other famous American artists who were working there. Benjamin West (whom he had met in Paris in the spring of 1785), Mather Brown and John Singleton Copley. Jefferson conferred with all four artists on the advisability of having the sculptor Houdon show General Washington in modern or ancient dress and hairstyle. Jefferson "was happy to find ... that the modern dress of your statue would meet with your approbation. I found it strongly the sentiment of West, Copley, Trumbull and Brown, after which it would be ridiculous to add that it was my own. I think a modern in an antique dress as just [as much] an object of ridicule as an Hercules or Marius with a periwig or chapeau bras." T.J. to G.W, August 14, 1787; G.W to T.J., August 1, 1786.

19. Lucy Paradise was a thirty-five year old scatter-brained Virginia heiress who had lived in England since the age of nine. She is reputed to have been beautiful but with a temper so violent that she was frequently out of control. By the age of eighteen she married John Paradise, an intellectual, whose world revolved around scholars, professionals and artists. John Paradise had a great facility for making friends and Jefferson took an immediate liking to him. When Jefferson left London to return to Paris, John Paradise accompanied him as far as Greenwich. The Paradises called on Jefferson for help: financial, political, and in Lucy's case, emotional.

20. Butterfield, L.H., ed. *The Diary and Autobiography of John Adams*, Cambridge: 1961, III: 184.

21. *Jefferson's Memorandum Books.*

22. *Papers*, IX: 373; Whately, Thomas. *Observations on Modern Gardening*, London: 1770, 4-5. [Hereafter cited as Whately.] Jefferson's library contained a 1770 first edition of Whateley's book. He obtained this book from the collection of Reverend Samuel Henley, a former professor of moral philosophy at William and

Mary College who left for England at the outbreak of the war, leaving behind a substantial library. In 1778 Jefferson was permitted by the president of the college to make selections of Henley's books for his own library. In 1785 Jefferson wrote Henley from Paris describing the books that he had selected and offering to either buy or return them. Henley agreed to sell Jefferson over fifty titles.

23. Chiswick was designed by Richard Boyle, the Third Earl of Burlington (1694-1753). The villa and gardens have been restored and are open to the public. For a detailed history of the Chiswick estate see John Harris', *The Palladian Revival, Lord Burlington, his Villa and Garden at Chiswick*, Montreal: 1994.
24. For an account of the life of Andrea Palladia see Bruce *Bourcher's Andrea Palladio, The Architect and His Time,* New York: 1994.
25. *Jefferson's Memorandum Books; Papers,* IX: 369.
26. William Kent (1685-1748).
27. *Alexander Pope and the Arts of Georgian England,* Oxford: 1978 ed., Ascending Villas: Pope's Influence on Twickenham Neighbors," 146-55.
28. *Papers,* IX: 369-70. The house and gardens of Twickenham's most famous citizen no longer exist. A girls school and convent were built on the site in the last century. But the tunnel which Pope used to visit his garden and grotto is still in place. A high school occupies the gardens and a preparatory school is on the site of the house. The tunnel is used as a passage for the children moving from their school to the playing fields and swimming pool. The grotto remains but can be seen only by appointment. The decorations have disappeared. Letters to the author from John Ives, Twickenham, March 12, 1992 and Sister Christina, St. Catherine's Convent, Twickenham, July, 1992.
29. Lancelot "Capability" Brown (1716--1783).
30. *Papers,* IX: 369.
31. *Jefferson's Memorandum Books; Papers,* IX: 370. The dwelling house at Claremont is now a school and at Esher-Place only the gatehouse survives.
32. *Whately,* 184-89; *Papers,* IX: *370; Jefferson's Memorandum Books.*
33. *Papers,* IX: *370;Jefferson's Memorandum Books;* University of Virginia, Alderman Library, *Jefferson Papers,* tavern bill, April, 1786. [Hereafter cited as tavern bills, UVA.] The Postman's Arms no longer exists.
34. Burke, Thomas. *Travel in England,* London: 1942, 23.
35. Turner, W J. *The Englishman's Country,* London:1935, 258-260. [Hereafter cited as Turner.] The coming of the railroads was the death knell for many English inns. It made its own road and built in its wake the railway hotel near important railway stations. These often ugly buildings were eventually replaced by the larger and more comfortable downtown hotels. The automobile reopened the roads and accounts for the survival of many old inns.
36. William Kent was a fashionable architect of formal buildings in the Palladian style but, paradoxically, he was the first important pioneer in the creation of the informal English garden. He was opposed to the stiff, regular English garden

patterns of the 17th century and was one of the first to eliminate walls or boundaries. He replaced them with sunken fences or what became known as "ha-has"—to express surprise at finding a sudden and unnoticed barrier. Kent's guiding principle was that "nature abhors a straight line." The man who made the greatest impact on 18th century English landscape gardens was Lancelot "Capability" Brown whose nickname derived from his habit of saying of nearly every garden he was asked to improve that it "had great capabilities." He worked at Stowe under Kent and made it one of the most talked about gardens of that day. Brown was a fervent advocate that gardens should display their natural beauty and give the appearance of freedom and employed the use of "ha-has" as a method of disguising boundaries. Turner, 238-42. At age 35, Brown was appointed Royal Gardener at Hampton Court.

37. *Jefferson's Memorandum Books; Papers*, IX: 370.
38. *Papers*, IX: 370; tavern bills, UVA; Andrews, C. Buryn, ed., *Torrington Diaries, John Byng, 5th Viscount,* 4 Vols., London: 1934-38, Vol. 2. [Hereafter cited as *Torrington Diaries.]* There was a Bear Inn on Castle Street in Reading in the 15th and 16th centuries. At some time in the late 18th century, it moved to new premises (just around the corner) on Bridge Street. I have not been able to establish whether the Bear Inn was on Castle Street or Bridge Street in 1786. It is mentioned as being on Bridge Street in the early 19th century and my feeling is that it was the newer Bear Inn on Bridge Street when Jefferson and Adams stayed there. I am told that until recently the Bear Inn building on Bridge Street was part of Cowage's Brewery offices but the brewery has now moved to the edge of town and most of its buildings have been demolished or built-over. The Bear Inn no longer exists. Letters to the author from Mary Butts of Reading, England, April 5, 1992, and John A. Becker, Reading, England, April 13, 1992.
39. Tavern bills, UVA. John Byng, who stayed at the Bear Inn one year later, complained that his punch was sour and weak and his bed was wrapped in damp sheets.
40. *Jefferson's Memorandum Books*; Burke, *Travel in England,* 56-89.
41. *Jefferson's Memorandum Books; Papers,* IX: 370-71; tavern bills, UVA.
42. Simone, Andre L. *Bottlescrew Days,* London: 1927, 144-198.
43. *Papers,* IX: 371-75. Jefferson did not actually record climbing the Pillar with Adams, but given his penchant for seeing things from the highest point we can assume that he did. The Stowe gardens are one of the best preserved landscape gardens that Adams and Jefferson saw.
44. The William Pratt Inn no longer exists and the local museum and library have no records of its existence. Letter to the author from Mary Butts, Banbury, England, April 7, 1992. Tavern bills, UVA; and *Jefferson's Memorandum Books.*
45. Letter to the author from Robert Bearman, Senior Archivist, the Shakespeare Birthplace Trust, March 31, 1992. *Torrington Diaries,* Vol. 2, 224. The White Lion did not survive the coming of the railroads and was closed in the 1860s. The

46. "Shakespeare and Pope, he [Jefferson] said, gave him perfection of imagination and judgment, both displaying more knowledge of the human heart-the true province of poetry-than he could find elsewhere." Bernard, John. *Retrospections in America 1797-1811,* New York: 1887, 238.

47. Shakespeare's flat tombstone lies at the channel of the choir with his lines pronouncing a curse on anyone who might remove his bones:
    "Good Friend, for Jesus' sake forbear
    To dig the dust enclosed here:
    Blest be the man that spares these stones
    And curst be he that moves my bones."

48. *Diary of John Adams,* III: 184-185. At the time of their visit to Shakespeare's house it was owned and operated by the Hart family, lineally descended from Shakespeare's sister. The peripatetic Englishman, John Byng, visited Shakespeare's house a year before the American ministers' visit, and recorded an interesting experience with the old chair. "How do you Mrs. Hart? Let me see the wonders of your house. 'Why, there, sir is Shakespeare's old chair, and I have been often bid a good sum of money for it. It has been carefully handed down on record by our family; but people never thought so much of it till after the jubilee, and now see what pieces they have cut from it, as well as from the old flooring of the bedroom!' I bought a slice of the chair equal to the size of a tobacco stopper; and I eagerly eyed the lower cross bar of the chair, curiously wrought, which Mrs. Hart would not be tempted to part with." Later that evening Byng passed the house and "Mrs. Hart took my offer and I carried off with me this curious morsel of theatrical antiquity, viz. the cross bar of Shakespeares chair; which is now hung in my dining room, in a mulberry frame." When Byng returned to Stratford-upon-Avon in 1792 he was shocked to learn that the Harts had sold the old chair and "they have discovered that they have sold the goose that laid the golden egg!! Had they been makers of Italian policy, they had always kept an old chair ready to succeed the one sold; or rather, kept the old one and parted with the substitute." The old chair is no longer a part of Shakespearean lore. *The Torrington Diaries,* Vol. 1, 224; Vol. 3, 152-53, 181; also E. Law, *Shakespeare's Garden,* 1922, 8-10.

49. *Jefferson's Memorandum Books;* tavern bills, UVA; *Diary of John Adams,* III: 185; Clarke, Edward Daniel. *A Tour Through the South of England,* London: 1783, 376-77.

50. Dodsley, R., II. *A Description of Leasowes, The Seat of the Late William Shenstone, Esquire,* London: 1775, 285-320.

51. *Jefferson's Memorandum Books; Papers,* IX: 371-73; *Diary of John Adams,* III: 185. Little of the Leasowes' estate survives today.

52. *Jefferson's Memorandum Books;* tavern bills at UVA; letters to the author from

James S. Pizey, Yarhampton, England, March 18, 1992; B. Chatterton, Stourbridge, England, April 8, 1992; *A Gentleman at the Talbot Stourbridge,* H.E. Palfrey, 1927 and Mark Moody, 1952. The brick front of the inn is the same today as when the two American ministers entered on April 7, 1786. Restoration has also preserved the stone mullioned windows, tudor beams, balusters, newel posts and, in some rooms, the original oak panelled walls and molded ceilings. Early 18th century (1702 and 1707) wine inventories reveal its wines were Claret, Sherry, Renish (white German wine), Sack (a form of Sherry), Tent (a red Spanish wine), and Canary (a form of Sherry from the Canary Islands).

53. *Papers,* IX: 372; Whately, 194-203. Jefferson had no doubt prepared himself for his visits to Leasowes and Hagley by reading Joseph Heeley's two volume work *Heeley on the Gardens of Hagley,* 1777, which he owned. Heeley also discussed the beauties of the gardens at Leasowes and Envil.
54. *Diary of John Adams,* III, 185; *Papers,* IX: 374-75.
55. Tavern bills, *UVA; Jefferson's Memorandum Books.* Letter to the author from Mary Butt, April 7, 1992; Worcester *Evening News,* July 6, 1979. John Byng had lodged at the Hop-Pole two years earlier and complained that it was so crowded and noisy that he criticized himself for a lack of good judgment in choosing it as a place to stay. Like so many English inns that were driven out of business by the coming of the railroads, the Hop-Pole closed in 1840. *Torrington Diaries,* Vol. 2, 44, 188.
56. The Marlborough Arms remains a handsome inn and is located an easy walk from the palace.
57. *Papers,* IX: 374-75. John Byng, when visiting Blenheim a year later, had a similar complaint: "The Duke is sparing of plantations, and it is evident that his great planner Brown is dead: all the sides of the lake should be planted, as well as numbers of acres, and thousands of single trees, and thorns, in the grand front ... and why all beaches? Variety is the life of planting." *Torrington Diaries,* Vol. 3, 332. Adams, however, thought Blenheim superb. The palace and gardens are open to the public and are worth a special visit.
58. *Jefferson's Memorandum Books;* tavern bills, UVA.
59. See Wilson, Douglas L. *William and Mary Quarterly,* Vol. 41, 1984, "Sowerby Revisited," 626-27. John Adams also carried his own copy of Whately's book. *Papers,* IX: 444-46; T.J. to John Page, May 4, 1786.
60. John Adams thought Stowe, Hagley and Blenheim superb; Woburn, Caversham and Leasowes beautiful and Wotton both great and elegant though neglected, but he also hoped "It will be long, I hope before Ridings, Parks, Pleasure Grounds, Gardens and ornamental Farms grow so much in fashion in America. But Nature had done greater Things and furnished nobler Materials there. The Oceans, Islands, Rivers, Mountains, Valleys are all laid out upon a larger Scale." *Diary of John Adams,* III, 187.
61. T.J. to Charles Wilson Peale, August 20, 1811.

62. *Diary of John Adams*, III: 186-87. The bridge derives its name from an ancient monastery of the Black Friars that dates from about 1276, located on the bank of the Thames River. Shakespeare is said to have once lived at Blackfriars and in 1599 acted at a theatre which occupied a part of the monastery.
63. *Papers* XI: 43-45; T.J. to St. John de Crevecoeur, January 15, 1787.
64. Sowerby, No. 4225; *Papers*, IX: 373.
65. *Jefferson's Memorandum Books*; Lewis, W S. *Three Tours Through London in the Years 1748, 1776, 1787,* London: 1941, 25; *Baedeker's London and Its Environs,* London, 13th ed., 1902, 377-378. The Ranelagh grounds were purchased in 1690 by Richard Jones, 3rd Viscount of Ranelagh. The Viscount built a mansion and gardens, and it was opened to the public in 1742 and later developed into a place of public entertainment.
66. *Jefferson's Memorandum Books.*
67. *Diary of John Adams*, III: *188-89; Jefferson's Memorandum Books.* The original Theatre on this site opened in 1732. In its early years opera was emphasized, but by the time of Jefferson's visit the focus was on plays.
68. Syon House has been the estate and seat of The Dukes of Northumberland since the 16th century. Capability Brown was responsible for the present lay-out of the Syon gardens. The gardens and estate house are open to the public.
69. *Diary of John Adams*, III: 190; *Jefferson's Memorandum Books.* Drury Lane Theatre was built under a charter from Charles II and opened May 7, 1663. It is the oldest English theatre still in use. The theatre Jefferson attended had been built in 1674 with Sir Christopher Wren as architect. It was replaced by a "fireproof" theatre in 1794 that burned down fifteen years later. The Irish playwright and politician, Richard Brinsley Sheridan (1751-1816) is supposed to have said while drinking a glass of wine in the street while the Drury Lane Theatre burned: "A man may surely be allowed to take a glass of wine by his own fireside." It reopened in 1812. Drury Lane celebrated its tercentenary on May 7, 1963. Sarah Siddons had become the "tragedy" queen of the English stage when Jefferson saw her perform.
70. *Jefferson's Memorandum Books.* The afterpiece was Isaac Jackson's farce, *All the World's a Stage.*
71. *Papers,* IX: 453.
72. *Papers,* IX: *453;Jefferson's Memorandum Books.* Jefferson paid Stockdale £40-10-6 and Mather Brown £10.
73. *Jefferson's Memorandum Books;* invoices, March 14 and April 1 and April 24, 1786, UVA.
74. T.J. to John Paradise, May 4, 1786.
75. William Smith to T.J., April 28, 1786.
76. T.J. to William Smith, May 4, 1786; T.J. to John Paradise, May 4, 1786; *Papers,* IX: 542. Passage from Dover to Calais was usually made in less time than vice versa because of more favorable sea conditions. Three to five hours was consid-

ered good time and six hours was common. Dutens, M. Louis. *Journal of Travels made through the Principal Cities of Europe,* translated from the French by John Highmore, London: 1782. [Hereafter cited as Dutens.] Jefferson's and Smith's passage from Calais to Dover took nine and a half hours. T.J. to Short, March 28, 1786.

CHAPTER FOUR

1. T.J. to Lefevre, Roussac & Cie, August 8, 1786. The term Malmsey is a corruption of Malvasia or Monemvasia, the name of a fortified town in the bay of Epidaurus Limera from where the grape is supposed to have originated. Malmsey was and is a sweet Madeira. Henderson, 249, 287.
2. Jean Baptiste Pecquet to T.J., December 9, 1785; T.J. to Pecquet, May 5, 1786; Lefevre Roussac & Cie to T.J., July 1 and July 11, 1786; T.J. to Achard Freres, August 7, 1786; T.J. to Anthony Garvey, August 7, 1786; T.J. to Lefevre, Roussac & Cie, August 8, 1786; Lefevre, Roussac & Cie to T.J., September 12, 1786; T.J. to Achard Freres, October 15, 1786; *Jefferson's Memorandum Books,* November 23, Malmsey and 450 livres for an assortment of another 140 bottles.
3. Trumbull, John. *The Autobiography of Colonel john Trumbull, 1756-1843,* New Haven: 1953, 96, 120. [Hereafter cited as Trumbull, *Autobiography.*]
4. Trumbull, *Autobiography,* 96.
5. *Jefferson's Memorandum Books,* August 14, 1786.
6. Trumbull, *Autobiography,* 98-99; *Papers,* X: 251-252; *Jefferson's Memorandum Books,* Sunday, August 5, 1786.
7. As a result of Jefferson's recommendation, Jean Antoine Houdon (1741-1828) had recently returned from the United States. He had stayed at Mt. Vernon and personally made measurements and studies of General Washington for the marble life-size statue of Washington that now stands directly under the dome of the Capitol in Richmond, Virginia. It is a remarkable sculpture.
8. Charles Bulfinch (1763-1844). Like so many young American men from wealthy families, Bulfinch was in Paris preparatory to his Grand Tour of Europe. Through Trumbull he met Jefferson. Bulfinch became a New England architect whose works include the Connecticut, Massachusetts and Maine state houses, the Hollis Street Church, the New South Street Church in Boston and the Massachusetts General Hospital.
9. *Trumbull, Autobiography,* 114-15.
10. Trumbull, *Autobiography,* 116.
11. *Trumbull, Autobiography,* 116.
12. T.J. to Ezra Stiles, September 1, 1786.
13. *Trumbull, Autobiography,* 106.
14. Trumbull, *Autobiography.* The church was completed in 1790 and the National Assembly voted in 1791 to turn the church into a pantheon for the burial of dis-

tinguished men. Voltaire, Rousseau, Mirabeau and Hugo are buried here. Trumbull's *Autobiography* and Jefferson's accounts do not specifically record that Jefferson accompanied Trumbull to the Invalides and climbed to the top of the scaffolding at St. Genevieve, but given the fact that Trumbull was in Paris at Jefferson's invitation, it is likely that Jefferson would have served as his personal guide. Trumbull mentions in his *Autobiography* that Jefferson joined him nearly everyday.

15. Rice, Howard C. *Thomas Jefferson's Paris*, Princeton: 1976, 18-20,30,43-44. [Hereafter cited as Rice.]
16. T.J. to Maria Cosway, October 12, 1786, "My Head and My Heart." See Diana Ketcham's book, *Le Desert de Retz* for an account of Jefferson and Maria's visit to the Desert, near Chambourcy, 10 miles west of Paris.
17. Rice, 107-08; Morris, *Diary*, 1:83.
18. Rice, 104.
19. On a clear day the terrace provides a sweeping view of the countryside and Paris. An extra bonus of a visit to St. Germain is the attractive town itself.
20. *Jefferson's Memorandum Books.*
21. Rice, 111-12.
22. The precise cause of Jefferson's dislocated wrist is not known. Attempting to jump over a fence in the Cours-la-Reine while walking along the Seine with Maria seems to have become the romanticized version. Jefferson's daughter, Martha, said it occurred while on a "ramble" with a male friend, and Mazzei said it happened when he fell from a horse. A recent biography has yet another version of Jefferson vaulting "over a small fountain" in his garden and tripping. When William Stephen Smith told Jefferson that John Adams was "anxious to know how you hurt yourself," Jefferson's enigmatic answer of "How the right hand became disabled would be a long story for the left to tell. It was by one of those follies from which good cannot come but ill may" sheds no light on how it happened. For a more detailed account of how it might have happened see *William and Mary Quarterly*, January, 1948, "Jefferson's Earliest Note to Maria Cosway With Some New Facts and Conjectures on His Broken Wrist," by L.H. Butterfield and Howard C. Rice, Jr.
23. T.J. to Maria Cosway, October 5, 1786; Maria Cosway to T.J., October 5, 1786.
24. T.J. to Maria Cosway, October 12, 1786, "My Head and My Heart."
25. Sparks, Jared. *Memoirs of the Life and Travels of John Ledyard*, N.Y: 1828, 212, 227. Ledyard received so much encouragement and support from Lafayette for his proposed exploration of the western part of the continent that he wrote Jefferson, "If I find in my travels a mountain as much above the mountains as he is above ordinary men I will name it LaFayette." John Ledyard to T.J., August 16, 1786; *Papers*, IX: 259-61.
26. *Trumbull, Autobiography,* 103-04; T.J. to John Ledyard, August 16, 1786; Ledyard to T.J., August 16, 1786; *Papers* IX: 259-60.

27. T.J. to Wm. Carmichael, March 4, 1789; *Papers,* IX: 261.
28. John Trumbull to T.J., October 9, 1786; T.J to Trumbull, October 13, 1786. Probably Monsieur Dorsay's wine cellar that Jefferson would visit on a trip to Champagne two years later.
29. T.J. to John Adams, January 11, 1787; T.J. to William Smith, January 15, 1787; T.J. to John Jay, February 8, 1787; T.J. to C.W F. Dumas, February 9, 1787; T.J. to William Carmichael, February 18, 1787; T.J. to William Barclay, February 18, 1787.
30. A principal source of the King's revenues came from taxes levied on all goods sent into Paris, and though Jefferson was diplomatically exempt, he still had to apply to the French ministers, Counts Vergennes and Montmorin, for a wine "passport" each time wine was shipped to him.
31. Le Veillard to T.J. [before January 26, 1787]; T.J. to Vergennes, February 11, 1787. Three days after Jefferson's passport request, Count Vergennes died and Count Montmorin was appointed his successor. T.J. to John Adams, February 14, 1787.

CHAPTER FIVE

1. T.J. to William Short, March 15, 1787.
2. Duetens, Louis M. *Journal of Travels made through the Pincipat Cities of Europe, translated from the French by John Highmore.* London: Printed by J. Willis, 1782. [Hereafter cited as Duetens *Journal.]* On this trip Jefferson carried with him the French version of Duetens' *Journal of Travels.* This detailed travel guide gave the time and distances between towns, e.g., "Dijon to Beaune 23 miles, 3 hours 15 minutes." It recommended the best inns and taverns, e.g., "Fountainebleau-The Dauphine ... Beaune-Post House has a fine garden." It provided monetary rates of exchange between countries, a description of the towns and cities and sights to see, and a variety of other useful hints and advice.
3. *Papers,* XI: 415.
4. Redding, Cyrus. *A History and Description of Modern Wines,* London: 1833, 127. [Hereafter cited as Redding.] Biographical Note: As a young man, Cyrus Redding (1785-1870) moved from Cornwall to London to become a journalist. He became successful as an author of a variety of books and poems, including *A Biography of William IV,* and *A History of Shipwrecks and Disasters at Sea.* Redding's involvement with wine, and French wine in particular, came about by accident. In 1814 he was sent to Paris as correspondent for *The Examiner* and remained in Paris as editor of *Galignani's Messenger* until1819. Redding spent his time visiting the vineyards of France and Italy and recalled in the introduction to *A History and Description of Modern Wines,* "I cannot look back without pleasure to seasons spent in lands of the vine, not in the town, but in the heart of the country."
5. Henderson, Alexander. *The History of Ancient and Modern Wines,* London: 1824,

167. [Hereafter cited as Henderson.] Biographical Note: Alexander Henderson (1780-1863) graduated as a doctor of medicine from Edinburgh University in 1803. Although he established a medical practice in London, he applied himself chiefly to literature, contributing to the *Encyclopedia Britannica* and other publications. Before writing this book, Henderson had visited the principal wine-growing districts of France, Germany and Italy. Henderson devotes fourteen chapters and 228 pages to modern wines and many of his observations are as valid now as then.

6. A 1989 white Clos da la Chainette was found to be full-bodied, with a rich buttery taste and aftertaste, a wine that could easily be confused with the better known white Burgundies from Puligny or Chassagne Montrachet.
7. Henderson, 167; Redding, 105.
8. M'Bride, Duncan. *General Instructions for the Choice of Wines and Spirituous Liquors*, London: 1793.
9. Henderson, 168; Jullien, Andre. *The Topography of all the Known Vineyards… Translated from the French and abridged.* London: 1824, 62-64. [Hereafter cited as Jullien.] Biographical Note: Jullien (1766-1832) was a wholesale wine merchant in Paris who regularly visited the principal wine-producing districts of France. According to Andre Simon, "he obtained a vast amount of practical knowledge about the vineyards he visited, the different species of vines he saw and the different wines he tasted, and he made it a practice to write down everything that interested him; later on in life he undertook to visit most of the vine-growing districts of Europe, and even passed into Asia. In 1816, he published in Paris a book entitled *Topographic de taus les Vignobles Connus*, which is of the highest interest because most of the information it contains is absolutely original."
10. *Papers*, XI: *415-16;Jefferson's Memorandum Books;* T.J. to Short, March 15, 1787; T.J. to Short, March 27, 1787.
11. *Papers*, XI: 416-18; 484; T.J. to Short, March 15, 1787.
12. *Papers*, XI: 416; Letter to the author from Louis Latour, Sr., May 27, 1974.
13. See *The Great Wine Blight* by George Ordish, 1972 for a detailed account of the cause, cure, social and economic effects this dreadful pest wrought on the world's wine industry. Unfortunately, Phylloxera is still present in many wine regions throughout the world. In recent years Phylloxera has again become a serious problem for vineyard regions in California, especially in Napa Valley and Sonoma County.
14. *Papers*, XI: 417. Chambertin was the favorite wine of King Louis XIV and Napoleon. But perhaps Chambertin's greatest praise was sung by an obscure English writer, Maurice Healy, who got up before a group of fellow wine enthusiasts, known as the Saintsbury Club, at Vintners Hall in London in the 1930's, and concluded his remarks by saying, "I can't remember the place and I can't remember the girl, but the wine was Chambertin."
15. Grand Cru is French for "great growth," and in Burgundy it stands for thirty of

Chapter Notes

the Cote d'Or's finest wines plus seven from Chablis.

16. Parker, Robert M., Jr. *Burgundy,* New York: 1990, 404-08. [Hereafter cited as Parker, *Burgundy.*]
17. Seward, Desmond. *Monks and Wines,* London: 1979, 66-69.
18. *Papers,* XI: 418.
19. Parker, *Burgundy,* 409.
20. Henderson, 164; Jullien, vii-viii. The monks realized that the quality of Vougeot's wines varied depending on the part of the vineyard from which the grapes came: "The wine made from those in the middle selling for one-third more than that made in the upper part, and three times as much as that made from those at the lower end." During the Revolution the house of Tourton and Ravel bought Clos de Vougeot for a million livres and indiscriminately blended the wines resulting in an immediate loss in quality.
21. Henderson, 163-64; Jullien, vii-viii.
22. Parker, *Burgundy,* 421-23.
23. *Papers,* XI: 417.
24. *Jefferson's Memorandum Books;* T.J. to Short, March 15, 1787.
25. *Papers,* XI: 418.
26. T.J. to Etienne Parent, March 13, 1787.
27. L.C. Reel3.
28. Parker, *Burgundy,* 558-60.
29. Henderson, 167-68; Jullien, 77.
30. For vineyard sizes, see Parker, *Burgundy,* 558-62.
31. Henderson, 167-168; Redding, 122-24.
32. *Papers,* XI: 417; Letter to author from Jacques d'Angerville, December 30, 1990.
33. Lavalle, M.J., *Histoire de la Vigne, et Statistique et des Grand Vins de la Cote d'Or,* 1855, p. 152. Letters to author from Jacques d'Angerville, November 27, 1990 and December 30, 1990.
34. Jullien, 78.
35. *Papers,* XI: 417.
36. Shannon, R[obert], M.D., *Practical treatise on brewing, distilling and rectification, ... of making wines, ... With an appendix on the culture and preparation of foreign wines, ...* London: 1805, 126--127. [Hereafter cited as Shannon.] Shannon's section on the wines of Burgundy is plagiarized word for word from a work by Claude Arnoux, *Dissertation Sur La Situation de la Bourgogne,* written in 1728.
37. Barry, Edward. *Observations, Historical, Critical and Medical on the Wines of the Ancients and the Analogy between them and Modern Wines,* London: 1775, 430. [Hereafter cited as Barry.] Barry reported that Volnay grapes (Pinot Noir) were so delicate that they were not allowed to ferment in the vat for more than 12 to 18 hours resulting in a color reminiscent of "the eye of a partridge." Barry confirmed that the wines could be drunk within one year of the vintage. This is the earliest major work in English on the wines of the ancients and the first book in

English that discusses modern wines.
38. *Papers*, XI: 417.
39. Shannon, 122-23.
40. Fisher, S.l. *Observations on the Character and Culture of the European Vine*, Philadelphia: 1834, 225; Notes to author from Danny Shuster, Australian winemaker, 1990, through correspondence with Warren Winiarski, proprietor of Stag's Leap Wine Cellars, Napa, California.
41. Shaw, Thomas George. *Wine, The Vine and the Cellar*, London: 1864, 342. [Hereafter cited as Shaw.] Biographical Note: Thomas George Shaw, a Scotsman, worked his way up from a position as a London wine dock clerk, to salesman for a port and sherry house, to his own business as a London wine merchant. Shaw has been credited with almost single-handedly bringing about the reduction of duties on wines imported into Great Britain and Ireland from France.
42. Notes to author from Danny Shuster, September, 1990. Mr. Shuster is an Australian winemaker.
43. Lavalle, M.J. *Histoire et Statistique de la Viene et des Grand Vins de la Cote d'Or*, Paris: 1855, 144.
44. *Papers*, XI: 418.
45. Simon, Andre L. *Bottlescrew Days. Wine Drinking in England During the 18th Century*, London: 1926, 164-71. [Hereafter cited as Simon, *Bottlescrew Days*.] Biographical Note: Andre L. Simon (1877-1970), bibliophile, gourmet, wine connoisseur, historian and writer is unrivaled in his contribution to the "art of good living." Born in Paris, he came to London in 1902 as the English agent for the champagne house of Pommery and Greno. Bitten by the bug of "printer's ink," Simon went on to write over 100 books and pamphlets on wine and food. Simon's knowledge of wine was encyclopedic. In 1935, at the age of fifty-five, he came upon the idea of forming a wine and food society. Although started at the height of the depression, the idea quickly proved to be popular and within three weeks of its inception there were 232 members. Today the International Wine and Food Society has over 150 chapters throughout the world and over 8,000 members. There were three types of Burgundy wine barrels or casks: *the feuillette* held 125 bottles; the *piece* held 250 bottles and the *queue* or *botte* held 500 bottles.
46. *Jefferson's Memorandum Books*.
47. Espalier-a method of training vines to grow.
48. *Papers*, XI: 418-20. Beaujolais is still one of the most beautiful and romantic of all of France's wine regions. The historic towns that dot this region are encircled by rolling hills, many with at least one first-class bistro serving hearty local food and fruity, thirst-quenching Beaujolais.
49. T.J. to Short, March 15, 1787; *Papers*, XI: 418-20. In his notes Jefferson states that the seignory of Château de Laye was about 15,000 arpents and in a letter to Short dated March 15, 1787, writes that it consisted of about 15,000 acres. The

size of an arpent (an old French unit of land measurement) seems to depend upon what reference is used. Some dictionaries place it at% of an acre, others at .85 of an acre, and still others at 1.25 acres. Obviously Jefferson considered one arpcnt equal in size to one acre.

50. *Papers*, XI: 420.
51. Short to T.J., October 2, 1788.
52. Inspection of dining room during visit to Château de Laye in June, 1991.
53. Conversation between the author and Christian de Fleurieu, the present owner of Château de Laye, June, 1991.
54. Letter to the author from Christian de Fleurieu, December 10, 1990.

CHAPTER SIX

1. *Jefferson's Memorandum Books; Papers*, XI: 420; T.J. to Short, March 15, 1787.
2. T.J. to Madame de Tesse, March 20, 1787.
3. T.J. to Parent, March 13, 1787. The wine was sent to Jefferson's Paris residence in care of his maitre d'hotel, Petit, but Parent thought the season too cold to risk sending the vines.
4. *Jefferson's Memorandum Books*.
5. *Jefferson's Memorandum Books; Papers*, XI: 423; XIII: 273; T.J. to Madame de Tesse, March 20, 1787.
6. *Papers*, XI: 423; Smollett, Tobias. *Travels Through France and Italy from The Miscellaneous Works of Tobias Smollett*, London: 1856, 785. [Hereafter cited as Smollett.] Biographical Note: Tobias Smollett (1721-1771) was born in Scotland, educated as a physician but gave up medicine to pursue a highly successful literary career. Because of ill health, Smollett and his wife left England in June of 1763 for the milder climates of Italy and France where he spent two years. In 1776 *Travels Through France and Italy* was published in the form of a series of letters written from June 23, 1763 to June 13, 1765. Smollett's travels took him along many of the same roads and towns that Jefferson followed 24 years later. The letters describe his views, opinions and observations of the people, customs, religion, government, arts, antiquities, etc. and fill in many factual gaps not mentioned by Jefferson; Wechsberg, Joseph. *Blue Trout and Black Truffles*, New York: 1953, 261-62.
7. *Papers*, XI: 421.
8. Johnson, Hugh. *Vintage: The Story of Wine*, New York: 1989, 89, 283. [Hereafter cited as Johnson, *Vintage*.] Livingstone-Learmonth, John and Master, Melvyn, C. H. *The Wines of the Rhone*, London: 1978, 1-2. [Hereafter cited as Livingstone-Learmonth.]
9. Henderson, 169. The aristocracy of England had imported the best wines of the Rhone long before 1788. The household accounts of John Hervey, first Earl of Bristol, for the years 1700 to 1739 reveal that he imported from France the

wines of Cote Rotie, Condrieux, Hermitage, Burgundy, Claret, Champagne and St. George. See Simon, *Bottlescrew Days,* 71.
10. L.C. reel 3.
11. *Papers,* XI: 421.
12. Henderson, 171; Redding, 39.
13. The wines of Cote Rotie are available throughout the United States and are of consistent high quality and represent good value. The wines of such top producers as Guigal and Jasmin are not only receiving the recognition and respect that has been traditionally reserved for the Grands Crus Burgundies and Bordeaux but also the prices that go with greatness. The characteristics of a mature, quality Cote Rotie are a dark, ruby-purple hue, a concentrated scent of raspberries, or some would say a fragrance resembling a combination of strawberries and violets, a full body and an intensely fruity taste and after-taste. It is a wine to be drunk with rich meat dishes.
14. Letter to author from E. Guigal, March 1, 1992.
15. Johnson, *Vintage,* 1989, 302-03.
16. For an interesting account of the history of wine bottles, corks, and corkscrews, see Johnson, *Vintage,* 194-198; also Simon, 252-55.
17. For a complete list of articles carried by Jefferson and the comments of a contemporary chemist as to the probable uses of the chemicals and other apparatus that shared space in this box, see Appendix E. The dimensions of the box were 8¼ x 6²/₄ x 3½."
18. Livingstone-Learmonth, 14; Parker, Robert M., Jr. *The Wines of the Rhone Valley and Provence,* New York: 1987, 74 [hereafter cited as Parker, *The Wines of The Rhone Valley];* personal observation.
19. Livingstone-Learmonth, 15.
20. The Viognier is a low yielding temperamental grape that requires a great deal of attention and care. It produces a dry wine that combines a delicate bouquet and taste that goes well with seafood and is popular in local restaurants. Its popularity and limited production causes it to be expensive and of limited availability in the United States, although it can be found in wine stores in metropolitan areas such as New York, Washington, D. C., San Francisco, and Los Angeles. An increasing number of winemakers in California are growing the Viognier grape and making interesting wines.
21. Letter to author from Monsieur Neyret-Gachet (owner of Château Grillet), April 22, 1974.
22. Henderson, 172.
23. Denman, James L. *The Vine and Its Fruit,* London: 1864, 270-71; Henderson, 172; Redding, 139.
24. *Papers,* XI: 421.
25. *Papers,* XI: 421-22; XIII: 273.
26. *Papers,* XI: 422; Parker, *The Wines of the Rhone Valley,* 85.

27. Johnson. *Vintage,* 88-89, 283; Livingstone-Learmonth, 27-28.
28. Henderson, 172. Jefferson described "White Hermitage of the growth of M. Jourdan; not of the dry kind, but what we call silky, which in your letter just received you say are called doux. But by our term *silky* we do not mean *sweet,* but sweetish in the smallest degree only. My taste in this is the reverse of Mr. Butler's, who you say likes the dry and sparkling, I the *non mousseux* and *un peu doucereux.*" T. J. to Stephen Cathalan, February 1, 1816.
29. Henderson, 172.
30. *Papers,* XI: 422; L.C. Reel, 3.
31. Denman, 282; Henderson, 172. Thiebaut De Berneard, Arsenne. *The VineDresser's Theoretical and Practical Manual, on the Art of Cultivating the Vine,* New York: 1829, 150. Constantia was a sweet white and red wine made near the Cape of Good Hope in South Africa and highly esteemed in the 18th century, especially the white.
32. L.C. reel 3.
33. *Jefferson's Memorandum Books;* letters to author from Robert Bailley, July 27, August 14 and September 15, 1974.
34. Parker, *The Wines of the Rhone Valley,* 89.
35. *Papers,* XI: 422.
36. Henderson, 171 and 335.
37. Allen, Warner H. *History of Wine,* London: 1961, 215-16. See also Thiebaut De Berneard, 120.
38. Saintsbury, George. *Notes on a Cellar-Book,* London: 1920.
39. Johnson, Hugh. *The World Atlas of Wine,* London: 1994, 4th ed., 127.
40. *Papers,* XI: 422; Henderson, 170.
41. Parker, *The Wines of the Rhone Valley,* 88-89.
42. Henderson, 176.
43. Henderson, 175; Redding, 124.
44. *Papers,* XI: 421-22.
45. Young, Arthur. *Travels During the Years 1787, 1788 and 1789,* London: 1792. [Hereafter cited as Young.]
46. *Jefferson's Memorandum Books; Papers,* XI: 423; T.J. to Madame de Tesse, March 20, 1787.
47. Peter Mayle in his book *Toujours Provence* describes his attendance at a Pavarotti concert held at the Roman Theatre in Orange.
48. Redding, 120-21; Henderson, 172; Jullien, 150.
49. Today as many as thirteen different grape varieties are permitted in the blending of Châteauneuf-du-Pape, with the principal red grapes being Grenache, Syrah, Mourvedre and Cinsault.
50. Henderson, 175; Jullien, 129 and 149.
51. Livingstone-Learmonth, 153-55.
52. *Papers,* XI: 424.

CHAPTER SEVEN

1. *Jefferson's Memorandum Books; Papers,* XIII: 274.
2. *Jefferson's Memorandum Books.*
3. Young, 34-35.
4. Smollett, 710-11.
5. *Papers,* XI: 424.
6. Redding, 121-22; Jullien, 129.
7. Redding, 122.
8. *Papers,* XI: 424; XIII: 274; T.J. to Madame de Tesse, March 20, 1787; T.J. to Short, March 29, 1787; T.J. to John Jay, May 14, 1787. Slodtz was born ReneMichel in Paris in 1705 to Sebastien Slodtz, a sculptor, and Madelene Cucci. He sculpted under the name of Michel Ange Slodtz. He grew up in Paris and lived at the Louvre where his father resided from 1699 until his death in 1726. His twin brothers were also sculptors and two other brothers became painters.
9. Young, 34.
10. The Nimes arena is the best preserved of all the Roman amphitheatre and in 1989 it was equipped with a "big top" that can be used to completely cover the interior, allowing it to be used for indoor as well as outdoor events. Bullfights are one of the more popular outdoor events.
11. Church of St. Honorat.
12. Papers, XI: 424-25.
13. Jullien, p. 139.
14. T.J. to Madame de Tott, April 5, 1787.
15. The identification of Jefferson's room at the Cheval Blanc in St. Remy is not based on historical documentation but on the spontaneous utterances of an elderly woman who was serving as the hotel manager/concierge an early morning in May 1991, when I visited there. Although she spoke only French, I was able to convey to her my interest in the age of the hotel. She told me that the section of the hotel where we were standing was 18th century. She beckoned me to follow her into a room located just to the left of the entrance to the old section of the hotel. After I had looked around she said in French: "Your president slept here." As she struggled to recall the name, I suggested "Thomas Jefferson." Excitedly, she explained "Yes, that is the name." She reported that no hotel records remained of Jefferson's visit, so obviously her knowledge of his stay was based on word of mouth, handed-down, information.
16. *Papers,* XIII: 274; *Jefferson's Memorandum Books.*
17. Pope-Hennessy, James. *Aspects of Provence,* London: 1952, 43-45.
18. Bailey, Martin. *Van Gogh: Letters from Provence,* London: 1990, 101-135.
19. T.J. to Martha Jefferson, March 28, 1787.
20. Smollett, 783.

Chapter Notes

21. Short to T.J., April 4, 1787.
22. T.J. to Short, April 7, 1787.
23. Jefferson's comment about a man who shoots himself is an obvious reference to a comment made by Short in a letter to him dated March 13, 1787. Short reported: "I saw M. de Lafayette yesterday morning at his house. He hopes you will not follow the example of M. de Simiane (the husband of the beauty of that name) who lately put an end to himself by a *coup de pistolet* [pistol shot] at Aix."
24. Fisher, M.F.K. *Map of Another Town*, Boston: 1964, 22.
25. Fisher, M.F.K. *Map of Another Town*, Boston: 1964, 258-60.
26. T.J. to Short, March 29, 1787.
27. Jullien, 138-39.
28. Parker, *The Wines of the Rhone Valley*, 434-36.
29. Jullien, 138-40.
30. Jullien, 140. James Boswell on returning from Italy and approaching Marseilles in 1765 describes a *vin cuit* that he drank with his breakfast calling it "the best vin cuit in France. This is a particular sort of wine, which, after having been boiled is excellent to drink a glass with a crust of bread by way of breakfast." See *Boswell On The Grand Tour Italy, Corsica, and France 1765-1766*. Frank Brady and Frederick A. Pottle, editors, New York: 1955, 239. [Hereafter cited as Boswell.]
31. T.J. to Chastellux, April 4, 1787; T.J. to Philip Mazzei, April 4, 1787.
32. Young, 35.
33. This was a time in history when the French and English were not friendly with each other so it may be that Young was ignored because he was an Englishman. France and America were undergoing a period of unprecedented friendship and goodwill. Jefferson wrote to Madison, January 30, 1787: "Its inhabitants [France] love us more, I think, than they do any other nation on earth." Therefore, it is quite possible that Jefferson's reception at the inn dinner tables was more cordial than that experienced by Young.
34. Young, 37.
35. T.J. to Short, 9 April 1787.
36. Young, 178.
37. *Jefferson's Memorandum Books; Papers*, XI: 427-29; XIII: 273-74; T.J. to Short, April 7, 1787; T.J. to John Jay, May 4, 1787. The present Basilica of Notre Dame de la Gard was built in the 19th century replacing the medieval pilgrimage chapel that Jefferson visited.
38. T.J. to Mazzei, April 4, 1787.
39. *Papers*, XI: 427-28. Jefferson's notes give the cellar temperature at 9½ degrees Reaumur, a scale developed in 1730 by French scientist Rene-Antoine Ferchault de Reaumur. Reaumur's temperature scale was fairly widely used in the 18th century but has now practically disappeared. See O.T. Zimmerman and Irvin Lavin, *Industrial Research Services Conversion Factors and Tables*, Dover, N.H.,

1961, 539. Stephen Cathalan, the American Consul in Marseilles, accompanied Jefferson to dinner at Bergasse's. Stephen Cathalan to T.J., June 5, 1816.
40. *Papers*, XI: 428.
41. T.J. to Mazzei, April 4, 1787.
42. T.J. to John Jay, May 4, 1787.
43. *Papers*, XI: 429.
44. *Papers*, XI: 429.
45. *Papers*, XI: 430; Jullien, 137.
46. *Papers*, XI: 430-31; XIII: 274.
47. *Papers*, XI: 430-31; Young, 185-87.
48. Horace-Benedict de Saussure (1740-1799). Saussure is credited with introducing the word "geology" into scientific nomenclature in the publication of his work, *Travels in the Alps*, containing over 30 years of geological studies.
49. *Papers*, XI: 431; Young, 185-87.
50. *Jefferson's Memorandum Books; Papers*, XIII: 27. The Hotel York no longer exists and its exact location cannot be established from the Nice City Archives because, the archives of this period were destroyed in the Revolution. It was located, however, on the sea front in a section of Nice now called Croix de Marbre. Croix de Marbre is an area of Nice loosely bordered by the sea to the south, Boulevard Gambetta to the west, Boulevard Victor Hugo to the north and Rue Dalpozzo Royale to the east. Letter to the author from M. de Bodman, Nice Tourist Office, October 25, 1990.
51. *Papers*, XI: 287; Young, 188.
52. *Papers*, XI: 432.
53. T.J. to Victor Aldolphus Sasserno, May 26, 1819.
54. Jullien, 188.
55. Parker, *The Wines of the Rhone Valley*, 401-402. Parker states that it is believed that these vineyards were originally planted by Phocaean Greeks who colonized the area in 500 B.C.
56. Parker, *The Wines of the Rhone Valley*, 402.
57. Parker, *The Wines of the Rhone Valley*, 402. The Bagnis family produces red, white and rose wines under the label of Château de Cremat on 49 acres of vineyards in the hills behind Nice. Robert Parker calls the wines of Château de Cremat the finest of the Bellet Appellation. The wines of Château de Cremat are exported to the United States.
58. T.J. to Lafayette, April 11, 1787.

CHAPTER EIGHT

1. T.J. to Short, April 12, 1787; Young, 192.
2. *Papers*, XI: 432.
3. *Jefferson's Memorandum Books; Papers*, XI: 432; XIII: 271; T.J. to Maria Cosway,

Chapter Notes

July 1, 1787.

4. *Papers*, XI: 432-33; Young, 191-192. Jefferson did not record where he stayed in Tende and the quote is from Young's account of his stay in Tende two years after Jefferson's visit. However, because travelers had few options as to where they could lodge in small villages, it is probable that Jefferson stayed in the same or a similar type inn.
5. Young, 192.
6. Smollett, 706-708.
7. *Papers*, XI: 433.
8. *Papers*, XI: 434.
9. *Jefferson's Memorandum Books; Papers*, XI: 435; XIII: 272; Young, 194 and 254-55.
10. Redding, 246; Johnson, *Vintage*, 419; Jullien, 189; letter to author from Burton Anderson, October 19, 1992. Mr. Anderson is the author of *The Wine Atlas of Italy and Traveller's Guide to the Vineyards*, 1990 and other books on Italian wines.
11. Young, 194-95.
12. T.J. to John Page, May 4, 1786; Malone, *Rights of Man*, 60.
13. *Jefferson's Memorandum Books; Papers*, XIII: 272; Baedeker's *Northern Italy*, 1903 ed., 36-67.
14. *Papers*, XI: 435; XIII: 272. Jullien reports that Montferrat produced both red and white wines from around the town of Casal about 40 miles east of Turin and that the whites were much better than the reds. Jullien, 189. See also Haraszthy, 178; Simon, *Bottlescrew Days*, 114.
15. *Jefferson's Memorandum Books; Papers;* XIII: 272; Young, 197. The Bascilica of Superga was built between 1717 and 1731.
16. *Papers*, XI: 436; T.J. to John Jay, 4 May 1787; T.J. to Edward Rutledge, July 14, 1787; Ralph Izard to T.J., November 10, 1787; Leon Drayton to T.J., November 25, 1787.
17. T.J. to Andre Limozin, March 27, 1788.
18. Letter to author from Burton Anderson, October 19, 1992.
19. *Papers*, XI: 435; XIII: 272.
20. Letter to author from Burton Anderson, October 19, 1992.
21. *Papers*, XI: 436-37.
22. This observation is from Arthur Young's account.
23. *Jefferson's Memorandum Books; Papers*, XI: 441; Young, 199-200.
24. *Papers*, XI: 437; XIII: 272.
25. *Jefferson's Memorandum Books; Papers*, XI: 437-40; XIII: 272; T.J. to J. Skinner, February 24, 1820.
26. Boswell, 43.
27. T.J. to Sir John Sinclair, July 2, 1787.
28. *Jefferson's Memorandum Books; Papers*, XIII: 272; Baedeker's *Northern Italy*, 1903, 187.
29. Jullien, 192; Redding, 276; Shannon called the local wine of Pavia, "Vino

Piccanti."
30. *Jefferson's Memorandum Books; Papers,* XI: 440-41; XIII: 270.
31. Bemelmans, Ludwig. *Holiday In France,* 1957, 232-37; Smollet, 745-46.
32. *Jefferson's Memorandum Books;* Smollett, 203-04. Boswell also left Genoa aboard a felucca and because of contrary winds had to put ashore. Boswell describes the felucca as having a crew of twelve sailors: a master, ten rowers and a boy who acted as coxswain. He describes it as a well-built vessel with a wood railing around it over which could be thrown canvas to protect the passengers from rain or the sun. Boswell, 225.
33. T.J. to Short, May 1, 1787; T.J. to Martha Jefferson, May 5, 1787; T.J. to Mazzei, May 6, 1787; *Papers,* XI: 441.
34. *Papers,* XI: 441; XIII: 271. Jefferson called the Noli tavern miserable but does not tell us why. Smollett stayed in Noli and reported having "after a very odd kind of supper, which I cannot pretend to describe, we retired to our repose; but I had not been in bed five minutes, when I felt something crawling on different parts of my body, and, taking a light to examine, perceived above a dozen of large bugs." Smollett, 748.
35. Conversations with Noli restaurateurs, June 1991; Anderson, Burton. *The Wine Atlas of Italy,* New York: 1990, 71-75.
36. *Papers,* XI: 441-42.
37. *Papers,* XI: 442; T.J. to Martha Jefferson, May 5, 1787; T.J. to Short, May 1, 1787. A "gite" is a French term to designate a certain type of accommodation: villa, apartment, room, tavern.
38. *Papers,* XI: 441-42; Anderson, Burton. *The Wine Atlas of Italy,* New York: 1990, 75.
39. *Papers,* XI: 442. Boswell noted that the commerce of Port Maurice was supported by olive oil and that the figs were the best that he had ever eaten. He drank a wine there that he called "a little inferior to Madiera." Boswell, p. 233.
40. *Papers,* XI: 442; XIII: 271; Jullien, 190.
41. *Papers,* XI: 442-43; XIII: 271.

Chapter Nine

1. *Papers,* XIII: 271.
2. *Jefferson's Memorandum Books; Papers,* XI: 443; XIII: 273-74.
3. Boswell, who had stayed at the St.Omer some 22 years earlier, described his room as cold and smokey but found the food excellent. He speaks of being comforted by some warm wine and bread. However, on returning from Italy, Boswell again stayed at the St. Omer and found the company at dinner disagreeable. Boswell, 274.
4. *Jefferson's Memorandum Books; Papers,* XI: 443; XIII: 273-74; Young, 173.
5. *Jefferson's Memorandum Books;* Young, 173-74.

6. T.J. to Martha Jefferson, May 21, 1787.
7. *Papers*, XI: 443; XIII: 273; letters to the author from Robert Bailey, July 12 and 27, 1974.
8. *Papers*, XI: 443; Jullien, 184.
9. Letters from Robert Bailey to the author, July 12 and 27, 1974.
10. Jullien, 138; Livingstone-Learmonth, 77-85. Today one other sweet lightly fortified wine is made in this region around the village of Rasteau. Sold as Appellation Rasteau Controlee it is made more in the port style from Grenache grapes: noir, gris or blanc. No mention is made of this wine in old wine books, and in taste, style, color and grape varietal it does not fit Jefferson's or the Marquis' description of "vin blanc de Rochegude."
11. Chapoutier, Domaine de Durban, Paul Jaboulet Aine, Domaine de Coyeux and Vidal-Fleury are five of the best.
12. *Jefferson's Memorandum Books.*
13. *Jefferson's Memorandum Books; Papers*, XIII: 274.
14. *Jefferson's Memorandum Books; Papers*, XI: 443-44; L.C. Reel3.
15. Henderson, 177; Jullien, 133-34.
16. *Jefferson's Memorandum Books; Papers*, XI: 443-44; XIII: 274; Young, 34.
17. Young, 34.
18. *Jefferson's Memorandum Books.*
19. Henderson, 175; Redding, 128-29.
20. *Papers*, XI: 444-45; XIII: 274; Shaw, 355.
21. Lambert to T.J., June 11, 1787.
22. The Muscat grape is an ancient Greek variety thought to have been introduced to France by the Romans. Jullien, 133.
23. Henderson, 176-77.
24. Frontignan, like the other popular sweet Muscat wines of Lunel, Rivesalte and Vin Blanc de Rochegude were fortified wines, having their fermentations stopped by the addition of brandy. This process leaves the wine sweet.
25. *Papers*, XI: 445-46.
26. See Penzer, N.M. *The Book of the Wine Label*, London: 1947, 88.
27. Thudichum, 98.
28. Here is a recipe for making Frontignan wine taken from a book published in 1838. "An artificial Frontignac may be made of raisin wine, in which the proportion of sugar, or malt spirits, to the raisins, is large and the whole body weaker; the muscadel flavor being communicated by an infusion of the flowers of meadow sweet."
29. Shaw, 361.
30. *Jefferson's Memorandum Books; Papers*, XI: 445-46; XIII: 274; Denman, *Wine and Its Adulterations*, London: 1867, 15-16; Shaw, 359. Shaw said Sète had become a by-word for wine adulterations and there were over 200 so-called wine merchants and increasing in number every year.

31. Harasthzy, Agoston, *Grape Culture, Wines, and Wine-making,* New York: 1862, 209.

Biographical Note: Agoston Harasthzy (1812-1869) immigrated to Sauk City, Wisconsin in 1842 from Hungary. Seven years later he left for California and for the next nineteen years proved himself one of the most remarkable of the '49ers. He first went to San Diego where he became sheriff and town marshall. In 1852 he was elected to the State Assembly and moved to San Francisco. He became director of the San Francisco Mint, and experimented with a variety of agricultural activities on a farm in San Mateo County, south of San Francisco. His interest in making wine commercially didn't take root until he purchased the Buena Vista Ranch in Sonoma Valley in 1856. Although Harasthzy was not the first to establish a vineyard in Sonoma Valley, his letters to San Francisco newspapers and articles for agricultural journals on everything from planting vines and growing grapes to making and bottling wine probably did more to focus attention on Sonoma Valley as a prime grape-growing area than those of any other person.

By 1858 Haraszthy had planted nearly 140 acres, mainly in the mission grape. Because Haraszthy knew great wine could not be made from that grape, he convinced Governor Downey to send him to Europe to collect grapevines. During his travels, Haraszthy collected and imported over 1,400 vinifera vine varieties. When the California legislature rejected his request for reimbursement for his expenses and the costs of the vines, Haraszthy planted the vines at Buena Vista and published a catalog for their sale. Many of the vines were purchased and planted throughout California. However, there remains to this day serious dispute as to how much influence Haraszthy's collection of foreign vines has had on the development of today's California wines.

Haraszthy went on to incorporate his vineyards into the Buena Vista Viticultural Society and he became its superintendent. Three years later, after a series of financial setbacks, the Society's directors removed him.

Ever restless, he went to Nicaragua in 1868 and bought a sugar plantation with the intention of distilling rum. He disappeared one day in 1869, and it is believed that while attempting to cross an alligator-infested stream he fell and drowned.

Thudichum, John Louis William & Dupre, A., *A Treatise on Wine,* Abridged ed. London and New York: 1894, 394; Shaw, 356.
32. *Papers,* XI: 446.
33. *Jefferson's Memorandum Books; Papers,* XI: 446.
34. T.J. to John Rutledge, Jr., March 25, 1789.
35. *Papers,* XI: 446-47; T.J. to Martha Jefferson, May 21, 1787.
36. *Papers,* XI: 446-47;
37. Henderson, 178; Redding, 148.
38. *Papers,* XI: 446-47; Redding, 127-28. Jullien says, however, that around Nar-

bonne a red wine was made that had "a good colour, not harsh, much body, firmness, spirit, and good flavour." Jullien, 135.

39. Henderson, 178.
40. Henderson, 178.
41. Henderson, 174-75; Redding, 130-36.
42. Actually one can climb the hillside facing lower Carcassonne and enter *El Cite*, but it is easier and more romantic to enter by the drawbridge.
43. Today's visitor can stay in the old section of Carcassonne at the elegant Hotel de la Cite with a castle-like decor and a garden-patio that overlooks the ramparts, lower Carcassonne and the surrounding countryside.
44. Vizetelly, Henry. *A History of Champagne with Notes on other Sparkling Wines of France*, London: 1882, 257. Utilizing the *methode champenoise*, Sparkling Limoux has AOC designation and is dry with the aroma of fresh-cut grass. Stevenson, Tom. *Southeby's World Wine Encyclopedia*, London: 1988, 186. Blanquette de Limoux is still made from the Marzac grape with a small percentage of Chardonnay and Chen-in Blanc for acidity and bouquet. Biographical Note: Henry Vizetelly (1820-1894) was a journalist and publisher. Vizetelly's first serious exposure to wine came in 1869 when he was commissioned by the *Pall Mall Gazette* to write a series of articles on the French vintage. Eventually he took up residence outside of Paris and "resumed my studies of the more famous wines of the world and every succeeding autumn for the next half dozen years I visited scores of celebrated vineyards in Champagne, the center and south of France, along the Rhine and Moselle and in the Palatinate."
45. *Jefferson's Memorandum Books; Papers*, XI: 447-48; XIII: 275.

CHAPTER TEN

1. T.J. to William Lee, April 28, 1806.
2. Redding, 125-26.
3. Denman, 289.
4. Johnson, *The World Atlas of Wine*, London: 1994, 4th ed., 112.
5. *Jefferson's Memorandum Books; Papers*, XI: 454-55, 457.
6. T.J. to Francis Eppes, May 26, 1787.
7. Johnson, *Vintage*, 201-03.
8. Simon, Andre L. *The History of the Wine Trade in England*, Vol. III, London: 1909, 270.
9. Henderson, 185; Redding, 154.
10. No mention of the Pontac or du Lamon vineyards of Blanqueford is made in the 1986 English Edition (13th) of Feret's *Bordeaux and Its Wines*.
11. For a detailed account of the rise into wealth and power of the Chartrons wine merchants see *The Winemasters* by Nicholas Faith.
12. Faith, Nicholas. *The Winemasters*, London: 1978, 47-50; Price, Pamela Vandyke.

French Vintage, London: 1986, 149.
13. Lichine, Alexis. *Alexis Lichine's Encyclopedia of Wines and Spirits,* New York: 1967, 347-53. In 1855 the *Exposition Universelle* was held in Paris. At the request of the French authorities, a group of Bordeaux wine merchants prepared and submitted a list of the leading wines of Bordeaux. All 61 of the red wines listed, except for Château Haut-Brion from Graves, were from the Medoc, and all of the 23 white wines listed were sweet and from Sauternes and its surrounding communes. This classification or ranking was based primarily on the prices the wines had sold at over many years. The 61 red wines were divided into five groups: First Growths (four châteaux); Second Growths (15 châteaux); Third Growths (14 châteaux); Fourth Growths (10 châteaux); and Fifth Growths (18 châteaux). Sauternes and its surrounding communes were listed in three categories. Château d'Yquem was classified a Great First Growth to distinguish it from its competitors. Thereafter, 11 châteaux were ranked as First Growths and 12 châteaux as Second Growths. One hundred and forty years have passed since the original classification, and extraordinary changes have taken place at many of the vineyards, but the classification remains with one exception: Mouton-Rothschild was, by order of the French Government, promoted in 1973 from a Second Growth to a First Growth.
14. Letter to author from Elie de Rothschild, January 23, 1974.
15. Letter to author from Jean Delmas, January 30, 1974.
16. Letter to author from Jean-Paul Gardere, March 12, 1974.
17. Henderson, 184-85.
18. Parker, Robert M., Jr. *Bordeaux,* N.Y: 1991, Revised ed., 206, 213, 371, and 514.
19. The vineyard of Gruard-Larose was planted in 1757 by Monsieur Gruard, whose heir, Monsieur de Larose, added his name just nine years before Jefferson's visit. It was later split into two distinct vineyards, Gruard-Larose-Faure and Gruard-Larose-Sarget but has been reunited into one vineyard and is now owned by Domaine Cordier. See Andre L. Simon, *A Concise Encyclopedia of Gastronomy,* Section VIII, "Wine," London: 1946, 86.
20. Letter to the author from Henri Martin, July 3, 1974.
21. *Papers,* XI: 456; T.J. to John Bondfield, Dec. 18, 1787; T.J. to d'Yquem, Dec. 18, 1787.
22. Letters to author from Count Alexandre de Lur-Saluces, April 2, 1974 and July 22, 1974.
23. Jefferson recorded that one tonneaux was equal to 1000 bottles and that d'Yquem produced 150 tonneaux.
24. *Papers,* XI: 455-57. Pichard's ownership of Lafite ended in 1793 when he was guillotined. He had purchased the Lafite estate in 1785 for the extraordinary sum of one million livres.
25. Henderson, 185-186.
26. *Papers,* XI: 45Cr57.

27. *Papers,* XI: 455. Although Château Carbonnieux produces red and white wines today, it is still better known for its dry white wine.
28. *Papers,* XI: 457. See page 148 for an explanation of why 18th century white wines were able to keep for such long periods.
29. T.J. to Alexander Donald, September 17, 1787.
30. Letter to author from Elie de Rothschild, January 23, 1974.
31. Redding, 152. Beni Carolos was a course, dark, alcoholic red wine from the Provence of Valencia, Spain, that was very popular in the 18th century as a "blending" wine.
32. T.J. to John Rutledge Jr., March 25, 1788.
33. Henderson, 181.
34. Henderson, 181-82; Redding, 140; Shaw, 293-94.
35. Lichine, 477.
36. *Papers,* XI: 457.
37. Butterfield, L.H. ed. *The Diary and Autobiography of John Adams, 1771-1781,* Vol. 2, 370-71.
38. *Jefferson's Memorandum Books.*
39. Young, 87-91.
40. Roger, Dion. *Histoire de la Vigne et du Vin en France des Origines au Siecle,* Paris: 1959, 45Cr57. [Hereafter cited as Dion.]
41. Lichine, Alexis. *Guide to the Wines and Vineyards of France,* New York: 1967, 236; Johnson, *The World Atlas of Wine,* London: 1971, 106. Muscadets have a crisp, fruity, acidic bite that goes well with oysters and other seafoods and are reasonably priced.
42. *Jefferson's Memorandum Books.*
43. *Papers,* XI: 459-460; Dion, 451-455.
44. *Papers,* XI: 461.
45. *Jefferson's Memorandum Books; Papers,* XI: 462.
46. *Papers,* XI: 462; XIII: 275; Young, 53-54.
47. T.J. to John Bannister, June 19, 1787.

CHAPTER ELEVEN

1. T.J. to Parent, June 14, 1787.
2. Parent to T.J., June 20, 1787; Parent to T.J., July 30, 1787; Jullien, 71.
3. *Papers,* XI: 670.
4. Letter to the author from Michel Jaboulet-Vercherre, October 18, 1990; Lavalle, M.J. *Histoire et Statistique de la Vigne et des Grand Vins de la Cote d'Or,* Paris: 1855, 144. The name *Commaraine* comes from the Counts of Vienne, Lords of Commaraine who owned this property before 1100, when it was known as Chevanche de Pommard. The château was built by the Duke of Eudes, III.
5. Betts, Edwin Morris. *Thomas Jefferson's Garden Book,* 1776-1824, Philadelphia:

1944, 423. The wines of Clos de la Commaraine are distributed throughout the United States and are generally available in major wine shops in large metropolitan areas.

6. Parent to T.J., June 20, 1787. Parent's addition is incorrect. The total cost of the Montrachet as listed is 333 livres.
7. Gruber, Anna and Shay, Hal. "Archaeology and Wine," Paper of the Thomas Jefferson Memorial Foundation, Inc., Monticello: c. 1985.
8. Parent to T.J., June 20, 1787.
9. T.J. to R & A Garvey, June 24, 1787; R & A Garvey to T.J., June 29, 1787; R & A Garvey to T.J., July 21, 1787.
10. T.J. to Lafayette, April 11, 1787.
11. T.J. to William Drayton, July 30, 1787.
12. T.J. to John Jay, August 6, 1787. The King did not succumb to the public outcry for a meeting of the States-General until a year later and then delayed its convocation until May 1, 1789.
13. T.J. to Madison, August 2, 1787; T.J. to James Currie, August 4, 1787.
14. T.J. to Moustier, July 24, 1787.
15. Moustier to T.J., September 3, 1787.
16. Bondfield notified Jefferson: "Enclosed is a Bill of Lading for two cases of Muscat forwarded to the care of Geo. Clymer of Philadelphia to whom I have wrote to dispose of them agreeable to orders he may receive from Le Cte. de Moustier." Bondfield to T.J., June 28, 1788.
17. Madison to T.J., December 8, 1788.
18. T.J. to Wilson Miles Cary, August 12, 1787.
19. T.J. to Alexander Donald, September 17, 1787.
20. A Donald to T.J., December IS, 1787.
21. T.J. to A Donald, February 15, 1788; T.J. to Callow Freres, Carmichael & Co., February 15, 1788.
22. T.J. to John Jay, September 17, 1789.
23. T.J. to Madame de Corny, June 30, 1787.
24. Dian, Roger. *Histoire de la Vigne et du Vin en France,* Paris: 1959, 215, 659, 673. The vineyards gave way to military fortifications in 1840, and following World War I it became the cemetery for Americans killed in the war.
25. Jefferson usually, but not always, went to Mt. Calvair on Fridays or Saturdays and his account book entries indicate that he made several visits to the retreat between September 5 and October 12, 1787. *Papers,* XII: 199; 214. Jefferson first called his home the "Hermitage" before settling on "Monticello," and two months after this visit to the "Hermites," he wrote William Carmichael from Paris: "I sometimes think of building a little hermitage at the Natural Bridge (for it is my property) and of passing there a part of the year at least." T.J. to William Carmichael, September 26, 1786.
26. Roger Dion fails to tell us whether *vin de Suresnes* was red or white, but given its

location, I think that it was a white wine.
27. Fremyne de Fontenille to T.J., October 23, 1787; T.J. to Fremyne de Fontenille, October 24, 1787.
28. *Diary of John Adams,* Vol. III, 37.
29. T.J. to John Trumbull, November 13, 1787.
30. Maria Cosway to T.J., December 7, 1787.
31. John Trumbull to T.J., August 28, 1787; Papers, XII: 60. The French officers that Trumbull painted from life were Lafayette, Rochambeau, De Grasse, De Barras, Viomenil, Chastellux, St. Simon, the young Viomenil, Choizy, Lauzun, de Custine, de Laval, Deuxponts, Pherson, and Damas. Trumbull, *Autobiography,* 152.
32. T.J. to Parent, December 17, 1787.
33. Parent to T.J., January 16, 1788.
34. Parent to T.J., February 3, 1788. Since the wines were bottled there were additional charges for the bottles and for corks, wax, straw and string.
35. T.J. to Parent, February 20, 1788; Parent to T.J., March 3, 1788; Short to T.J., March 10, 1788.
36. T.J. to Monsieur d'Yquem, December 18, 1787; T.J. to John Bondfield, December 18, 1787.
37. Bondfield to T.J., January 15, 1788; Lur-Saluce to T.J., January 7, 1788.
38. Moustier to T.J., November 3, 1787; Papers, XII: 319.
39. Jefferson's mention of "the kindness you extended to Mr. Barclay our counsel" is in reference to what had occurred in Bordeaux a few days before Jefferson's arrival there. Thomas Barclay, the American Consul and Jefferson's friend, had been arrested and put in prison for debts. Pichard, President of the Bordeaux Parliament and the owner of Chateau Lafite, had helped in securing Barclay's release. Fearful that he would be rearrested, Barclay escaped from Bordeaux on July 1, 1787 with the help of John Bondfield and sailed for America a month later.
40. T.J. to President Pichard, February 22, 1788; T.J. to Bondfield, February 22, 1788; Bondfield to T.J., March 7, 1788.

CHAPTER TWELVE

1. Malone, Dumas. *Jefferson and The Rights of Man,* Boston: 1951, 146-177.
2. Abigail Adams to T.J., February 26, 1788.
3. T.J. to John Adams, March 2, 1788.
4. *Jefferson's Memorandum Books.*
5. Lambert, R.S. *Grand Tour,* New York: 1937, 147. [Hereafter cited as Lambert.]
6. T.J.'s tavern bills, UVA.
7. T.J. to Short, March 10, 1788.
8. T.J. to Short, March 10, 1788. Although the road from The Hague to Amsterdam passed through Leyden, one of the neatest and pleasantest cities in Holland,

there is no evidence that they stopped there or that Jefferson returned to see Leyden. This is a curious gap in Jefferson's itinerary. Jefferson was aware that Leyden was the site of a great university, adjoining which were botanical gardens, a library founded by William of Orange and a museum of natural history. There was another, almost equally compelling reason why Jefferson would have wanted to go to Leyden. It was the home of a kindred spirit and intellect and political philosopher, Jean Luzac, a professor at the university and publisher and editor of the *Lieden Gazette*. Under Luzac's direction, the French language *Gazette*, one of the most influential newspapers in Europe, had been a strong supporter of the American Revolution. During Adams' earlier years in Holland, he and Luzac had become close friends. When William Short visited Holland three years earlier, he told Jefferson about the pleasures of Leyden. See Short to T.J., August 28, 1785.

9. Lambert, 141-142; Dutens, Louis. *Journal.*
10. Dumbauld, Edward. *Thomas Jefferson American Tourist,* Norman, Oklahoma: 1946, 110-115 for a more detailed account of their negotiations.
11. T.J.'s tavern bills, UVA.
12. Morris, G. *Diary of the French Revolution,* 449; Tharp, Louise Hall. *The Baroness and the General,* Boston: 1962: 406. If it was Riedesel, the conversation probably turned to one of Riedesel's sorest subjects, Burgoyne's reprehensible conduct in not insisting that his troops should be returned to Canada "because Gates would have certainly consented."
13. T.J.'s tavern bills, UVA. Except for a bottle of Rhine wine, and a couple of unidentified bottles, all of the wines he ordered were either Moselles or Graves.
14. Johnson, Hugh. *Vintage,* 184-87.
15. *Papers,* XIII: 8-10.
16. Short to T.J., August 28, 1785.
17. *Papers,* XIII: 11-12.
18. *Jefferson's Memorandum Books.*
19. T.J. to Trumbull, March 27, 1788.
20. T.J. to Geismar, March 18, 1788; Geismar to T.J., March 26, 1788.
21. *Jefferson's Memorandum Books; Papers,* XIII: 12; 264; T.J.'s tavern bills, UVA.
22. *Papers,* XIII: 12; Lambert, 139.
23. *Papers,* XIII: 264.
24. *Papers,* XIII: 13.
25. Lambert, 119-123.
26. *Papers,* XIII: 264.
27. *Papers,* XIII: 13.
28. T.J.'s tavern bills, UVA.
29. *Jefferson's Memorandum Books; Papers,* XIII: 14, 265.
30. Baedeker, Karl. *The Rhine from Rotterdam to Constance,* London: 1892, 27-35. [Hereafter cited as Baedeker.]

31. *Jefferson's Memorandum Books;* T.J.'s tavern bills, UVA; Lambert, 137.
32. Vineyards are no longer to be found around Cologne.
33. *Papers,* XIII: 14.
34. *Jefferson's Memorandum Books.*
35. Simon, Andre. *Bottlescrew Days,* London: 1926, 220-224; *A Survey of Wine Growing in South Africa,* Snider-Paarl: 1974, 2.
36. Redding, 397. Redding lists the alcoholic strength of white Constantia at 19.75% and red Constantia at 18.92% indicating that it was fortified.
37. Henderson, 259-60; Simon, *Bottlescrew Days,* 220-224.
38. *Papers,* XIII: 15.
39. *Papers,* XIII: 265; John Rutledge, Jr. to T.J., July 8, 1788; Thomas Lee Shippen to T.J., July 31, 1788.
40. *Papers,* XIII: 15-16, 265.
41. "… 100 years ago [it was] reckoned the greatest wine of the Mosel, perfectly satisfying the taste for wine that was full-bodied and golden." Johnson, Hugh. *The World Atlas of Wine,* 4th ed., London: 1994, 150. [Hereafter cited as Johnson, *The World Atlas of Wine.*]
42. *Papers,* XIII: 15-16, 265.
43. T.J.'s tavern bills, UVA. It is not clear how many ounces a pot contained but it probably was the equivalent of a liter, i.e., 33.8 ounces.
44. *Papers,* XIII: 20; 266. This calculation assumes that Jefferson used the American wine measure, i.e., one tun being equal to 252 gallons and the bottle capacity about the same as today's bottle, i.e. 750 mi.
45. *Papers,* XIII: 16. See wine list of John Adam Dick & Son, *Papers,* XIII: 20-21.
46. T.J.'s tavern bills, UVA.
47. *Papers,* XIII: 17.
48. T.J. to Short, April 9, 1788.
49. *Papers,* XIII: 16-20; 266.
50. T.J.'s tavern bills, UVA.
51. *Papers,* XIII: 18-21. Actually, Jefferson's notes reveal that the wines of Rudesheim of the same year (1783) sold for a little more than those of Hochheim.
52. Johnson, *The World Atlas of Wine,* 156.
53. *Papers,* XIII: 19.
54. *Papers,* XIII: 19. Meinhard, Heinrich. *Wines of Germany,* N.Y: 1976, 218. The Bishop of Fulda can also lay claim to another historic footnote, the designation "cabinet" wine. The Prince-Bishop of Fulda decreed that the best wines were to go into his private cellar under a separate label known as the "secret cabinet." Over time the best wines came to be known as "cabinet wines."
55. *Papers,* XIII: 21.
56. T.J. to Geismar, July 13, 1788.
57. There is no evidence that he took them with him or that they were ever planted

at Monticello.
58. T.J.'s tavern bills, UVA. His tavern bills do not reveal what he ate, but it would appear that he drank wine with his meals and not after the meal as was the American custom.
59. *Papers*, XIII: 22.
60. Letters to the author from Fritz (S.F.) Hallegarten, February 28, 1974 and March 21, 1974.
61. Letter to the author from Harold P. Olmo, March 21, 1974.
62. *Papers*, XIII: 16. The best wine Jefferson drank was a thirteen year old Johannisberg.
63. See Johann Carl Leuchs, *Treatise on Wines and Wine-Making*, Nurenberg, 1847, extracted and included as Appendix B in Agoston Haraszthy's *Grapes Culture, Wines and Wine-Making*, New York: 1862, 210.
64. Letter to the author from Hans Ambrosi, April 17, 1974.
65. Letter to the author from the late Fritz Hallgarten, March 21, 1974.
66. The Spatburgunder is now grown in several other of Germany's wine regions, and there is a renewed interest in its planting.
67. *Papers*, XIII: 21 and wine list of John Adam Dick & Son, 16; Jullien, 203.
68. *Papers*, XIII: 21-22; Johnson, Hugh. *The Atlas of German Wines*, New York: 1986, 92; Johnson, *The World Atlas of Wine*, 163.
69. *Papers*, XIII: 22-25; 266-67.
70. Baedeker, 243.
71. *Papers*, XIII: 22-24; 267.
72. *Papers*, XIII: 25. The palace still forms the base for the town's radiating streets.
73. *Papers*, XIII: 267. Koenig's bookshop was located on Rue des Garendes Arcades at the corner of Rue des Hallebardes but the building was destroyed in 1944 by aerial bombing.
74. *Papers*, XIII: 267. Today's visitor must climb 330 triangular stone steps to reach the top. Miller, Luree. "Retracing Thomas Jefferson's 1788 Journey," *Washington Post*, April II, 1993.
75. *Papers*, XIII: 26. At nine livres per bottle it was three times as expensive as a First Growth Bordeaux or a Grand Cru Burgundy.
76. Letter to the author from Jean Hugel, June 19, 1974.
77. Redding, 185-86.
78. T.J.'s tavern bills, UVA.
79. Redding, 184; Jullien, 36-40, but they probably had in mind the *Vin de Paille*.
80. *Papers*, XIII: 28.
81. *Papers*, XIII: 29.
82. *Papers*, XIII: 30.
83. *Papers*, XIII: 30-31.
84. *Papers*, XIII: 30.
85. *Papers*, XIII: 31.

Chapter Notes

86. Johnson, Hugh. *World Atlas of Wine*, London and New York: 1971, 100.
87. *Papers*, XIII: 32.
88. Letters between the author and Christian Bizot at Bollinger resulted in Mr. Bizot enclosing pages from Jean Nollevalle's book, *Ay en Champagne un bourg viticole ala fin de l'Ancien Regime* which referenced Monsieur Dorsay's 18th century vineyard in Ay. Over time Dorsay's small Ay vineyard became the property of the Dueil family. In 1951 Mme. Lily Bollinger purchased the Dueil vineyard. Bollinger uses the grapes from the former Dorsay vineyard in its *vin claire* from which Bollinger's Special Cuvee, Grande Annee, Rose and R.D. are made.
89. *Jefferson's Memorandum Books; Papers*, XIII: 31-32.
90. *Papers*, XIII: 31. Jefferson reported that Dorsay produced 1,100 pieces of Champagne a year. Since a piece held 200 bottles, Dorsay's annual production was 220,000 bottles. Dorsay's Champagne was so popular that he sold it as soon as it was bottled. Arthur Young visited Dorsay's winery a year later and reported that Dorsay had from 30,000 to 40,000 bottles in his cellar.
91. *Papers*, XIII: 32, 33.

CHAPTER THIRTEEN

1. T.J. to George Washington, May 2, 1788.
2. Bondfield to T.J., April 19, 1788; *Papers*, XIII: 96; from the vineyard part of Haut-Brion owned by Le Cte. De Fumel.
3. T.J. to Bondfield, November 3, 1788.
4. Bondfield to T.J., September 6, 1788.
5. T.J. to Bondfield, December 14, 1788.
6. T.J. to William Shippen Jr., June 19, 1788; T.J. to John Rutledge Jr., June 19, 1788. These notes, which have come down to us as "Hints On European Travel," were invaluable to the two young travelers. *Papers*, XIII: 264-276. Jefferson's letters of introduction included Andre de Sasserno in Nice, Stephen Cathalan in Marseilles and Geismar in Frankfurt. *Papers*, XIII: 356-57.
7. Thomas Lee Shippen to T.J., July 31, 1788.
8. Thomas Lee Shippen to T.J., July 31, 1788; John Rutledge, Jr. to T.J., August 1, 1788; *Papers*, XIII: 454.
9. Thomas Lee Shippen to T.J., July 31, 1788.
10. T.J. to Thomas Lee Shippen, September 28, 1788.
11. Short to T.J., September 24, 1788.
12. Before Jefferson left for France, the Virginia Legislature had asked him to design a building to be used as the State Capitol. Jefferson had drawn up tentative plans, but in order to finish the project he decided that he needed help and sought the assistance of Charles-Louis Clerrisseau, a distinguished French architect and the author of a book on French antiquities. They chose as their model a Roman temple called the Maison Carrée located in Nimes. Clerrisseau

prepared the plans and constructed the plaster model, but Jefferson adapted the building to the needs of the Virginia Legislature. Using a Roman antiquity as the struc ture for a legislative building was a bold departure from any previous form of governmental colonial architecture. In a letter to Madison he explained why. "We took for our model . . . one of the most beautiful, if not the most beautiful and precious morsels of architecture left us by antiquity. It is very simple but it is noble beyond expression." T.J. to Madison, September 20, 1785.

13. Julian P. Boyd, the first editor of the *Papers of Thomas Jefferson*, has suggested that Jefferson's failure to give a copy of the askos to Clerriseau resulted perhaps from a sudden realization that it was an inappropriate gift because "the object he saw in M. Seguier's cabinet was indeed an elegant and fairly uncommon form of a familiar type of Greek pottery and bronze work discovered chiefly in Etruscan excavations. The earlier samples were in clay and in the shape of a duck, of which excellent specimens exist in the Louvre. The bronze askos of Nimes is of a later period, as is another almost identical with it in the *Museo Etrusco Gregoriano* in Vatican City. Scholars have given more attention to the form than to the function of the askos, but the duck shape itself suggests the use. So does the Greek root of askos, meaning bag, wineskin, bladder. George Dennis, in his *Cities and Cemeteries of Etrusia* was unquestionably correct in concluding that such vessels 'seem to have been employed for the toilet alone'-in a word, as urinals." With all respect to Julian P. Boyd, a renowned Jeffersonian scholar, the Greek root definition of askos "bag, wineskin, bladder," defines its use as a wine vessel. Wineskins had been used for thousands of years to hold and transport wine, and predate the origin of this askos by at least a thousand years. Alexander Henderson, the author of *The History of Ancient and Modern Wines*, reports that the most ancient receptacles for wine were probably the skins of animals, and that when Ulysses went to the cave of the Cyclops, he was carrying with him a goat-skin, filled with a rich black wine he received from Maron, "the priest of Apollo." Hugh Johnson, the modern day chronologist of the history of wine, tells of wine being delivered to the cellar of King Nestor of Pylos in animal skins. Jefferson had inscribed on the lid of the silver askos, "Copied from a model taken in 1787 by/Th. Jefferson/from a Roman Ewer in the/Cabinet of Antiquities at/Nimes." The reference to "Ewer" is a clear acknowledgement of what Jefferson considered its function to be. *Papers*, XV: 172. Henderson, 47-48; Johnson, *Vintage: The Story of Wine*, 36, 47.

14. Short to T.J., April 21, 1789; *Papers*, XV: 67.

15. Short to T.J., October 28, 1788. I have not been able to identify the "little treatise" that Short refers to.

16. Short to T.J., November 19 and 29, 1788; T.J. to Thomas Lee Shippen, January 5, 1789.

17. T.J. to Moustier, March 13, 1789; T.J. to Madame de Brehan, March 14, 1789.

18. T.J. to Parent, January 22, 1789; Parent to T.J., February 16, 1789; T.J. to Parent, March 11, 1789.

19. Goubert, Pierre. *The Ancient Regime French Society 1600-1750*, New York: 1973, 12-15; Lefebvre, Georges. *La Grande Peur de 1719*, 44; Rude, George. *Paris and London in the Eighteenth Century*, New York: 1971, 85-86. In Paris, the normal price of a four pound loaf of bread was 8 or 9 sous. Between August and September of 1788 the price went to 11 sous, and by the end of January it had reached 14½ sous and remained at that level until the storming of the Bastille.
20. Jefferson had been away from Paris in 1786, 1787 and 1788 during the Easter holidays so this was the first time he had seen the *fete* from his house on the Champs-Elysées. Gouverneur Morris in his diary under date of April 8, 1789 records, "Dine early with Jefferson to see the Procession to Longchamps."
21. *Diary of John Quincy Adams*, Vol.1: 239.
22. *Diary of John Adams*, Vol. 4: 62-63. Young Nabby apparently was not given the same version by her protective father since her diary tells an anecdote of a "young woman opera dancer whose carriage was superior to any other or to the Queen's. The wheels of her carriage were washed with silver, and her horses were shod with silver. The next day the Queen sent her word, if she ever appeared in such a manner again she should be taken care of." Nabby went on to wonder, "whether this was not descending from the dignity we should suppose in the character of the Queen of France, I will not decide."
23. Lefebvre, Georges. *La Grande Peur de 1719*, 50; Gaubert, Pierre. *The Ancient Regime French Society 1600-1750*, New York: 1973, 12-14.
24. T.J. to Madison, June 18, 1789.
25. T.J. to John Jay, June 24, 1789.
26. *Papers*, XV: 240-41; XV: 354-55. Lafayette to T.J., August 25, 1789; Morris, Gouverneur, July 4, 1789, 134.
27. T.J. to Montmorin, July 8, 1789; T.J. to John Trumbull, August 5, 1789; *Papers*, XV: 260-61.
28. T.J. to Thomas Paine, July 13, 1789.
29. The Bastille held only seven prisoners; four charged with forging bills of exchange, two lunatics and a young nobleman who had been committed by *lettre de cachet* at his father's request because of dissipation and bad conduct. Rude, George. *Paris and London in the Eighteenth Century*, New York: 1971, 93.
30. T.J. to John Bondfield, July 16, 1789; T.J. to John Mason, July 16, 1789; T.J. to Thomas Paine, July 17, 1789; T.J. to Richard Price, July 17, 1789.
31. T.J. to Richard Price, July 17, 1789. Jefferson said that "should this revolution succeed, it is the beginning of the reformation of the governments of Europe."
32. T.J. to C.W.F. Dumas, July 27, 1789.
33. T.J. to Maria Cosway, July 25, 1789.
34. Lafayette to T.J., August 25, 1789.
35. *Papers*, XV: 354-55.
36. T.J. to John Jay, September 17, 1789; *Papers*, XV: 375-77.
37. Randolph, Sarah N. *The Domestic Life of Thomas Jefferson*, New York: 1871, 150-

51.

CHAPTER FOURTEEN

1. T.J. to George Washington, December 15, 1789; George Washington to T.J., January 21, 1790; T.J. to George Washington, February 14, 1790; T.J. to Madame de Tesse, March 11, 1790; T.J. to Madame de Corny, April 2, 1790.
2. T.J. to George Washington, February 14, 1790; T.J. to Short, March 12, 1790; T.J. to Lafayette, April 2, 1790; T.J. to Mazzei, April 5, 1790.
3. T.J. to J. Madison, February 14, *1790;Papers*, XVI: 183.
4. T.J. to James Brown, January 3, 1789.
5. Alexander Donald to T.J., January 9, 1790.
6. T.J. to Elizabeth Wales Eppes, March 7, 1790.
7. T.J. to Thomas Mann Randolph, Jr., March 28, 1790.
8. T.J. to Madame d'Houdelot, April 2, 1790; T.J. to LeVeilland, April 5, 1790; T.J. to Ferdinand Grand, April 4, 1790 and April 23, 1790.
9. T.J. to Thomas Mann Randolph, Jr., March 28, 1790.
10. T.J. to Madame de Tesse, March 11, 1790; T.J. to Madame de Corny, April 2, 1790; T.J. to Madame d'Enville, April 2, 1790; T.J. to Lafayette, April 2, 1790; T.J. to Abbes Arnoux and Chalut, April 5, 1790; T.J. to Short, May 27, 1790 and June 6, 1790.
11. T.J. to Thomas Mann Randolph, Jr., April 18, 1790.
12. George Mason to T.J., March 16, 1790. George Mason had set in motion the replacement of John Bondfield as American Consul in Bordeaux in favor of his son's partner, Joseph Fenwick, with letters to George Washington, October 28, 1789, and to Rufus King, October 28, 1789. What Mason did not know was that George Washington was annoyed with him because of a "want of manly candor" which prevented him from admitting "an error in his opinions" of The Constitution. See George Washington to Dr. James Craik, September 8, 1789. Still, their lifelong friendship won out and Fenwick got the appointment.
13. T.J. to George Mason, June 13, 1790. John Mason (1766-1849) in Georgetown and Joseph Fenwick in Bordeaux were partners in the trading firm of Fenwick, Mason and Co. which was dissolved in 1800.
14. T.J. to Bondfield, August 31, 1790.
15. John Bondfield to T.J., October 7, 1790.
16. Jefferson may have met Hamilton in Philadelphia in early 1783 when Hamilton was a member of Congress. *Papers*, VI, 217.
17. T.J. to Francis Eppes, July 1, 1790; T.J. to Short, July 1, 1790; *Papers*, XVI: 598.
18. T.J. to James Brown, August 8, 1790.
19. *Papers*, XVII: 322.
20. T.J. to Short, August 12, 1790.
21. Jefferson's estimate of 3000 livres as the total cost for the 1,161 bottles of wine he

Chapter Notes

ordered for the President was pretty close. The actual cost of the wines was 3080 livres but there were additional charges of 702.12 livres for packaging, transportation, etc. for a total cost of 3782.12 livres or about 3.25 livres per bottle. See *Papers*, XXIII: 325, for an itemized breakdown.

22. T.J. to Short, September 6, 1790.
23. T.J. to Joseph Fenwick, September 6, 1790.
24. T.J. to Madame Rozan, September 6, 1790.
25. T.J. to Count Miromenil, September 6, 1790.
26. T.J. to Comte de Lur Saluce, September 6, 1790.
27. Letter from Miromenil to T.J., January 18, 1791.
28. Fenwick to T.J., February 10, 1791; *Papers*, 18:630.
29. Lambert to T.J., February 10, 1791.
30. Countess de Lur Saluce to T.J., February 25, 1791.
31. T.J. to Tobias Lear, Nov. 22, 1791. Before shipping charges and other expenses, 350 bottles of Yquem cost 525 livres; 240 bottles of Lafite cost 720 livres and the 451 bottles of Dorsay Champagne cost 1,680 livres. Dr. Lambert's 120 bottles of Frontignan at 155 livres was almost as expensive as Yquem. The prices of the great French wines today have increased dramatically relative to the costs of some food items and not so dramatically relative to the cost of other food items. A bottle of 1989 Château d'Yquem sells at retail in 1995 for about $250 compared to thirty sous in 1791, roughly the equivalent of about 30¢ in 1791 Philadelphia dollars. Thirty cents then would have bought about a pound and a half of butter. Today the price of a bottle of Château d'Yquem would buy more than 100 pounds of butter. Lobsters, on the other hand, cost pennies in 1791 and now sell for about $10.00 per pound, an increase in price more in keeping with expensive French wines.
32. Madame de Rausan to T.J., January 30, 1791.
33. Thomas Lee Shippen to Dr. William Shippen, Jr., September 15, 1790.
34. Thomas Lee Shippen to Dr. William Shippen, Jr., September 15, 1790.
35. Gordon, Winifred. *Maryland Historical Magazine*, "The Dome of the Annapolis State House," Vol. 67, No.3, 1972, 294-97.
36. Thomas Lee Shippen to Dr. William Shippen, Jr., September 15, 1790.
37. Thomas Lee Shippen to Dr. William Shippen, Jr., September 15, 1790.
38. *Papers*, XVII: 571-72.
39. T.J. to James Brown, October 29, 1790.
40. *Papers*, XVI: 512; *Papers*, XVIII: 33-39; T.J. to Sharp Dulaney, January 15, 1791.
41. T.J. to Short, March 12, 1790; Short to T.J., December 24, 1790; T.J. to Short, April 6, 1790; Short to T.J., July 7, 1790; T.J. to Short, January 24, 1791; *Jefferson's Memorandum Books*. Petit arrived in Philadelphia on July 19, 1791. *Papers*, XVI: 321-23. William Short let it be known that he desired the appointment as minister to France. Over time Jefferson received a barrage of letters from Short reflecting concern in not having heard whether he was to be appointed minister.

Because he was performing the same duties, and the diplomatic corps considered him Jefferson's successor, Short reported that he had "gotten used to the idea." The appointment, however, went to Gouverneur Morris who became the minister to France after confirmation by the Senate on January 12, 1792. On the same day President Washington nominated, and the Senate confirmed, Short as minister resident to The Hague.

42. *Jefferson's Memorandum Books*, January 19, February 11 and March 9, 1791. Each bottle of Madeira held 26.5 oz., about the same capacity as today's 750 mi. bottle of 25.4 oz.
43. T.J. to Alexander Donald, May 13, 1791.
44. T.J. to Gouverneur Morris, April 28, 1792.
45. T.J. to H. Remsen, Jr., May 16, 1791; *Papers*, XVIII: 555.
46. Stephen Cathalan, Jr. to T.J., January 22, 1791.
47. T.J. to Guide, May 1, 1791.
48. T.J. to Guide, May 16, 1791.
49. Weld, Isaac Jr. *Travels Through the States of North America*, New York: Johnson Reprints, 1968, Vol. 2, 31.
50. Rice, Kym S. *Early American Taverns: For the Entertainment of Friends and Strangers*, Chicago, 1983, p. 102. [Hereafter cited as Rice, Kym S.]
51. Rice, Kym S., 105-106.
52. Rice, Kym S., 115.
53. *Jefferson's Memorandum Books* record the purchase of several corkscrews. In addition, Jefferson carried with him a multi-purpose knife that included a corkscrew.
54. Stein, Susan R. *The Worlds of Thomas Jefferson*, New York: 1993, 344-45. Elbridge Gerry thanked Jefferson for a gift of an "elegant traveling box." Gerry to T.J., August 24, 1784.
55. Madison to T.J., May 12, *1791; Jefferson's Memorandum Books*.
56. N. Hazard to Alexander Hamilton, November 25, 1791.
57. *Jefferson's Memorandum Books*; T.J. to T.M.R., June 5, 1791; Chastellux, 1: 200-0 I, 346.
58. The Saratoga Historical National Park tour of the battle sites covers nine miles with ten tour stops.
59. T.J. to Martha Jefferson Randolph, May 31, 1791.
60. In 1820 William Ferris Pell bought the land to preserve the ruins and in 1908-09, his descendant, Steven Pell, conceived the idea of restoring the fort and began the archaeology, reconstruction and assembly of the fort, the museum and library collections. The museum contains one of the finest collections of prerevolutionary and revolutionary weapons, uniforms and related artifacts.
61. T.J. to T.M.R., June 5, *1791; Jefferson's Memorandum Books*.
62. *Papers*, XX: 455; T.J. to M.J.R., May 31, 1791.
63. T.J. to T.M.R., June 5, 1791; Chastellux, 1: 216, 353.
64. *James Madison's Papers*, Volume 14, *25-29; Jefferson's Memorandum Books*.

65. Dewey's Walloomsac Inn stands on a hill just above the Bennington Museum on Monument Avenue in Old Bennington. It is a private residence now and there have been additions and alterations in the intervening years. Elijah Dewey is buried across the street in a small, private cemetery.
66. T.J. to George Washington, June 5, 1791.
67. Jefferson rated the inns and taverns where he and Madison stayed by assigning * for good, + for middling, and - for bad. Of the twenty-eight inns he rated in this manner, five were noted as bad, twelve middling and eleven good. Dewey's in Bennington and Fred Bull's Tavern in Hartford got top ratings.
68. *Jefferson's Memorandum Books; Papers*, XX: 467-70.
69. Joseph Fey to T.J. August 9, 1781; T.J. to William Prince, July 6, 1791; T.J. to James Brown, November 28, 1791; Mass. Hist. Soc., Jefferson Papers; Betts, 166-69.
70. Gabler, James M. *Wine Into Words*, Baltimore: 1985, 213. William Prince's son, William Robert Prince (1795-1869), published in 1830 a text titled, *A Treatise on the Vine; embracing its history from the earliest ages to the present day ... with a complete dissertation on the establishment, culture, and management of vineyards.*
71. James Madison to James Madison, Sr., July 2, 1791.
72. *Jefferson's Memorandum Books.*
73. T.J. to Tobias Lear, June 24, 1791.
74. *Jefferson's Memorandum Books.*
75. *Jefferson's Memorandum Books; Pennsylvania Journal,* June 29, 1791.
76. *Papers,* XX: 685.
77. T.J. to Madame de Rausan, September 1, 1791. In letters of the same date Jefferson wrote Short and Fenwick providing for payment, 1000 livres Tournois and another bill for 40 pounds sterling. It appears that half of this order, i.e., 250 bottles of 1785 wine and a cask of 250 bottles of 1790 wine were ordered for Henry Knox. See T.J. to William Short, September 1, 1791 and *Papers,* XX: 118-19.
78. T.J. to William Short, November 25, 1791.
79. Joseph Fenwick to T.J., August 31, 1791; *Papers,* XXII: 122-23.
80. David Humphreys to T.J., September 10, 1791; *Papers,* XXII: 138.
81. *Jefferson's Memorandum Books.*
82. L.C. reel.
83. Jefferson is mistaken about the cost of Goutte d'Or. At 6 sous a bottle his cost per feuillette (125 bottles) would have been only 37.5 livres and that would have been before the additional costs for bottling the wine. He usually paid 100 livres per feuillette or about 16 sous a bottle.
84. *Jefferson's Memorandum Books,* January 13 to October 13, 1792. He bought a quarter cask of Madeira for $70.83 on January 5.
85. T.J. to Short, April 24, 1792; T.J. to Fenwick, April 24, 1792.
86. T.J. to Short, October 14, 1792.
87. T.J. to David Rittenhouse, August 12, 1792.
88. Petit remained in Jefferson's service until 1794 when he returned to France.

89. Adrien Petit to T.J., July 28, 1792; T.J. to Petit, August 13, 1792; T.J. to John Taylor, Jr., 1792; Taylor to T.J., September 10, 1792.
90. Lipscomb, Andrew A *The Writings of Thomas Jefferson,* Vol. I: "The Anas," 315-19. [Hereafter cited as Lipscomb, Vol. 1: "The Anas."]
91. David Humphreys to T.J., September 9, 1792; October 31, 1792.
92. T.J. to Humphreys, November 6, 1792.
93. Simon, Andre. *A Dictionary of Wine,* 43; Shaw, 95-97.
94. Jullien, 184. Shaw, 195. Shaw talks of another wine called Arinto that was "usually half and half of mellow Lisbon and Bucellas."
95. Goncalves, Francisco Esteves. *Le Portugal Pays Vinicole,* Lisbon: 1983, 145-48.
96. The Carcavellos vineyards appear to be not more than ten acres surrounded by residential and business buildings bordering the Lisbon suburb of Orieas.
97. *Papers,* XXV: 29. See Bulkeley to T.J., February 20, 1793 confirming the shipment of "3 Pipes of the best Termo cased and bound for Norfolk to James Brown." *Papers,* XXV: 236, 549; T.J. to Richard Curson, April 21, *1793; Jefferson's Memorandum Books,* April 21, 1793.
98. *Papers,* XX: 361-62.
99. T.J. to Lafayette, April 2, 1790.
100. Gouverneur Morris to T.J., September 10, 1792. See Jefferson's ' dam and Eve" letter to Short of January 3, 1793 for an expression of his opinions on the French Revolution.
101. T.J. to Charles Coatsworth Pinckney, December 2, 1792.
102. T.J. to Joseph Fenwick, October 10, 1792; Fenwick to T.J., December 28, 1792; T.J. to Alexander Donald, October 11, 1792.
103. Trumbull, *Autobiography,* 173-75. William Branch Giles (1762-1830) at the time was a member of the House of Representatives, later a Senator and Governor of Virginia. He was a Jeffersonian Democrat and an ardent opponent of Alexander Hamilton. William Maclay of Pennsylvania wrote in his journal on January 20, 1791 about Giles: "The frothy manners of Virginia were ever uppermost. Canvas-back ducks, ham and chickens, old Madeira, the glories of the Ancient Dominion, all fine, were his constant themes."
104. T.J. to Benjamin Rush, January 16, 1811.
105. Jefferson had witnessed manned balloon flights in Paris in September, 1784 and June, 1786.
106. T.J. to Albert Gallatin, January 25, 1793; Pinney, Thomas. *A History of Wine in America from the Beginnings to Prohibition,* Berkley: U. of Calf Press, 1989, 107-114. Jefferson wrote this information to Albert Gallatin, his future secretary of the treasury, because Gallatin was one of a committee of five of the Pennsylvania House of Representatives to consider a plan from Legaux approving the "incorporation of the society for the promotion of the culture of the vine and the raising of silk worms and silk." On the day he wrote to Gallatin, the committee urged the Pennsylvania House to authorize an "association of persons" to pro-

mote viniculture in Pennsylvania. The recommendation was enacted into law in March, 1793. *Papers,* XXV: 93.
107. Weld, 207-09.
108. T.J. to Elbridge Gerry, February 26, 1793. The note from Gerry to Jefferson has not been found. *Papers,* XXIV: 269n.
109. T.J. to Martha Jefferson Randolph, January 26, 1793; March 10, 1793; T.J. to Madison, March 31, 1793; T.J. to Henry Leiper, April 11, 1793; T.J. to Martha Jefferson Randolph, May 26 and July 7, 1793.
110. See Lipscomb, Vol. I: "The Anas," 384-89.
111. T.J. to John Bulkeley, October 11, 1792; John Bulkeley to T.J., January 7, 1793; James Brown to T.J., April 10, 1793; T.J to Alexander Donald, October 11, 1792.
112. T.J. to Joseph Fenwick, August 22, 1793.
113. Weld, 37-38; 206--08.
114. T.J. to John Adams, February 28, 1796.
115. *Jefferson's Memorandum Books* note that on January 4th he paid Joseph Mussi, in addition to five weeks board, $8.00 for wine and on the 5th, just before leaving Philadelphia, he paid Henry Sheaff $5.62 for wine.
116. T.J. to G.W, May 14, 1794.
117. T.J. to J. Adams, April 25, 1794.
118. *Jefferson's Memorandum Books.*
119. T.J. to Yznardy, September 7, 1793.
120. T.J. to Mazzei, May 30, *1795; Jefferson's Memorandum Books,* May 27, 1795.
121. Henderson, 230-238; Redding, 242.
122. T.J. to Maria Jefferson Eppes, March 3, 1802.
123. The inaugural ceremonies for Jefferson and Adams took place in Philadelphia on March 4, 1797. While attending Congressional sessions as Vice-President, Jefferson usually boarded at the home of John Francis and his memorandum books and receipts show that accounts between them included charges and payments for wine. Early in 1799 Jefferson paid Francis $19.00 for wine and on another occasion $40.00 for wine.
124. Jefferson was inaugurated Vice-President on March 4, 1797.
125. Dufour, John James. *The American Vine Dresser's Guide, being a Treatise on the Cultivation of the Vine, and the Process of Wine Making Adapted to the Soil... of United States...* Cincinnati: 1826. John Dufour came to America from Switzerland at the age of 33 to engage in grape growing and winemaking. Before forming the Kentucky Vineyard Society, Dufour made an inspection tour of America's vineyards. What he saw is set out in this book and is the most accurate account of grape growing in the United States at the beginning of the 19th century.
126. T.J. to Spencer Roane, September 6, 1819.

Chapter Fifteen

Passions

1. The horseraces were held on an oval track west of the White House. *Jefferson's Memorandum Books.*
2. Roosevelt, Theodore. *Gouverneur Morris, American Statesmen Series*, Vol. III, Boston: 1899, 287. Morris was in Washington as a U.S. Senator.
3. Smith, Margaret Bayard. *The First Forty Years of Washington Society,* New York: 1906, p. 12. [Hereafter cited as Smith, Margaret Bayard.]
4. Davis, John. *Travels of Four Years and a Half in the United States of America; during 1798, 1799, 1800, 1801, 1802,* 177.
5. Jefferson remained at Conrad's for fifteen days and moved into the White House on March 19, 1801.
6. The President's residence was not known as the White House until later. During Jefferson's time it was called the President's House.
7. Edmond Charles Edouard Genet [Citizen Genet] [1763-1834] arrived in the United States in April 1793 as the French Minister and his immediate attempts to enlist America's support for France in its war with England so angered President Washington that he asked for Genet's recall in August, 1793. Genet married a daughter of Governor Clinton of New York and never returned to France.
8. Legaux to T.J., March 4 and March 25, 1801. T.J. to Legaux, March 24, 1801. Betts, Edwin Morris, ed. *Thomas Jefferson's Garden Book*, Philadelphia, 1944: 277-78. *Jefferson's Memorandum Books,* May 11, 1802 reads: "Pd. Anthony Giannini for planting grape vines for Legaux I.D."
9. Hedrick, Ulysses Prentice. *The Grapes of New York,* Albany: 1908, 1 18, 161-162.
10. T.J. to Adlum, January 13, 1816 and June 13, 1822. Adlum, John. *A Memoir on the Cultivation of the Vine in America and the Best Mode of Making Wine,* 2nd Edition, 1828. The Alexander grape, a native hybrid, is no longer grown in the United States.
11. Jefferson's White House wine cellar was located in the west wing basement and helped form an underground corridor to an icehouse situated on the west lawn. It no longer exists and could have been filled in when the White House underwent extensive repairs and restoration following its burning by the British in 1814.
12. The new President moved into the unfinished presidential mansion on March 19th and quickly assembled a chef, steward, coachman, valet-porter, housekeeper and later added a footman, a stable boy, washer woman and apprentice cooks. Jefferson initially brought with him as head of his household, Joseph Rapin, but by mutual agreement, Rapin was replaced by Lemaire. Seale, William. *The President's House,* Washington, D.C.: 1986, 193. [Hereafter cited a Seale.]
13. Jefferson did away with levees, so the Adams levee room on the west end, today's State Dining Room, became Jefferson's office. Seale, 90-91.
14. Stanton, Lucia C. "Wine and Food at the White House, The Presidential Table," from *Jefferson and Wine,* 1976, 202-212, edited by Treville Lawrence, Sr.

Chapter Notes

15. Bacon, Edmund. *Jefferson at Monticello*, edited by James A Bear, Jr., 1967.
16. Brown, Everett Somerville, ed. *William Plumer's Memorandum of Proceedings in the United States Senate, 1803-1807*, New York: 1923, 211-12. [Hereafter cited as Plumer.] Young, James Sterling. *The Washington Community 1800-1828*, New York: 1966, 168. [Hereafter cited as Young, James Sterling.]
17. Seale, 86, 102.
18. Jefferson had first become acquainted with macaroni (known as spaghetti today) at the tables of his aristocratic French friends, and he introduced it to the White House along with balls of ice cream served in a warm pastry. *See* Seale 102-03.
19. Seale, 104-05; 108.
20. Young, James Sterling, 169; Seale, 104. Smith, Margaret Bayard, 388.
21. Bernard, John. *Retrospections of America, 1797-1811*, New York: 1887, 235-36. [Hereafter cited as Bernard.]
22. Bernard, 235.
23. Plumer, 543.
24. Young, James Sterling, 167-169.
25. The current value of Jefferson's $25,000 presidential salary can be arrived at by using the Consumer Price Index, United States, 1700-1991 Table A-2, set out in John J. McCusker's *How Much Is That in Real Money? A Historical Price Index for Use as a Deflator of Money Values in the Economy of the United States*, Worcester: American Antiquarian Society, 1992. I took an average of the composite consumer price numbers in Col. 6 for the years in question, 1801-1808, and calculated the ratio between those numbers and the same numbers for 1991 (1629 ÷ 142 = 11.47). Using the ratio as a multiplier, the value of Jefferson's $25,000 presidential salary in 1991 dollars is about $286,750, which seems low. For a detailed but easy to understand explanation of how the figures are arrived at, see *How Much Is That in Real Money?*
26. This approximate 20,000 bottle figure was arrived at by calculating the equivalent number of bottles contained in each barrel.
27. T.J. to Fulwar Skipwith, May 4, 1803.
28. T.J. to Yznardi, May 10, 1803.
29. Jefferson purchased his Hungarian wines from J. Erick Bollman. Bollman had helped the Marquis de Lafayette temporarily escape from an Austrian prison after the Marquis' revolutionary sentiments were outpaced by the radicals of his country.
30. Bryans, Robin. *Madeira*, London: 91. One pipe lasted sixteen months; another, ten months.
31. Plumer, 543-545.
32. Plumer, 547.
33. *Diary of John Quincy Adams*, November 23, 1804. John Quincy Adams was elected a Federalist senator from Massachusetts on February 3, 1803.
34. Bergasse was so frightened by the mob's violence that he sold his thriving wine

Passions

business to other local wine merchants and moved to his native city of Lyons, never to return. His son later revived the Bergasse wine business in Marseilles. See Stephen Cathalan to T.J., June 4, 1816.

35. Martha Jefferson Randolph to T.J., July 12, 1803.
36. Dr. William Thornton (1759-1828) was born in the Virgin Islands, raised in England, came to America in 1787 and became a citizen the following year. Although Thornton had been educated as a physician, his architectural and scientific talents led him away from medicine. He was the designer of the United States Capitol, and in 1802 became the Director of the United States Patent Office, which position he held until the time of his death twenty-six years later. On March 6, 1803, Jefferson appointed Benjamin Henry Latrobe, an architect, Surveyor of The Public Buildings of the United States. Though Latrobe's first duty was the completion of the Capitol, Jefferson employed his talents on projects at the President's House. See Seale, II 0-118.
37. These narrow steps exist today at Monticello but because they violate existing fire regulations, visitors are not allowed above the first floor.
38. Peterson, Merrill D., Editor. *Visitors to Monticello,* "A Querulous Guest from Washington," Anna Thornton, 1989: 33-35.
39. Smith, Margaret Bayard, 65-81.
40. T.J. to William Short, November 15, 1807.
41. T.J. to C.P. de Lasteyrie, July 15, 1808.
42. T.J. to Albert Gallatin, June 3, 1807.
43. T.J. to Peter Walsh, March 27, 1811.
44. T.J. to William Lee, April 28, 1806.
45. T.J. to William Lee, June 25, 1807; Lee to T.J., August 21, 1806.
46. T.J. to Cathalan, June 7, 1807.
47. T.J. to Cathalan, June 29, 1807.
48. Cathalan to T.J., October 14, 1807.
49. T.J. to James Monroe, February 18, 1808.

Chapter Sixteen

1. T.J. to DuPont de Nemours, March 2, 1809.
2. T.J. to General Thaddeus Kosciuszko, February 26, 1810.
3. Berman, Eleanor D. *Thomas Jefferson Among the Arts,* New York: 1947, 79.
4. T.J. to [probably William Short], November 24, 1821. Julien, remained in Washington, established a successful catering business and from time to time would send Jefferson a delicacy. On one occasion Julien prepared and sent his former employer wild canvasback ducks. Obviously pleased, Jefferson responded: "They came sound and in good order, and enabled me to regale my friends here with what they had never tasted before. Their delicious flavor was new to them, but what heightened it with me was the proof they brought of your kind recollection

of me." T.J. to Julien, January 27, 1825.

5. Wiltse, Charles M. and Moser, Harold D., eds. *Papers of Daniel Webster,* Correspondence I, 370-380; Smith, Margaret Bayard. *The First Forty Years of Washington Society,* New York: 1906, 66-89 [hereafter cited Smith, Margaret Bayard.]; Ticknor, George. *Life, Letters and Journals,* Boston: 1876, 1-36.
6. Smith, Margaret Bayard, 66-89.
7. *Jefferson's Memorandum Books.*
8. T. J. to Cathalan, June 6, 1817.
9. Vizetelly, Henry. *The History of Champagne,* London: 1867, 257; Redding, 127-28.
10. A small amount of red wine was produced (Jefferson's cellar records show six bottles of red Limoux) but far more white Blanquette was sold and at twice the price of the red. Today the best wines of Limoux are white, a still wine and two sparkling wines, Blanquette de Limoux and Vin de Blanquette. Parker, Robert M., Jr. *Parker's Wine Buyer's Guide,* 3rd ed., New York: 1993, 465-66. Parker calls Blanquette de Limoux "close to a high-quality, nonvintage champagne at one-third the price." *The MacDonald Guide to French Wines, 1986,* London: 1985, 425. [Hereafter cited as MacDonald's Guide.]
11. T.J. to Cathalan, June 6, 1817, to which Jefferson added: "and I am as partial to it now as then."
12. Redding, 12; Henderson, 174-75.
13. T.J. to Monroe, April 8, 1817.
14. T.J. to Monroe, April 5, 1817.
15. The vineyards of Muscat de Rivesaltes are located four miles north of Perpignan and it was considered similar to Frontignan, one of Jefferson's favorite sweet wines, but lighter. Today it carries an Appellation Contrôlée designation.
16. T.J. to Stephen Cathalan, February 11, 1816. In commenting on the taste of some Roussillon wine that he had ordered for Jefferson through M. Durant of Perpignan, Stephen Cathalan said it had the "taste of old Madeira wine." Cathalan to T.J., June 9, 1816.
17. T.J. to Cathalan, July 3, 1815.
18. With his annual wine order he usually also ordered macaroni, olive oil, anchovies, and seedless raisins.
19. T.J. to Cathalan, January 18, 1818.
20. T. J. to Stephen Cathalan, February 1, 1816.
21. No wine grapes are grown in this region of Maryland today.
22. T.J. to Major John Adlum, Oct. 7, 1809.
23. Adlum to T.J., February 15 and March 13, 1810.
24. Adlum to T.J., April 10, 1810.
25. T.J. to Adlum, April 20, 1810.
26. T.J. to John Dortie, October 1, 1811.
27. Pelluci, Emanuele. *Antinori: Vintners in Florence,* Florence: 1981, 18-19, 25.

28. Although the wines of Artimino are not generally imported into the United States some are available in the San Francisco area.
29. Anderson, Burton. *The Wine Atlas of Italy and Traveller's Guide to the Vineyards*, New York and London: 1990, 201.
30. *Jefferson's Memorandum Book*, February 23, 1823. In Jefferson's time the Pomino vineyards were a far larger area, and included much of what is now Chianti Rufina. The Frescobaldi family has been cultivating vineyards in these hills for over 400 years and is today the sole commercial producer of Pomino wines. Modern red Pomino has Cabernet, Merlot, and Pinot Nero added to its Sangiovese base and can be found in most metropolitan wine stores. Anderson, Burton, *The Wine Atlas of Italy*, 1980, 202-04.
31. T.J. to Thomas Appleton, January 14, 1816.
32. T.J. to Samuel I. Harrison, September 18, 1817; T.J. to Monroe, April 5, 1817. The Montepulciano wines that Appleton purchased for Jefferson were "produced on the grounds formerly belonging to the order of Jesuits and sold for the benefit of the government in 1793." Jefferson instructed that his Montepulciano be shipped to Monticello "in black bottles, well corked and cemented, and in strong boxes..." T.J. to Thomas Appleton, January 14, 1816.
33. Appleton to T.J., April 15, May 30, July 30, September 27 and October 20, 1816.
34. T.J. to Appleton, August I, 1817.
35. The principal red grapes are Prugnolo Gentile, Canaiolo and Mammolo with an allowance for up to ten percent of white grapes. See Burton Anderson's *The Wine Atlas of Italy and Traveller's Guide to the Vineyards* for a more detailed account of modern Montepulciano.
36. T.J. to Samuel H. Smith, September 11, 1814.
37. A fire in the 1840s destroyed about two-thirds of Jefferson's books. The original Library of Congress building is named after Jefferson and the other two principal Library of Congress buildings are appropriately named for John Adams and James Madison.
38. *Jefferson's Memorandum Books.*
39. T.J. to Madison, April II, 1820.
40. John David to T.J., November 26, 1815.
41. T.J. to John David, December 25, 1815.
42. T.J. to Adlum, January 13, 1816.
43. Adlum to T.J., February 27, 1816; Levin Gale to T.J., March 30, 1816; T.J. to Levin Gale, May 7, 1816.
44. T.J. to John David, January 13, 1816. The neighbor was General John Hartwell Cocke of Bremo, Fluvanna County, Virginia, whose diary under date of March 27, 1817, reflects"... sent to Monticello some Marseilles figs and Paper Mulberry, and at the same time sent Mr. Jefferson some wine made from the Scuppernong grape of North Carolina, a fruit which must be well worthy to be cultivated. The wine is of delicious flavor resembling Frontinac..."

45. T.J. to Monroe, January 16, 1816; Lawrence, R. de Treville, Sr., *ed., Jefferson and Wine,* The Plains, VA: 1989, "Quality No Matter the Wine," by James A. Bear, Jr., 13-14; and "Restoring the Vineyards," by Peter Hatch, 52-59; T.J. to Monroe, January 16, 1816. Monroe's home, Ashlawn is located about three miles up the mountain from Monticello. Apparently Monroe's success with growing *vinifera* vines was a little better than Jefferson's, although there is no evidence that Monroe was any more successful in making wine from his vineyard than was Jefferson. Three probable reasons Jefferson failed to make wine from his two small vineyards involved the presence of vine diseases, the lack of a sufficient number of grapes of a single varietal, and the small amounts grown were eaten soon after they ripened. Although he received the vine cuttings, there is no evidence that Jefferson ever successfully made wine from his Monticello vineyards.
46. T.J. to Judge William Johnson, May 10, 1817; T. W Eppes to T.J., April 28, 1817; T.J. to Thomas Coxe, June 3, *1823; Jefferson's Memorandum Books,* May 1, 1817: "Enclosed to T. W. Eppes an order on Gibson & Jefferson for 26.D. to pay for a barrel of Scuppernon wine bot. for me by Mr. Burton of Halifax N.C."
47. T.J. to Samuel Maverick, May 12, 1822. See also letters from Maverick to T.J., August 11, 1821 and March 4, 1822 covering viticulture and wines.
48. T.J. to Thomas Cox, June 3, 1823.
49. T.J. to Monroe, April 5, 1817; T.J. to Cathalan, June 6, 1817.
50. T.J. to Cathalan, April 5, 1818.
51. T.J. to Victor Aldolphus Sasserno, May 26, 1819.
52. T.J. to Cathalan, May 26, 1819. Jefferson's statement that "I should much prefer a wine which should be *sweet* and *astringent,* but I know of none_," conflicts with a description by Henderson of Jefferson's favorite Tuscan wine, Montepulciano. "[I]ts sweetness is generally tempered with an agreeable sharpness and astringency. It is in fact, one of the best specimens of the *dolce-piccanti* wines." See Henderson, 237-8.
53. Eighteenth century wine glasses were much smaller than present wine glasses. The six wine glasses that remain at Monticello (all of which descend through Jefferson's family) when filled to $^3/_8$" from the top vary in capacity from about three ounces (85 ml.) to two ounces (55 ml.). Assuming Jefferson drank from the larger wine glass (a reasonable assumption given his love of wine) and that he drank three to four and a half glasses of wine a day, his daily wine consumption was in the range of a third to a half of a bottle of wine-less than during his days in Europe. The volume measurements were not taken with scientifically precise equipment and should be considered approximate:

    Object: Wine Glasses (2)
    Date: Late 18th century
    Description: Funnel-shaped champagne flutes with plain foot. Both glasses have a band of narrow oblong cuts around the rim. One glass (a) has broad petal-like cuts around the base of the bowl and

	hexagonal stem. (b) has a plain round stem.
Dimensions:	Height—6" and 5¾"
Volume:	105 ml and 90 ml filled to the brim; 85 ml and 75 ml filled to ³/₈" from top
Provenance:	Items descended through family of Jefferson's granddaughter Virginia Jefferson Randolph Trist. Probably owned by Jefferson.
Location:	Visitors Center exhibition
Object:	Wine Glasses (2)
Date:	1810-1840
Description:	Both glasses have squat wafered stems, and bowls with a nine-sided base and cut roundel and ray design.
Dimensions:	Height—4³/₈"
	Volume—¼ cut or 75 ml
Volume:	95 ml at brim; 70 ml at ³/₈" from top
Provenance:	Items descended through family of Jefferson's grandson, Thomas Jefferson Randolph.
Location:	Tea Room
Object:	Wine Glass
Date:	1770-1780
Description:	Glass has trumpet bowl and double wafered stem with a heavy plain foot.
Dimensions:	Height—4³/₄"
Volume:	90 ml at brim; 65 ml at ³/₈" from top
Provenance:	Items descended through family of Jefferson's grandson, Thomas Jefferson Randolph.
Location:	TeaRoom
Object:	Wine Glass
Date:	1760-1770
Description:	Glass has trumpet bowl with eight petal-shaped cuts around the base; double wafered stem with a heavy plain foot.
Dimensions:	Height—4 ⁵/₄"
Volume:	75 ml at brim; 55 ml at ³/₈" from top
Provenance:	Items descended through family of Jefferson's granddaughter, Virginia Jefferson Randolph Trist.
Location:	Tea Room

The wine glass information was furnished by Lucia Stanton, Director of Research at Monticello.

54. Julius Oliver to T.J., September 27, 1819.
55. T.J. to Joshua Dodge, July 13, 1820. For further wine orders to Dodge see T.J. to Dodge, June 11, 1822 and June 6, 1824.

56. Henderson, 297; Redding, 193.
57. T.J. to William H. Crawford, November 10, 1818.
58. T.J. to Monsieur de Neuville, December 13, 1818.
59. T.J. to John Adams, October 12, 1823.
60. *The New York Times,* Architecture View/Paul Goldberger, "Jefferson's Legacy: Dialogues with the Past," Sunday, May 23, 1993. Jefferson was proud of his architectural designs for the University of Virginia. In November, 1821 he wrote, "You enquire also about our University. All it's buildings except the library will be finished by the ensuing spring. It will be a splendid establishment, would be thought so in Europe, and for the chastity of it's architecture and classical taste leaves everything in America far behind it." T.J. to [probably William Short], November 24, 1821.
61. T.J. to Dr. Vine Utley, March 23, 1819.
62. T.J. to John Adams, June 1, 1822.
63. The exact number of bottles remaining at the time of Jefferson's death is not known, but five months before his death his cellar inventory showed 586 on hand, all but 22 bottles from Lanquedoc. Based on his average household consumption of about 50 bottles per month, it would appear that he died leaving only a few hundred bottles.
64. T.J. to Madison, January 13, 1821.
65. Adlum to T.J., June 5, 1822.
66. T.J. to Adlum, June 13, 1822. During the early stages of his viticultural efforts, Adlum experimented with native wild grapes and strains of European *Vitis vinifera. After* failing with the European wines, he eventually concentrated on native grapes.
67. Adlum to T.J., March 14 and March 24, 1823; T.J. to Adlum, April 11, 1823. During President Monroe's administration, Adlum proposed "a lease of a portion of the public ground in the city [Washington] for the purpose of forming a vineyard, and of cultivating an experimental farm. It was my intention, had I been successful, to procure cuttings of the different species of the native vine, to be found in the United States, to ascertain their growth, soil, and produce, and to exhibit to the Nation, a new source of wealth, which has been too long neglected. My application was, however, rejected, and I have been obliged to prosecute the undertaking myself, without assistance and without patronage, and this I have done to the full extent of my very limited means. A desire to be useful to my countrymen has animated all my efforts, and given stimulus to all my exertions."
68. T.J. to B. Peyton, November 21, 1824.
69. T.J. to Roger Weightman, June 24, 1826.
70. His friend and revolutionary colleague, John Adams, died the same day uttering, "And Jefferson still lives." Actually, Jefferson had died a few hours before Adams.

Appendices

APPENDIX A

Jefferson's Favorite Wines—Available Today

FRANCE

Red Burgundies

Chambertin – Jefferson rated Chambertin the best of Burgundy's red wines. He imported 100 bottles of Chambertin during the third year of his presidency.

Clos de Vougeot – When Jefferson visited Clos de Vougeot in 1787 it was still owned by the monks of Citeaux. Its annual production was 50,000 bottles and the wines had a reputation for excellence. Jefferson rated it second in quality behind Chambertin. During the French Revolution the monks were evicted and the vineyards and château were sold at public auction. A loss of quality was soon reported following the divestiture. The reason for the loss of quality is clear. The monks knew that the quality of Clos de Vougeot's wines varied depending on the part of the vineyard from which the grapes came, and they priced their wines accordingly. "The wines made from those in the middle selling for one-third more than that made in the upper part, and three time as much as that made from those at the lower end." The new owner of Cos de Vougeot did not follow the monks' practice but blended the wines together.

Vosne-Romanée – Jefferson did not designate the order of rank but one did exist. Alexander Henderson writing during Jefferson's time singled out Romanée-Conti, La Tache, Richebourg, and Romanée St. Vivant for "their beautiful color and exquisite flavor and aroma, combining ... qualities of lightness and delicacy with richness and fullness of body," a remarkably accurate description of these wines today.

Volnay – Jefferson considered Volnay the equal in flavor to Chambertin but relegated it to fourth place because it was lighter in body, lacked longevity, and did not bear transportation as well. However, it had two advantages over the wines of Chambertin and Clos de Vougeot; it cost only one-quarter as much and was ready to drink after one year. Jefferson never identified a particular vineyard from which he purchased his Volnay wines but vineyards of special recognition then were Cailleret and Champans.

Pommard – Clos de la Commaraine. This wine was sent to Jefferson in fulfillment of an order for Volnay. He was not told that it was from neighboring Pommard, and not a Volnay, just that it was of the "best element."

White Burgundies

Montrachet – Jefferson was first introduced to Montrachet when he traveled to Burgundy in March 1787. He called it the best white wine of Burgundy, a distinction it still retains. It sold then at a price that was equal to the best Bordeaux, i.e., Lafite, Haut-Brion, Latour and Margaux.

Meursault – Jefferson thought the best wine of Meursault came from the vineyard of Goutte d'Or (Drop of Gold). Other Meursaults of equal reputation at the time were Les Perrières, Les Combettes, Les Charmes, and Les Genevrières. These five vineyards continue to make outstanding dry white Burgundies and along with ten other Meursault vineyards enjoy Premiers Crus classification. The main exporters of Goutte d'Or today are Arnaud Ente, Bouchard, Buisson-Charles, Comtes Lafon, Francoise Gaunoux, Louis Jadot, Louis Latour, René Emanuel, Vincent Bouzereau.

Rhone Valley

Côte Rôtie – Although the red wines of Côte Rôtie were recognized for their color, strength, bouquet, taste and ability to age, Jefferson made the comment that they were not yet of such high "estimation to be produced commonly at the good tables of Paris." Eighteenth century winemakers recognized their merit, however, often blending them with Bordeaux and Burgundy wines to add strength and character.

Château Grillet – Jefferson called Grillet the best white wine of the northern Rhone, a distinction that is in dispute today.

Red Hermitage – Although Jefferson did not single out the red wines of Hermitage for special praise, he did acknowledge their high quality. He listed the owners of the best vineyards, and the great red Hermitages of today come from those same vineyards.

White Hermitage – Jefferson so esteemed white Hermitage "marked with a touch of sweetness" that he called it the "first wine in the world without exception." During his presidency he purchased 550 bottles of white Hermitage from the House of Jourdan. The Jourdan vineyards were eventually inherited by the Monier family who, because of their ancestry, revived the name Chastaing de le Sizeranne. The Jourdan vineyards presently belong to M. Chapoutier who calls his red Hermitage La Sizeranne. Chapoutier produces two white Hermitage wines, Chante-Alouette (Lark's Song) and the more expensive Ermitage de l'Orée. A sweet white Hermitage was also made during Jefferson's time.

Provence and Languedoc

Bellet (near Nice) – Jefferson was first introduced to these wines before starting over the Alps on the back of a mule on his 44th birthday. He found Bellet wines good "though not of the first quality." He later called them "remarkably good." Robert M. Parker, Jr. describes the wines of Bellet as "Nice's best-kept secret." Red, rosé and white wines are made in this small appellation, but the whites are the wines that excel today. The best white wines are made from a grape called the Rolle. Most of the wines of Bellet are consumed at restaurants along the French Riviera but some are exported and can be found in major wine markets.

Frontignan – a fortified sweet white dessert wine made from the white Muscat grape. Jefferson first tasted this wine on the spot over dinner at the home of Monsieur Lambert, a physician and vintner. Jefferson remarked, "It is potable the April after it is made, is best that year . . . It is not permitted to ferment more than half a day, because it would not be so liquorish [sweet]. The best color, and its natural one, is amber." The sweet Muscat wines of Frontignan were enjoying their greatest popularity at the time of Jefferson's visit to this small Mediterranean town. Although still available, there aren't many Monsieur Lamberts making Muscat de Frontignan today. Its production is now dominated by cooperatives.

Nimes – In Nimes Jefferson drank an "excellent" red vin ordinaire from nearby vineyards called Ledenon, and according to Jefferson "served pure at tables of the finest rank in France." Known for its agreeable bouquet, it was considered the equal in quality and taste to the wines of Châteauneuf-du-Pape. It was one of his favorite wines in retirement. The wines from this region are known today as Costieres de Nimes and are reasonably priced and readily available.

Vin Blanc de Rochegude – A sweet fortified white wine, probably the ancestor of today's Beaumes-de-Venise. Jefferson thought highly of this wine and sent it as a gift to President George Washington.

Muscat de Rivesaltes – A variety of wines were produced (and still are) in Roussillon, but those Jefferson liked best were the sweet wines of Muscat de Rivesaltes. They were considered "lighter on the stomach than Frontignan." In his seminal wine treatise (1816), André Jullien ranked Muscat de Rivesaltes "first" of all Vins de Liqueur. Jefferson first drank this wine when he traveled on the Canal du Midi in May 1787. Its taste lingered on his palate because he continued to import it until the last year of his life.

Blanquette de Limoux – from vineyards around the town of Limoux near the medieval city of Carcassonne. Jefferson spent a night in Carcassonne and it was probably here that he became acquainted with the wines of Limoux that he imported in retirement. Blanquette de Limoux, made from the mauzac grape, was sweet and sparkling, the same as it is today.

Red Bordeaux

Châteaux Haut-Brion, Lafite, Latour, Margaux – Jefferson drank all four of these wines and referred to them as "first growths." He also mentioned for special recognition Rozan (Rauzan-Segla), Larose (Gruard-Larose), Dabbadie, ou Lionville (now three châteaux: Leoville-Las-Cases, Leoville-Poyferre, Leoville-Barton and then owned by Monsieur d'Abadie), Quirouen (Kirwan), Durfort (Durfort-Vivens), followed by a "third class" of wines consisting of Calons (Calon-Segur), Mouton (Mouton-Rothschild), Gassie (Rauzan-Gassies), Arboete (LaGrange), Pontette (Pontet-Canet) de Terme (Marquis-de-Terme) and Candale (d'Issan). From this group Madame Rauzan's was his favorite. He wrote Madame Rauzan, "I had the opportunity on a tour I made during my stay in Paris of visiting the canton of the best Bordeaux wines, among which was de Rozan, your cru, of excellent quality." In a letter of wine advice to a friend he said, "Rozan-Margaux which is made by Madame de Rozan. This is what I import for myself, and consider it equal to any of the four crops [growths]."

White Bordeaux

Carbonnieux – Several other white wines that Jefferson mentioned no longer exist having been lost to urban development.

Sauternes

Château d'Yquem – Jefferson praised Yquem as the best. On his return to Paris he ordered 250 bottles of Yquem. While secretary of state he ordered it for himself and 360 bottles for President Washington. When he became president he served Yquem at White House dinners. Two other Sauternes he mentioned were President du Roy's vineyards, now known as Château Suduiraut, and President Pichard's, now Lafaurie Peyraguey and Haut-Peyraguey. While president he shared 150 bottles of Filhot with dinner guests.

Champagne

Monsieur Dorsay's in Ay – Jefferson preferred non-sparkling Champagne. There is evidence that Monsieur Dorsay's vineyard in Ay is now owned by Champagne Bollinger.

Appendices

GERMANY

Mosel

Brauneberg – followed in order by Wehlen, Grach, Piesport, Zelting, Bernkastel.

Rheingau

Schloss Johannisberg – He also singled out for praise the wines of Rudesheim and Hochheim. To a German friend who accompanied him on this part of his German vineyard trip he wrote, "I take the first moment to inform you that my journey was prosperous: that the vines which I took from Hochheim and Rudesheim are now growing luxuriously in my garden here, and will cross the Atlantic next winter, and that probably, if you ever revisit Monticello, I shall be able to give you a glass of Hock or Rudesheim of my own making." There is no evidence that Jefferson took these vines with him when he left France in September 1789 to return to America.

ITALY

Piedmont

"Nebiule" – Jefferson's phonetic spelling of the Nebbiolo grape which makes many of Italy's best wines, Barolo, Barbaresco, Gattinara and Ghemme. He found the "Nebiule" wine singular, melding three contradictory characteristics. "It is about as sweet as the silky Madeira, as astringent on the palate as Bordeaux, and as brisk as Champagne. It is a pleasing wine." The full-bodied, dry, tannic Barolos and Barbarescos of today are not sweet and do not effervesce because the style the wines has changed. Throughout the 18th century, and well into the 19th century, in the Piedmont region of Italy, the fermentation was not allowed to finish, leaving the wines sweet. The incomplete fermentation also left them frizzanti, which probably explains Jefferson's "brisk as Champagne" comment.

Tuscany

Montepulciano – also Chianti, Carmignano, Artimino and Pomino. Jefferson's "very favorite" Tuscan wine, which he sometimes referred to as a Florence wine, was Montepulciano. He described Montepulciano as a high-flavored, light bodied wine "equal to the best Burgundy."

SPAIN

Dry Sherry – Saying "that if I should fail in the means of getting it, it will be a privation which I shall feel sensibly once a day." Jefferson's taste in Spanish wines ran from Malaga and Pedro Ximenes, both sweet, to pale and dry sherry and dry and sweet

Paxarete. Paxarete (also spelled Pacharetti) was made from the Pedro Ximenes grape at an ancient monastery about fifteen miles from Jerez. Pedro Ximenes made sweet and dry wines that resembled sherry in taste. Its name comes from a grape said to have been imported from the Rhine by a man named Pedro Simon (corrupted to Ximenes). Jefferson also drank a red, sweet wine made from the muscadine grape called Tinto di Rota, which was known in England as Tent, and was made near the village of Rota north of Cadiz. Jefferson imported substantial amounts of these Spanish wines during his eight years as president.

PORTUGAL

Madeira – Like most of the Founding Fathers, Jefferson was a Madeira enthusiast. While in Paris Jefferson and Marquis de Lafayette agreed to share a pipe (110 gallons) of Madeira "of the nut quality and of the very best."

APPENDIX B

The White House Wine Cellar with Annotations

Wines provided at Washington, their costs and names of the suppliers. TJ's brackets indicate wines that were sent to Monticello.

1801

May	3.	A pipe of Brazil Madeira[1] from Colo. Newton	350.
	20.	⌈A pipe of Pedro Ximenes Mountain[2] from Yznardi. 126.	
		⌊galls. @ 2.D. 424 bottles of it sent to Monticello. Feb. 1803.	252.
		A Quartr. cask of Tent[3] from do. 30. galls. @ 1.50	45.
		A keg of Pacharetti[4] doux. from do.	
		15. doz. Sauterne from H. Sheaff[5] @ 8.D.	120.
		doz. of claret from do.[6]	
June	12.	2. pipes of Brazil Madeira from Taylor & Newton[7]	700.
		148. bott. claret @ 10.D. pr. doz. 123.33	195.33
		72.do @ 12.D. 72.	
		220.	
Sep.	28.	2. pipes of Brazil Madeira from Taylor & Newton[8]	700.
Nov.	28.	30. doz. = 360. bottles of Sauterne from Sheaff[9]	240.

1802

Jan.	7.	A tierce (60. galls.) Malaga from Mr. Yznardi. Lacryma	
		Christi. The above is 46. years old viz. vintage of 1755.[10]	106.
		2 doz. bottles of claret from Mr. Barnes @ 8.D.	16.
Feb.	24.	1. pipe dry Pacharetti from Mr. Yznardi	202.
		⌈1. pipe Sherry of London quality 10. y. old	188.
		⎱½ pipe of Sherry of a different quality	94.
		⌊ 278 bottles of it sent to Monticello. Feb. 1803.	
		½ pipe of white Sherry[11]	84.
		D.	
		Insurance on the wines of Feb. 24 22.72	
May	6.	Duties pd. Yznardi on do. 156.	178.72
		Claret from J. Barnes.	
Nov.		A half barrel of Syracuse[12] from Capt. McNiel	

Dec.	1.	100. bottles Champagne from the Chevalr. Yrujo.	
1803			
Jan.	10.	100 do. @ 86¼ viz. .75 first cost+ 11¼ duty)	172.50[13]
		2. half pipes of wine of Oeyras[14] from Mr. Jarvis at Lisbon. Sent to Monticello	98.17
Mar.	3.	2 pipes of Brazil Madeira from James Taylor Norfolk.	700.
	21.	12. doz. Sauterne from Sheaff@ 8 ⅔ D. 104.33	
Oct.	21.	50. bottles white Hermitage @ 73⅓ cents + 8¾ duty= 82 cents + 9½ freight = 91½.	45.80
	23.	150. bottles Rozan Margau[15] @ 82½c. + 8¾ duty = 91¼ cents + 8¾ = I.D.	150.00
		150. do. Sauterne[16] @ 64⅙ + 8¾ duty = 72⁹⁄₁₀ + 8¾frt. = 8¾ c.	122.57

                                                                             cost   duty   frt.

Dec. 1. 400 do. Champagne d'Aij[17]   .68¾   .07½   .19 = .95)
(153. broke) 484.
100 do. Burgundy of Chambertin .59½   .07½   .19 = .86)

	10.	A quarter cask Mountain of crop of 1747. from Kirkpatrick of Malaga frt. 19.	
	30.	2 pipes Termo one the crop of Carrasqeira, the other of Arruda. Jarvis. 170 millreis =	196.35
		1. butt of Pale Sherry from Yznardi	194.85
1804			
Mar.	19.	A pipe of Brazil Madeira from Taylor	354.07
		A box Champagne from do. 5. doz.@ 62½ cents	37.50
June	20.	138. bottles of wines from Florence (123 Montepulciano) frt. & duty 25½c. cost 26 c.	33.17[18]
July		400 bottles Champagne from N.Y same as Mar. 19.@ I.D. (23 broke)	400.
July	20.	98. bottles claret from Sheaff	82.
Nov.	28.	240 bottles of Hungary wine @ 1.70)	
		36 do. Tokay 3.31) from Bollman[19]	546.43
		12 do. other wines 4.36)	
Monticello			
Dec.	1	pipe dry Pacharetti prime cost 194.85	
		1 Sherry 15. yr. old	
		147 bottles Port	
		53. Bucellas 10. y. old) from Fernandes[20]	152.25
		1 pipe Arrudae wine from Jarvis. Lisbon.	
		36. bottles Château Margaux of 98. @ 7tt)	
		72. do. Rozan Margaux of 98 @ 4 tt-10s) 778f-50 (Lee)[21]	
		72. do. Salus Sauterne@ 2tt-5s)	

1805

Apr.	17.	38 bottles Aleatico 3. do. Santo 3.)
		do. Artemino. 19. do. Chianti. 10.)from Joseph Barnes = 73.
		do. Montepulciano)
May	30.	100. bott. vino del Carmine[22] Appleton
		1. hhd. (i.e. half pipe) Marsalla Preble
Oct.	19.	⎡ 1. Qr. cask old Termo from Jarvis 26.20)
		⎣ 1 do. Bucellas from do. 28.60) + frt. duties &c. 73.83
Nov.	9.	473 bottles Montepulciano. Cost Leghorn .25= 118.50=.25 pr. bottle
		duties 35.60 freight 46.38 port charges 6.08=88.06=.18112 pr. bottle
		100 bottles hermitage[23]

1806

Jan.	2.	pipes Marsalla wine. Higgins 212.D. cost+ 69.60 duty
Apr.	22.	100. bottles white Hermitage cost at Marseilles 76.62 + 21. duty frt.
		6. do. vin de paille do. 7.82 + 1.22
June	7.	100. do. White Hermitage cost at Marseilles 76.62 + frt.
		8.91 + dut. 12.835 = 98.365[24]
		Barrique 45 galls. Cahusac cost @ Bordeaux 22.85 +
		frt. 14.725 + dut. 22.275 = 60 D.
July		50. bottles Nebioule shipped by Thos. Storm for Kuhn cost
		200. bottles Nebioule from Kuhn.25 Cost delivered at
		Genoa .54 cents pr. bottle.

1807

Feb.		200. bottles Hermitage from Marseilles
June	4.	350. bottles (80. galls.) Montepulciano[26] from Leghorn
		91.55 D. + frt. 40.42 + duties 29.85 + port charges
		2.25 = 164.07 or .47 pr. bottle
	13.	A cask Cahusac (23. galls.) cost at Bordeaux 29.51 + frt.
		4.88 + duties 7.36 + D. c.
		Port charges 4.83 = 46,58 or 2.02 pr. gallon.
		120. bottles St. George[27] sent to Monto.) cost at
		Cette @ 24 pr. bottle 42.875
Oct.	8.	Do. from Mr. Barnes 60.bottles) charges .15 26.847
		69.722
Dec.	2.	3. kegs Nebioule yielding 134 bottles

1808

Apr.	4.	100. bottles wine of Nice cost there	30.84
			1.96 freight to Marseilles
			24.42 to Phila.
			17.69 duty & permit
			.67 potage
			75.58

Madeira

No.	recd.	broached	finished	lasted excludg. absence
1.	1801. May 3.	1. May 15.	01. Nov. 3	3½ months
2.	1801. June 12	Nov. 3	02. June 6	6. months
3.	do.	02. Jun 6	03. Apr. 10	7. months
4.	Sep. 28	03. April 10	04. May 28	10. months
5.	do.	04. May 28	05. May 15. sent remains 76 b. Montico.	
6.	1803. Mar. 3	05. May 15	06. July	10-17
7.	do.	06. July	07. Nov. 25	10-19
8.	1804. Mar. 19	07. Nov. 25		

ANNOTATIONS ON THE WHITE HOUSE WINE CELLAR

1. Brazil Madeira was named for the wooden cask in which it was aged, Brazilian Satinwood. Shortly after receiving this Brazil Madeira, T.J. ordered two more pipes of it. Thomas Newton to T.J., May 13, 1801, August 28, 1801; T.J.'s Memorandum Book, "desire J. Barnes to pay Mr. Taylor of Norfolk for 2 pipes wine"; James Taylor to T.J., June 4, 1801.
2. Pedro Ximenes gets its name from a grape said to have been imported from the Rhine by a man named Pedro Simon (corrupted to Ximenes}.It was one of the richest and most delicate of the sherry-like wines.
3. Tinto di Rota known as "Tent" in England was a rich, lucious red wine made from the Muscadine grape in vineyards around Rota, about fifteen miles from Cadiz, Spain. T.J. to Josef Yzardi, March 24, 1801; Josef Yzardi to T.J., April 7, 1801.
4. Pacharetti, also spelled Paxarete, was an ancient monastery about five miles from Xeres de la Frontera, near Cadiz, which gave its name to highly regarded sweet and dry wines. Sweet Pacharetti was made from the Pedro Ximenes grape. It resembled sherry in taste.
5. Henry Sheaff was a Philadelphia merchant from whom Jefferson bought wine. When Secretary of State, Jefferson gave Sheaff guidance on the quality, prices and sources of the best European wines. See Chapter 14.
6. This line refers to the 220 bottles of claret itemized under date of 12 June. T.J.'s Memorandum Book, 28 Aug. 1801.
7. T.J.'s Memorandum Book under January 7, 1802, records: "Enclosed James Taylor of Norfolk 705D in bank bills cut in two. One set of halves sent now the other to follow by another post. This to pay for the fourth and fifth pipes of Madeira."

Appendices

8. James Taylor to T.J., June 4, 1801.
9. T.J.'s Memorandum Book, August 28, 1801 shows payment to "Henry Sheaff for wine 553.80." This reflects payment for the 15 dozen Sauternes and one dozen Claret under May 20, 120 bottles of Claret under June 12, and 360 bottles of Sauternes, November 28, 1801; T.J. to H. Sheaff, July 27, 1801. T.J.'s Memorandum Book, March 9, 1802: "Enclosed a checkof220.50 to Henry Sheaff to pay him for wines"-for the 360 bottles of Sauternes.
10. This sweet, dark Malaga wine had arrived in Baltimore and General Samuel Smith paid T.J.'s cost of freight and duties. On December 20, 1801, Jefferson entered in his Memorandum Book "gave ord. on J. Barnes in favor General Sam Smith $22.29" as reimbursement; Robert Oliver invoice, November 25, 1801. T.J.'s Memorandum Book records February 1, 1802: "J. Barnes is to remit 403D for me to Josef Yznardi for wines." This was in payment for the Pedro Ximenes sherry, a quarter cask of Tent and the Tierce of Malaga.
11. T.J.'s Memorandum Book, March 9, 1802; "Enclosed a check of 590.72 to Yznardi to pay his bill of wines," for a pipe of dry Pacharetti, a pipe and two half pipes of three kinds of sherry.
12. Syracuse wine was produced at the foot of Mount Etna on the island of Sicily. Both red and white wines were made from the Muscadine grape and produced a variety of wines according to different soils and exposures. Syracuse wines were often adulterated by the addition of brandy and Henderson reported that Sicilian brandy had a "particularly harsh flavor, which no treatment will mellow, and no age subdue." Consequently, it fell into disrepute.
13. T.J.'s Memorandum Book, February 6, 1803 reads, "Enclosed to General Muhlenberg the bank post note of Jan. 17 for 22.50 to pay the duty 200 bottles Champagne bought of M. de Casa-Yrujo." John Peter Gabriel Muhlenberg (1746-1807) had served with distinction in the Revolutionary War and rose to the rank of General. He was appointed by Jefferson as collector of customs for the port of Philadelphia in 1802 and held that post until his death. Muhlenberg to T.J., February 11, 1803.
14. Oreiras was a town southwest of Lisbon, and the vineyards surrounding it had a reputation for making rich wines from the Muscatel grape which were often brandied. Although Oreiras still exists as a suburb, its vineyards have disappeared. T.J.'s Memorandum Book, February 14, 1803 reads, "Enclosed is said note for 42.42 to Messrs. Smith and Buchanan of Baltimore for duties, freight from Lisbon & porterage of 2 hhds. of wine d'Oeyrias sent to me by Mr. Jarvis." Jefferson found this wine a bit too sweet and when next ordering from William Jarvis, U.S. Consul at Lisbon, he ordered Termo. T.J. to Jarvis, May 10, 1803.
15. Vintage 1798.
16. 1798 Filhot instead of the Yquem requested. T.J. to William Lee, June 14, 1803.
17. Champagne from his favorite maker, Dorsay.
18. The freight and duty alone came to $35.14 (MB 20 June 1804).

19. J. Erick Bollman was a Hungarian adventurer who had risked his life in devising and executing the scheme that allowed the Marquis de Lafayette to escape temporarily from an Austrian prison after the Marquis' revolutionary sentiments were outpaced by the radicals of his country. Lafayette barely escaped the guillotine. Less than three years after purchasing the wine, Jefferson had Bollman arrested as a conspirator along with Aaron Burr, in a plan to revolutionize the western states. Burr had served as Jefferson's vice president during his first term as President.
20. John F. Oliveira Fernandes was a Portuguese physician and merchant in Norfolk, Virginia. T.J.'s Memorandum B.book, Februray [7, 1805] shows: "For a draught on bk. Norfolk favr. Oliveira Fernandes 152.25 wine." See T.J. to Fernandes, January 4, 1805; Oliveira Fernandes & Co. to T.J., January 24, 1805.
21. William Lee was U.S. Consul at Bordeaux. The "Salus Sauterne" referred to Yquem of the 1798 vintage. Lee to T.J., September 12, 1804, August 21, 1806; T.J. to Lee, April 28, 1806 and June 25, 1807.
22. Carmignano from Tuscany.
23. T.J.'s Memorandum Book, May 7, 1805: "231.09 to be remitted to Ludlow in N.Y for Wm. Hazard, holder of Cathalan's bill." Cathalan's bill was for 100 bottles of white Hermitage and assorted Mediterranean foodstuffs. Cathalan to T.J., December 8, 1804; T.J. to Cathalan, May 5, 1805.
24. The white Hermitage of the 1802 vintage from the vineyards of Jourdan was, in the opinion of Jefferson, "the very best I ever received: It is exactly to our taste, neither too dry nor too sweet. The vin de paille was judged not to American taste." Cathalan to T.J., January 4, 1806; T.J. to Cathalan, April 28, 1806.
25. Peter Kuhn, Jr. was a merchant in Genoa who supplied Jefferson with these 250 bottles of Nebbiolo wine which turned out to be undrinkable. In spite of this disappointment, a year and a half later he ordered three kegs of Nebbiolo from Kuhn. T.J.'s Memorandum Book entry of December 9, 1809 reads: "Enclosed to Genl. Sam. Smith ord. on dk. US. for 200.68 to pay a draught to Peter Kuhn in favor. of Mr. Patterson of Baltimore for Nebioule wine heretofore furnished."
26. Even though T.J.'s Montepulciano was shipped in bottles, he gives the gallon content of 350 bottles at 80 gallons. Therefore, each bottle contained 29.26 ounces of wine, or about four ounces more than the current 750 ml. wine bottle.
27. T.J.'s Memorandum Book, January 5, 1808 shows: "drew on bank in favr. Isaac A Coles 219.73 to wit 150. for a quarter's salary plus 69.73 to pay Philetus Havens for three cases St. George wine." This wine, which came from vineyards around Montpelier in southern France, was imported by New York merchant Philetus Havens from Peter Walsh in Sète, France. Jefferson liked it so much that three years later he wrote directly to Walsh ordering a pipe of it to be sent to him annually. T. J. to Walsh, March 27, 1811.

APPENDIX C
Currency Values—Equivalents

Jefferson's memorandum books confront one with an assortment of different currencies: French, English, Dutch, Italian and Colonial, i.e., Virginia, Maryland, Pennsylvania.

In attempting to make currency comparisons several cautions should be kept in mind. First, an understanding of the French monetary system in the 18th century is complicated by the fact that both gold and silver coins were in circulation. There is also the problem of establishing exact currency values for specific years. The value of currency still changes on a daily basis so an exact value can never be given. Attempts to make currency comparisons are further complicated by changes in the value of goods and services over time.

Another caution applies to the use of the term "dollar." In the 1780's individual states and the United States Government were still issuing their own currencies and there were different conversion rates for each of the states. With these and other variables in mind, the following currency values are offered. The most helpful sources of information were Jefferson's memorandum books, correspondence, and miscellaneous accounts; Franz Pick and Renee Sedillot's *All the Monies of the World*, 2nd ed., N.Y: Pick Publishing, 1971; John J. McCusker's *How Much Is That in Real Money? A Historical Price Index for Use as a Deflator of Money values in the Economy of the United States*, Worchester: American Antiquarian Society, 1992.

FRANCE

The livre Tournois was the unit of account of the French monetary system from the 13th century until 1795 and the coin called the "franc" was not in use during Louis XVI's reign. Therefore, a Jefferson entry, "15 f 10s," for example, should be read as 15 livres 10 sous and not 15 francs 10 sous.

12 deniers = 1 sou
1 sou = slightly less than one cent American but for conversion purposes,
    1 sou = 1 cent.

20 sous = 1 livre Tournois
I livre= about 19 cents
5 livres, 5 sous = 1 dollar
24 livres = 1 Louis d'Or
25 livres = I pound sterling
1 Louis d'Or = 19 shillings
6 livres = 1 ecu

ENGLAND

12 pence = 1 shilling
20 shillings = 1 pound sterling
21 shillings = 1 guinea
1 pound sterling = 25 livres

HOLLAND

60 kreitzer = 1 florin
20 stivers = 1 florin
1 florin = 2 shillings

PORTUGAL

810 reis = 1 dollar
432 reis = 3 livres

MONETARY SYMBOLS OR ABBREVIATIONS

d—denier or pence
s—sou or stiver
for #—livre Tournois
D—dollar

APPENDIX D

Wine Measures

ENGLISH WINE MEASURES

Tun	Pipes	Puncheons	Hogshead	Tierces	Gallons	Quarts	Pints		Liters
1	2	3	4	6	252	1008	2016	=	953.9208
	1	1½	2	3	126	504	1008	=	476.9604
		1	1½	2	84	336	672	=	317.9736
			1	1½	63	252	504	=	238.4802
				1	42	168	336	=	158.9868

THE STANDARD GAUGE FOR FOREIGN WINES

The pipe of	Port	138 gallons
	Lisbon, Bucelas, and Carcavelos	140*
	Madeira	110
	Barcelona and Vidonia	120
The butt of	Sherry	120**
	Mountain	126
The hogshead of	Claret	57
	Tent	63
The ohm of	Hock	36
	Cape	20

* Jefferson in a note calculated a pipe of Lisbon at 117 gallons, a hogshead at 58 gallons and a quarter cask at 29 gallons.

** Jefferson entered a butt of Sherry at 108 gallons, a hogshead at 54 gallons and a quarter cask at 27 gallons.

FRENCH WINE MEASURES

Barrique—In Bordeaux a wooden barrel that held 128 liters; in Hermitage 120 liters.

Burgundy Wine Bottle—30.8 ounces or about 5½ ounces more than todays standard 750 ml. bottle of 25.4 ounces.

Feuillette—A Burgundian wooden barrel or cask that held the equivalent of 125 bottles or 114 liters.

Liter—33.8 ounces or 1.057 quarts

Piece—A Burgundy wooden barrel that held the equivalent of 250 bottles. In Champagne a piece held 200 bottles.

Puncheon—A barrel holding the equivalent of 250 Burgundy bottles, but in Cote Rotie and Hermitage it held only 210 bottles.

Queue or Botte—A Burgundy barrel that held the equivalent of 500 bottles or 456 liters.

Tonneau—In Bordeaux the equivalent of four barriques or 512 liters.

GERMAN WINE MEASURES

German Wine Bottle—32 ounces or the equivalent of an American quart.

Aume—A German wooden cask or barrel that held the equivalent of 170 bottles or 421h gallons.

Foudre—A German wine cask containing six aumes of 170 bottles each.

Tun—Eight aumes

AMERICAN LIQUID MEASURES

Four Gills—A pint
Two pints—A quart
Two quarts—A pottle
Two potties—A gallon
Eight gallons—A firkin
Thirty-two gallons—A hogshead
Two hogshead—A pipe, butt or puncheon
Two pipes—A ton

APPENDIX E

Jefferson's Travel Box

Jefferson carried with him a travel box that measured 8¼" by 6¾" by 3½" and, in TJ's hand, contained:

[First column]
looking-glass
2 razors
razor-strop
shaving brush
tooth brush
dentifrice
combs
courtplaister
sponge
toothpicks
scissors
pins
needles pen
[s?]ilk
thread
beeswax
phosphoric matches
corkscrew
2 launcets

[Second column]
pen
ink
paper
p[?]ce [pounce, puince, pumice?]
wafers
sealing wax
penknife
platting scale
dividers
draw-pen
black lead
red lead pencil
air pencils
elastic gum
red ink
Indian i[nk?]
verdigris
gamboge
red orpim[en?]t
Oltramarine
gum Arabic
money scales
money steelyards

[Third column]
borax
fixed alkali
nut-galls
syrup of violets
Nitrous   }
Virtriolic }acids
Muriatic   }
Magnet
pounding hammer
pounding ream
hammering plate
a file
blowpipe
candle
steel
flint
agaric tinder
graphometer
[quandrant?]
geometrical square
dial
ringdial
pendulums. 1" and ½"
sand glass 15"
lenses, convex, concave
mppers
glass tub[es?] F[es?]
microscope
thermometer

Unable to determine what use Jefferson might have had for the chemicals and apparatus listed in the third column, I asked a chemist and metallurgist, Alfonso Baldi, to speculate on how Jefferson might have used them.

As a scientist specializing in the field of chemistry and metallurgy, I have tried to put myself in TJ's shoes to decide how he would have used his package of materials. I feel comfortable with this since TJ was an empirical scientist much as I have been throughout my career. We both carried out experimentation in a test tube style to establish facts and build upon those facts with additional experimentation.

Throughout his life TJ had an interest in viticulture. While in Europe he visited vineyards in France, Germany and Italy. Of the major factors to be considered in producing good wine, namely, climate, soil, variety of grape, skill in growing the vines and making the wines, the greatest unknown factor is the soil. Jefferson knew that the soil in which the grapes grew was critically important to the quality of the wine. I considered the various phases of wine making and concluded that his primary use of the chemicals and apparatus was for a qualitative analysis rather than a quantitative analysis of the soils in which the vines grew. With this assumption in mind I feel comfortable in speculating on how he might have used his materials when visiting vineyards.

Chemicals and apparatus

(1) Borax and Blow Pipe

Borax is a salt chemically known as sodium tetra borate ($Na_2 B_4O_7 \cdot 10H_2O$). It is colorless and has a low melting point of 741°. When heated with metal oxides it dissolves them and gives a color characteristic of the particular metal oxide i.e.

Copper oxide—Blue
Iron oxide (magnetic)—Green
Iron oxide (nonmagnetic)—Brown
Nickel oxide—Yellowish brown
Manganese oxide—Violet

With the aid of a Blow Pipe TJ could blow air into a flame to increase the temperature in order to adequately melt the Borax to react with the metal oxide to develop the color.

(2) Acids

Mun•atic (Hydrochlon•c Acid)
Nitrous (Nitric Acid)
Vitriolic (Sulfuric Acid)

One or a combination of these acids could be used to dissolve certain minerals in the soil. For example chalk (calcium carbonate) will readily react with muratic acid and liberate carbon dioxide gas. The quantity of gas released could be observed which would give TJ an idea of how much chalk was present in the soil.

Iron oxide would dissolve in the acids. With muriatic acid, a green color would result and with a mixture of muriatic or vitriolic and nitn'c acid the iron would be oxidized to give a red-brown color.

Most silicates such as quartz and silica sand would be unaffected by the acids. Any car-

bonaceous material in the clay in soil would give a charred color upon adding vitriolic acid to the soil.

(3) *Fixed Alakli*

Alkalis such as Sodium Hydroxide (caustic soda) in very strong concentrations would have little effect on minerals such as iron oxide and chalk but would tend to dissolve silica sand and other silicon dioxide containing materials such as some quartz. Also adding some fixed alkali to acid solutions to lower the acidity might be necessary in some of TJ's analytical approaches.

(4) *Pounding Ream, Pounding Hammer, Hammering Plate*

These implements could be used to evaluate the texture of the soil to determine the presence and quantity of stones, gravel and other hard materials which permit good drainage. This is an important factor in producing good wine.

(5) *File*

In addition to being of general use for smoothing down or removing burrs etc. from materials, the file was useful in determining the relative hardness of minerals (if large enough) in the soil. Those materials when scratched with a file would show that talc is the softest mineral followed by gypsum, then chalk and calcite and finally quartz being the hardest.

(6) *Candle*

Used for light and mild heating when carrying out soil-chemical reactions.

(7) *Steel, Flint, agaric tinder*

Rubbing flint against a steel plate would cause a spark to ignite the tinder to start a fire with wood fuel.

(8) *Magnet*

Used for determining the presence of any magnetic material in the soil. For example, it could differentiate between any magnetic iron oxide in the soil and non-magnetic iron oxide.

(9) *Thermometer*

TJ could have used his thermometer in many ways.

(a) To measure the temperature in his environment to give indication of the comfort index.

(b) Record the temperature in any soil-chemcial reaction.

(c) Establish the approximate alcoholic content in wine by measuring the temperature at which it would boil.

100%	Alcohol	78.5°c B Pt.
20%	Alcohol	86.0°c B Pt.
17%	Alcohol	87.0°c B Pt.
15%	Alcohol	88.0°c B Pt.
12%	Alcohol	89.0°c B Pt.
10%	Alcohol	90.0°c B Pt.
8%	Alcohol	92.0°c B Pt.
6%	Alcohol	93.0°c B Pt.
100%	Water	100.00°c B Pt.

(10) Glass Tubes

These were probably what we call today test tubes. These could be used for observing chemical-soil reaction, boiling point of wine, and as a volume measuring device.

(11) Microscope and Lenses

Could have been used to examine soil under high magnification to identify (by inference) the approximate Crystal structure* of mineral which was present. For example the following are given:

Hexagonal crystals	*—Calcium carbonate (chalk)*
	—Silcon dixoide (Quartz)
Cubic crystal	*—Iron oxide (Non magnetic)*
Monoclinic	*—Magnesium silicate (Talc)*
	—Calcium sulfate (Gypsum)

*Crystal structure is the way in which atoms are assembled and can only accurately be determined by x-ray or electron diffraction studies.

(12) Nipper

General cutting purposes or to hold something.

(13) Graphometer, Geometric square

Drawing of graphs, etc.

(14) Sand Glass

Similar to an hour glass to establish a time element.

(15) Nut galls

For polishing or smoothing purposes

(16) Dial and Ring dial

Used in instrumentation for regulating speed, time, etc.

(17) Pendulum

As a time counting device.

Glossary

Aix-en Provence (Eks-ahn Pro-vahnss) —A beautiful old city that is the unofficial capital of Provence.

Alsace (Al'zas) —The easternmost wine province of France situated between the Rhine River and the Vosges Mountains.

Appellation Contrôlée (Ah-pel-ah-see-awn Cawn-trol-lay) —See AOC.

AOC —Appellation d'Origine Controlee (Ah-pel-ah-see-awn Dor-ee-Jeen Cawntrol-lay). French laws created by the *Institut National des Appellations d'Origine* that regulate virtually everything concerned with the production of wine in France. Wine is organized into four broad quality divisions. The best is *Appellation d'Ongine Controlee* (AOC) and is the most strictly controlled. Virtually all the French wines that Jefferson drank now fall into this category. Next in line is *Vin Delimite de Qualite Superieure* (VDQS). The third division is *Vin de Pay* (country wines) which are much less regulated particularly as regards grape variety and vineyard yield. The final category is *Vin de Table*. Unlike the others, table wines do not carry a place name and need only have a minimum alcoholic strength.

Arpent (Ar-pahn) —An ancient French measure of land equal to about one acre.

Auslese (Ouse-lay-zuh) —A superior German white wine with a high concentration of sweetness made by vinifying only the ripest bunches from late harvested grapes; generally a dessert wine.

Barsac (Bar-sack) —One of the five communes that make up the sweet white wine district of Sauternes; its two most famous vineyards being Châteaux Climens and Coutet.

Barolo (Bar-o-low) —Italian wines made from the Nebbiolo grape in the Piedmont section of Northern Italy. Barolos are usually full-bodied, tannic red wines that are long-lived.

Beaujolais (Bo-juh-lay) —A light, fruity, easy to drink red wine from Burgundy's most southern district made exclusively from the Gamay grape.

Beaumes-de-Venise (Bohm-duh-Veh-neez) —A village in the southern Rhone famous for a sweet white wine of that name made from the Muscat grape.

Beaune (Bone) —Ancient and picturesque city in the middle of the Cote d'Or that is the center for the Burgundy wine trade.

Beerenauslese (Bear-en-ouse-lay-zah) —A very sweet and expensive German white wine made by vinifying only the ripest grapes from late harvested bunches; generally a dessert wine.

Blaye (Blay) —A town on the right bank of the Gironde River about thirty miles west of Bordeaux surrounded by vineyards that produce good everyday quality wines, mostly reds.

Bommes (Bom) —One of the five communes that make up the district of Sauternes. Its most famous vineyards are Châteaux Lafaurie-Peyraguey, La Tour Blanche and Rayne-Vigneau.

Bordeaux (Bor-doe) —City in southwestern France surrounded by five of the world's greatest vineyard areas, Medoc, Graves, St. Ernilion, Sauternes, and Pornerol.

Botrytis Cinerea (Bo-try-tiss Sin-eh-ray-ah) —The name for the fungus that sometimes affects the grapes in Sauternes (and certain other wine regions) increasing the porosity of the grape skins allowing the water to evaporate and leaving behind a very sweet and concentrated juice.

Burgundy —The modern name for what remains of the ancient Duchy of Burgundy. It is best known today for its great red and white wines, excellent cuisine and some of the most beautiful châteaux in France. The region extends from Chablis and Auxerre in the north to Beaujolais in the south. Burgundy's most famous wines come from the vineyards along the Cote d'Or, a thirty mile stretch of hillsides that begin just below Dijon in the north and extend to Santenay in the south.

Calon-Segur (Ca-lawn Say-goor) —A Third Growth Medoc from St. Estephe, a red wine.

Carcavelos (Car-ca-vel-oss) —Red and white wines from vineyards near Lisbon, now but a shadow of their former size.

Chablis (Shab-lee) —A crisp, dry white wine made from the Chardonnay grape from vineyards that surround the town of the same name; the most northern wine region of Burgundy.

Chambertin (Shahm-bear-tan) —World-famous red wine of Burgundy, from the Cote de Nuits. A Jefferson favorite.

Chardonnay (Shar-doe-nay) —The grape that makes all of the great dry white Burgundies and an important grape in Champagne.

Château Grillet (Shat-toe Gree-yay) —The smallest vineyard in France with its own Appellation Contrôlée, located in the northern Rhone Valley near Ampuis. Thought to make the finest white wine of Condrieu.

Château d'Yquern (Shat-toe dee-Kern) —The most famous and expensive wine of Sauternes, a Jefferson favorite and a favorite today with wine lovers who can afford it.

Châteauneuf-du-Pape (Shat-toe-nuff dew Pahp) —A full-bodied red wine from the town of that name in the southern Rhone located between Orange and Avignon.

Glossary

Chianti (Key-ahn-tee) —A red wine from Tuscany whose principal grape is the Sangiovese.

Chusclan (Sheuss-clahn) —A village in the southern Rhone near Tavel and Châteauneuf-du-Pape known mainly for its Rose wines.

Cote d'Or (Coat door) —French for "golden slope." Takes its name from the Burgundy vineyard hillsides that extend about thirty miles from just south of Dijon in the north to Santenay in the south.

Cote de Beaune (Coat duh Bone) —The southern half of the Cote d'Or which produces, among others, the great whites of Puligny-Montrachet (Poo-leen-yee Mawn-rasch-shay), Chassagne-Montrachet (Shass-anya Mawn-rasch-shay) and Meursault (Mere-so); also the charming reds of Volany, Pommard and Beaune.

Cote de Nuits (Coat duh N'wee) —The northern section of the Cote d'Or where the Grand Cru red Burgundy vineyards are located.

Cote Rotie (Coat Ro-tee) —The most northern Rhone vineyards terraced up steep hillsides that produce rich full-bodied red wines.

DOC —The abbreviation for Denominazione di Origine Controllata, a category of Italian laws that regulate grape growing and wine making.

Durfort-Vivens (Dyr-fort Vee-vahn) —A Second Growth vineyard in Margaux.

Épernay (A-pair-nay) —City in the Champagne region and home to some of the most famous producers, such as Bollinger, Moet et Chandon, Perrier-Jouet and Pol Roger.

Fargues (Farg) —One of the five communes of the Sauternes district with Château Rieussec being the most famous.

Feuillette (Foy-yet) —Burgundian barrel that held 125 bottles or 114 liters of wine. Goutte d'or (Goot door) -A Meursault vineyard that still produces elegant dry wines; Jefferson's favorite dry white table wine.

Graves (Grahv) —An area south of the city of Bordeaux now famous for both its red and white wines-especially Château Haut-Brion, one of Jefferson's favorites.

Gruaud-Larose (Grew-oh La-roz) —Second Growth red wine of St. Julien, Medoc.

Haut-Brion (Oh Bree-ohn) —First Growth red wine from Graves and a Jefferson favorite.

Haut-Peyraguey (Oh Pay-rah-gay) —First Growth of Sauternes from Bommes district.

Hectare —One hectare equals 10,000 square meters or 2.471 acres.

Hermitage (Air-mee-taj) —Located about fifty miles south of Lyon near the village of Tain l'Hermitage. The Syrah grape makes the red wines, although splendid full-bodied white wines are made from the Marsanne and Roussane grapes.

Hochheim (Hawk-hime) —A German town which is famous for the white wines its six hundred acres of vines produce. The term "Hock" has become synonymous with white German wine. d'Issan (dee Sahn) -Third Growth of Medoc from Cantenac but sold under the AOC of the adjoining commune, Margaux.

Lafaurie Peyraguey (Lah-foh-ree Pay-rah-gay) —First Growth of Sauternes from Bommes district.

Lafite-Rothschild (La-feet-Rot-sheeld) —First Growth red wine of Medoc in Pauillac. Most Americans pronounce it as spelled but without the "s." A Jefferson favorite red wine.

La Tache (La Tahsh) —A famous red Burgundy wine that is located a stone's throw from its more famous neighbor, Romanée-Conti.

Languedoc (Lang-doc) —An ancient French province that extends from the Rhone River in the east to Toulouse in the west with its southern border following the Mediterranean. Produces large quantities of good, everyday wines. A favorite source of Jefferson's retirement wines.

Latour (La-toor) —First Growth of Medoc in the commune of Pauillac and a Jefferson favorite red wine.

Léoville -Barton (Lay-oh-veel Bar-tawn) —Second Growth red wine of St. Julien.

Léoville-las-Cases (Lay-oh-veellas Cass) —Second Growth red wine of St. Julien.

Léoville Poyferre (Lay-oh-veel Pwa-fuh-ray) —Second Growth red wine of St. Julien. Lettre de cachet (Lettra duh ca-shay) -The King's right to order any subject arrested and indefinitely detained or imprisoned without cause or a hearing.

Limoux (Lee-moo) —A small hill town near Carcassonne in Languedoc. Jefferson imported white wines from this area in his retirement years.

Loire (Lwahr) —The longest river in France and along its borders in the Loire Valley are many famous châteaux and vineyards producing white, red and rose wines.

Lur-Saluces (Lur-Sa-lus) —The name of the family that has owned Château d'Yquem since Jefferson's time.

Margaux (Mar-go) —A commune in the Medoc whose vineyards produce many great wines including Château Margaux, a First Growth and a Jefferson favorite red wine.

Macon (Mah-cawn) —A city in southern Burgundy most famous for the good, inexpensive dry white wines of its name, such as Macon-Villages, Macon-Lugny, Macon-Vire, and Macon-Prisse.

Medoc (May-dock) —The narrow strip of land north of the city of Bordeaux which continues to make great red wines.

Mise en bouteille au château (Meez-ahn-boo-tay oh shat-toe) —Bottled at the château.

Montepulciano (Mohn-teh-pool-chee-ano) —A red wine from southern Tuscany that Jefferson liked.

Moselle (Mó-zell) —The German wine district that produces crisp, fruity, white wines whose steep-terraced slate vineyards are almost perpendicular to the Moselle River.

Mousseux (Moo-sir) —Literally, "foamy," but, in wine, sparkling, as in Champagne.

Mouton-Rothschild (Moo-tawn-Rot-sheeld) —Famous First Growth red Medoc; most Americans pronounce Rothschild as spelled but without the "s."

Muscat (Moos-cah) —Wines made from Muscat grapes are sweet, fruit-scented, dessert wines.

Nebbiolo (Neb-be-oh-low) —Italian red grape which makes some of Italy's finest dry red wines in the Northern Italian Piedmont.

Nimes (Neem) —Ancient French city that borders Languedoc on the west and Provence on the east. Formerly a principal Roman city that has more Roman antiquities than any place outside of Italy.

Nierstein (Neer-stine) —The most famous wine of the German Rheinhessen region.

Phylloxera (Fil-lox-err-ah) —An insect that attacks and destroys the vine, especially its roots. In the later 1860's and 1870's it almost destroyed the world's vineyards. It is again causing great destruction to California vineyards, especially in Napa and Sonoma Counties.

Pinot Noir (Pee-no Nwahr) —The grape that makes all of the great red Burgundies and the principal grape of Champagne.

Pommard (Po-mar) —A little village in Burgundy's Cote de Beaune whose vineyards produce light and elegant red wines.

Posthouses —Inns, taverns and way-stations along the roads in France that provided horses, postillions, drivers, guides and, usually, overnight room and board.

Pouilly-Fuisse (Poo-yee Fwee-say) —Well-known white wine from the southern section of Burgundy near the town of Mikon, and made from the Chardonnay grape.

Preignac (Pray-nyac) —One of five communes that make up the Sauternes district. Two well-known sweet white wines from here are Châteaux Guiraud and Suduiraut.

Provence (Pro-vahnss) —A beautiful, sun-kissed ancient French province that extends from Aix-en-Provence in the west to Nice in the east with its southern border following the Mediterranean.

Rausan-Segla (Roh-san-Say-glah) —Classified a Second Growth of Margaux was Madame Rausan's estate. A red wine Jefferson esteemed.

Rauzan Gassies (Roh-sahn Gah-see) —Classified a Second Growth of Margaux.

Rheingau (Rhine-gow) —A German wine district whose vineyards grow on the hillsides facing the Rhine opposite Mainz and Bingen.

Rheinhessen (Rine-hess-en) —The largest of the eleven German wine regions.

Richebourg (Reesh-boor) —A famous red Burgundy that abuts Romanée-Conti.

Riesling (Rees-ling) —The white grape that makes the famous German wines of the Moselle and Rheingau.

Rivesaltes (Reev-sahlt) —A town north of Perpignan in Roussillon whose name is on wines that come from the surrounding vineyards. Muscat de Rivesaltes, still popular, was a favorite wine of Jefferson in his later years.

Romanée-Conti (Roh-mah-nay Con-tee) —Burgundy's most expensive red wine and, many say, its best.

Romanée St.-Vivant (Roh-mah-nay San Vee-vahn) —A Grand Cru red Burgundy once prescribed for Louis XIV by his Burgundian physician.

Roussillon (Roo-see-yawn) —An area of southern France with extensive vineyards that borders the Mediterranean on the east and south, Languedoc to the north and the Pyrenees Mountains in the west. One of Jefferson's favorite wine sources in his retirement and still producing fine white Muscat dessert wines.

Rudesheim (Roo-des-heim) —A quaint town in the Rheingau that borders the Rhine and is surrounded on three sides by many of Germany's great vineyards. The restaurants and pubs that line its narrow, crooked streets are perfect spots for the visitor to enjoy the local wines.

Sangiovese (Sahn-jo-vay-zay) —The principal grape that makes red Chianti wines from Italy's famed Tuscany region.

Saint Estephe (San Es-Tef) —One of the four most important wine producing communes of Medoc and especially noted for the red wines of Châteaux Cos d'Estournel, Montrose and Calon-Segur.

Sauternes (Saw-tairn) —A wine district about thirty miles southeast of the city of Bordeaux that has long been famous for its sweet white wines. The district consists of five communes—Barsac, Bommes, Fargues, Preignac and Sauternes. The most famous wine of Sauternes, and Jefferson's favorite, is Château d'Yquem.

Sauvignon Blanc (So-veen-yohn Blahn) —The principal grape from which the dry white wines of Bordeaux and Sancerre are made.

Semillon (Say-me-awn) —The principal white grape of Sauternes wines.

St.-Emilion (San-tay-mee-lee-awn} —The quaint and beautiful ancient town on the right bank of the Dordogne River. It is literally surrounded by vineyards. Many great red wines come from its vineyards with the two most famous being Châteaux Cheval-Blanc and Ausone.

Syrah (See-rah) —The principal grape that makes the rich red wines of Cote Rorie and Hermitage and a principal grape of Châteauneuf-du-Pape.

Tent —Sometimes called Rota Tent, it was known as the darkest of all Spanish wines.

Termo —White wines from vineyards from around the Lisbon region.

Traminer (Trah-mee-ner) —Alsatian grape whose best known variety is Gewurtztraminer (Guh-vertz-trah-mee-ner), makes a spicy, pungent white wine.

Trockenbeerenauslese (Trok-en-bear-en-ouse-lay-zuh) —The richest, sweetest and most expensive German white wine made from a special selection of over-ripe grapes that have been affected by Botryis Cinerea.

Tun (Ton) —A large wine cask that held about 252 gallons; the equivalent of two pipes or four hogsheads.

Volnay (Vol-nay) —A little village in Burgundy's Cote de Beaune whose vineyards produce light and elegant red wines.

Vosne (Vone) —The vineyards that surround the town of Vosne-Romanée located in the Cote de Nuits district are responsible for producing many great red Burgundies such as Romanée-Conti, La Tache, Richebourg, Romanée Saint-Vivant, and La Romanée. Although Jefferson did not list the best wines of Vosne, he did single out Vosne wines for special distinction.

Vougeot (Voo-joh) —A little village in the Cote d'Or best known for the red wines of Clos de Vougeot which Jefferson noted as one of the best red wines of Burgundy. The Château du Clos de Vougeot is the headquarters of the famous Burgundian wine society, the Confrerie des Chevaliers du Tastevin.

Yquem (ee-kem) —Classified a First Great Growth of Sauternes and Jefferson's favorite Sauternes.

Index

Account Books 2, 61
Acid Wines 93
Adams, Abigail 18-20, 22, 25, 27, 35,44,46, 139,169,228
Adams, Abigail (Nabby) 18, 21, 22,25,26,27
Adams, John 8, II, 12, 13, 17, 18,20-22,25-28,30,35,39, 42-46, 124, 139-40, 162, 169, 189,191,193, 19 210,225
Adams, John Quincy, 18, 19, 22, 25, 27,203
Adams, Margaret 175
Adams, Samuel 13
Adams, Thomas 4, 5
Adirondack Mountains 179
Adlum, John 196,214, 219, 226,227
Agde I 06, 159
Aigle d'Or 15, 165
Aix-en-Provence 56, 85-88, 103,224
Albenga 101, 102
Alberes 111
Albergo Reale Inn 99
Aleatico grape 217
Alexandergrape 196, 214, 227
Alicante grape 109
Allen, Ethan 180
Alpilles Mountains 85, 86
Alps 95, 96, 102,145
Alsace and wines 143, 151, 152
Alychamps 84
Amboise Forest 127
Ambrosi, Hans 148
American Philosophical Society 193

American Root Stocks 62
American Taverns 177, 178
Amphitheatre 71, 72, 74, 83, 85, 89, 106
Amsterdam 24, 98, 139-41, 146, 171, 185,218
Amsterdam Arms 140
Ancenis 125
Andernach 143, 144
Anderson, Burton 99
Angers 126
Anjou 126
Annapolis 11-13, 173-75
Antoinette, Marie (Queen) 162, 188, 199
Antwerp 54, 56, 139
Apennines 98, 100, 101
Appellation Contrôlée (AOC) 74, 106, 107, 213
Appleton, Thomas 215, 217, 221-22
Aqueria, Robert d' 105
Arboete 120
Argiles 111-12
Arimo grape 187
Arles 83-85, 104
Arnold, Benedict 179-80
Arnaud (Valet) 145-46
Arno 217 (see also Val d'Arno di Sopra)
Arnoux, Abbe 20, 22, 23, 51, 69, 92
Artimino 215-17
Askos 83, 159-60
Assmanshausen 149
Au Grand Gaillon I 09
Auberge de la Postea 102
Aubergiste de l'hotel de Rohan 152

Aude River 113
Ausleses 148-49
Auteuil 19, 27-30
Auvillij 154
Auxerre 60, 159
Avignon 79, 103-06, 165
Ay 152-55, 170, 184

Bachet, Jeans Joseph and wines 65, 67, 129, 135-36, 160-61
Bacon, Edmund 198
Bacon, Francis 189, 210
Bagatelle 30, 54
Baltimore 177, 191
Banalite du Moulin 162
Banbury 40
Barbaresco 97, 99
Barclay, Thomas 19, 33, 136
Barolo 97, 99
Barsac 120-21, 185, 187, 189
Bastille 51, 54, 162, 164
Batard-Montrachet 65
Baum, Colonel 181
Beaujolais and wines 68, 70, 83
Beaumarchais 23, 50
Beaumes 76, 77
Beaumes-de-Venise 106
Beaune 61, 62, 64, 66, 71, 159, 201
Bedell (winery) 152
Beer 6, 33, 212, 218
Beerenausleses 145, 148
Bellet 92, 93, 183, 202, 206, 213, 221-23
Bellevue 133, 134
Bellini, Charles 28
Bemis Heights 179
Benedictine Monks 154, 184
Beni Carlos 2, 122
Bennington, Vermont 181
Bergasse, Henry (see also Claret de Bergasse) 89, 90, 203, 212-13, 222-24
Bernkastel 144-45
Bessards, Les 76
Bezier 106, 109, 111
Bidwell (winery) 182
Bienvenues-Batard-Montrachet 65
Birmingham 42

Bishop of Fulda 147
Bladensburg 175
Blanchard, Jean Pierre 189
Blanqueford 117
Blanquette de Calvisson 82
Blanquene de Limoux 212
Blaye 123
Blenheim Palace 43
Blois 126, 127
Bodenheim 145, 149
Bois de Boulogne 19, 23, 29, 54, 133, 162
Bommes 120-21
Bondfield, John 25, 33, 34, 133, 136, 157-58, 168
Bonn 143
Bonnes Mares 64
Bordeaux 5, 18, 21, 25, 27, 28, 32, 33, 57, 72, 75, 76, 89, 110, 112-20, 122-23, 126, 130, 132, 136, 140, 152, 168, 171, 172, 176, 177, 184-85, 189-90, 196, 200, 213, 222-23
Bordeaux de Segur (see Latour, Château)
Bordighera 102
Boston 13, 15, 180
Boswell, James 100
Botrytis Cinerea 74, 120-22
Bourg 123
Boyd, Julian P. I
Bradley, Stephen (Senator) 200
Braine-le-Comte 139
Brandy 19, 106, 167, 175, 178, 184, 187, 188, 220, 226-27
Brauneberg 144-45, 158, 185-86
Brazil Madeira 202
Brazilian Madeira 200
Breymann, Colonel 181
British Museum 46
Brown, James 167, 169, 175, 189, 191
Brown, Lancelot "Capability" 38, 39, 43
Brown, Mather 36, 37, 46
Brownberg (see Brauneberg) Brussels 139
Bucelas 187
Buckingham House 45
Buffon, Comte de 23, 33
Bulfinch, Charles 50
Bulkeley, John 176, 188, 191

Burgoyne, General John 8, 181
Burgundy 4, 5, 18, 32, 40, 60-68, 71-72, 75-76, 109, 112-13, 125, 129-30, 152, 165, 184-85, 196, 200-01, 214-15, 219, 221-22, 227
Burr, Aaron 193, 196
Burton, Colonel G. Hutchins 220

Cabernet Franc grape 126
Cadiz 169, 202
Cahuzac 28, 57, 115, 176, 202, 206
Calais 35, 47
California 149
Calon-Segur 120
Calons 120
Calvert, B. 192
Campbell's (tavern) 2
Cammazes 113
Campomarone 100
Canaiols Rosso 215
Canal-du-Midi 106, 109, 110, 114, 185, 212
Canal of Lanquedoc (see Canal du-Midi)
Candale 120
Cannes 102
Cannon, Robert 47
Canon 123
Cap d'Antibes 102
Cape of Good Hope 143, 196
Cape wine 143
Capitaineries 130
Carcavelos 97, 99, 169, 187, 188
Carmignano 5, 215, 217
Carcassonne 106, 111, 113, 212
Cartei 5
Cary, Wilson Miles 132
Cassel 143
Cassis 88
Castelnaudary Ill, 113-14
Castres 115
Catawba 227
Cathalan, Stephen 93, 189, 203, 205-06, 212-14, 221-22, 224
Cathedral of Milan 100
Caumartin 129, 219, 227
Caversham 39

Ceasar, Julius 141, 189
Ceres 15
Cette (see Sète) Cevennes 109
Chablis 60
Chalon 67
Chalut, Abbe 20, 22, 23, 51, 69
Chambertin 4, 61-63, 66, 71, 109, 130, 136, 184-85, 200, 201, 214
Champagne 5, 21, 32, 40, 56, 67, 75, 77, 97, 113, 143, 152-55, 158, 165, 170-71, 173, 177, 183-85, 196, 199, 200-01, 212, 215, 221
Champs-Elysées 17, 19, 22, 30, 47, 51, 129, 162
Chante-Alouette 76
Chapoutier, M. 76
Chardonnay 60, 64, 68, 153
Charente River 123
Charlemagne 141
Charlottesville 2, 5, 8, 9, 141
Charlton's (tavern) 2
Chase-Lloyd House 173
Chassagne-Montrachet 64, 65
Chastellux, Marquis de 10, 11, 22, 33, 89, 135, 178, 179
Château Borely 89
Château Chanteloup 126
Château d'If 89
Château d'Issan 120
Château d'Yquem (see Yquem)
Château de Laye 68, 69, 70, 83
Château de Madrid 54
Château de Suduiraut 34, 121
Château de la Rochefoucauld
Château Fortia 79
Château Gloria 120
Château Grillet 74
Château Kirwan 120, 123, 185
Château LaGrange 120
Château Marquis de Terme 120, 123
Château Palmer 123
Château Peyraguey 121
Château Pontac Montplaisir 122
Château Simone 88
Château of Valkhof 141
Châteauneuf-du-Pape 79, 82

Chaumont, Le Ray de 18
Chaumont, M. 211
Chenin Blanc grape 126
Chermont, M. de 64, 184, 201
Chesapeake Bay 173
Chestertown, Maryland 173
Cheval Blanc 85
Chevalier, M. 224
Chevalier-Montrachet 65
Chez un Anglois Inn 141
Chez Zimmerman 142
Chianti 215, 217
Chimney Point 180
Chiswick 38
Chusclan 79
Ciandola 96
Cider 2, 6, 33, 212, 226
Cinsault grape 79, 106
City Tavern (New York) 168
City Tavern (Philadelphia) 7
Clairctte of Limoux 224
Claremont 38
Claret 21, 109, 185-86, 189, 192, 200, 215, 217, 228
Claret de Bergasse 203, 212, 222, 226
Clark Museum 182
Classification of 1855 118, 120
Clermont 165, 167
Clermont, Monsieur 64, 136
Clerriseau, Charles-Louis 159, 160
Clos Vougeot (see Vougcot)
Clos de la Chainette 60
Clos de la Commaraine 129
Coblenz 140, 144-45, 158, 185
Cohoes Falls 179
Col de Tende 96
Colle 5, 190
Cologne 142-43
Columbus, Christopher 100, 210
Colvins Tavern 181
Comartin (see also Caumartin) 129
Comedic Francais 50
Condorcet, Marquis de 23, 29
Condrieux 72, 74
Congress 7, 8, 11-13, 140, 169, 193, 195, 198, 214, 223, 225

Coni 95, 96
Connecticut 13, 182
Conrad and McMunn's 195-96
Constantia 75, 143
Coopers Wine Recipe 215
Coppinger 218
Corbieres 111
Corkscrew 73, 178
Cornas 77
Cornwallis 9, 10
Costiere 82
Costiere du Gard 82
Cosway, Maria 37, 50, 52-54, 56, 59, 135
Cosway, Richard 50, 52, 56
Cote d'Or 60-62, 66-67
Cote de Beaune 64, 66
Cote de Nuits 62-63
Cotes-du-Rhone-Villages 106
Cote Rorie 72-74, 189
Cour du Plantin (tavern) 150
Cours Mirabeau 87
Court of St. James's 26, 27, 36
Countess d'Houdetot 23
Cousin, Monsieur 152, 171
Covent Garden 45
Cowes, England 18
Cox, Thomas 220
Crawford, William H. 225
Criots-Batard-Montrachet 65
Croce Bianca 96, 100
Crown Point 180
Crozes Hermitage 77
Cuers 91
Cul-de-Sac Taitbout 19, 25, 30
Cumieres 153, 155
Currants 219
Custis, John Park 5
Cutler, Senator 199

da Vinci, Leonardo 100
d'Abadie, Monsieur 120
d'Aqueria, Robert (see Agueria)
d'Issan 120
d'Yquem (see Yquem)
Dalton, CT 182
Dariste 117

Index

David, John 219-20
David, Jean-Louis 23, 50, 51
De Barras, Admiral 135
Declaration of Independence 18, 22, 36, 135, 193
De Grasse, Admiral 135
Delamon, Château 122
Delmas, Jean 119
Dessin, Pierre 35, 47
Dewey, Elijah 181
Dick, John Adam 145, 149
Dijon 60, 61
Dion, Roger 126
Diquem, M. (see Yquem, Monsieur)
Dizy 153, 155
Dolly's Chop House 36, 37
Domaine Des Comtes Lafon 65
Domaine Francois Gaunoux 65
Domaine Rene Manuel 65
Domaine de la Romanée-Conti (see Romanée-Conti)
Domenger, Seigneur 172
Donald, Alexander 33, 132-33, 167, 176
Dorchester Heights 180
Dorsay, Monsieur 154-55, 171, 184
Dorsay's Champagne 154-55, 170, 173, 183-84
Dossenheim 150
Dover 36, 47
Downs in Morichies 182
Droit du Four 162
Drury Lane 125
du Roy, President (vineyards) 34, 121
Duchesss d'Anville 23
Duchess of Rochefoucauld 206
Dufour, John James 193
Duisberg 142
Duke of Chartes 24, 50, 163
Duke of Choiseul 126
Duke of Marlboro 43
Duke of Normandy 26
Duke of Rochefoucauld 23, 29, 115, 188
Duke of Tuscany (see Grande Duke of)
Dulamon (du Lamont) 117, 122
Dulany, Lloyd 11, 12
Dunmore, Governor Earl 5

Durand, M. 221, 224
Durfort 120, 185
Durfort-Vivens 120, 185
Dusmond, 144, 185
Dusseldorf 142, 150, 158

Edgehill 48
Edy 211
El Cite 113
Elbling grape 152
ElkRidge 9
Elkton, Maryland 191
Elysian Fields 84
Enfield Chase 37
English Wine Merchants 5, 100, 109, 117, 135, 158, 177
Épernay 152, 153, 155
Eppes, Elizabeth 13, 168
Eppes, Francis 13, 25, 33, 115, 117, 130, 132-33, 167
Eppes, John Wayles 193
Erbach 147, 240
Erbaluce grape 99
Esher Place 38
Espagnol (Valet) 139
Esterel Mountains 91
Etang de Thau 109
Etauliers 124
Ezekiel Ensign's Tavern 179

Failli, Monsieur de 154
Falernian 109
Fanny 211
Fargues 120-21
Fauquier, Governor Francis
Federal City 195-96
Federalists 190, 193, 200
Felucca 101
Fenwick, Joseph 168, 171-73, 183, 185-86, 189-91
Ferger, Gramont and Cie 117, 130
Filhot 200
Fleurieu, Christian de and family 70
Florence 4, 5, 215, 217, 221-22
Floyd, William 182
Flushing, Long Island 183

Folie Blanche grape 125
Fontainebleau 31, 60
Fort Carillon 179
Fort George 179
Fort Ticonderoga 179-81
Fort William Henry 179
Foster, Augustus 204
Fountain of Vaucluse 104-05
Fourth of July 163, 183, 228
Foxgrape 214, 219
Frankfurt 141, 145-46, 218
Franklin, Benjamin 1, 4, 5, 8, 11-13, 17, 18, 20, 22, 25-27, 44, 51, 133, 168, 210-11
Frederick Bull's 182
Fredericksburg 175
Frejus 91, 103
French Revolution 63, 89, 104, 117, 159, 164, 188-89, 203
French Riviera 93
French Wine Merchants 117
Frontenac 27, 28, 33, 108
Frontignan 27, 32, 93, 106-09, 111, 131, 151, 165, 171, 189, 217

Gaillac 28, 32, 11S, 202
Gale, Levin 219
Gallatin, Albert 205
Gamble, Robert 191
Garden Book 2, 34, 129
Gardere, Jean-Paul 119
Garonne River 110, 114-15, 123
Garvey, Anthony 28, 130
Gassies, Château 120
Gattinara 97, 99
Geismar, Baron de 9, 141, 146, 158
Genet, Citizen 196
Genoa 95-96, 98, 100
Gentil grape 152
Gentile, Monsieur 126
George Wythe I, 2
Georgetown 175, 197-98, 214, 219, 226
Germany 40, 109, 141, 142, 147, 152-53, 158, 224
Gerry, Elbridge 190
Ghesseland, Mrs. II Ghemme 97

Giannini, Anthony 34, 196
Giles, William Branch 189, 198
Gironde 117, 122-23
Glanum 85
Gobelin tapestries 127
Goldberger, Paul 226
Goutte d'Or 65, 129, 135-36, 160, 184
Graach (Crach) 144-45
Graeco-Roman Theatre 84
Grand Theatre, Bordeaux 118
Grand Corniche 102
Grand Duke of Tuscany 4, 8, 215
Grand Echezeaux 64
Grands Crus 64, 118, 122
Grave (see Graves)
Graves 115, 117, 122-23, 140, 176, 185, 189
Gray's Ferry 183, 196
Gray's Gardens 183
Great Falls 175
Great Tun of Heidelberg ISO
Green Mountain Boys 180-81
Green Mountains 179
Greenport 182
Gregory, Capt. 115-16
Grenache grape 79, 105, 112
Grey, Edward Whitker 46
Griffin's in Riverhead 182
Grillé de Chaillot 17, 30, 37
Grimm, Baron 23
Gros Plant grape 125
Gruaud-LaRose 120, 185
Guide, Pierre 177, 183
Guide, Jean Baptiste 177
Guilford 182

Haarlem 141
Hagley 42
Halifax, N.C. 220
Halle aux Bleds 52, 53
Hallgarten, Fritz 148-49
Hamilton, Alexander 168, 176, 186, 189-91, 196
Hammond-Harwood House 173
Hampton Court 38
Hanau 146

Haraszthy, Agoston I 09
Hargrave (winery) 182
Harrison, Samuel!. 221
Hartford 182
Hattenhcim 147
Haut-Brion, Château 21, 33, 34, 65, 115-18, 122, 154, 157, 185
Haut-Peyraguey 121
Hautviller 184
Havre 15, 165, 184-85, 201
Havre de Grace, Maryland 214, 219
Heidelberg 150-51
Heidelberg Castle 150
Hemings, James 15, 19, 165
Hemings, John 192
Hemings, Peter 219
Hemings, Sally 165
Henderson, Alexander 76, 119, 121, 123, 213
Hendrickson's Tavern 179
Henry, Patrick 1, 33, 60, 64, 76
Hermitage 72, 75-77, 112, 122, 185, 189, 200, 203, 221
Hermitage, The 133-34
Hermites 133, 135
Het Wapen van Amsterdam 140
Histoire de la Vigne et des Vins en France 126
Ho Bryan (see Haut-Brion) 117
Hoban, James 196
Hock 145, 147, 185
Hochheim 145-47
Holland 139-40
Holy Ghost, Chez Ingel Tavern 143
Hop-Pole Inn 43
Hope, Henry 141
Hôtel a l'Esprit 151
Hôtel d'Angleterre 35, 47, 51, 97
Hôtel d'Orleans 17, 26
Hôtel d'York 18
Hôtel de la Princesse 89
Hôtel de Henri N 125
Hôtel de Langeac 30, 31, 162, 176
Hôtel de Luxembourg 106
Hôtel de Notre Dame 113
Hôtel de Richlieu 115

Hôtel de Salm 23, 51
Hôtel de St. Omer 104
Hôtel de Valentinois 18
Hôtel de l'Epee Royale 124
Hôtel des Invalides 50, 51
Hôtel du Griffon d'Or 114
Hôtel du Louvre 81, 82, 89
Hôtel du Palais Royal 68, 71
Hôtel of the Three Kings 99
Hôtel Grand Cerf 100
Hôtel ayence 146, 201
Hôtel Pomme de Pin 15
Hôtel St. Jacques 103
Hoosick Falls 181
Houdon, Jean Antoine 23, 50
House of Burgesses 1
House of Representatives 193
Hugel, Jean 151-52
Humphreys, David 12, 19, 21, 22, 184, 187
Hungary 205, 220
Hyeres 91

Independence Hall 7
Invalides 51
Italian Riviera 101, 102
Italy 72, 90, 91, 95, 102, 109, 158, 190, 202, 220, 224
Izard, Ralph 98

Jaboulet-Vercherre Family 129
Jamaica 183
Jamesport (winery) 182
Jane Brice House 173
Jardin de la Fountaine 83
Jay, John 12, 105, 131, 165
Jefferson, Lucy Elizabeth 13, 25
Jefferson, aria (Polly) 13, 168, 191-93, 226
Jefferson, Martha (Patsy) 13, 15, 17, 86, 167, 191
Jefferson, Martha (wife) 8, 11
Jefferson, Thomas (see below)
   Jefferson as Governor of Virginia 9
   Jefferson as President 195-207
   Jefferson as Secretary of State 167-91

Jefferson as Vice President 193
Jefferson in Alsace 151-52
Jefferson in Champagne 152-55
Jefferson in Bordeaux 115-23
Jefferson in Burgundy 59-70
Jefferson in England 35-47
Jefferson in Germany 142-51
Jefferson in Holland 139-41
Jefferson in Italy 95-102
Jefferson in Languedoc 106-14
Jefferson in Loire Valley 124-27
Jefferson in Paris 15-34, 49-57,129-37,157-65
Jefferson in Provence 81-94, 103
Jefferson in Retirement 209-28
Jefferson in the Rhone Valley 71-79,104-06
Johannisberg, Schloss 145-48, 158,186
John Shaw House 173
Johnson, Hugh 76, 144, 147, 154
Johnson, Nathaniel 76
Jones, John Paul 20, 124
Jouett 9
Jourdan (vineyard) 75, 76, 213, 221
Julien, Honore 197-98,211
Jullien, Andre 60, 187,213

Kaeferthall 150
Karlsruhe 151, 175
Kent, William 38, 39
Kew Gardens 44,45
Killock's (tavern) 182
King (Louis XVI) 25-26, 31-32, 59, 77, 91, 130, 154, 161, 163-64
King George III 36
King's Garden and Cabinet 33, 50, 54
Klein berger grape 148
Klemmer grape 148
Klemperien grape 148
Kleve 142
Knox, Henry 169,180
Koenig's, Amand (bookstore) 151

La Comarenne 129
La Grange 120
La Nerthe 79

La Reole 115
La Rochelle 124
La Saumal 111-13
LaTache 64
La Trappe, Society of 158
Lacryma Christi 202
Lafaurie Peyraguey 121
Lafayette, adame de 20, 26
Lafayette, arquis de 20, 22, 23, 25, 29, 32, 56, 94, 135, 163-64, 178, 226-28
Lafite, Château 21, 65, 76, 109, 115-19, 122, 136-37, 154, 157, 173, 183, 211
Lake Champlain 179-80
Lake Como 100
Lake George 179-81
Lambert, Doctor 107-09, 131, 171-73
Lamarque 123
Lamont,. de 122,185
Lampy 113
Langon 115
Languedoc 60, 77, 79,106,110, 212,221
Larose 120, 185
Last Supper 100
Latour, Château 21, 65, 115, 118-19, 122, 154, 171, 172, 185
Latour, Sr. Louis 62
La alque (vineyard) 91
la Tour, Monsieur de 64, 129, 136, 184
Laubenheim 145, 149
Laura 104
Laura's Tomb 104
Layc-Epinaye, Monsieur and Madame 68, 69
Lc Desert de Retz 54
Lc Havre (see Havre) Lear, Tobias 183
Leasowes 42
Ledenon (see Ledenon) Ledenon 82,212-14,221, 223-24,226
Ledyard, John 56
Lee, William 206
Lefevre, Roussac & Cie 244
Lcgaux, Peter 190, 196
Leghorn 4, 100, 192, 215-16, 222
Leiper, Thomas 175
Lemaire, Etienne 197-98

Index

Lenz (winery) 182
Léoville 34, 185
Léoville-Barton 34, 120, 185
Léoville-Las-Cases 34, 120, 185
Léoville-PoyfCrrc 34, 120, 185
Les Charmes 65
Les Combettes 65
Les Epenots 129
Les Genevrieres 65
Lés Greffieux 76
Lés Miserablcs 90
Les Muret 76
Lés Perrieres 65
Lés Rocoules 76
Les Rugiens 129
Lctombe, Philipe 197
Lewis, Victor 118
Lewis, Francis 32
Library of Congress 23, 218
Libourne 123
Limone 96
Limoux (wine of) 110-11, 113, 212-13, 224, 226
Limozin 98
Lirac 79, 213
Lisbon 49, 187, 188, 202
Lisbon Malmsey 202
Lisbon Wine 2, 3, 33, 105, 169, 175, 184, 186-88, 202, 206
Livingston, Robert 8
Locke, John 117, 189, 210
Loire 67, 124, 126
London 4, 5, 18, 24, 27, 35, 36, 44, 46, 89, 117, 140, 145, 176, 183-84, 218, 221
Long Island 182-83
Longchamps 133, 162
Lorient 29, 124
Louano 101
Louis Latour 65
Louis, M. 170
Louis XVI (see King) Louvre 50, 51
Lunel (wine) 106-09, 111, 189, 224
Lur-Saluce (see Lur-Saluces)
Lur-Saluces, Countess 173, 190
Lur-Saluccs, Monsieur de 120, 136, 157, 171, 176, 185
Lur-Saluces, Alexandre de 120
Luxembourg Palace and Gardens 49, 50
Lyon (see Lyons) Lyons 71, 72, 87

Macon 67, 68
Macon-Lugny 68
Macon-Prisse 68
Macon-Village 68
Macon-Virc 68
Madame Hclvetius 22, 23
Madame de Corny 23
Madame de Pichard 136
Madame de Pompadour 127
Madame de Rausan 171-73
Madame de Tesse 23, 27, 29
Madame de la Marquise de Erehan 131-32
Madame la Vcuvc Pcyrousc 74
Madere 93
Madeira 2, 3, 6, 27, 28, 32, 33, 93, 97, 105, 109, 165, 169, 175-78, 184, 187-88, 202-03, 212-14, 222, 226
Madison, James 31, 36, 131, 162, 167, 169, 171, 173, 176, 178, 181, 183, 192, 203, 207, 219, 226
Madrid 218
Mainz 146--49, 158
Maison Carrée 72, 83, 106, !59
Malaga 21, 107, 109, 202, 224
Malause 115
Malcshcrbcs 23, 32, 46
Malmscy 49, 224
Malvasia 215
Mann, George 12
Mann's Tavern 12, 175
Mannheim 150
Mantes 16
Marans 124
Marc (Valet) 19, 33
Marcobrunn 145, 147
Margaux, Château 21, 65, 109, 115, 117-19, 122-23, 130, 132, 154, 185
Marly 16, 52, 54
Marmande 115
Marquis de Lur-Saluccs (see Lur-Saluces)

323

Marquis-de-Terme 120
Marsala 202
Marsannc grape 75, 77
Marseilles 84, 87-89, 90, 93, 109, 203, 205-06, 212-13, 221-22
Marscillestte 111-12
Martin, Henri 120-22
Martin, Mrs. Joseph 3
Maryland 146, 173, 214-15, 219
Maryland Gazette 12
Maryland Inn 173
Maryland State House 173
Mason, George 5, 168
Massachusetts 13, 26
Mattituck Hills (winery) 182
Mayencc (see Mainz)
Mazzei, Philip 3, 4, 5, 6, 8, 29, 34, 89, 132, 163, 189, 192, 200, 215
McCieod, Major 9
McHenry, James 13
Mead, Le 76
Medab Stone's Tavern 182
Mediterranean 86, 91, 100-01, 107, 109-10, 114, 177, 202, 206, 220-21
Medici Villa Ferdinanda 215
Medoc 115, 117-18, 122-23, 191
Melon grape 125
Memoir on the Cultivation of the Vine in America and the Best Mode of Making Wine 227
Menton 102
Mercier, Sebastien 24
Meursault 61-62, 64-66, 71, 129, 136, 159-60, 165, 184
Middleton Tavern 173
Mifflin, Thomas 12, 13
Milan 99, 100
Miller, Joseph 218
Minister Plenipotentiary 26, 30
Mirabeau, Honore-Gabriel Riqueti 23, 89, 199
Mirambeau 124
Miromenil, M. de 171-72
Moissac 115
Monaco 102
Moncaglieri 98

Monnieres 125
Monroe, James 11, 13, 207, 219-20, 224
Mont Calvaire 54, 133-34
Mont Valerien 133-34
Montauban 115
Montelimar 77
Montepulciano 202, 215, 217-18, 221-22
Montferrat 98
Montmorin, Count 23, 188
Monticello 2, 3, 4, 5, 6, 7, 9, 10, 11, 31, 34, 43, 69, 85, 107, 110, 119, 147, 159, 167, 169, 175, 186, 189, 190-93, 198-99, 203-04, 207, 211, 214, 219-20, 224, 227-28
Montpelier 106-07
Montrachet (also Monrache) 4, 61, 62, 64, 65, 71, 105, 129-30, 136, 165, 184 201
MoorPark 37
Morris, Gouverneur 161-64, 176, 188, 195
Mosel (see Moselle) Moselle 140, 144, 185
Moselle wines 144-45, 148, 158
Mount Calvaire 52
Mount Vernon 12, 175
Mountain wine 21
Mourvedre 106
Moustier, Count de 49, 131-32, 136, 173
Mouton 120
Mouton-Rothschild 120
Mouzillon 125
Mt. Brois 95
Mt. Braus 95
Muscadine grape 220
Muscadet 125
Muscat Blanc de Lunel 224
Muscat de Rivesaltes (see also Rivesaltes) 212-13, 217, 224
Muscat grape and wine 106, 108-09, 112, 143, 173, 217, 224
Muscatel 187
Musigny 64
My Head and My Heart 56

Nanearrow, John 176

Nancy 152
Nanterre 16
Nantes 29, 87, 124-25
Naples 187, 202, 224
Napoleon 83, 102
Narbonne 106, 111-12
Nassau 145
Naurouze 114
Nebbiolo 97, 99, 177, 202
Nebiule (see Nebbiolo)
Neckar River 150, 151
Necker, Jacques 23, 163, 199
Netherlands 142
New England 178, 189, 196
New Hampshire 93
New Jersey 13, 44
New York 13, 178
New York City 13, 168-69, 171, 178, 183, 196
Newton, Isaac 85, 189, 210
Neyret-Gachet 74
Nice 91, 95, 100, 102-03, 177, 202, 206, 214, 221-22
Nierstein 145, 149
Nijmegen 141
Nîmes 71, 81-83, 85, 89, 106, 159, 185, 212
Noir Mountains 113
Noli 101
Norfolk 165, 167, 227
North Carolina 220, 227
North Hampton 182
Notes on a Cellar Book 76
Notes on the State of Virginia 22
Notre Dame 50, 51
Novaro 99
Novi 100
Nuits 61, 71

Oeiras 187
Oidium 188
Oliver, Julius 224
Ollioules 90, 91
Olmo, Harold 148
Oneglia 102
Oppenheim 149-50

Orange 77-79
Oregon 149
Orient Point 182
Orleans 126-27, 143
Orleans grape 148-49
Osterly House 45
Oxford 43
Oyster Pond Point 182

Pacharetti 93, 200, 202, 213, 222
Page, John 43
Paine, Thomas 163
Painshill Park 38
Place of the Popes 106
Palais Royal 17, 23-26, 52, 163
Palladio 38
Palmer 182
Palmer (winery) 182
Panthemont 17
Paradise, Lucy 36, 37, 158
Paradise, John 36, 37, 47, 158, 163
Parent, Etienne 64, 67, 71, 129, 136, 159, 160-61, 201
Paris 16, 17, 19, 23-26, 28-31, 35-37, 47, 49, 51, 54, 56, 57, 59, 60, 67-68, 69, 71, 72, 73, 83, 86, 87, 105, 107-08, 119, 127, 129, 130, 133, 146, 188, 201, 206, 216, 218, 226
Parker, Jr., Robert M. 76, 88, 93
Passy 17, 18, 30, 51
Paumanok (winery) 182
Pavarotti, Luciano 78
Pavia 100
Paxerete (see Pacharetti)
Peconic Bay (winery) 182
Pecquet, Jean Baptiste 49
Pedro Ximenes 21, 200, 202
Pennsylvania 146
Pepys, Samuel 117
Peronne 139
Perpignan 112, 221 Pessac 115
Peters, Richard 37
Petit 28, 176, 186, 192
Petitjean (Valet) 61
Petrarch 104-05, 151
Peyton, Capt. Bernard 222

Philadelphia 6, 8, 11, 13, 15, 89, 168-69, 171-72, 175-76, 183-85, 187, 189, 191, 192, 197, 204
Philip Wyckin & Co. 192
Phylloxera 60, 62, 188
Picardan de la Marine (grape) 111
Picardan de la Montagne (grape) 111
Pichard, Madame 136
Pichard, President 121, 136, 157
Picpoul grape 125
Piedmont 59, 90, 97, 98
Pierrij [Pierry] 153-54, 155
Piesport 144-45
Pigato grape 102
Pinckney, Charles Coatsworth 188-89
Pindar (winery) 182
Pinot Noir 149, 153
Pinto, Chevalier de 36
Place Louis XV 17, 23, 163
Plumer, William 198, 200, 202-04
Po River 97, 98
Poggio a Caiano 215
Pomerol 123
Pomeroy's 182
Pomino 215, 217
Pommard 61, 62, 64, 66, 71, 129
Pomme de Pin 15
Pons 124
Pont de Neuilly 16, 30
Pont du Gard 81
Pont St. Esprit 79
Pontac, Arnoud de and wines 116-17, 122, 185
Pontet-Canet 120
Pontette 120
Pope, Alexander 42
Poplar Forest 221
Port wine 3, 6, 33, 169
Port Maurice 102
Porter 169, 175
Portugal 35, 40, 49, 99, 109, 187, 202
Portugese wine 122, 176, 187, 188
Posthouses 59, 60, 74
Posting Houses 39
Postman's Arms 38
Poughkeepsie 178-79

Pouilly-Fuisse 68
Pouilly-Sur-Loire 126
Preignac 115, 120-21, 185
Premiers Crus 65
President Washington 170-71, 177, 183
President's House 76, 107, 196-97, 199
Pretorian Palace 72
Prevost (bookseller) 151
Prince Heredittair tavern 151
Prince Nursery 183
Prince William 183
Promenade a Longchamps 162
Provence 105
Pugliese (winery) 182
Puligny-Montrachet 64, 65
Puteaux 133
Pyramide 72
Pyrenees 111

Quai Des Chartrons 117, 122
Queen Anne's, Maryland 175
Quirouen 185

Raleigh's (tavern) 2
Randall, Paul Randolph 26, 27
Randolph, Benjamin 7
Randolph, Edmund 6, 167
Randolph, Sarah N. 3
Randolph, Thomas 5
Randolph, Thomas Mann 167-68
Ranelagh 44
Rausan, Madame de 120, 171-73, 176, 183, 185-86, 200
Rausan-Segla, Château 120, 123, 185, 200
Rauzan-Gassies, Château 120, 123
Reading 39
Red House Tavern 145-46
Redding, Cyrus 32, 97, 152, 217
Redi, Francesco 217
Remoulins 81
Remsen, Jr., Henry 177
Rennes 124
Republican (now the Democratic) Party 193
Republicans 200

Index

Rheingau 148-49
Rheinhessen 149
Rhine 140-42, 145-47, 151-52, 158
Rhine Wine 142-44, 148-50
Rhone Valley and wines 105-06, 200
Rhysslin (see Riesling) Richebourg 64
Richmond, Virginia 83, 132, 167, 179, 189, 191-92, 222-23
Riedesel, General Frederick 6, 9, 190
Riedesel, Baroness Friderike 9
Riesling 148-49, 152, 187
Riquet, Pierre Paul 110-11
Rivesalte (see Rivesaltes)
Rivesaltes 110-12, 212, 221-22
Robinson, Moses 182
Rochambeau, General H, 135
Rochefort 124
Rochegude, Marquis de and Wines 105-106, 160-65
Rock Hall 173
Rolle grape 93
Roman baths 83
Roman Mausoleum 85
Roman Theatre 77, 78
Romanée 61, 62, 71, 136
Romanée-Conti 64
Romanée St. Vivant 64
Rome 100-01, 109, 160
Rose, La 119
Roseneck (wine) 147
Rothen House Tavern 141, 145-46
Rothschild, Elie de 118, 122
Rotterdam 139
Rottland (wine) 147
Rouen 15, 16, 27, 49, 67, 98, 130
Roussanne grape 75, 77
Roussillon 110, 112, 185, 213-14, 221-22
Royal Palace 62
Royal Palace Hotel 77
Royal Theatre 45
Rozan (see Rausan, Madame de)
Rozzano 100
Rubens 142
Rudesheim 145-47
Rue Saint Honore 17, 23
Ruggieris 52

Rum 2, 3, 178
Rush, Benjamin 196, 226
Rutledge, Edward I 58, 160
Rutledge, Jr., John 104, 110, 144, 151, 158-59

Saint Cloud 52, 133
Saint Emilion 123
Saint-Germain-en-Laye 16, 20, 26, 54, 56
Saint Patrice 79
Saintsbury, George 76
Salus (see Lur-Saluces) Salussola 99
San Remo 102
Sancerre 126
Sandy Hill Falls 181
Sangiovese 215
Santa Maria Delle Grazie 100
Saorge 95
Sarah Williams Marsh's 182
Saratoga 179, 181
Sardinia 177
Sarsnet, Marquis de 64, 184, 201
Sasserno, Andre de 92, 93, 206
Sasserno, Victor Aldolphus 93, 221-22
Saussure, Horace-Benedict de 91
Sauterne (see Sauternes) Sauternes 34, 105, 115, 118, 120-22, 157, 171, 185, 189, 190, 200
Sauvignon Blanc 126
Schlossberg (wine) 147
Schuykill River 183, 190
Schylerville 179
Schwelbach 145
Schwetzinger 150
Scuppernon (see Scuppernong)
Scuppernong 220, 227
Seguier, Jean Francois 83, 159
Seine 16, 23, 54, 67, 155, 184
Senate 193, 196
Sète (Cette) 106-07, 206
Sevre-et-Maine 125
Sevres 133
Shaaff 173
Shadwell 2, 3
Shakespeare, William 40, 41

327

Shaw, Thomas George 67, 108
Sheaff, Henry 176, 184
Sheaff, Henry-Notes To 184-86
Sherman, Roger 8
Sherry 105, 169, 178, 184, 192, 202
Split Rock 180
Shippen, Jr. William 158
Shippen, Thomas Lee 104, 144, 151, 158-59, 160, 173, 175
Short, William 20-22, 26, 29, 30, 50, 69, 86, 87, 146, 159, 160, 170-72, 176, 186, 204
Siddons, Sarah 45
Silky wines 93
Sion House (see Syon House)
Sizeranne, La 76
Skelton, Bathurst 3
Sleepkoets 140
Slodtz, Michael Angelo 83
Small, William 1, 2
Smith, Daniel 7
Smith, William Stephen 35, 37, 38, 46, 47
Smith's Inn 182
Smollet, Tobias 86, 101
Smyrna, Turkey 4, 90
Sospello 95
Souche 159-60
Spain 109, 187, 219, 224
Spatburgunder 149
Spreafico, M. 92, 93, 223
Square Peyrou, Le 107
St. Cloud 52
St. Denis 56
St. Ferreol 113
St. Genevieve 50, 51
St. George d'Orques 107, 202, 205-06
St. Gilles 82, 85
St. Hermines 124
St. Joseph 77
St. Julien Inn 125
St. Laurent des Arbes 213
St. Omer 47
St. Paul's Cathedral 45
St. Peray 77, 113, 212
St. Remy 85

St. Sulpice 50, 51
St. Veran 68
Stark, Colonel John 181
State House (Maryland) 12
Sterimberg, Gaspard de 75
Stern, Lawrence 35
Stockdale, John 46
Stourbridge 42
Stowe 40, 42
Strasbourg 141, 151-52
Stratford-upon-Avon 40, 42
Straw Wine (see Vin de Paille)
Superga 98
Suresnes 50, 133
Swan Tavern 42
Swanwick, John 183
Sweet wines 93, 107, 108, 112-13
Switzerland 193
Syon House 45
Syrah grape 72, 75, 76, 106
Syracuse 202

Table Mountain 143
Tains 74, 77
Talbot Inn 42
Tarlton, Colonel 9
Tavel 79, 82
Tavern Accommodations 177-78
Tavern Food 178
Taylor, John 186
Temple of Diana 83
Tende (see Col de Tende)
Tent 200, 202
Termo 176, 178, 184, 186-88, 191
The Hague 27, 28, 139-40
Thornton, Anna 203
Thornton, William 203
Tinto di Rota 202
Tokay 88, 202-03, 205, 221, 224
Tonneins 115
Toulon 90, 91
Toulouse 106, 109-10, 114-15
Touraine 126
Tour Magne 81, 83, 84
Tourneron, M. 224
Tournus 68

Tours 126
Tower of London 44
Tracy, Nathaniel 15
Traminer 152
Treaty of Peace 12
Trebbiano 215
Triel 16
Triumphal Arch 85
Trockenbeerenauslese 145, 148
Trumbull, John 36, 37, 49, 50, 51, 52, 56, 135, 189
Tuileries 17, 51, 135
Tuileries Gardens 17, 23, 52
Tupple's Inn 182
Turin 96-99
Tuscan wines 5, 217
Tuscany 4, 202, 215, 217

University of Virginia 212, 225-26, 228
Unquachog Indians 183
Usseau 124
Utrecht 141
Uzes 81

Val d'Arno di Sopra 215
Vallet 125
Van Gogh, Vincent 85, 86
Vaucluse 151
Vaughan's (tavern) 2
VDQS Appellation 82
Vercelli 99
Vermont 181-82
Vergennes, Count 23, 30, 49
Versailles 25, 26, 27, 29, 50, 51, 54, 163
Vespucci, Arnerico 210
Via Aurelia 101
Vienne 72
Villa Simonetta 100
Villefranche 102
Villeneuve-les-Avignon 106
Vin Blanc de Rochegude 105-06, 160, 165
Vin Cuit 88, 224
Vin d'Oporto 93
Vin de Graves 33, 34, 93
Vin de Hochheim 93

Vin de Paille [straw] 75, 151, 152
Vin de Rhin 93
Vin de Segur (see Latour, Château)
Vin de Suresnes 133, 135
Vins de la Cote de Toulon 91
Vin uscat de Lunel 106
Vin ordinaire 82, 102, 133, 189
Vin Vieux Rouge de Nice 177
Vino Nobile di Montepulciano 217
Viny, John 44
Viognier 74
Virginia 6, 8, 34, 130, 132, 159, 171, 190-91
Virginia Assembly 4, 8, 11, 179
Vizetelly, Henry 212
Volnay 61, 62, 64, 66, 67, 129, 135-36, 159
Vosne (also Veaune) 61, 62, 64, 67, 71, 184, 201
Vosne-Romanée 62, 66
Vougeot (also Voujeau) 61, 62, 63, 66, 71, 130, 136, 184, 201

Waal River 141
Walloomsac Inn 181
Walsh, Peter 205-06
Wanderwerff, Adriaen 142
Warner, Seth 181
Washington, D. C. 119, 193, 195, 218-19, 225, 228
Washington, George 5, 7, 12, 13, 19, 26, 105, 157, 165, 167-69, 175, 180, 185, 187-90, 192, 197, 199, 204, 210-11
Wayles, John 3
Wayles, Martha 2
Webster, Daniel 212
Wehlen [Vialen] 144-45
Weld, Isaac 6, 190
West, Benjamin 26, 37
Whateley, Thomas 43
White Elbling 148
White Hermitage 75, 76, 206, 213, 221-22
White House 110, 196-99, 204, 210-11, 218, 225
White Lion Inn 40, 41

Wildman au l'Homme Sauvage Tavern 144
Wildman, The 144-45, 158
Wiley, John 42
Willard, Elias 179
William and Mary College 1, 20, 28, 225
William Paca House 173
William Pratt Inn 40
Williamos, Charles 20, 30
Williams College 182
Williamsburg 1, 2, 4
Williamstown 182
Wilmington, Delaware 173
Windsor Castle 37
Wine bottles/bottling 68, 73, 201
Wine Cellar 2, 18, 19, 31, 108, 154, 159, 176, 186-87, 192, 197, 200, 203, 222, 224-25
Wine Glasses 6, 31, 167, 203, 223

Wine Theft 67, 68
Wing's Falls 181
Woburn 39
Woodstock 43
Wooton 40
Worcester 42, 43
Worthington 182
Wythe, George 1, 2

Yarmouth 167
Young, Arthur 15, 16, 28, 82, 83, 88, 89, 98, 104
Yquem, Château 118, 120-22, 136, 158, 171-73, 200
Yquem, Monsieur 136
Yznardy, Joseph 184, 192, 202

Zaandam 141
Zelting [Selting] 144-45

Made in the USA
Middletown, DE
16 May 2017